COMPOSERS
AT WORK

COMPOSERS
AT WORK

The Craft of Musical Composition 1450 – 1600

Jessie Ann Owens

New York   Oxford   •   Oxford University Press   1997

Oxford University Press

Oxford   New York

Athens   Auckland   Bangkok   Bogota   Bombay   Buenos Aires
Calcutta   Cape Town   Dar es Salaam   Delhi   Florence   Hong Kong
Istanbul   Karachi   Kuala Lumpur   Madras   Madrid   Melbourne
Mexico City   Nairobi   Paris   Singapore   Taipei   Tokyo   Toronto

and associated companies in
Berlin   Ibadan

Copyright © 1997 by Jessie Ann Owens

Published by Oxford University Press, Inc.,
198 Madison Avenue, New York, New York 10016

Oxford is a registered trademark of Oxford University Press

Library of Congress Cataloging-in-Publication Data
Owens, Jessie Ann.
Composers at work : the craft of musical composition 1450–1600 /
Jessie Ann Owens.
p.   cm.
Includes bibliographical references and index.
ISBN 0-19-509577-4
1. Composition (Music)—History.   2. Music—15th century—History
and criticism.   3. Music—16th century—History and criticism.
I. Title.
ML430.094   1997
781'.3'09031—dc20   95-38533

The publication of this book has been supported by a grant from the National
Endowment for the Humanities, an independent federal agency, and by the
American Musicological Society.

1 3 5 7 9 8 6 4 2

Printed in the United States of America
on acid-free paper

for Jinny

PREFACE

I first began work on "compositional process" while I was writing my dissertation on Cipriano de Rore and had the opportunity to examine the set of autograph partbooks in the Biblioteca Ambrosiana in Milan in 1975. Perhaps because of the intense interest in compositional process that characterized musicology in general during the 1970s (for example, Robert Marshall's *The Compositional Process of J. S. Bach: A Study of the Autograph Scores of the Vocal Works* appeared in 1972, and many of the fundamental studies of Beethoven's compositional process came into print following the "Beethoven" year in 1970), and my training in particular (I participated in Lewis Lockwood's Beethoven seminar at Princeton University), I was able to recognize what had apparently gone unnoticed before: the revisions and cancellations meant that the Milan partbooks were Rore's composing manuscripts. The changes were not easy to interpret, and since the manuscript was not central to my dissertation, I put the topic aside until 1979–1980 when I had the luxury of a year at Villa I Tatti and the opportunity to spend more time with the manuscript. In 1980 I presented a preliminary study of the partbooks at the annual meeting of the American Musicological Society. I argued that Cipriano de Rore was able to compose by writing in separate parts, without using a score. But it was not until the summer of 1981 that I finally solved the most important and revealing of the corrections and not until 1984 that the study appeared in the *Journal of the American Musicological Society*. In some ways, this book fleshes out ideas that I could only hint at in a short article and indeed only barely understood. The Milan partbooks now are just one small piece of a much larger picture. The evidence assembled here leaves me more convinced now than I could ever have been earlier of the correctness of my hypothesis. At the same time, I came to see that the picture is far more complex than I had imagined: this book is presented not as the last word, but as a first attempt to sketch some of the principles that govern how composers from roughly 1450 to 1600 composed.

Since in effect I have been working on this topic during my entire career, I have the pleasure of thanking virtually all the granting agencies that have given me generous financial support: in 1975–1976 the Martha Baird Rockefeller

Fund, in 1979–1980 the Leopold Schepp Foundation to support my fellowship at Villa I Tatti, during the summer of 1981 the American Philosophical Society, in 1983–1984 the American Council of Learned Societies, and in 1991–1992 the National Endowment for the Humanities. The Mazer Fund at Brandeis University provided research support in 1990, 1992, 1993, and 1995. My work was interrupted from 1987 until 1990 while I served as Dean of the College at Brandeis University; I am grateful to the University for administrative leave in 1990.

I thank the staff of the many libraries and archives where I have worked; I am grateful for permission to reproduce photographs of their holdings (as specified): Augsburg, Staats- und Stadtbibliothek (pl. 3.4); Barcelona, Biblioteca de L'Orfeó Català (pl. 7.3–4); Basel, Öffentliche Bibliothek der Universität (pl. 6.4 and 7.5); Bergamo, Biblioteca Civica "A. Mai" (pl. 7.7); Berlin, Staatsbibliothek zu Berlin, Preußischer Kulturbesitz, Musikabteilung (pl. 7.23 and 10.1); Bologna, Civico Museo Bibliografico Musicale; Bologna, Archivio Musicale della Fabbriceria di San Petronio; Bruges, Stadarchief (pl. 6.3); Cambridge, Harvard University, Houghton Library (pl. 4.1) and Harvard Art Museums, Fogg Art Museum (pl. 5.5, gift of Belinda L. Randalla from the collection of John Witt Randall); Castell'Arquato, Chiesa Collegiata, Archivio parocchiale (thanks to Prof. Lina Pagani for allowing me to spend parts of two days in the archive; pl. 7.6, 7.14–7.20); Chicago, Newberry Library (pl. 5.10); Coimbra, Biblioteca Geral da Universidade (pl. 7.9); Dublin, National Museum of Ireland (pl. 5.3); Erlangen, Universitätsbibliothek (pl. 7.24); Florence, Archivio San Lorenzo (pl. 8.1); Florence, Biblioteca Nazionale Centrale (pl. 7.8, 8.2–8.8); Florence, Duomo, Archivio Musicale dell'Opera di Santa Maria del Fiore; Hradec Králové, Muzeum východních Čech (Museum of East Bohemia) (pl. 6.1–2); Leiden, Rijksuniversiteit, Prentenkabinet (pl. 5.4); Lille, Archives départementales du Nord (pl. 7.20); London, British Library, Reference Division, Department of Manuscripts (pl. 7.1–2); Mantua, Archivio di Stato (thanks to Dott.ssa Daniela Ferrari); Milan, Biblioteca Ambrosiana, courtesy of The Medieval Institute of the University of Notre Dame (pl. 9.1–3); Milan, Biblioteca del Conservatorio di Musica (thanks to Dott.ssa Agostina Zecca Laterza); Modena, Archivio di Stato; Munich, Bayerische Staatsbibliothek, Musikabteilung (pl. 7.10–11); New York, Hispanic Society of America (pl. 3.7); Nuremberg, Stadtbibliothek (pl. 5.1); Parma, Archivio di Stato; Rochester, Eastman School of Music, Sibley Music Library (pl. 2.1 and 5.9); Rome, Biblioteca Musicale Governativa del Conservatorio di Musica "Santa Cecilia" (pl. 11.2–3); Rome, San Giovanni in Laterano, Archivio Musicale (thanks to M.o Giancarlo Rostirolla for arranging limited access to the archive, pl. 11.4–5); Uppsala, Universitetsbiblioteket (pl. 7.12, 7.21–22); Vatican City, Biblioteca Apostolica Vaticana (pl. 11.1); Vienna, Österreichische Nationalbibliothek (pl. 5.11); Washington, Library of Congress, Music Division (pl. 2.2–4, 3.1–3, 3.5–6, 3.8, 5.6–8, 7.25); Wells (Somerset), Wells Museum (pl. 5.2). I benefited a great deal from the expert assistance of Ross Wood (Sibley Music Library, Eastman School of Music, University of Rochester), Kathryn Bosi (Biblioteca Berenson, Villa I Tatti), John Howard (Isham Memorial Library, Harvard University), and Robert Evensen, Vera Deak, and Bradley Short (Creative Arts Library, Brandeis University). I am grateful too for the very profitable time I spent at the Musicological Archives for Renaissance Manuscript Studies at the University of Illinois and for the help I received from Herbert Kellman and Jerry Call. This project would not have been possible without these superb libraries and their dedicated staff.

The list of people to whom I am indebted is so long that to record the specifics of my indebtedness would have doubled the length of the footnotes. I take the liberty of listing them here and ask their understanding: Carolyn Abbate, the late Courtney Adams, M. Elizabeth Bartlet, Phyllis Benjamin, Lawrence Bernstein, Stanley Boorman, Susan Boynton, the late Howard Mayer Brown, Jerry Call, Tim Carter, Matthew Cron, Frank D'Accone, Carroll Durand, Margot Fassler, Alan J. Fletcher, Wolfgang Freis, Margareta Fulton, Irving Godt, John Griffiths, James Haar, Frederick Hammond, Donna Cardamone Jackson, Peter Jeffery, Robert Judd, Herbert Kellman, Robert Kendrick, Ursula Kirkendale, Warren Kirkendale, James Ladewig, Harry Lincoln, Robert Marshall, Roberta Marvin, Timothy McTaggart, Scott Milner, Oscar Mischiati, Christopher Mossey, Arthur Ness, Noel O'Regan, Daniel B. Page, Claude Palisca, Pierluigi Petrobelli, Adriana Ponce, Harold S. Powers, Isobel Woods Preece, Mary Rasmussen, Owen Rees, Christopher Reynolds, Joshua Rifkin, Emilio Rós-Fabregas, Gregory Shesko, Richard Sherr, H. Colin Slim, Debra Sowul, Louise Stein, Edmond Strainchamps, Gary Towne, Andrew Wathey, Tom Ward, and Charles Warren. A special word of thanks to the graduate students in musicology at Brandeis who took a crack at some of the autograph manuscripts, and in particular to Roberta Marvin, Wendy Heller, David Farris, Beverly Stein, Matthew Cron, Dana Dalton, Craig Thomas, Rachel Golden, Megumi Nagaoka, and Jennifer Stinson.

A number of scholars sent me material in typescript in advance of publication or shared other research materials. I would like to acknowledge their generosity: Jane Bernstein, Bonnie J. Blackburn, Margot Fassler, Wolfgang Freis, Paula Higgins, Peter Jeffery, Daniel Leech-Wilkinson, Lewis Lockwood, John Milsom, Megumi Nagaoka, Lilian Pruett, H. Colin Slim, and Gary Towne. I would like to offer special thanks to John Kmetz, M. Jennifer Bloxam, and Daniel B. Page, who participated in a symposium at Brandeis University, "The Creative Process in Renaissance Music," in 1992 and allowed me to refer to their unpublished papers.

There are a few colleagues whose special assistance I would like to recognize. Lewis Lockwood, a friend and mentor for many years, offered encouragement from the beginning; his careful reading of individual chapters and then of the entire first draft (completed in October 1993) was extremely helpful for the final shaping of the book. My friend and colleague Jane Bernstein read several chapters in their earliest stages and listened countless times to just about everything in the book and much else besides. My European "families"—Egon and the late Maggie Hanfstaengl in Munich, Edvige Masini and Alberto Spisni in Parma—offered warm hospitality and assistance on many occasions. Two graduate students were very generous with their time: Megumi Nagaoka read the entire first draft—especially the musical transcriptions—with great care and offered helpful criticisms; Susan Boynton read portions of the revised draft, with particular attention to the translations and to prose style. The three anonymous readers for Oxford University Press turned out to be Lewis Lockwood, M. Jennifer Bloxam, and Bonnie J. Blackburn. Their detailed and substantive criticisms challenged me to rethink major elements of the book's structure.

Oxford University Press received two generous subventions to help finance the publication of this book. I am indebted to the American Musicological Society and to the National Endowment for the Humanities for their support.

The material in Chapter 10 first appeared in *Music in the German Renaissance: Sources, Styles, and Contexts*, ed. John Kmetz (Cambridge University Press, 1994). It is presented here by permission of Cambridge University Press.

There are a number of people whom I thank for helping turn the manuscript into a book. Hyunjung Choi showed uncommon resourcefulness in designing and producing the very complicated musical examples. Patrick Fairfield helped to prepare the final typescript. L. A. Holford-Strevens corrected and improved many of the translations. The editorial and production staff of Oxford University Press worked with exemplary professionalism at every stage of the process. Bonnie J. Blackburn contributed in many ways to this book: as a colleague responding to my inquiries and requests for unpublished material, as a reader for Oxford University Press, and as the copy editor (a title that in no way describes the extent of her contributions). Her profound understanding of the field and her generosity in helping me shape my arguments have greatly improved this book.

The final stages of work coincided with the death of my father, William A. Owens, on 8 December 1990 and then just over a year later of my mother, Ann W. Owens, on 31 January 1992. I am sorry that they did not live to see this book published; without their encouragement and love it would never have been written. I thank Alice Kearney and Gertrude Schlachter, their neighbors in Nyack, for their kindness to them and to me during difficult times.

Jinny Fitzgerald, my partner these last six years, has helped me in countless ways. I dedicate this book to her with my thanks.

CONTENTS

List of Plates xiii
List of Musical Examples xvi
Abbreviations xviii

ONE
Introduction 3

PART I. EXPLORING THE EVIDENCE

TWO
Teaching Composition 11

THREE
Reading and Writing Music 34

FOUR
Composing without Writing 64

FIVE
Erasable Tablets 74

Appendix:
Selected Documents Concerning Erasable Tablets (Cartelle) 101

SIX
Autograph Composing Manuscripts 108

SEVEN
Sketches, Drafts, Fair Copies 135

PART II. FOUR CASE STUDIES

EIGHT
Francesco Corteccia   205

NINE
Cipriano de Rore   244

TEN
Henricus Isaac   258

Appendix:
Isaac, Sanctissimae virginis votiva festa   277

ELEVEN
Giovanni Pierluigi da Palestrina   291

Appendix:
Excerpts from the Correspondence between
Palestrina, the Duke of Mantua, and Annibale Capello   311

Postscript   313
Bibliography   315
Index   334
Index of Manuscripts   343

PLATES

2.1 Philomathes, *De nova domo* (1512), sig. e iii^v 18

2.2 Aaron, *Thoscanello* (1523), sig. K 2^r 25

2.3 Lampadius, *Compendium musices* (1554), sig. F vii^r 26

2.4 Lampadius, *Compendium musices* (1554), sig. F vii^v 29

3.1 Gaffurius, *Practica musice* (1496), sig. dd ii^r 35

3.2 Lampadius, *Compendium musices* (1554), sig. B iii^v 40

3.3 Lampadius, *Compendium musices* (1554), sig. B iiii^r 41

3.4 Agricola, *Musica instrumentalis deudsch* (1529), foldout   43

3.5 Sebastiani, *Bellum musicale* (1563), sig. N 1^v-2^r 47

3.6 Burmeister, *Musica poetica* (1606), p. 58   49

3.7 Valderrábano, *Libro de música de vihuela, intitulado silva de sirenas* (1547), fol. 42^v 53

3.8 Bermudo, *Declaración* (1555), fol. 134^v 63

4.1 Bálint Bakfark, *Intabulatura* (1553), title page   72

5.1 Anonymous, *Music Lesson* in *Latinum ideoma Magistri Pauli Niavis* (1501)   83

5.2 Slate: Wells   84

5.3 Slate: Smarmore   84

5.4 Dirck Volkertszoon Coornhert (after Maarten van Heemskerck), *Allegory of Good and Bad Music* (detail)   85

5.5 Johann Sadeler (after Martin de Vos), *Annunciation to the Shepherds*   86

5.6 Gregor Reisch, *Margarita philosophica* (1508), sig. n ii^r 87

5.7 Ornithoparcus, *Musice active micrologus* (1517), title page   88

5.8 Banchieri, *Cartella musicale* (1614), pp. 12-13   90-91

5.9 Coclico, *Compendium musices* (1552), sig. K ii^r 92

5.10 Diruta, *Seconda parte del Transilvano* (1609), p. 3   94

5.11 Gumpelzhaimer, *Compendium musicae* (1625), portrait (woodcut by Lucas Kilian, 1622)   96

6.1 Matous Radous, *Music Scribe*, HradKM 13   114

6.2 Radous, *Music Scribe* (detail)   115

6.3 BrugS 538, leaf C^r: anonymous, chansons, sketches and drafts   118

6.4 BasU F.VI.26h, fol. 4^r: Fabri, unidentified compositions, sketches   119

7.1 LonBLR A23, fol. 43^r: Gerarde, unidentified composition, sketch   137

7.2   LonBLR A23, fols. 43^v–44^r: Gerarde, unidentified composition, sketch   138

7.3   BarcOC 28, fol. 57b: Pujol, Kyrie, sketch   142

7.4   BarcOC 28, fol. 2: Pujol, Kyrie, draft   142

7.5   BasU F.VI.26d, fol. 4^r: Fabri, Magnificat, draft   143

7.6   CastellC 2 [= Slim fasc. I], fol. 2^v: anonymous, unidentified keyboard piece, sketch   145

7.7   BergBC 1143, fols. 37^v–38^r: Fogliaris, organ versets, sketches and drafts   146

7.8   FlorBN II.I.295, fol. 51^v: Del Rio(?), ricercar, sketch   148

7.9   CoimU 48, fols. 21^v–22^r: anonymous, Magnificat, draft   149–150

7.10   MunBS 267, fol. 32^r: anonymous (Herwart?), ricercar, fair copy with revisions   152

7.11   MunBS 267, fol. 48^v: anonymous (Herwart?), ricercar, sketches   152

7.12   UppsU 76b, fols. 145^v–146^r: Morlaye(?), Nul n'est, drafts in tablature, sketch in mensural notation   153–154

7.13   VatV 5318, fol. 245^r, cantus and tenor: Spataro, Ave gratia plena, fair copy   156

7.14   CastellC 47, tenore I, fol. 1^r: Rosso(?), Magnificat, sketch   165

7.15   CastellC 32c, fol. [6^v]: Rosso(?), unidentified composition, sketch   166

7.16   CastellC 32a, fol. [6^v]: Rosso(?), De utero matris meae, draft   166

7.17   CastellC 12a, fol. [6^v]: Rosso(?), unidentified composition, keyboard score   167

7.18   CastellC 33, fol. 5^v: Rosso(?), unidentified composition, open score   167

7.19   CastellC 33, fol. 11^v: Rosso(?), unidentified compositions   168

7.20   LilleA 1081: Bouchel(?), A quoy passerai, draft   170

7.21   UppsU 76a, fol. 77^v: Anonymous, En contemplant, draft   172

7.22   UppsU 76a, fol. 78bis^v: Anonymous, En contemplant, fair copy   175

7.23   BerlS 40021, fol. 257a^r: Anonymous, In grandi cenaculo, sketches and draft   176

7.24   ErlU 473/4, fols. 242^v–244^r: Othmayr, Der Tag der ist so freudenreich, unfinished fair copy   180–183

7.25   Frosch, Qui de terra est, segments: Rerum musicarum, sig. E iv–ii^r 194

7.26   Frosch, Et testimonium (2.p. of Qui de terra): Rerum musicarum, sig. E iii^v–iiii^r 195

8.1   FlorASL 2129, fol. 72^{r-v}: Corteccia autograph   206–207

8.2   FlorBN Magl. 117, fol. 37^r: Corteccia, Amanti i 'l vo pur dir, sketches   212

8.3   FlorBN Magl. 117, fol. 39^v: Corteccia, Amanti i 'l vo pur dir, draft   212

8.4   FlorBN Magl. 117, fol. 20^r: Corteccia, unidentified composition, sketch   216

8.5   FlorBN Magl. 117, fol. 44^r: Corteccia, Fammi pur guerr'Amor, sketch   223

8.6   FlorBN Magl. 117, fol. 29^r: Corteccia, Fammi pur guerr'Amor and Con quel coltel, sketches   226

8.7   FlorBN Magl. 117, fols. 58^v–59^r: Corteccia, Fammi pur guerr'Amor, sketches   230

8.8   FlorBN Magl. 117, fols. 38^v–39^r: Corteccia, Con quel coltel, sketches   236

8.9   FlorBN Magl. 117, fol. 34^v: Corteccia, Con quel coltel, sketches   238

9.1   MilA 10, fol. 17^v: Rore, textless fragment (altus), draft   246

9.2 MilA 10, fol. 10ᵛ: Rore, *Miserere mei, Deus* (cantus), draft   250

9.3 MilA 10, fol. 4ʳ: Rore, *Sub tuum praesidium* (tenor), fair copy   257

10.1 BerlS 40021, fols. 255ᵛ–256ᵛ: Isaac, *Sanctissimae virginis*, fair copy   264–266

11.1 VatV 10776, fols. 55ᵛ–56ʳ: Palestrina, *Dixit Dominus*, fair copy   298–299

11.2 RomeSC O.232, tenor (chorus secundus): Palestrina, *Omnis pulchritudo*, fair copy   300

11.3 RomeSC O.231, tenor (chorus secundus): Palestrina, *Beatus es (2.p. Ave Maria)*, fair copy   301

11.4 RomeSG 59, fol. 1ʳ (after Casimiri): Palestrina, Lamentation, *Miserere mei*   304

11.5 RomeSG 59, fol. 94ᵛ: Palestrina, *Benedictus Dominus*   307

MUSICAL EXAMPLES

NOTE ON MUSICAL EXAMPLES

I retain the original note values but change the clefs to conform to modern usage. The text is underlaid as it appears in the source. Earlier versions are given on a small staff above the main staff.

♭/♮ c1c3c4F4 indicates system (*cantus mollis/cantus durus*) and cleffing (the clef and the line of the staff on which it appears, counting from the bottom).

2.1 Philomathes, *De nova domo* 18

2.2 Lampadius, *Compendium musices*: (a) "Exemplum cuiuslibet regulae": ten-line staff, with literal transcription of note values; (b) realization of verbal rules, based on version (a) (black notes = altus) 27

2.3 Lampadius, *Compendium musices*: (a) "simplex concordantiarum compositio": transcription of version on ten-line staff; (b) "resolutio": transcription of version in parts 28

2.4 Buchner, "Fundamentum": (a) chant melody; (b) chordal setting; (c) florid version (Buchner, *Sämtliche Orgelwerke*, 22–23) 31

5.1 Coclico, *Compendium musices*: (a) good counterpoint; (b) bad counterpoint 93

7.1 [Gerarde], unidentified composition 140–141

7.2 Spataro, *Ave gratia plena* 157–162

7.3 Anonymous (Rosso?), Magnificat 165

7.4 Anonymous (Bouchel?), *A quoy passerai* 171

7.5 Anonymous, *En contemplant* 173

7.6 Anonymous, *In grandi cenaculo* 178–179

7.7 Othmayr, *Der Tag der ist so freudenreich* (4 vv.) 184–186

7.8 Othmayr, *Der Tag der ist so freudenreich*, melody: (a) two-voice setting; (b) four-voice setting 187

7.9 Pujol, Kyrie 188–192

7.10 Anonymous (Frosch?), *Et testimonium* (2.p. of *Qui de terra*): motet and "aliud" segments 197–202

8.1 Corteccia, *Amanti i 'l vo pur dir*, mm. 1–20 213–215

8.2 Corteccia, unidentified composition from FlorBN Magl. 117, fol. 20ʳ 216

8.3 Corteccia, *Fammi pur guerr'Amor* 218–220

8.4 Corteccia, *Fammi pur guerr'Amor*,
    mm. 1–7   224–225

8.5 Corteccia, *Fammi pur guerr'Amor*,
    mm. 8–14   228

8.6 Corteccia, *Fammi pur guerr'Amor*,
    mm. 19–29   231

8.7 Corteccia, *Con quel coltel*,
    mm.1–12   234

8.8 Corteccia, *Con quel coltel*,
    conclusion   239

9.1 Rore, textless composition, mm.
    66–73   247

9.2 Rore, textless composition, mm.
    1–13   248

9.3 Rore, *Miserere mei, Deus*, mm.
    113–122   252

9.4 Rore, *Sub tuum praesidium*, mm.
    1–4   254

9.5 Rore, *Sub tuum praesidium*, mm.
    21–37   255–256

10.1 *Sanctissimae virginis votiva festa*:
    (a) *Graduale Pataviense*, fol. 267^r
    and (b) Isaac, discantus (and tenor),
    BerlS 40021, fols. 255^v–256^v
    262–263

10.2 Isaac, *Sanctissimae virginis votiva
    festa*   277–290

11.1 Palestrina, *Christe redemptor . . .
    conserva*, str. 5, mm. 29–30   308

ABBREVIATIONS

AfMw	*Archiv für Musikwissenschaft*
CC	*Census-Catalogue of Manuscript Sources of Polyphonic Music 1400–1550*
CEKM	Corpus of Early Keyboard Music
CMM	Corpus mensurabilis musicae
CS	Charles Edmond Henri de Coussemaker, *Scriptores de musica medii aevi*
CSM	Corpus scriptorum de musica
EM	*Early Music*
JAMS	*Journal of the American Musicological Society*
MD	*Musica disciplina*
MGG	*Die Musik in Geschichte und Gegenwart*
MQ	*Musical Quarterly*
MSD	Musicological Studies and Documents
NG	*New Grove Dictionary of Music and Musicians*

Library and Manuscript Sigla[1]

BarcOC	Barcelona, Biblioteca de L'Orfeó Català
28	Item 12-VII-28
BasU	Basel, Öffentliche Bibliothek der Universität
F.I.8a	MS F.I.8a
F.VI.26	MS F.VI.26
BergBC	Bergamo, Biblioteca Civica "A. Mai"
	Misericordia Maggiore (MIA)
	989, 1143, 1207, 1208, 1209
BerlS	Berlin, Staatsbibliothek zu Berlin
1175	Mus. ms. theor. 1175
Dressler	Mus. ms. autogr. theor. Dressler

---

1. The sigla are taken from the *Census-Catalogue* (*CC*) or are newly created in accordance with the principles followed in the catalogue.

	Preußischer Kulturbesitz, Musikabteilung
40021	Mus.ms. 40 021
40027	Mus.ms. 40 027
40028	Mus.ms. 40 028
BolC	Bologna, Civico Museo Bibliografico Musicale
	B57, B140, Q25, Q116
BolSP	Bologna, Archivio Musicale della Fabbriceria di San Petronio
	29, 31, 38, 40, 45, 46
BrugS	Bruges, Stadarchief
	538
BrusC	Brussels, Bibliothèque du Conservatoire Royal de Musique
	27731
CastellC	Castell'Arquato, Chiesa Collegiata, Archivio
	2, 3, 5, 6, 12a, 32, 33, 47
CoimU	Coimbra, Biblioteca Geral da Universidade
	8, 18, 33, 36, 48, 242
EdinNL	Edinburgh, National Library of Scotland
	5.1.15
ErlU	Erlangen, Universitätsbibliothek
	473/4
FlorSL	Florence, Archivio San Lorenzo
	2129
	N
FlorBN	Florence, Biblioteca Nazionale Centrale
AG	MS Ant. di Galileo
	1, 6, 9
Magl.	Magliabechi XIX.
	106bis, 107, 117
II.I.295	II.I.295 (=Magl.107)
FlorD	Florence, Duomo, Archivio Musicale dell'Opera di Santa Maria del Fiore
	21
GdańPAN	Gdańsk, Biblioteki Polskiej Akademii Nauk
	E.2165
GöttU	Göttingen, Niedersächsische Staats- und Universitätsbibliothek
IV.3000	Mus. IV 3000 Rara
103	Ms. Philos. 103
GuatC	Guatamala City, Catedral, Archivio Capitular
	1
HradKM	Hradec Králové, Muzeum východních Čech
13	MS 11 A 13
JenaU	Jena, Universitätsbibliothek
	33
KönS	Königsberg, Stadtbibliothek
	Gen. 2.150

KrakPAN   Kraków, Biblioteka Polskiej Akademii Nauk
                1716
LilleA   Lille, Archives départementales du Nord
    1081   MS 4 G 1081
LonBLR   London, British Library, Reference Division, Department of
           Manuscripts
    A   MSS Royal Appendix
                17-22, 23-25, 26-30, 31-35, 49-54, 74-76
MilA   Milan, Biblioteca Ambrosiana
    10   MS A.10.sup.
MilC   Milan, Biblioteca del Conservatorio di Musica "Giuseppe Verdi"
           MS Santa Barbara
                42, 55, 109, 142, 143, 164, 166, 195/17, 195/18
ModE   Modena, Biblioteca Estense e Universitaria
                C.311
MunBS   Munich, Bayerische Staatsbibliothek, Musiksammlung
           Musica MS
                239, 266, 267, 1503f, 1627, 2987, 3155, 9437
OaxC   Oaxaca Catedral
                s.s.
OxfB   Oxford, Bodleian Library
    MSe.420-2   MSS Music School e.420-2
ParBN   Paris, Bibliothèque nationale, Fonds du Conservatoire
    429   Rés. 429
ParA   Parma, Archivio di Stato, Raccolta manoscritti
    75/2   Busta 75, n.o 2
RegB   Regensburg, Bischöfliche Zentralbibliothek
    205-210   Butsch 205-210
RomeSC   Rome, Biblioteca Musicale Governativa del Conservatorio di Musica
           "Santa Cecilia"
    G.384   MSS G.384
    O.231   G.MSS O.231
    O.232   G.MSS O.232
RomeSG   Rome, San Giovanni in Laterano, Archivio Musicale
                59
SegC   Segovia, Archivio Capitular de la Catedral
                s.s.
Sib   Sibton Abbey, private possession (J. E.Levett-Scrivener)
    HA3   H.A.3:50/9/15.7(1)
UppsU   Uppsala, Universitetsbiblioteket
           MS Vokalmusik i Handskrift
                76a, 76b, 76c, 87, 412
Vat   Vatican City, Biblioteca Apostolica Vaticana
    G   MS Cappella Giulia
                XIII.24, XV.19

S   MS Cappella Sistina
                42, 57
V   MS Vaticani Latini
                5318, 10776
VienNB   Vienna, Österreichische Nationalbibliothek, Handschriften- und
             Inkunabelsammlung
                MS 5094, 11883, 18744
WashF   Washington, Folger Shakespeare Libraries
                V.b.280
WolfA   Wolfenbüttel, Herzog August Bibliothek
   499   MS 499 (=W₃)
WoodS   Woodford Green, private collection of Robert Spencer
YorkM   York, Minster Library
   91   MS M 91 S

COMPOSERS
AT WORK

CHAPTER ONE

INTRODUCTION

In the past two or three decades, studies of "compositional process" have become a familiar staple of musicology. In a paper entitled "Sketch Studies," presented at the American Musicological Society meeting in 1981, Joseph Kerman traced the development of this sub-discipline within musicology.[1] Listing some twenty composers whose sketches had received scholarly attention—none earlier than Bach—he noted, "Then there was Jessie Ann Owens's paper last year about Cipriano de Rore. Who would have thought of sketches surviving from *that* period? It just goes to show that if you know what you are looking for, you may find it."[2] Kerman's remark reflects the view that prevailed until recently that none of the manuscripts actually used in composition of music from before 1600 had survived.

Some composer autographs, of course, were known.[3] During the late eighteenth and nineteenth centuries, autographs had become valuable objects, desired by collectors. Peter Jeffery, in his study of Francesco Cavalli's autographs, traced the emergence of this phenomenon, and offered a useful overview of autographs or manuscripts alleged to be autograph from Cavalli's period or earlier.[4] Despite the fascination with composer autographs, there was relatively little interest in seeing what clues they might hold for understanding compositional process.[5] The

1. Joseph Kerman, "Sketch Studies," in *Musicology in the 1980s: Methods, Goals, Opportunities*, ed. D. Kern Holoman and Claude V. Palisca (New York, 1982), 53–65.

2. Kerman, "Sketch Studies," 57. I presented the paper to which he referred at the American Musicological Society meeting in 1980 and published it in 1984 ("The Milan Partbooks: Evidence of Cipriano de Rore's Compositional Process," *JAMS* 37 (1984): 270–298).

3. See, for example, the surveys given by Heinrich Besseler and Peter Gülke, *Schriftbild der mehrstimmigen Musik*, Musikgeschichte in Bildern 3/5 (Leipzig, 1973), 152–155; and by Wilhelm-Martin Luther, "Autograph," *MGG*.

4. Peter Jeffery, "The Autograph Manuscripts of Francesco Cavalli" (Ph.D. diss., Princeton University, 1980), 1–2. Working with what was then thought to be the earliest substantial collection of composer autographs, Jeffery developed a rigorous methodology for identifying and authenticating autographs, and offered an important interpretation of their use in the process of composing and producing operas.

5. Raffaele Casimiri's investigation of the Palestrina autograph RomeSG 59, *Il "Codice 59" dell'Archivio Musicale Lateranense, Autografo di Giov. Pierluigi da Palestrina* (Rome, 1919), and H.

lack of a systematic consideration of the manuscript evidence did not keep scholars from speculating about how composers worked. The primary concern was the
format employed by composers for writing their music. Otto Kinkeldey, for
example, thought that they were able to read music in separate parts and might
therefore have composed in parts; he believed that scores for composition first
came into use toward the end of the sixteenth century.[6] Rudolf Schwartz challenged this view, finding it implausible that composers or performers could read
in parts; he believed that they must have used scores.[7] Edward Lowinsky, in several controversial but influential articles, affirmed Schwartz's position and added
evidence of his own in support. In a 1948 article he drew attention to the existence of a score in the 1537 treatise (actually a textbook) by the German schoolteacher Auctor Lampadius.[8] The role of the score became one of the corner-
stones of his view of music history. He believed that there was a major distinction
between music conceived "successively" and that conceived "simultaneously"; he
argued that composers began to use scores in about 1500 as a means of control-
ling the new complex style of imitative polyphony found in the works of Josquin
des Prez. He supported this hypothesis with a study (published in 1960) of sixteenth-century manuscripts notated in score.[9] As it turns out, however, only one
of these manuscripts shows evidence of use in composition, and only two others
can be linked to composers.[10]

Other evidence was beginning to turn up that revealed important information about some of the tools composers used for their work. Suzanne Clercx's
discovery of an erasable slate tablet led her to speculate that composers worked
not in score but in a kind of score without barlines ("partitions sans barres"), a
format that is sometimes referred to as "pseudo-score" or "quasi-score."[11] Siegfried
Hermelink made a major contribution to our understanding of slates—he called
them "tabulae compositoriae"—linking their use to actual composers through

---

Colin Slim's of Veggio's manuscript in Castell'Arquato, CastellC 2, "Keyboard Music at Castell'-
Arquato by an Early Madrigalist," *JAMS* 15 (1962): 35–47, are important exceptions.

6. Otto Kinkeldey, *Orgel und Klavier in der Musik des 16. Jahrhunderts* (Leipzig, 1910), 188.

7. Rudolf Schwartz, "Zur Partitur im 16. Jahrhundert," *AfMw* 2 (1919–1920): 73–78.

8. "On the Use of Scores by 16th-Century Musicians," *JAMS* 1 (1948): 17–23; reprinted
with minor changes in Edward E. Lowinsky, *Music in the Culture of the Renaissance and Other
Essays*, ed. Bonnie J. Blackburn (Chicago, 1989), 797–800. The article generated an acerbic
exchange between Ruth Hannas and Lowinsky in ensuing issues of *JAMS*.

9. "Early Scores in Manuscript," *JAMS* 13 (1960): 126–173, reprinted with minor changes in
Music in the Culture, 803–840.

10. Portions of FlorBN Magl. 106bis may have been used for composing keyboard music; see
chap. 6. Three manuscripts are composer autographs not used for composition: FlorBN AG 9
(Vincenzo Galilei) and BerlS 40027 and BerlS 40028 (Adam Gumpelzhaimer). BolC B140, a
manuscript Lowinsky believed to be an autograph of Costanzo Porta, was not written by Porta;
see chap. 2.

11. Suzanne Clercx, "D'une ardoise aux partitions du XVIe siècle . . . ," in *Mélanges d'histoire
et d'esthétique musicales offerts à Paul Marie Masson* (Paris, 1955), I: 157–170. This article contains an
extensive bibliography of the older secondary literature on the use of scores.

documentary evidence and assembling information about them that he culled from the writings of music theorists.[12] Working only from the German theoretical evidence and from what he considered common sense, Hermelink concluded that composers wrote either on a ten-line staff (a staff large enough to incorporate the entire tonal system) or in score. Since the publication of Hermelink's article, other slates have been discovered, some with music, some without: none use score or the ten-line staff format; the one with most legible music is in quasi-score.[13]

In the past decade, perhaps partly as a consequence of the great interest in sketch studies for other periods of music history, a number of scholars have begun to study the manuscript evidence for compositional process in music that dates from before 1600. In the 1984 study to which Kerman alluded, I argued that Cipriano de Rore had used a set of autograph partbooks for drafting three compositions and hypothesized that he was able to compose even complex, five-voice polyphony without using a score.[14] In the years since then other composing manuscripts have come to light, none of them in score. In 1987 Howard Mayer Brown discovered a draft of a three-voice chanson in a manuscript now in Uppsala (UppsU 76a).[15] In 1991 I identified a Florentine manuscript (FlorBN Magl. 117) that Francesco Corteccia had used for sketching several madrigals, a motet, and other unidentified compositions.[16] In 1992 John Kmetz and M. Jennifer Bloxam reported on their discovery of early sixteenth-century manuscripts containing sketches and drafts of polyphonic music found in Basel and Bruges.[17]

As this brief account indicates, more manuscripts actually used in composition have survived than anyone had ever suspected. Including these recent discoveries and others presented here for the first time, I can identify manuscripts in the hands of over thirty composers. This work has been aided in no small measure by the publication of new bibliographical tools that allow better access to the sources and of modern critical editions that make the music itself avail-

---

12. Siegfried Hermelink, "Die Tabula compositoria. Beiträge zu einer Begriffstimmung," in *Festschrift Heinrich Besseler zum sechzigsten Geburtstag* (Leipzig, 1961), 221–230.

13. Judith Blezzard, "The Wells Musical Slates," *Musical Times* 120 (1979): 26–30; A. J. Bliss, "The Inscribed Slates at Smarmore," *Proceedings of the Royal Irish Academy* 64 (1965–1966), Section C, 33–60; and Jacques Chailley, "Tabulae Compositoriae," *Acta musicologica* 51 (1979): 51–54.

14. "The Milan Partbooks."

15. Howard Mayer Brown, "Emulation, Competition, and Homage: Imitation and Theories of Imitation in the Renaissance," *JAMS* 35 (1982): 1–48.

16. I first presented my findings at a colloquium at the University of Illinois (Urbana) in December 1991, and subsequently at a symposium at Brandeis University, "The Creative Process in Renaissance Music" in February 1992, and finally at the American Musicological Society meeting in Pittsburgh in November 1992.

17. John Kmetz, "The Drafts of Jodocus Fabri and Company: New Evidence of Compositional Process from Renaissance Basel," presented at the 1992 Brandeis symposium and at the annual meeting of the American Musicological Society, 1994; M. Jennifer Bloxam, "Newly-discovered Fragments of Renaissance Polyphony in Bruges: A Glimpse of Sixteenth-Century Composers at Work," presented at the 1992 Brandeis symposium and at the 1992 meeting of the American Musicological Society.

able.[18] I fully expect that many more composer autographs will be identified as we learn how to look for them.

The core of this book is an examination of the extant autograph manuscripts used for composing. The focus on manuscript evidence compels me to set the early boundary of this study at roughly 1450; most of the manuscripts in fact date from the sixteenth century. Before 1450 the manuscript evidence appears to be too sparse to permit well-founded conclusions.

I set the late boundary at roughly 1600. The fundamental changes in musical style taking place during the second half of the sixteenth century and the beginning of the seventeenth toward a strong soprano–bass polarity characteristic of "baroque" music suggest different (and in fact, score-based) methods of composing.

The temporal boundaries of this study—1450 to 1600—invite use of the term "Renaissance." It is a term I would like to avoid because it better reflects the views of the nineteenth-century German cultural historians who first coined it than it does any particular period in music history.[19] I believe that some of the observations that I make about music during the period 1450 to 1600 may well be valid for earlier music. Indeed, I think it is helpful to see the period from 1250 or 1300 to 1550 or 1600 as being unified, in a general way, by systems of notation, pitch, and harmonic organization (namely, by the Guidonian diatonic, the mensural system, and counterpoint, the weaving together of lines to form harmonies). Setting the boundary at 1450 reflects the evidence currently available about music manuscripts, not a stylistic divide.[20]

Manuscript evidence tells only part of the story. Other evidence comes from documents, from iconography, and from music treatises and textbooks. The evidence is fragmentary, and often requires special consideration of its limitations. Rarely, for example, do we have more than one manuscript for any given composer, making generalizations risky. Perhaps the biggest limitation of all is that we are trying to capture something that is inherently elusive. At best we may be able to see the craft of composition, the "poetics" in the sense of making something. Trying to pin down the imagination or the spark of creativity is doomed.

The work on compositional process for music of this period is in its infancy. My goal is to examine the existing evidence systematically and to weave it together to construct a paradigm about how composers worked. While I have tried to cast the net widely and assemble a variety of different kinds of evidence, I know full well that there are many manuscripts, treatises, and documents that

18. For example, *Census-Catalogue of Manuscript Sources of Polyphonic Music 1400–1550*, Renaissance Manuscript Studies 1, 5 vols. (American Institute of Musicology, 1979–1988), and the editions in the series Corpus mensurabilis musicae and the Corpus of Early Keyboard Music, published by the American Institute of Musicology.

19. I have addressed this view in my study, "Music Historiography and the Definition of 'Renaissance,'" *MLA Notes* 47 (1990): 305–330.

20. Scholars who have worked more than I have with sources from before 1450 may be able to identify additional autograph manuscripts. Like many other "Renaissance" musicologists I have concentrated on the period from ca. 1430 to 1600, surely one of the drawbacks of the traditional definition of "Renaissance."

I have not considered. Since this is the first attempt at a synthesis, the conclusions are inevitably provisional.

The book consists of two parts. In the first I explore the evidence concerning compositional process and address some of the basic questions about how composers worked: how they learned; how they read music and wrote it down on the page; how they planned their music in the earliest, unwritten stages; what kinds of tools they used, especially the erasable tablet; what sorts of manuscripts they used for composing; and finally, what their sketches, drafts, and fair copies looked like. In the second, I try to apply the results of these investigations in four case studies. The four composers are different from one another not only in musical style and structure but in their working methods as well. So while the first part of the book seeks to establish certain norms, the second challenges the norms by revealing the complexity of individual approaches.

There is no single "compositional process" in music of this period, but there are certain overriding principles and approaches that in turn reveal basic attitudes about the construction of music and the relationship among the voices. The most fundamental is the fact that composers of vocal music did not use scores for composing, but instead worked in separate parts or quasi-score. Only keyboard composers, who were accustomed to performing from score, composed in score. It is hard for us to imagine composing without scores: we are accustomed to thinking in terms of scores, and our modern editions of early music invariably translate separate parts into score format. I believe that composing in separate parts reflects the basic character of the music: lines woven together to form harmonies, and not a series of sonorities. Composers heard harmonies but did not see them arrayed in columns on the page. As we shall see, the implications of this basic fact vary from repertory to repertory, from decade to decade. The challenge is to see how composers "composed," literally, "put together" their music.

PART I

EXPLORING THE EVIDENCE

CHAPTER TWO

TEACHING COMPOSITION

My teacher Josquin . . . never gave a lecture on music or wrote a theoretical work, and yet he was able in a short time to form complete musicians, because he did not keep back his pupils with long and useless instructions but taught them the rules in a few words, through practical application in the course of singing. And as soon as he saw that his pupils were well grounded in singing, had a good enunciation and knew how to embellish melodies and fit the text to music, then he taught them the perfect and imperfect intervals and the different methods of inventing counterpoints against plainsong. If he discovered, however, pupils with an ingenious mind and promising disposition, then he would teach these in a few words the rules of three-part and later of four-, five-, six-part, etc. writing, always providing them with examples to imitate. Josquin did not, however, consider all suited to learn composition; he judged that only those should be taught who were drawn to this delightful art by a special natural impulse.[1]

---

1. "Item Praeceptor meus Iosquinus de Pratis nullam unquam praelegit aut scripsit musicam, brevi tamen tempore absolutos musicos fecit, quia suos discipulos non in longis & frivolis praeceptionibus detinebat, sed simul canendo praecepta per exercitium & practicam paucis verbis docebat. Cum autem videret suos utcunque in canendo firmos, belle pronunciare, ornate canere, & textum suo loco applicare, docuit eos species perfectas & imperfectas, modumque canendi contra punctum super choralem, cum his speciebus. Quos autem animadvertit acuti ingenii esse & animi laeti his tradidit paucis verbis regulam componendi trium vocum, postea quatuor, quinque, sex &c appositis semper exemplis, quae illi imitarentur. Non enim omnes ad componendi rationem aptos iudicavit Iosquinus, eos tantum eam docendos statuit, qui singulari naturae impetu ad pulcherrimam hanc artem ferrentur . . ." *Compendium musices descriptum ab Adriano Petit Coclico discipulo Iosquini de Pres in quo praeter caetera tractantur haec: De modo ornate canendi, De regula contrapuncti, De compositione* (Nuremberg, 1552; reprint, Kassel, 1954), sig. F ii^v. This translation, adapted from Smijers, is found in Gustave Reese and Jeremy Noble, "Josquin Desprez," *The New Grove High Renaissance Masters* (New York, 1984), 20. The passage concludes with the sentence: "because he said that many pieces had been composed with great sweetness, than which scarcely one out of thousands could compose something similar or better" ("quia multa dulciter composita esse aiebat, quibus similia aut meliora, vix unus e millibus componere posset").

W ith these words the German theorist and composer Adrianus Petit Coclico explained how Josquin taught music: first singing, then counterpoint, and finally composition. Whether or not Coclico was actually a pupil of Josquin and an eyewitness, his account shows us how a sixteenth-century musician thought composition should be taught—and, possibly, had been taught by one of the great composers of the period. Despite the promise of Coclico's remarks, we have remarkably little direct evidence about the teaching of composition. No diaries have survived to record an actual course of study, no manuscripts preserve compositions marked with a teacher's corrections.

Yet we do know something about the social and institutional structures in which music education—and, by implication, its most advanced topic, composition—took place.[2] Many students learned music in schools, some of which were associated with cathedrals. The character both of the institution and the curriculum varied according to the region as well as the religious doctrine.[3] Students could also receive private instruction, serving as apprentices to professional composers or performers. A number of contracts recording various kinds of private instruction have survived.[4]

2. Music education in general remains an area badly in need of further investigation. For a general overview, with bibliography, see Iain Fenlon, Nan C. Carpenter, and Richard Rastall, "Education in Music (II and III)," NG. See also Bernarr Rainbow, Music in Educational Thought and Practice: A Survey from 800 BC (Aberystwyth, 1989), chs. 4–5; J. Smits van Waesberghe, Musikerziehung: Lehre und Theorie der Musik im Mittelalter, Musikgeschichte in Bildern 3/3 (Leipzig, 1969); and the papers and discussion of the round table "La musica nella storia delle università," in Atti del XIV Congresso della Società Internazionale di Musicologia (Turin, 1990), 1, 27–89. Kristine Forney, "'Nymphes gayes en abry du Laurier': Music Instruction for Women in Renaissance Antwerp," paper read at the annual meeting of the American Musicological Society, 1992, shows the wide variety of institutions in which education took place in sixteenth-century Antwerp.

3. As an example of music education in a cathedral school, see Craig Wright, Music and Ceremony at Notre Dame of Paris 500–1550 (Cambridge, 1989), 174–180. For education in Protestant Germany, see K. W. Niemöller, Untersuchungen zu Musikpflege und Musikunterricht an den deutschen Lateinschulen vom ausgehenden Mittelalter bis um 1600 (Regensburg, 1969). See also Édith Wéber, "L'Enseignement de la musique dans les écoles humanistes et protestantes en Allemagne: Théorie, pratique, pluridisciplinarité," L'Enseignement de la musique au Moyen Age et à la Renaissance (Fondation Royaumont, [1987]), 108–129. Jeremy Yudkin, in his translation and edition of the chapter on music in Johannes Thomas Freig's Paedagogus (Basel, 1582), MSD 38 (Neuhausen-Stuttgart, 1983), described the place of music in a four-year school curriculum; Freig's schoolbook was intended to be an introduction to all the subjects the student was to learn. On music education in the Jesuit schools, see Thomas D. Culley, S.J., Jesuits and Music I: A Study of the Musicians connected with the German College in Rome during the 17th Century and of their Activities in Northern Europe (Rome, 1970). Concerning music education in England, see Jane Flynn, "A Reconsideration of the Mulliner Book (British Library Add. MS 30513): Music Education in Sixteenth-Century England" (Ph.D. diss., Duke University, 1993) and Flynn, "The Education of Choristers in England during the Sixteenth Century," in English Choral Practice, 1400–1650, ed. John Morehen (Cambridge, 1996).

4. They include: a 1478 contract for instruction in organ in L. Frati, "Memorie per la storia della musica in Bologna dal secolo xv al xvi," Rivista musicale italiana 24 (1917): 451; a 1594 contract for instruction by Giovanni Maria Nanino in singing, counterpoint, and composition in A. Cametti, "L'insegnamento privato della musica alla fine del Cinquecento," Rivista musicale italiana 37 (1930): 76–77; a 1504 contract for teaching organ repertory in Renato Piattoli, "Un documento fiorentino di apprendistato musicale dell'anno 1504," in Collectanea Historiae Musicae 2 (Florence, 1957), 351–353.

One particularly interesting document concerning music instruction in mid-sixteenth-century Italy comes from legal proceedings taken against Pietro Pontio, a composer, music theorist and *maestro di cappella*.[5] In 1566, a number of witnesses—Pontio's colleagues, pupils, and other musicians—were called to testify in an investigation. There were evidently serious concerns that he had not fulfilled adequately his obligations as *maestro di cappella* at Santa Maria Maggiore in Bergamo, one of which was to teach counterpoint and *canto figurato*. Pontio was obligated to teach ten of the young clerics as part of his responsibilities, but he also took on private students. There were several complaints about his teaching. One was that he gave his private students more attention, making the other students sing in a group, not individually (despite a bribe of pigeons and artichokes by the father of one of the aggrieved students). Another was that he did not teach properly: one student explained that he had marked with an 'x' passages that were perfectly good and left errors uncorrected.[6] The comments of the witnesses reveal the expectations of the students: that Pontio would hear them sing their part by themselves, not in a group; that he would correct their exercises; and that he would meet with them daily.

A number of manuscripts have survived that record the activities of students.[7] Several of them contain compilations of rules, which are in effect notes from counterpoint lessons. One of these, BolC B140, was previously thought to be an autograph by Costanzo Porta.[8] The title—"Trattato di Contrapunto, o sia Instruzioni di contrappunto date dal P. Costanzo Porta al P. Tomaso Gratiano da Bagnacavalla. Est liber domini Innocentii de Ravenna"—led both Oscar Mischiati and Paolo Fabbri to speculate that it was *written* by (as well as owned by) Innocenzo da Ravenna. However, comparison of the manuscript with BolC Q116, a choirbook signed by Tomaso Graziani, reveals that BolC B140 was in fact written by Graziani, and may be a record of his studies with Porta.[9] It contains several different sections of counterpoint rules as well as music that would have

---

5. The document was discovered by Russell E. Murray; the full text is found in his dissertation, "The Voice of the Composer: Theory and Practice in the Works of Pietro Pontio" (Ph.D. diss., University of North Texas, 1989), 2: 23–50; see also his article, "On the Teaching Duties of the Maestro di Cappella in Sixteenth-Century Italy: The Processo against Pietro Pontio," *Explorations in Renaissance Culture* 14 (1988): 115–128, parts of which I draw on here.

6. Although the original does not survive, we know that Palestrina wrote comments and crosses on the music of his royal pupil, Duke Guglielmo Gonzaga; see chap. 11.

7. These sources merit further study both individually and as a group.

8. Lowinsky, "Early Scores in Manuscript," *Music in the Culture*, 824–825, including several facsimiles.

9. Oscar Mischiati, "Un'antologia manoscritta in partitura del secolo XVI. Il ms. Bourdeney della Bibliothèque Nationale di Parigi," *Rivista italiana di musicologia* 10 (1975): 271. (Lowinsky, in a long footnote added to the 1989 version of his article (823, n. 51a), disputed Mischiati's assessment and continued to adhere to his original interpretation. Paolo Fabbri, "Vita musicale nel Cinquecento ravennate: Qualche integrazione," *Rivista italiana di musicologia* 13 (1978): 44, noted that Innocenzo was in Ravenna between 1592 and 1595 and possibly longer (both earlier and later pay registers are missing); he proposed a possible date for the manuscript of 1594–1596, the dates when Graziani was teaching counterpoint. See also Fabbri, *Tre secoli di musica a Ravenna dalla controriforma alla caduta dell'Antico Regime* (Ravenna, 1983), 16. Graziani's role as scribe of BolC B140 was suggested to me by Bonnie Blackburn and confirmed by Robert Kendrick.

been useful for a church musician (settings of *Miserere*, *Benedictus*, psalm intonations, tuning for the violin and viola). Another example is the manuscript
RomeSC G.384. Written in several different hands, it contains a music treatise
("Regule de contrapuncto"), extensive examples of cadences for two to four
voices, and consonance tables with numbers on the staves. Portions of the manuscript have the appearance of a workbook, with erasures and corrections. There are
also collections of musical phrases ("punti diversi").[10] Other examples include the
notebook of Georg Donat, a student from Wittenberg, and the Basel manuscripts
recording some aspects of Amerbach's studies with Piperinus.[11]

A few manuscripts may record actual counterpoint exercises. The fragments
of polyphonic music recently discovered in the binding of a mid-fifteenth-
century account book in Bourges contain music that appears to be counterpoint
exercises (two-voice, with a cantus firmus sometimes in long notes).[12] Another
example, FlorBN Magl. 117, has brief examples of two-voice counterpoint, written probably in the middle of the sixteenth century by two unknown musicians;
one of them wrote in score, while the other used quasi-score format (without
alignment or barlines).[13] A third example is the score manuscript kept by an
organist at the Santa Cruz Monastery in Coimbra (CoimU 48).[14] For example,
fol. 126[r] contains fragmentary four-voice sketches of counterpoint exercises over
a cantus firmus in long notes.

The manuscript evidence does not reveal as much as we would like about music
instruction. The best evidence that has survived consists of the music textbooks
used in instruction, as well as the treatises aimed at a more sophisticated audience.
The discussion of "composition" is typically found in the counterpoint sections of
musica practica treatises or, within the German tradition, in *musica poetica* treatises.[15]

But neither textbooks nor treatises offer the kinds of practical advice about the
craft of composition that we would like to find. Even a treatise with the promising title "Rules How to Compose" offers elementary instruction in counterpoint

10. The manuscript, to my knowledge, has not received close scrutiny, beyond a brief mention
because of a canon by Costanzo Festa. It does contain several pieces in score that seem to be later
additions (e.g., fols. 68[v], 21[r]).

11. Adolf Abert, "Das musikalische Studienheft des Wittenberger Studenten Georg Donat (um
1543)," *Sammelbände der Internationalen Musikgesellschaft* 15 (1913–1914): 68–98; John Kmetz, "The
Piperinus–Amerbach Partbooks: Six Months of Music Lessons in Renaissance Basle," in *Music in the
German Renaissance*, ed. John Kmetz (Cambridge, 1994), 215–234.

12. Paula Higgins, "Music and Musicians at the Sainte-Chapelle of the Bourges Palace,
1405–1515," *Atti del XIV Congresso della Società Internazionale di Musicologica* (Turin, 1990), 3: 692.
Professor Higgins plans a detailed account of the fragments; the pages carry the names of two clerks,
Jean du Bois and Robinet Paindavoine.

13. See Table 8.1.

14. See chap. 6.

15. "Treatise" is the conventional term for a book that deals with music theory; in reality, most
of the books are textbooks intended for use by schoolboys. The principal systematic account of
theoretical writings about composition is Ernst Apfel's *Geschichte der Kompositionslehre von Anfängen
bis gegen 1700* (Wilhelmshaven, 1981); he offers synopses of many of the treatises. As limited as this
study is, it nevertheless offers a useful point of departure. See also Hans Haase, "Komposition,"
MGG.

and not advice about composition.[16] As Howard Mayer Brown has noted, "no treatises on 'free composition,' no books that tell the budding composer precisely how to go about his craft were written so early as the first half of the sixteenth century."[17] Still, some of the writers were composers themselves—Tinctoris, Aaron, Coclico, Vicentino, Zarlino, Pontio, Galilei, Cimello, to name a few; they may have left reflections of their teaching (if not of their own compositional methods) in their writing.[18]

It is difficult to make generalizations about instruction in "composition" because it differs dramatically according to the length of the treatise, its intended audience, and the purposes and attitude of the writer. Nevertheless, certain features of these treatises were standard both in Italian and German traditions over a number of decades. Many, perhaps most, of the treatises/textbooks contain rules to govern both the vertical and horizontal aspects of music. There are rules (often eight) for voice-leading (prohibitions against parallel perfect consonances, for example) and for constructing chords (sometimes expressed as tables). There are also rules governing distinct segments of compositions (beginning, middle, end) as well as the various components or techniques found in Renaissance music (*fuga*, canon, cadences). Still others concern the text on various levels (meaning, structure, syllable length).

The table of contents of "Praecepta musicae poeticae" by the mid-sixteenth-century German composer and theorist Gallus Dressler is both characteristic in its contents and exemplary in its clarity:

Dividimus praecepta musicae poeticae in XV capita.	*We divide the precepts of* musica poetica *into fifteen chapters.*
I. caput agit de definitione et divisione contrapuncti	I. The first chapter addresses the definition and types of counterpoint
II. de sonis et consonantiis	II. Concerning sounds and consonances
III. de dissonantiis et syncopatione	III. Concerning dissonances and suspensions
IV. de differentia inter vera et falsa intervalla	IV. Concerning the difference between true and false intervals
V. de usu sextae et quartae	V. Concerning the use of the fourth and the sixth
VI. de partibus cantilenarum	VI. Concerning the parts [or voices] of songs

16. John Coprario, *Rules How To Compose: a facsimile edition of a manuscript from the library of the Earl of Bridgewater (circa 1610) now in the Huntington Library, San Marino, California*, introduction by Manfred F. Bukofzer (Los Angeles, 1952).

17. "Emulation, Competition, and Homage," 9–10.

18. James Haar addresses the issue of the composer-teacher in "Lessons in Theory from a Sixteenth-Century Composer," in *Altro Polo: Essays on Italian Music in the Cinquecento*, ed. Richard Charteris (Sydney, 1990), 51–81, a study of a treatise attributed to the Neapolitan composer Giovan Tomaso Cimello. Murray, "The Voice of the Composer," offers an interesting view of Pontio as both teacher/writer and composer.

VII. de commixtione consonantiae	VII. Concerning the combining of consonances
VIII. de constitutione et divisione clausularum	VIII. Concerning the structure and types of cadences
IX. de usu clausularum	IX. Concerning the function of cadences
X. de pausis	X. Concerning rests
XI. de inventione fugarum	XI. Concerning the construction (*inventione*) of points of imitation (*fuga*)
XII. de fingendis exordiis	XII. Concerning the composition of the opening (*exordium*) of a composition
XIII. de media parte cantilenarum constituenda	XIII. Concerning the construction of the middle part of songs (*cantilenarum*)
XIV. de fine harmoniarum	XIV. Concerning the end of compositions (*harmoniarum*)
XV. qua ratione tyrones in hoc studio cum fruge progredi possint.	XV. By what methods students may progress with profit in this subject.[19]

The opening seven chapters deal with the basic vocabulary of music—consonance, dissonance, suspensions, voices or parts, and chord formation. Within chapter 6, which addresses the range and function of the four voices, two other topics of great interest are considered: "which voice is the first of all to be made?" and "how many lines do *poetae* (i.e., creators and thus composers) use on which to compose?" The next four (8–11) discuss music in terms of its structural components—cadences, imitation, and rests. Dressler concludes the treatise with three chapters on how to write the beginning, middle, and end of a composition, and a final chapter that gives five recommendations on how to proceed in learning *musica poetica*.

It would be interesting to compare systematically all the "rules how to compose" and to trace the changes over time.[20] I suspect that the recommendations will prove to illustrate the accepted norms of style—how the voices relate to one another, what musical space they occupy, what relationship music has to the words—and show us what music teachers thought beginners needed to know about musical language. Far from being literal accounts of how to compose, they instead reflect the prevailing views about music.

---

19. "Praecepta musicae poeticae," praefatiuncula; the treatise was completed in 1564 but never published. For an edition, see Bernhard Engelke, *Geschichtsblätter für Stadt und Land Magdeburg* 49–50 (1914–1915): 214–250. A new edition and translation are sorely needed; a translation of part of chap. 13 is found in Ellen Beebe, "Text and Mode as Generators of Musical Structure in Clemens non Papa's *Accesserunt ad Jesum*," in *Music and Language*, Studies in the History of Music 1 (New York, 1983), 93.

20. For example, a study comparable to Ann Moyer's *Musica scientia: Musical Scholarship in the Italian Renaissance* (Ithaca, 1992) would be very welcome.

To illustrate this point, let us consider one of the topics that most of the writers included: which voice to compose first. The early sixteenth-century German theorist Venceslaus Philomathes offered the following advice, using the hexameter verse that is characteristic of much didactic writing:

De ordine vocum formandarum

Incipe sic: trahe per pluteum bis quinque lituras:
In certisque locis signatas construe clavis:
Demum que primum tibi vox ponenda videtur:
Pone. sed in primis mediam posuisse licebit.
Nam basis est vocum: sine qua tepet omne poema.
Qua recta posita: tractu perpendiculari
(Ne seducaris) distingue a tempore tempus.
Supremam cura vocem posuisse subinde: ut
Cum media resonet quovis in tempore recte.
Tum gravis harmoniam vocis suppone decenter:
Sic ut cum media sonet et cum voce suprema.
Postremum tandem vocem formabis acutam:
Ut cum voce gravi tantummodo consona fiat.
Et forme coeant ubi congruit: utque videtur.

[margin:] Concerning the order for forming the voices Begin this way: draw on the board twice five marks [lines], and draw the signed clefs at the specified places. Then place the voice you think should go first, but you may place the *media* [tenor] first, for it is the foundation of the voices, without which every composition [*poema*, i.e., thing created] is lukewarm. Once it has been correctly placed, divide the *tempora* from one another with perpendicular lines lest you be deceived. Then take care to place the *suprema* [discantus] immediately so that it will sound correctly with the *media* [tenor] in whatever *tempus*. Then place below the harmony of the *gravis* [bassus] properly such that it will sound with the *media* and the *suprema*. Finally, you will form the *acuta* [altus] so that it makes consonance only with the *gravis*. And let the forms meet where it is suitable and as you see fit.[21]

A nearby example illustrating the construction of cadences helps to clarify the instructions concerning the order of voices (see plate 2.1). The example shows a ten-line staff ("twice five lines") with the customary clefs (Gamma, b, F, b, c, g, b, dd);[22] it has four voices, labeled (from top to bottom) *suprema, acuta, media,* and *gravis* (see example 2.1).

The advice seems simple enough. While the student can begin with any voice, Philomathes offers directions that start with the tenor. Once the entire tenor has been written, barlines are added. Then the discantus is added to the

---

21. *De nova domo musicorum libri quattuor compendioso carmine elucubrati* (Vienna, 1512), sig. e iii[v]–iv[r].
22. On this format, see the discussion in chap. 3.

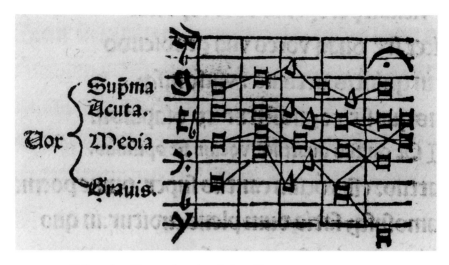

PLATE 2.1   Philomathes, *De nova domo* (1512), sig. e iii[v]

tenor, reaching a cadence at the octave. Then comes the bassus, which must go with both. Finally the altus is added, fit into the small space that remains.

In reality, the recommendations are quite complex—and therefore difficult to interpret—because they serve several different functions. Taken quite literally, they seem to describe the order in which the parts were to be composed. Such a view does not sufficiently account for the complexity of musical thought. The actual steps taken in creating a composition or even an exercise must be considerably more complex. A process that involves notating first one part in its

EXAMPLE 2.1   Philomathes, *De nova domo*

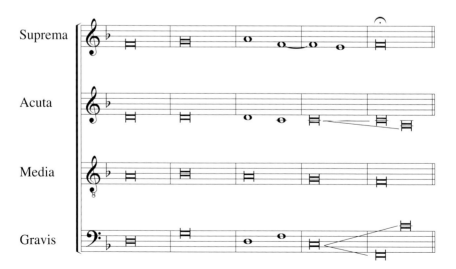

entirety and then another does not necessarily mean that the composer was literally hearing the music the way he wrote it down.[23] Even a raw beginner writing down a tenor could have been thinking about the possibilities for its paired discantus or for the other voices. Every note, every line has a potential harmonic context.

Philomathes, while apparently prescribing an order, is also explaining the function and character of the voices. The tenor serves as point of departure, the bassus as the foundation. The voices work in pairs: the altus goes with the bassus in the same way that the discantus goes with the tenor, but unlike the bassus, which must go with both discantus and tenor, the altus needs to go only with the bassus. (In other words, the interval between the altus and bassus must be a consonance, while the interval between the altus and the other two voices could be a fourth.)

In early music, as a rule, something—a line, a motive, a canon, in short, a "subject," the term used by the mid-sixteenth-century Italian theorist Gioseffo Zarlino—served as the compositional point of departure. Zarlino's explanation reflects the great diversity not only of technique but also of kinds of "subject" found in sixteenth-century music:

Incominciando adunque dalla prima dico, che il soggetto di ogni compositione musicale si chiama quella parte, sopra laquale il compositore cava la inventione di far le altre parti della cantilena, siano quante si vogliano. Et tal soggetto può essere in molti modi: prima può essere inventione propia, cioè, che il compositore l'haverà ritrovato col suo ingegno; dipoi può essere, che l'habbia pigliato dalle altrui compositioni, accommodandolo alla sua cantilena, & adornandolo con varie parti, & varie modulationi, come più gli aggrada, secondo la grandezza del suo ingegno. Et tal soggetto si può ritrovare di più sorte: percioche può

Beginning then with the first requirement [i.e., the subject], I say that the subject of every composition is that part of a composition upon which the composer exercises his inventiveness to produce the other parts, however many voices these may be. The subject may be one of several kinds. It may be a creation of the composer himself, a product of his genius. It may be taken from a composition of another, fitted to his own and adorned by various parts, as he pleases to the best of his talent. Such a subject may be of several kinds: it may be a tenor or other plain-chant part, or a part from a polyphonic

---

23. Thus, Daniel Leech-Wilkinson, "Machaut's *Rose, Lis* and the Problem of Early Music Analysis," *Music Analysis* 3 (1984): 10: "Is it conceivable that a composer of the calibre of Machaut was unable to imagine a piece of music; that, rather, he had to assemble it a line at a time according to a set of rules . . . in the hope that the result would sound acceptable? And must we therefore assume, as has been usual, that he and his contemporaries somehow managed to perceive polyphony principally in a single horizontal dimension, remaining largely insensitive to vertical coincidences? So simplistic a view of medieval polyphony could never adequately explain the complexity of much of the surviving music." See also his *Compositional Techniques in the Four-Part Isorhythmic Motets of Philippe de Vitry and his Contemporaries* (New York, 1989). My views have been shaped to a large extent by Leech-Wilkinson's arguments.

essere un tenore, overo altra parte di qualunque cantilena di canto fermo, overo di canto figurato; overo potranno esser due, o più parti, che l'una seguiti l'altra in fuga, o consequenza, overo a qualunque altro modo: essendo che li varii modi di tali soggetti sono infiniti.

Ritrovato adunque che haverà il compositore il soggetto, farà poi le altre parti, nel modo che più oltra vederemo; il che fatto tal maniera di comporre si chiamerà, secondo li prattici, far contrapunto. Ma quando non haverà ritrovato prima il soggetto; quella parte, che sarà primieramente messa in atto; over quella con la quale il compositore darà principio alla sua cantilena, sia qual si voglia, & incomincia a qual modo più li piace; o sia grave, overamente acuta, o mezana; sempre sarà il soggetto, sopra il quale poi accommodarà le altre in fuga, o consequenza, overo ad altro modo, come più li piacerà di fare; accommodando le harmonie alle parole, secondo che ricerca la materia contenuta in esse. Ma quando il compositore andrà cavando il soggetto dalle parti della cantilena, cioè quando caverà una parte dall'altra, & andrà cavando il soggetto per tal maniera, & facendo insieme la compositione, come vederemo altrove; quella particella, che lui caverà fuori delle altre, sopra laquale dipoi componerà le parti della sua compositione, si chiamerà sempre il soggetto. Et tal modo di comporre li prattici dimandano comporre di fantasia: ancorache si possa etiandio nominare contrapuntizare, o far contraponto, come si vuole.

composition. It may also consist of two or more voices, one of which may follow another in a fugue or consequence, or be organized in some other manner. Indeed, the types of such subjects are potentially infinite in number.

After a composer has found his subject, he proceeds to write the other parts in the manner we shall investigate. This process is called by musicians "making counterpoint." But should he not have a subject to begin with, the part that sounds first, or which he writes as a beginning, whatever it may be and however it may begin—whether a high, middle, or low part—this shall be the subject. Upon it he will adapt the other parts in fugue, consequence, or however he pleases, suiting the music to the words and to the meaning they contain. But when a composer derives his subject as he composes the parts of a composition, that is, when he derives one voice from another and arrives at the subject as he composes the parts all together, then that fragment of it from which he derives the parts of the rest of the composition is called the subject. Musicians call this "composing by fancy" (*comporre di fantasia*). It could well be called counterpointing, or making counterpoint, as one chooses.[24]

---

24. Gioseffo Zarlino, *Le istitutioni harmoniche* (Venice, 1558; repr. New York, 1965), 172, trans. Guy A. Marco and Claude V. Palisca under the title *The Art of Counterpoint. Part Three of* Le Istitutioni harmoniche, *1558* (New York, 1968), 52–53.

The "subject" changed over time, and within the same period from repertory to repertory, genre to genre. Burtius, for example, suggested two different scenarios for composing three-voice music, one for music that used a newly composed melody and one for music that was based on a pre-existent tune:

His igitur intellectis primo cantum sive, ut dicunt, supranum, investigatione praemissa, componas. Deinde tenorem, omnis castigatione tersum et examinatum. Postremo contrabassum, nullam dissonantiam ceteris procreantem. . . .

Igitur quando quis vellet super cantu plano mensuratum componere, nam ut primo dictum est, sic incipiendum. Nam necessum est quod cantus primo fabricatus sit. Secundo vero ut supranus magna sollertia, habendo respectum ad tenorem qui est planus cantus, edatur sive componatur. Exinde ad contrabassum deveniendum et mente et oculis ac ratione quicquid contra harmoniae dulcedinem obstiterit eradicando absolvendum.

When you have understood these things [that is, notation, properties of the tones, and have studied "an infinite number of songs"], compose first the cantus or soprano, as they say, with due care, then the tenor, amended and checked for any correction, and finally the contrabass, composed without making any dissonance with the other two. . . .

When one wants to compose a mensural composition on a plainsong the procedure is different than that above, for it is necessary that the plainsong be composed first. The soprano is created or composed second, with great care in regard to the tenor, which is the plainsong. Going from there to the contrabass, the latter must be observed by mind, reason, and eyes in order to remove anything that might disturb the pleasantness of the harmony.[25]

Burtius recommended that composers (presumably beginners) should compose (his terms are *fabricatio* and *componere*) in the order cantus, tenor, contrabass for freely composed music, and tenor, cantus, and contrabass for music based on a pre-existent melody.[26]

Frequently, writers contrasted older and newer practices. For example, Gallus Dressler described an older method, reflecting his awareness of an earlier style:

25. Nicolaus Burtius, *Musices opusculum* (Bologna, 1487; repr. Bologna, 1969), Trac. II, cap. 5, ed. G. Massera, *Nicolai Burtii Parmensis Florum libellus* (Florence, 1975), trans. Clement A. Miller, MSD 37 (Neuhausen-Stuttgart, 1983), 84–87.

26. A similar statement is found in an anonymous treatise now preserved in Cambridge, Corpus Christi College, MS 410: "in a motet the tenor should be composed first, but in rondeaux, virelais, and ballades the soprano should be written first." Cited by Miller, trans., Burtius, *Musices opusculum*, 18. Machaut, in *Le Voir Dit* (Letter XXXI), wrote: "I'm sending you a rondeau with music, of which I made the tune and the text a while ago. I have newly made a tenor and contratenor for it." Leech-Wilkinson, whose translation I have quoted ("*Le Voir Dit* and *La Messe de Nostre Dame*: Aspects of Genre and Style in Late Works of Machaut," *Plainsong and Medieval Music* 2 (1993): 48–49), proposed that the music might be Rondeau 18, stylistically quite different from Machaut's other music written at this time, and atypical also in how it came into existence.

Quae vox est omnium primo fingenda?	*Which voice is to be composed first of all?*

Veteres judicarunt Tenorem omnium primo inveniendum, secundo loco discantum tertio Bassum, ultimo Altum addendum. Inde Tenore nomen adeptus videtur a tenendo quod ad eum tanquam ad cerebrum (ceterae partes) respiciunt. In contrapuncto simplici vel florido haec veterum sententia potest et debet observari sed quilibet vox cui thema componendum attribuatur tenor iure quodam appellanda est sive Discantus sive Bassus vel quaecunque vox fuerit. Verum in contrapuncto colorato ubi mira varietas incidit, non Tenoris tantum sed et aliarum omnium vocum ratio habenda est, quando igitur figuralis harmonia componitur imprimis, Observetur ambitus tonorum qui per clausulas et repercussiones usitatas repraesentatur quo pacto omnium vocum ita ratio habeatur ut singulae suavitatem prae se ferre videa[n]tur. In cantionibus quae ex fuga constant, vox fugam incipiens vel continuans primaria et praecipua est, cui reliquae omnes quotquot fuerint parere coguntur, de qua re infra agetur.

The ancient [theorists] judged that the tenor was to be found first, the discantus in the second place, the bassus in the third, and the altus was to be added last. Whence the tenor appears to have acquired its name from *tenere*, "to hold," because the other parts look to it as if it were the brain. In simple or florid counterpoint this opinion of the ancient theorists can and must be observed but any voice to which the motive that is to be composed is given (whether it be the discantus or bassus or whichever voice) shall by a kind of right be called the tenor. But in ornamented counterpoint in which a remarkable variety occurs, not only the tenor but also all of the other voices must be taken into account. Therefore, when figural harmony is composed, above all you must observe the range of the modes which is represented by the cadences and by the *repercussio* [characteristic modal intervals], so that all the voices should so be taken into account that they each are seen to reveal sweetness. In songs composed of *fugae* [imitation] the voice beginning or continuing the *fuga* is primary and takes precedence, and all the rest, as many as there may be, are forced to obey it, about which matter see below.[27]

Recommendations about order explain both the compositional point of departure and the relationship among the voices in the ensemble: the number, range, and function. The specifics of the relationships changed from repertory to repertory. Pietro Aaron, for example, in his statements about the order of composition, made clear that his main issue was to find room for each of the voices in the sonority:

27. "Praecepta musicae poeticae," chap. 6; the discussion of *fuga* is in chap. 5. Dressler recognized that the essence of the tenor derived not from its location in the overall sonority but from its role as the presenter of the given line (*thema*).

La imaginatione di molti compositori fù, che prima il canto si dovesse fabricare, di poi il tenore, et dopo esso tenore il contrabasso. Et questo avenne, perche mancorno del l'ordine, et cognitione di quello, che si richiede nel far del contralto. et però facevano assai inconvenienti nelle loro compositioni, perche bisognava per lo incommodo, che vi ponessino unisoni, pause, salti ascendenti, et discendenti difficili al cantore, overo pronontiante: in modo che detti canti restavano con poca soavita, et harmonia. perche facendo prima il canto, over soprano, di poi il tenore, quando è fatto detto tenore, manca alcuna volta il luoco al contrabasso, et fatto detto contrabasso, assai note del contralto non hanno luoco. per la qual cosa considerando solamente parte per parte, cioè quando si fà il tenore, se tu attendi solo ad accordare esso tenore, et cosi il simile del contrabasso, conviene, che ciascuna parte delli luochi concordati patisca. Onde li moderni in questo meglio hanno considerato, come è manifesto per le compositioni da essi a quatro, a cinque, a sei, & a più voci fatte, delle quali ciascuna tiene luoco commodo, facile, et grato, perche considerano insieme tutte le parti, et non secondo, come di sopra è detto.

Many composers were of the opinion that the soprano should be composed first, then the tenor, and after the tenor the bass. This happened because they lacked the order and understanding of what was necessary to compose the alto. Thus they had many awkward places in their compositions because they had to insert unisons, pauses, and ascending and descending leaps that were difficult for the singer or performer, so that those works had little sweetness and harmony. For in composing the soprano first and then the tenor, once the tenor was made there was sometimes no room for the bass, and once the bass was made, there was no place for many notes in the alto. There, in considering only part by part, that is, when the tenor is being composed, if you pay attention only to harmonizing this tenor [with the soprano], and the same with the bass, it is inevitable that each part will suffer where they come together. Therefore the modern composers had a better idea, which is apparent from their compositions in four, five, six, and more voices, in which each part has a comfortable, easy and agreeable place, because they take all the parts into consideration at once and not as described above.[28]

Lowinsky took this passage to mean that the modern composers conceived all the parts together, that is, in score, using what he took to be a new harmonic conception of music. I suggest, however, that Aaron was concerned with the

---

28. *Thoscanello de la musica* (Venice, 1523; repr. New York, 1969), sig. I iᵛ. The translation is by Bonnie J. Blackburn, "On Compositional Process in the Fifteenth Century," *JAMS* 40 (1987): 215. In the next few sentences, Aaron explains that one can begin, as some do, with the bassus or with the tenor or with the contraltus, but he advises the student that because beginning part by part can be difficult he should follow the order and method proposed earlier (to consider the parts all together). For a more extended discussion of the entire passage and of the version published seven years earlier in Latin, see ibid., 212–219. Blackburn offers a modification of Lowinsky's interpretation (*Music in the Culture*, 11).

division of musical space into distinct realms in which each voice had its own place, a practice that was still relatively recent when he was writing.[29]

Recommendations about the order of composition generally appear within the context of counterpoint lessons. They inevitably reflect the conflict inherent in counterpoint between lines and chords, between the horizontal and vertical aspects of music.[30] Synthesizing these two components presents a challenge for students learning to compose.

The rules set forth by theorists, while often appearing to be concerned with lines, actually address chord formation as well. Writers had no simple way to describe sonorities consisting of more than two notes, or to present all the notes that could be used in a sonority. They offered instructions, often in chapters with titles such as "De modo componendi" (Vanneo), that were quite formulaic in character. Aaron's formulation for constructing a four-voice texture is typical. There are ten rules, one for each of the intervals separating the cantus and tenor (unison, third, fourth . . . to the thirteenth). Within each rule he listed all the options available to the bassus, and then the options for the altus according to the choice made for the bassus, for example:

Quando il tenore sara nel l'unisono col canto, poni il tuo contrabasso in quinta sotto del tenore: et il tuo alto in terza, ò in ottava, et (sel ti piace) in decima di sopra al basso: secondo quello, che sarà a te piu al proposito.	When the tenor is at the unison with the cantus, place your contrabassus a fifth below the tenor, and your altus a third, or an octave and (if it pleases you) a tenth above the bassus, according to what seems most appropriate.[31]

Virtually every counterpoint treatise from the end of the fifteenth century throughout the entire sixteenth century—in the Italian as well as the German tradition—contains some version of these rules.[32] They changed as the texture shifted from three voices to four, but the principles remained the same.

29. In taking this view of Aaron, I concur with a point made by Blackburn ("On Compositional Process," 212–219), though we reach different conclusions. A study—repertory by repertory, source by source—of the names, ranges, and character of the individual voices as well as the overall number would be a useful contribution to our understanding of the changes in musical style for the period ca. 1450–1550. Frank Carey, "Composition for Equal Voices in the Sixteenth Century," *Journal of Musicology* 9 (1991): 300–342, is a good example of the work that could be undertaken. Zarlino (*Le istitutioni harmoniche*, 260) wrote that the greatest difficulty in composing was to "accommodar le parti della cantilena in tal maniera, che l'una dia luogo all'altra, che siano facili da cantare, & habbiano bello, regolato, & elegante procedere"—a task not easily taught in books, but a matter requiring judgment and discretion on the part of the composer.

30. Klaus-Jürgen Sachs, "Contrapunctus/Kontrapunkt," *Handwörterbuch der musikalischen Terminologie* (1982–1983), 11, outlines the many meanings "counterpoint" can have, including a line, a composition, an object of study, a process. See also Frieder Rempp, "Elementar- und Satzlehre von Tinctoris bis Zarlino," in *Italienische Musiktheorie im 16. und 17. Jahrhundert,* Geschichte der Musiktheorie 7 (Darmstadt, 1989).

31. *Thoscanello,* sig. I iv.

32. Helen Bush ("The Recognition of Chordal Formation by Early Music Theorists," *MQ* 32 [1946]: 227–243) described the awareness of chords in music theory of the fifteenth and sixteenth

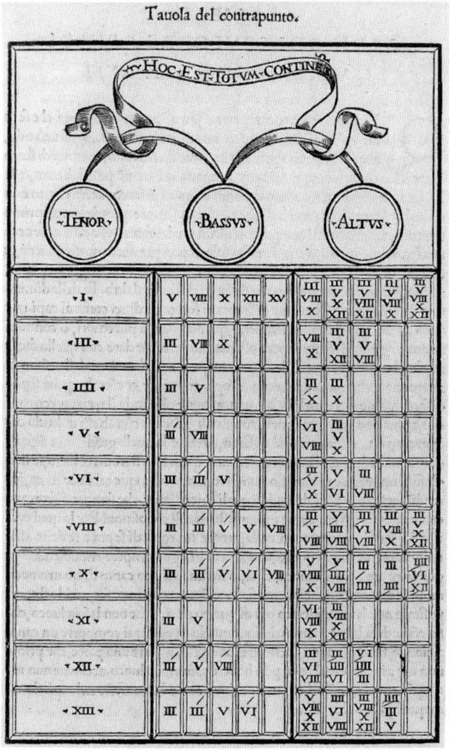

Tauola del cōtrapunto.

HOC·EST·TOTVM·CONTINE...

·TENOR·   ·BASSVS·   ·ALTVS·

PLATE 2.2   Aaron, *Thoscanello* (1523), sig. K 2[r]

Writers illustrated the rules in various ways. Some of them simply provided verbal accounts; others supplied musical examples[33] or chord tables. Aaron, for example, supplemented his prose account with a table containing three columns, for the tenor, bassus, and altus (see plate 2.2). For each interval between the cantus and tenor, all the options in the bassus and altus are shown with Roman numerals to indicate the intervals. Simon de Quercu illustrated the possible sonorities on a fourteen-line staff (!), showing the intervals beneath the chords in Roman numerals.[34] Galliculus drew chords without specific reference to pitch by using a staff without clefs.[35]

---

centuries. As Blackburn noted ("On Compositional Process," 219), Bush thought that her earliest witness, the anonymous "Ars discantus secundum Johannem de Muris" (CS 3: 93), dated from the fourteenth century; it is now thought to date from the middle of the fifteenth century.

33. For example, Franchinus Gaffurius, *Practica musice* (Milan, 1496; repr. New York, 1979), sigs. dd viii[r]–ee i[v], trans. Irwin Young under the title *The* Practica musicae *of Franchinus Gafurius* (Madison, 1969).

34. *Opusculum musices* (Landshut, 1516), fols. 2[v]-3[r]. This example is discussed and shown in facsimile by Benito Rivera ("Harmonic Theory in Musical Treatises of the Late Fifteenth and Early Sixteenth Centuries," *Music Theory Spectrum* 1 (1979): 87.

35. Johannes Galliculus, *Isagoge de composicione cantus* (Leipzig, 1520), sig. C iiii[v]–D ii[v], trans. Arthur A. Moorefield under the title *The Introduction to Song Composition* (Ottawa, 1992).

I II III IIII V VI VII VIII

Hæc eft fimplex concordantiarum
compofitio fecundam prædictas regu-
las, poffet enim multo fubtilius & uelo-
tius conftrui, hoc modo.

PLATE 2.3   Lampadius, *Compendium
musices* (1554), sig. F vii[r]

Sequitur Refolutio.

The German schoolteacher Lampadius illustrated his eight rules with specific chords, labeled I–VIII, shown on a ten-line staff[36] (see plate 2.3, top). He introduces it with the words "Here follows an example of each rule showing its essence and idea" ("Sequitur Exemplum cuiuslibet regulae vim & notitiam, declarans"). Example 2.2(a) gives a transcription.

There are four voices; the altus is identified by the use of black notes. The perpendicular lines divide the music into eight separate examples. Each of the eight has a specific rhythmic duration (I is one long, II one breve, III one semibreve, etc.). The musical examples conform almost exactly to Lampadius' verbal rules. Rule I, for example, provides two options for the altus, either a third or a fifth above the tenor, and both are shown. Example 2.2(b) shows the places where the verbal rules do not match the musical example. The verbal version of Rule II—"If the discantus touches a third above the tenor, the bass will have the octave below the tenor"—offers three options for the altus, while the example shows only one option. The verbal version of Rule III has only one, while the example shows two. A bigger discrepancy occurs in the seventh and eighth examples. The first chord in the seventh example illustrates Rule VII, while the second chord illustrates one of the options for Rule VIII. The eighth example does not illustrate any of the rules, though it is similar to Rule I.

36. Auctor Lampadius, *Compendium musices, tam figurati quam plani cantus ad formam dialogi, in usum ingenuae pubis ex eruditis musicorum scriptis accurate congestum* (Berne, 1537; edition consulted for this study: Berne, 1554).

Directly following the illustration of the chord tables, Lampadius provided a brief phrase notated twice, first on a ten-line staff with irregular barlines (bottom of sig. F vii[r]; see plate 2.3, bottom and example 2.3(a)) and then on five-line staves with no barlines (sig. F vii[v]; see plate 2.4 and example 2.3(b)). He introduces it as follows:

Haec est simplex concordantiarum compositio secundam praedictas regulas, posset enim multo subtilius & velotius construi, hoc modo.	This is the simple putting together (*compositio*) of the consonances according to the aforementioned rules, which may be constructed by far more subtly and quickly in this way.[37]

The "resolution" in separate parts then follows.

The "simplex concordantiarum compositio" is sometimes taken to be a chordal "reduction" or background draft of the chords given in example 2.2(a), but in fact the examples are not related.[38] Example 2.2(a) has Roman numerals to indicate the appropriate rule of chord formation and is barred by example rather than by rhythmic unit. The music in example 2.3(a), which is nearly identical to the version in Example 2.3(b), contains eight full measures, ending with a cadence on G. The juxtaposition of music notated first on a ten-line staff and then in parts next to the discussion and illustration of chord formation is significant, and suggests that beginners could have worked from a kind of chordal grid.

It is surely no coincidence that the order given for constructing a chord generally reflects the advice about the order for writing the parts. The point of departure is usually the interval between tenor and discantus, followed by bassus and then altus. But there are exceptions, just as there are exceptions to the rule

EXAMPLE 2.2   Lampadius, *Compendium musices:* (a) "Exemplum cuiuslibet regulae": ten-line staff, with literal transcription of note values; (b) realization of verbal rules, based on version (a) (black notes = altus)

37. Lampadius, *Compendium musices*, sig. F vii[r].
38. Siegfried Hermelink, *Dispositiones modorum* (Tutzing, 1960), 33–37.

EXAMPLE 2.3   Lampadius, *Compendium musices:* (a) "simplex concordantiarum composito": transcription of version on ten-line staff; (b) "resolutio": transcription of version in parts

1) notated as a minim directly on top of barline
2) notated with black notes

of beginning with the tenor.[39] Schanppecher devoted three chapters of his brief counterpoint treatise to rules for constructing first the tenor (what sort of shape it should have), then the discantus (giving the rules of voice-leading, for example, the prohibition against consecutive perfect consonances), and finally the contrapunctus. In discussing the contrapunctus he explained how to build sonorities, providing rules that are similar to those of the anonymous author of "Ars discantus":

Prima regula, si discantus ponitur cum tenore in unisono, bassus poni potest in 3, 5, 6, 10, 12 infra tenorem. Sic

The first rule: if the discantus is placed in unison with the tenor, the bassus can be placed a third, fifth, sixth, tenth,

39. Rivera ("Harmonic Theory") focuses on evidence concerning the interval between tenor and bass as part of an argument for a new harmonic function for the bass.

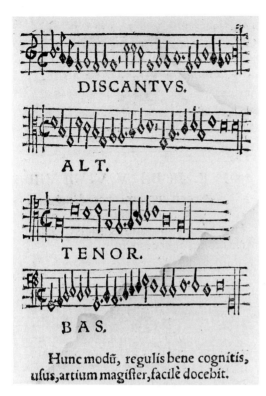

DISCANTVS.

ALT.

TENOR.

BAS.

Hunc modū, regulis bene cognitis,
usus, artium magister, facilè docebit.

PLATE 2.4   Lampadius,
Compendium musices (1554),
sig. F vii[v]

quoque, cum bassus positus fuerit cum tenore in unisono, discantus in simili forma poni poterit supra tenorem.

or twelfth below the tenor. Thus also, when the bassus is placed in unison with the tenor, the discantus can be placed in the same intervals above the tenor.[40]

Schanppecher offers two possibilities: the discantus–tenor pair to which a bassus can be added or a tenor–bassus pair to which the discantus can be added.

Ornithoparcus based his eight rules on the distance of the discantus from the tenor (unison, third, fifth, etc.). The final rule, however, notes that "if you make your Base first you shall make it with the Discantus."[41] Lampadius devoted the first five of his eight rules to the relationship between cantus and tenor, and the last three to the relationship between tenor and bassus.[42]

Writers working in a variety of different stylistic traditions explained how to

40. Parts III and IV of *Opus aureum* (Cologne, 1501), ed. K. W. Niemöller, *Die musica figurativa des Melchior Schanppecher. Opus aureum. Köln, 1501, pars III/IV,* Beiträge zur rheinischen Musikgeschichte 50 (Cologne, 1961), 25 and 37.

41. *Musice active micrologus* (Leipzig, 1517; repr. of 1517 edition and 1609 translation by John Dowland as Ornithoparcus/Dowland, *A Compendium of Musical Practice,* introduction by Gustave Reese and Steven Ledbetter (New York, 1973), in Dowland's translation sig. M 1[r-v].

42. *Compendium musices,* sig. F v[v]–vi[v].

use the chord tables in composition. In his treatise for beginning organists, Hans Buchner, himself an organist and student of Henricus Isaac, explained how to set a line of chant. He could have put it in the tenor or bassus, but chose to put it in the discantus.

Quanquam in plano cantu idem genus notarum pertuo [*sic*] sit: tamen sciendum est eas nos posse reducere vel ad brevium vel semibrevium figuras. Secundo sciendum est, liberum esse cuique, eum cantum, quem planum suscepit ludere, redigere vel ad tenorem vel discantum vel Bassum. Sed omnium istorum esto sequens exemplum. Choralis cantus. [ex. 2.4(a)]	Although in plain chant the notes are all of the same kind, nevertheless it must be known that we may reduce them either to the shapes of breves or of semibreves. Second, it must be known that anyone is free to adapt the melody which he undertakes to play as chant to the tenor or to the discantus or to the bassus. Let the following example [2.4(a)] represent all of them.
Ita redigatur ad symphonias trium vocum, servato Chorali in discantus voce et ducto per semibreves hoc modo. [ex 2.4(b)]	In this way let it be adapted to a composition for three voices, retaining the chant in the discantus, set out in semibreves in the following way [example 2.4(b)].
Haec est simplicissima ratio planum redigendi cantum in varias voces, quia vero nullam plane adhuc habet gratiam, ideo organistae addunt cuique voci suos colores, quos cuivis facile est invenire exercitatio [*recte* exercitato]: Sequentur quoque tabulae, ex quibus petere colorandi rationem licebit. Sed addamus et nostro hoc exemplo suum colorem. [ex. 2.4(c)]	This is the simplest way of fitting the melody in the various voices, but because it clearly still has no grace, organists give each voice its own "color," which any practiced person can find easily. There will also follow tables from which it is permitted to seek out a method for "coloring." But let us give our example too its own color [example 2.4(c)].[43]

Buchner used small barlines to divide a line of chant into separate sections corresponding to word divisions, and then decided which notes to treat as part of the melody and which to use for making the cadence. In the first phrase (*Te deum laudamus*), the cadence is an addition of G and A following the final note of the phrase, A; in the second phrase (*Te Dominum confitemur*), the final notes of the chant (A G) become G F G for the cadence. In both phrases, all the other notes of the chant are used in the setting. Next he created a chordal grid, writing the tenor line first and noting its distance from the discantus. The beginner

---

43. "Fundamentum," modern edition in Hans Buchner, *Sämtliche Orgelwerke*, ed. and trans. Jost Harro Schmidt, Das Erbe deutscher Musik 54–55 (Frankfurt, 1974), 54: 22–23. This passage is from the version of the treatise found in Basel, Öffentliche Bibliothek der Universität, MS F I 8a, copied by Christoph Piperinus (see John Kmetz, *Die Handschriften der Universitätsbibliothek Basel* [Basel, 1988], 33–34 and n. 11 above). The treatise covers many of the familiar components of instruction in counterpoint: a list of intervals, classification according to consonance and dissonance, rules of voice-leading, and rules about how to construct chords.

EXAMPLE 2.4   Buchner, "Fundamentum": (a) chant melody; (b) chordal setting; (c) florid version (Buchner, *Sämtliche Orgelwerke*, 22–23)

could consult the consonance tables to find pitches that would be available to the bassus. Finally, he "colored" each note, adding rhythmic and melodic variety to the basic grid. Again, the beginner could find specific examples of how to color such a grid by looking at the tables in the treatise.

Elementary instruction in composition helped the student achieve a synthesis of chord and line, something that an experienced composer knew intuitively. Zarlino, for example, in his chapter on composing for four or more voices, showed how a student might combine the information contained in the chord tables with what he has learned about voice-leading to write imitative polyphony:

. . . volendo dar principio alle compositioni nominate di sopra; primeramente si ritroverà il soggetto; dipoi ritrovato, si potrà incominciare il contrapunto da quella parte, che tornarà più commodo. La onde poniamo, che si volesse dar principio alla cantilena con la parte del basso; subito il compositore potrà conoscere il luogo del contralto, del soprano, & quello del tenore. Cosi ancora volendo dar principio per qualunque altra parte; sicome per il tenore, o per il basso; saprà i luoghi dell'altre parti per ordine, reggendosi secondo'l modo mostrato di sopra nella tavola; osservando anche quelle regole, che disopra in molti luoghi hò mostrato, quando fu ragionato intorno il modo di comporre a due, & a tre voci.

To begin a four-voice composition, a subject must first be chosen, and a counterpoint added to it in any convenient voice. Suppose that the bass begins the composition; the composer will quickly recognize the proper places for the contralto, soprano and tenor. Whatever part begins, he can locate the place for the remaining parts by consulting the table given above and by utilizing all the rules given in connection with two- and three-voice writing.[44]

Johannes Lippius, in *Synopsis musicae novae*, recommended a procedure for composing chordal music that recalled the idea of chord tables:

Colligitur ex his compendiosissimum esse τὸ μελοποιεῖν sincere discenti, si primo melodia fundamentalis quae est bassus in systemate coniuncto ipsi proponatur statuis punctis contra puncta in loca partium radicialium triadis harmonicae, cuius primam et basin tenet bassus. [example: *Laudate dominum*, bassus]

Ut huic melodiae fundamentali deinde per puncta ista proxime assignet

One gathers from all this that the most compendious method for the serious student of composition is first to establish on the great staff the fundamental melody, namely the bass. Dots should be placed against other dots to locate the radical parts of the harmonic triad, with the bass maintaining the prima or basis.

To this fundamental melody one melodiam principalem seu regalem

---

44. *Le istitutioni harmoniche*, 261; trans. Marco and Palisca, *The Art of Counterpoint*, 227.

tenorem: tum superiores altum, de-
nique discantum superaddat iuxta
modo praecepta et percepta pure componendi momenta. [example: *Laudate
dominum*, four voices]

should next, with the aid of those dots,
notate the principal or ruling melody
of the tenor. Then he should add the
alto and finally the discant, according to
the rules of pure composition that have
just been taught and learned.[45]

Lippius explained that once this method had been learned, it was possible to begin with the tenor or the discantus.

The order of composition has in the past loomed large in music historiography. Lowinsky's hypothesis of a dichotomy between successive and simultaneous composition has seemed attractive to many, and reasonable when considered from the perspective of musical style and structure. I believe that we should view the advice from writers about order as reflections of musical style, not as descriptions of the processes of actual composers.[46] While the process of *notating* music had to be successive by its very nature (it is possible to write only one note at a time), the music itself always has both a linear and a vertical component. It is time to leave this particular hypothesis behind. The recommendations are intended for beginners and thus explicate what any composer knew instinctively, for example, how to construct chords. It is risky to take advice such as "compose this line first" too literally; after all, one of the functions of the treatises is to explain the character of the music (the function of the voices, the kind of ensemble, the nature of the "subject").

Treatises and textbooks are important sources of information; in the next chapter we will consider the evidence they present about how musicians might have read and written music. But there are limits to what they can tell us about the practices of actual composers. Today, one would not turn to an elementary textbook to shed light on a professional composer's working methods; nor should we for earlier periods. Composers did not need rules, though they probably learned them during their own period of apprenticeship.[47] The rules should probably be thought of as reflections of contemporary musical language. We would do well to recall the words of the Bolognese composer, choir director, and music theorist Giovanni Spataro: "The written rules can teach the first rudiments of counterpoint well, but they will not make a good composer, inasmuch as the good composers are born just as are the poets."[48]

45. Johannes Lippius, *Synopsis novae musicae* (Strassburg, 1612), sig. G 7ᵛ–8ʳ]. The translation is from Benito Rivera, *German Music Theory in the Early 17th Century: The Treatises of Johannes Lippius* (Madison, 1980), 48–49.

46. Leech-Wilkinson, *Compositional Techniques*, 18–20, made the same point in dealing with an earlier repertory.

47. A point expressed several times in the Spataro correspondence. See Bonnie J. Blackburn, Edward E. Lowinsky, and Clement A. Miller, eds., *A Correspondence of Renaissance Musicians* (Oxford, 1991), for example, in Letter 11; see the discussion in chap. 5.

48. Blackburn et al., *A Correspondence*, Letter 22, para. 3; discussed also on p. 101. The passage was first discussed by Edward Lowinsky in "Musical Genius—Evolution and Origins of a Concept," *MQ* 50 (1964), repr. in *Music in the Culture*, 51.

CHAPTER THREE

READING AND WRITING MUSIC

READING MUSIC

How did musicians customarily see music? How was it arranged on the page? We know the answer when they were performing, but what about when they were reading by themselves or studying?[1] The musical examples in textbooks and treatises provide one kind of answer to these questions: they reflect the habits and skills of their readers, a group that presumably ranged from amateurs who could sing and play an instrument and who were interested enough in music to buy books about music to more sophisticated musicians.[2] Indirectly the examples mirror the techniques available to both composers and students of composition.

A survey of a small sample of music treatises and textbooks published between 1496 and 1597 over a wide geographical area reveals a number of different ways of positioning or arranging music on the page (see table 3.1).

Separate Parts

By far the most common method is to notate the music in separate parts. The deployment of the voices on the page depends on the length of the example. In short examples the voices are frequently notated side by side, on the same line (see plate 3.1). Longer examples have to be notated consecutively on several staves (either in "run-on" fashion, for example, with a voice beginning in the middle of one staff and continuing onto the next one,[3] or voice by voice, for example, staves 1–2 for the cantus, 3–4 for the altus, etc.

Another option frequently used for lengthy examples is to divide the page or

---

1. Besseler and Gülke (*Schriftbild der mehrstimmigen Musik*) present a rich collection of facsimiles, organized both chronologically and by genre.
2. Both Kinkeldey (*Orgel und Klavier*, 188) and Schwartz ("Zur Partitur," 73–78) considered this issue in connection with the debate about the use of scores in the sixteenth century.
3. An example in Gaffurius' *Practica musice* is found on sig. ll ii[v].

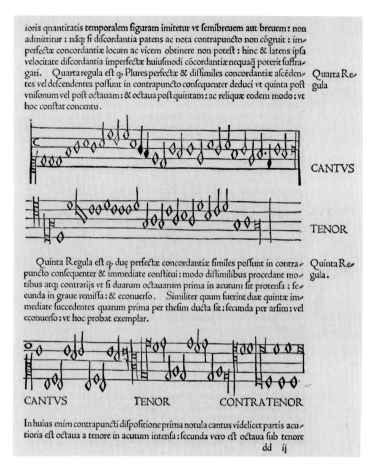

ioris qnantitatis temporalem figuram imitetur vt femibreuem aut breuem: non
admittitur : náq̃ fi difcordantia patens ac nota contrapunĉto non côgruit : imperfectæ concordantiæ locum ac vicem obtinere non poteft : hinc & latens ipfa
velocitate difcordantia imperfectæ huiufmodi côcordantiæ nequaq̃ poterit fuffra-
gari.   Quarta regula eft q̃, Plures perfectæ & diffimiles concordantiæ afcéden-   Quarta Re-
tes vel defcendentes poffunt in contrapuncto confequenter deduci vt quinta poft   gula
vnifonum vel poft octauam: & octaua poft quintam: ac reliquæ eodem modo: vt
hoc conftat concentu .

CANTVS

TENOR

Quinta Regula eft q̃, duę perfectæ concordantiæ fimiles poffunt in contra-   Quinta Re-
puncto confequenter & immediate conftitui: modo diffimilibus procedant mo-   gula.
tibus atq̃ contrarijs vt fi duarum octauarum prima in acutum fit protenfa : fecunda in graue remiffa: & econuerfo .   Similiter quum fuerint duæ quintæ immediate fuccedentes quarum prima per thefim ducta fit: fecunda per arfim: vel
econuerfo: vt hoc probat exemplar.

CANTVS   TENOR   CONTRATENOR

In huius enim contrapuncti difpofitione prima notula cantus videlicet partis acu-
tioris eft octaua a tenore in acutum intenfa: fecunda vero eft octaua fub tenore
                                                                    dd   ij

PLATE 3.1   Gaffurius, *Practica Musice* (1496). sig. dd ii[r]

opening into discrete blocks, each containing one part. The format is similar to
that used in the large choirbooks for performing vocal polyphony, and is generally referred to as choirbook format.

The crucial question about this format—not just for reading and studying
but also for composing—is whether musicians were able to read in separate
parts; it is a question we will consider in some detail later in this chapter.

Quasi-score

A second method is the format that might be referred to as quasi-score or
pseudo-score, in which the individual voices each occupy a single staff and are
superimposed one above the other, not necessarily in the order high to low, and
without barlines or vertical alignment (see plates 3.1 and 2.4). As far as I know,
there are no descriptions of this format in contemporary documents or treatises

TABLE 3.1 Formats of Music Examples in Selected Printed Treatises

Author, title (date)	Separate parts (short, on one staff)	Separate parts (long, more than one staff)	Choirbook	Quasi-score	Quasi-score, barred by example	Ten-line staff	Score	Other
Gaffurius, *Practica musice* (1496)	many	many	—	many	—	—	—	2v. on one staff, f. dd v^v
Ornithoparcus, *Micrologus* (1517)	many	many	f. L iv^v	many	—	f. L iii^r	—	—
Aaron, *Thoscanello* (1523)	many	—	f. L i^v	f. L ii^v	—	—	—	—
Vanneo, *Recanetum* (1533)	many	—	—	many	—	—	—	—
Glarean, *Dodecachordon* (1547)	p. 221, p. 231	many	many	p. 233	—	—	—	nine-line staff: p. 71; barring to show line endings in Latin verse (many)
Bermudo, *Declaración* (1555)	f. lix^v	f. cxxviii^v	many	many	—	—	ff. lxxxiii^r, cxxxiii^v	compact choirbook: f. cxxxix^r
Vicentino, *L'antica musica* (1555)	f. 91	many	ff. 69^v–70^r	ff. 91^v–92^r	many	—	—	compact choirbook: f. 93^r

TABLE 3.1 (continued)

Author, title (date)	Separate parts (short, on one staff)	Separate parts (long, more than one staff)	Choirbook	Quasi-score	Quasi-score, barred by example	Ten-line staff	Score	Other
Zarlino, *Le istitutioni harmoniche* (1558)	many	many	—	many	many	—	—	seven-line staff: p. 281; compact choirbook (many)
Sancta María, *Arte de tañer fantasia* (1565)	—	f. 79ᵛ	ff. 83ᵛ–84ʳ	many	many	—	—	keyboard score: f. 54ʳ
Pontio, *Ragionamento di musica* (1588)	many	many	—	many	—	—	—	compact choirbook: p. 151
Zacconi, *Prattica di musica*, I (1596)	many	many	many	many	f. 207ʳ	—	ff. 48ᵛ–49ʳ	eleven-line staff: f. 218ᵛ
Morley, *A Plaine and Easie Introduction* (1597)	—	many	many	many	many	—	many	—

Note: The table offers a rough approximation of the frequency of use of particular formats. "Many" indicates more than three occurrences, while the presence of foliation or pagination records the instances of formats used three or fewer times.

and therefore no term for it with any claim to authority.[4] Both quasi-score and pseudo-score are problematic as names because they suggest a relationship to the score, a format that developed considerably later.[5] Aside from the stacking of the voices, the two formats have little in common.

Quasi-score is a way of writing music out in separate parts that is appropriate to musical examples exactly one line long. It retains the features of notation in separate parts but brings the voices into physical proximity. There is no alignment to help the reader, but at least the parts are not in separate books or divided into separate quadrants on an opening. The decision to use this format in music treatises seems to be primarily a function of the length of the music and the amount of space available.

Ten-line Staff

A third method employs a ten-line staff—*scala decemlinealis*—to represent the entire tonal system, from Gamma ut to ee. The individual lines of the polyphonic fabric are written out, distinguished from one another by color, shape, or lines that show the connections between notes; most examples employ barlines (see plates 2.1 and 2.3).

In contrast to quasi-score format, for which there are a significant number of examples but no theoretical discussion, theorists working in the German-speaking realm frequently discussed the ten-line staff and used it for many of their musical examples.[6] The earliest references to this format use a variety of names. Cochlaeus referred to composing "per decem lineas," Philomathes to "bis quinque lituras."[7] Ornithoparcus was the first writer to use the term that

---

4. Hans Hoke ("Partitur," *MGG*) may have been the first to use the term pseudo-score (his words are "Pseudo"-Partitur, Pseudopartitur, unechte Partitur). Neither Clercx ("D'une ardoise," 165), who drew attention to this format, nor Lowinsky ("Early Scores," *Music in the Culture*, 807–808), who listed a number of other examples, referred to it by a specific name; Lowinsky argued that this format should not be considered a score.

5. Examples of quasi-score format occur in the sources of Notre Dame polyphony and continue to be used for some vocal repertories well into the fifteenth century. On the issue of format (parts versus quasi-score) and its relation to genre, see Rebecca Baltzer, "The Thirteenth-Century Motet and the Role of Manuscript Makers in Defining a Genre," paper read at the annual meeting of the American Musicological Society, Chicago, 1991.

6. The main witnesses are: anonymous, "Juxta artem conficiendi," GöttU IV. 3000, edited by Carl Dahlhaus, "Eine deutsche Kompositionslehre des frühen 16. Jahrhunderts," *Kirchenmusikalisches Jahrbuch* 40 (1956): 33–43; Johannes Cochlaeus, *Musica activa* (Cologne, ca. 1504; 3d ed., 1507); Philomathes, *De nova domo*; Ornithoparcus, *Musice active micrologus*; Galliculus, *Isagoge de composicione cantus*; Lampadius, *Compendium musices*; Heinrich Faber, "Musica poetica," BerlS 1175 (on the sources of this treatise see Bernhard Meier, "Eine weitere Quelle der 'Musica poetica' von H. Faber," *Musikforschung* 11 (1958): 76); Dressler, "Praecepta musicae poeticae"; Seth Calvisius, draft (ca. 1589) for *Melopoiia sive melodiae condendae ratio* (Erfurt, 1592), GöttU 103, edited by Carl Dahlhaus, "Musiktheoretisches aus dem Nachlaß des Sethus Calvisius," *Musikforschung* 9 (1956): 129–139.

7. *Musica activa*, fol. 28; *De nova domo*, sig. e iv. The anonymous author of "Juxta" also referred simply to "decem lineis."

became standard, *scala decemlinealis*.[8] Lampadius may have used *scala compositoria* to mean ten-line staff; it occurs, unfortunately without an accompanying musical example, in a section entitled "Rules concerning the forming of cadences and canons" ("De Clausulationibus & Canonibus formandis regulae"): "beware, lest you go beyond two octaves on the *scala compositoria*, because consonances within the range of two octaves are more frequent and are more pleasing by far than others."[9]

While the ten-line staff first began to be used as a pedagogical tool in the early sixteenth century, the idea of representing the pitches of the tonal system on a grid of ten lines and spaces was nearly as old as staff notation itself.[10] In the sixteenth century, the usual way of teaching the tonal system employed a grid similar to that on the ten-line staff. A typical example, a diagram of the *scala generalis* from Lampadius' *Compendium musices*, shows a system of nineteen pitches, from Gamma to dd, arrayed on ten lines and their contiguous spaces; a twentieth pitch, ee, is usually thought of as part of the basic system, while the twenty-first, FF (the F below Gamma ut), rarely notated in treatises, was frequently used in practice. The *scala generalis* (plate 3.2) shows the *claves* (letters) and the *voces* (solmization syllables); each letter has its place on a line or space. A diagram on the facing page (plate 3.3) shows the "signed" clefs, which situate the gamut on the staff; the other letters are understood but not written. This cleffing is characteristic. All of the examples of ten-line staves of which I am aware use the cleffing Gamma, F, c, g, dd, sometimes with a b in the three lines representing Bmi, ♭fa/♮mi, ♭♭fa/♮♮mi, sometimes without. The ten-line staff might be said to serve as a visual image of the tonal system of early music in much the way that the piano keyboard represents our system.

Not surprisingly, staves both with and without clefs offered a convenient way to present examples in treatises.[11] One of the first printed examples is the eleven-line staff in Burtius' *Musices opusculum* (1487).[12] Another one is in Schanppecher's *Musica figurativa*, where there are only empty lines; the examples were to be added by hand.[13] These examples do not concern the ten-line staff as a tool, but rather show its obvious utility as a way of representing the tonal sys-

---

8. *Musice active micrologus*, sig. L ii^v–iii. The passage was quoted by Claudius Sebastiani, *Bellum musicale* (Strassburg, 1563), chap. 30. The first six breves of the example are virtually the same as in Ornithoparcus; the final ten breves in Ornithoparcus are condensed and altered to five breves in Sebastiani. The term was subsequently used by Galliculus, *Isagoge de composicione cantus*, sig. D iii^v, and others.

9. "Cavebis, ne in scala compositoria Disdiapason transilias, quia consonantiae intra Disdiapason sunt frequentiores & multo suaviores aliis"; Lampadius, *Compendium musices*, sig. F viii^v. Lampadius drew his three rules on sig. F viii^r directly from Galliculus, *Isagoge de composicione cantus*, sig. D iii^v–iiii^r (without acknowledgment).

10. An example cited by Hermelink (*Dispositiones modorum*, 38) will suffice to illustrate the antiquity of this notion: a twelfth-century Italian manuscript of *Metrologus*, an anonymous commentary on Guido's *Micrologus*, shows the gamut set forth on a series of lines and spaces.

11. In some instances, the staves have more or fewer than ten lines. For example, John Playford, *An Introduction to the Skill of Musick* (London, 1655; 12th ed., London, 1694 [repr. New York, 1972], 38, used an eleven-line staff; Cochlaeus (*Musica activa*, fol. 31^v) used a nine-line staff.

12. Sig. c ii.

13. Sig. h ii^v.

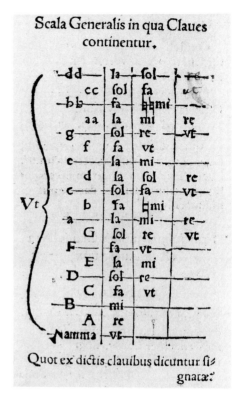

PLATE 3.2   Lampadius, *Compendium*
musices (1554), sig. B iiiᵛ

tem, either in its entirety or in segments. The examples notated with ten-line staves range from brief illustrations of chords or cadences (e.g., Cochlaeus, *Musica activa*) to entire segments of polyphonic compositions (e.g., Faber, "Musica poetica"). Martin Agricola, in *Musica instrumentalis deudsch* (1529), used the ten-line staff to illustrate tablature. Following the explanation of how to create an organ tablature from three-voice polyphony (work one voice at a time, beginning with the discantus, then tenor, then bassus), Agricola provided an example notated in two different formats, linked with barlines: a ten-line staff (mensural notation) and organ tablature (upper voice on a staff, lower voices using a combination of letters and strokes).[14]

The main advantage of the ten-line staff is that it presents the parts vertically aligned and thus shows the sonorities. The chief disadvantage is the difficulty in distinguishing among the individual voices. Philomathes solved the problem in his four-voice example by drawing lines to connect notes (see plate 2.1). Ornithoparcus used white and black notes in his two-voice example: white notes for the top voice, black for the bottom.[15] Cochlaeus used both white and

---

14. (Wittenberg, 1529, 2d ed., 1545; repr. of the 1529 ed., Hildesheim, 1969), trans. by William E. Hettrick under the title *The 'Musica instrumentalis deudsch' of Martin Agricola* (Cambridge, 1994), facsimile and transcription of the fold-out in appendices 7–8.

15. *Musice active micrologus*, sig. L iiiʳ.

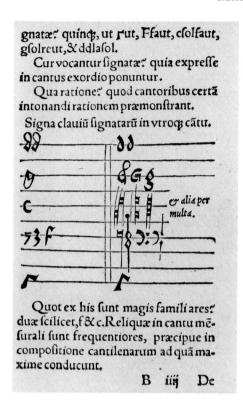

gnatæ? quinɋ, ut ɼut, Ffaut, cſolfaut,
gſolɼeut,& ddlaſol.

Cur vocantur ſignatæ? quia expreſſe
in cantus exordio ponuntur.

Qua rationeʔ quod cantoribus certā
intonandi rationem præmonſtrant.

Signa clauiũ ſignatarũ in vtroɋ cātu.

et alia per multa.

Quot ex his ſunt magis famíli aresʔ
duæ ſcilicet, f & c. Reliquæ in cantu mē-
ſurali ſunt frequentiores, præcipue in
compoſitíone cantilenarum ad quā maxime conducunt.

B iiɉ   De

PLATE 3.3   Lampadius, *Compendium musices* (1554), sig. B iiii^r

black notes and note-shapes in his four-voice example.[16] Lampadius distinguished the altus from the other three voices by making the notes black (see plate 2.3). While each of these writers solved the problem in his own way, none of them discussed it. Not until 1548 did a treatise contain explicit advice. Faber recommended the use of shapes (discantus and bassus: rectangular; media: triangular; altus: round); the examples in the Berlin copy of this treatise add the dimension of color (discantus and bassus: red; altus: green; tenor: black).[17] The use of colors and shapes was to be a feature of all the subsequent descriptions.[18] Rhythm is controlled by the use of barlines (*cancelli*) to distinguish one tempus from another; all of the examples use barlines, most of them at the interval of the breve.

16. *Musica activa*, fol. 31^v.

17. "Musica poetica." A facsimile of BerlS 1175, fols. 106^v–107^r is in Hermelink, *Dispositiones modorum*, 34.

18. Dressler, "Praecepta musicae poeticae" (shapes only); Calvisius, draft of *Melopoiia*; Wolfgang Schonsleder, *Architectonice musices universalis ex qua melopoeam per universa et solida fundamenta musicorum, proprio marte condiscere possis* (Ingolstadt, 1631); and J. A. Herbst, *Musica poetica sive compendium melopoeticum* (Nuremberg, 1643) (a paraphrase of Schonsleder). The passages from Calvisius and Schonsleder are quoted below.

Score

A fourth way of deploying music on the page is score format. A score consists of two or more staves, each containing the music for a single voice. The voices are typically ordered high to low. Barlines placed at regular intervals divide the score into measures. As is also the case with ten-line staves, the presence of barlines in scores forces compromises of various kinds for the notation of rhythmic values that cross the barline; notes are sometimes placed directly over the barline, or divided into smaller values, or placed entirely before the barline.

Score notation began to appear in treatises during the second quarter of the sixteenth century, often as a way of illustrating instrumental tablature notation. Theorists evidently realized that the easiest way to show how to translate mensural notation into tablature was to show the same passage in both notations. The earliest is an illustration included as an oversized folio folded into the 1529 edition of Agricola's *Musica instrumentalis deudsch* (see plate 3.4).[19] There are three voices: discantus, tenor, and bassus. Each voice appears in two versions: mensural notation and, directly beneath it, tablature. The mensural notation is labeled "Gesang," the tablature "Tabelthur" (these labels are only partially visible in this reproduction). The example has all the features associated with a score: an ordering of the voices from high to low (the clefs are g3, c3, F4), a separate staff for each voice (usually five-line, but in this case six-line in the bassus), and regular barring of every breve. Agricola has no name for this format, nor does he recommend its use in preparing a tablature: its purpose here is simply to illustrate tablature notation. Many of the examples of scores in sixteenth-century treatises are similar in function.[20]

Apart from the examples of scores associated with instrumental tablatures, the only other example of a score in a treatise dating from the first half of the sixteenth century is Lampadius' well-known "ordo distribuendi voces," containing the opening measures of Verdelot's four-voice motet *Sancta Maria succurre miseris*.[21] Lampadius included the example to show how he believed composers such as Josquin and Isaac wrote out compositions that they had first worked out

---

19. First discussed by Kinkeldey, *Orgel und Klavier*, 189. Kinkeldey mistakenly believed that the edition dated from 1528; on the dates and publication history, see Hettrick, trans., *The 'Musica instrumentalis'*. I am excluding the early repertories of polyphonic vocal music that are often referred to as being in score, but are actually in a form of quasi-score, without barlines and often without alignment.

20. Examples include Juan Bermudo, *El arte tripharia* (Osuna, 1550; repr. n.p., n.d.), fol. xxxviiᵛ; Luis Venegas de Henestrosa, *Libro de cifra nueva* (Alcalá de Henares, 1557), facsimile in Higinio Anglés, *La música en la Corte de Carlos V*, Monumentos de la Música Española 1, pt. 2 (Barcelona, 1944), 158; Vincenzo Galilei, *Fronimo dialogo . . . nel quale si contengono le vere et necessarie regole del intavolare la musica nel liuto* (Venice, 1568; 2d ed., Venice, 1584), fol. 12ʳ (1568 ed.); Adrian Le Roy, *A Briefe and easye instruction to learne the tableture* (London, 1568; 2d ed., London, 1574), fol. 5ʳ (1574 ed.), facsimile in *Oeuvres d'Adrian Le Roy, Les instructions pour le luth (1574)*, ed. J. Jacquot, P.-Y. Sordes, and J.-M. Vaccaro (Paris, 1977), 7; and Michele Carrara, [*Intavolatura di liuto*] (Rome, 1585), facsimile and edition by B. Disertori (Florence, n.d.).

21. *Compendium musices*, sig. G viʳ. This page has frequently appeared in facsimile; see, for example, Lowinsky, "On the Use of Scores," *Music in the Culture*, 799.

PLATE 3.4   Agricola, *Musica instrumentalis deudsch* (1529), foldout

in their minds.[22] This is the only instance where he used a score; the other examples were notated either in separate parts (including quasi-score) or on a ten-line staff.

By the second half of the sixteenth century, however, score format—or at least formats that bear close resemblance to score format—began to be used as a way to present certain aspects of music theory. Some of the instances usually thought to be in score are actually quasi-scores barred by example: the barlines demarcate musical segments rather than rhythmic units and thus are not really scores according to the usual definition. I would include in this category the format used by Zarlino, Tigrini, and others to illustrate block chords or intervals.[23] While the features fit the usual definition of score, the examples are not actual music; the barring, while regular, shows vertical relationships rather than musical time. The closest analogy is the use of the ten-line staff to illustrate cadences or chords.

A cursory survey of the use of scores and other formats in printed treatises suggests that the choice of format varied not only over time but also from region

22. For a more detailed discussion of this passage, see chap. 4 (on composing in the mind) and chap. 5 (on composers' use of tablets).

23. For example, Orazio Tigrini, *Il compendio della musica* (Venice, 1588; repr. New York, 1966), 40; Zarlino, *Le istitutioni*, 158.

to region. Morley, who published *A Plaine and Easie Introduction to Practicall Musicke* in London in 1597, used scores extensively in the portions of his treatise devoted to the study of counterpoint and composition, while generally presenting in separate parts complete compositions intended to be performed. He drew attention to the score format, which he called "partition," in three cases where he wanted the reader to grasp a complicated example: (1) "And to the ende that you may the more easelie understand the contryving of the parts, and their proportion one to another, I have set it downe in partition" (p. 34; a five-voice madrigal by Giulio Renaldi); (2) "Here it is set downe in partition, because you should the more easilie perceive the conveiance of the parts" (p. 97; Osbert Parsley, *Salvator mundi* for three voices); (3) "And although hee should assaie twentie several hymnes or plainsonges for finding of one to his purpose, I doubt if hee should any waie goe beyond the excellencie of the composition of this, and therefore I have set it downe in partition" (p. 103; Byrd, four voices).[24] In contrast, Zacconi, writing only a year earlier in Italy and covering a similar topic at a comparable length, used score format only twice, preferring instead a wide variety of notations involving separate parts.[25] A systematic examination of each writer's practices should yield valuable information not only about regional differences but also about individual habits. It is curious, for example, that Giovanni Battista Rossi, in his *Organo de cantori* (1618), usually used score format for the brief examples that illustrated his points, while presenting longer examples in separate parts. He gave pieces that he considered especially difficult in two different formats: first in separate parts in the body of the treatise, and then in score at the end of the volume:

Porrò nel fine la partitura di questa cantilena [Palestrina, *Missa Ecce sacerdos magnus*] in tempo imperfetto, acciò si veda quel che si dice nella seguente lettione appaia esser vero: è cosi partiremo il Duo del Rodio, come due cantilene difficili. Non hò partito ogni cosa, perche la dicchiaratione nostra è tanto chiara, che non fa bisogno di altra partitura, poi che ogni buon cantore lo saprà fare da se stesso.	I shall place at the end the score of this song [Palestrina, *Missa Ecce sacerdos magnus*] in imperfect tempus, so that one may see that what is said in the following section appears to be true. And so we will score the Duo of Rodio, since they are both difficult songs. I have not scored everything because our explanation is so clear that there is no need for other scores, since every good singer will know how to make one for himself.[26]

The comparatively infrequent use of score format before the end of the sixteenth century may be related to technical difficulties or to the expense of

24. The passages were cited by Klaus Haller, "Partitur," *Handwörterbuch der musikalischen Terminologie* (Wiesbaden, 1976).

25. Lodovico Zacconi, *Prattica di musica* (Venice, 1596; repr. Bologna, 1983).

26. *Organo de cantori per intendere da se stesso ogni passo difficile che si trova nella musica* (Venice, 1618; repr. Bologna, 1984), 41.

printing a score, as Lowinsky suggested.[27] In fact, Bermudo complained that the example showing cipher notation aligned with mensural notation in score had not been done as well as he had wished "por la dificultad, y tardança dela impression."[28] However, if printing technology were really the only difficulty, one might expect to find large numbers of scores in manuscript treatises, but even here they begin to appear in significant numbers only towards the end of the sixteenth century.[29] The main reason, I would argue, is that score format did not suit mensural notation well, particularly when voices differed from one another in character (slow-moving versus quick). Furthermore, it was antithetical to the very conception of the music as counterpoint, built from independent lines.

Tablature

A fifth category consists of instrumental tablatures: systems of notation that instruct the player how to position his hand on the instrument. There are many different forms of tablatures; they have in common the property of presenting the entire polyphonic composition so that it can be read and performed by a single player. Almost as old as the mensural notation developed for polyphonic vocal music, these instrumental notations often reflect the actual physical motions required to play the instrument and thus differ from instrument to instrument. Lute tablature, for example, showed the performer where to place his fingers on the fretboard. Unlike mensural notation in which each part is written on its own five-line staff without reference to other parts, instrumental notations present the entire melodic and rhythmic content of the composition in a single location. They also typically use some sort of barring to divide the composition into regular metrical units. While there were eventually virtually as many tablatures as there were instruments, the most common forms were keyboard and lute tablatures.

While scholars today tend to restrict the meaning of tablature to systems of notation employing letters, numbers, and signs, or a mixture of staff notation and other symbols, it is clear that, in the sixteenth and seventeenth centuries at least, all of the notations associated with instrumental performance were thought of as tablatures, both those employing letters, symbols, and numbers, and those employing staff notation.[30] For example, Claudius Sebastiani, in his *Bellum musi-*

---

27. Lowinsky ("Early Scores," *Music in the Culture*, 808) stated: "The reason why most treatises of the period publish their examples of counterpoint in single parts may be seen in the greater difficulty and expense of printing in score instead of in parts."

28. *El arte tripharia*, fol. xxxviii[v].

29. They are used, for example, in Galilei's treatises now preserved in Florence, Biblioteca Nazionale Centrale.

30. For example, Geoffrey Chew, "Notation," III.5, *NG*, explained that "the term 'tablature' generally signifies a notational system using letters of the alphabet or other symbols not found in ordinary staff notation, and which generally specifies the physical action required to produce the music from a specific instrument, rather than an abstract representation of the music itself. The latter qualification, though perhaps the primary one, does not apply to the German organ tablatures of the late Middle Ages and later: in these, letters are used to identify pitches rather than finger positions." See also Thurston Dart, "Tablature," *NG*; Dart did include a section on keyboard notations.

cale, set up a mock musical battle in which four captains—representing the four parts of music—were in three companies, each with its own kind of tablature:

... fueruntque praedicti capitanei in tres turmas distincti tabulaturae, videlicet notarum, literarum, & numerorum cyphrae: in prima numerabantur musici instrumentorum periti, Italiarum organoedi, & Galliarum cum suis componistis, qui per notas musicales, suas depingebant tabulaturas. In secunda turma penè totius Germaniae, Italiae, Hispaniae, &c. Testudinarii, quoniam Tabulaturas suas per cyphras formabant & literas. Caeteri omnia confundentes caracteres, notas, literas & numeros arithmeticos in una eademque tabulatura coniungebant, ut aliquanto difficilioris intellectus esse iudicarentur, & perspicatioris ingenii à plebecula passim haberentur.	And the aforementioned captains were assigned to the three companies of tablatures, that is, of notes, of letters, and of arabic numbers. In the first were counted expert instrumentalists, the organists of the Italian and the French lands with their composers, who were writing their tablatures with musical notes. In the second company were the lutenists of nearly all of Germany, Italy, Spain, etc., since they were forming their tablatures with numbers and letters. The others, combining all the marks, joined notes, letters, and arithmetic numbers in one and the same tablature, so that they were judged to be harder to understand and were held of more perspicacious wit by the common people.[31]

Sebastiani's verbal description does not agree very well with the illustration (plate 3.5). The difficulty is that there are *three* companies and *four* examples of tablature. The first company, illustrated by the first two examples on sig. N 1ᵛ, contains *two* kinds of tablatures using "notes" or mensural notation: open score ("Exemplum primi generis Tabulaturae notarum") and keyboard score ("Exemplum secundi generis Tabulaturae notarum"). The second company is illustrated by German lute tablature, the example given at the top of the facing page ("Exemplum Tabulaturae literarum & cyphrae, pro Testudine"). The third company, combining notes and letters, is the German organ tablature at the bottom of sig. N 1ᵛ ("Exemplum Tabulaturae Germanorum").

Two kinds of tablature employed a form of score notation. One of these, generally referred to today as *intavolatura*, keyboard *partitura*, or keyboard score, has two staves, one for each hand.[32] It was used as early as the fifteenth century, for example, in the Faenza codex.[33] The other employs an open score, in which

---

31. *Bellum musicale*, sig. N 1ᵛ-2ʳ.

32. On keyboard notations, see James Ladewig, "Frescobaldi's 'Recercari, et canzoni franzese' (1615): A Study of the Contrapuntal Keyboard Idiom in Ferrara, Naples, and Rome, 1580–1620," Ph.D. diss., University of California at Berkeley, 1978; Robert Judd, "The Use of Notational Formats at the Keyboard. A Study of Printed Sources of Keyboard Music in Spain and Italy c. 1500–1700" (D.Phil. thesis, Oxford University, 1988); and Alexander Silbiger, "Is the Italian Keyboard *Intavolatura* a Tablature?" *Recercare* 3 (1990): 81–103.

33. While the Faenza codex is generally thought to be a keyboard source, Timothy McGee, "Instruments and the Faenza Codex," *EM* 14 (1986): 480–490, argued that it could have been used

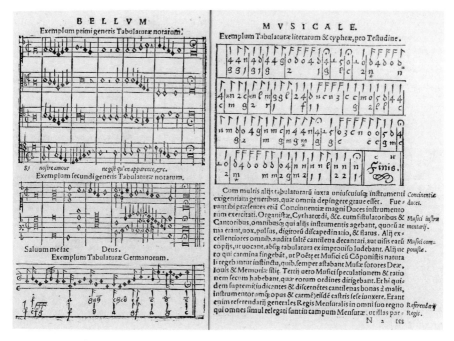

PLATE 3.5   Sebastiani, *Bellum musicale* (1563), sig. N 1^v-2^r

each line is notated on its own staff; the staves are placed one above the other, usually high to low. As far as we can tell from the extant sources, this format developed somewhat later: its earliest occurrence is in the Castell'Arquato manuscripts from the 1530s.[34] Seeing score notation as a form of instrumental tablature adds an important dimension to our earlier discussion.

Most examples of tablatures are found in treatises concerning specific instruments or in prefaces of collections destined for instruments. Thus, to cite just one example, the treatise in Jan of Lublin's organ book (KrakPAN 1716) employs German organ tablature.[35]

Some forms of tablature showed the full sonority at a glance and therefore had obvious advantages for presenting music examples. The German theorist Othmar Luscinius, for example, thought that tablature was a wonderful invention because it allowed the various voices to be put on a single page:

by two lutenists. See also Roland Eberlein, "The Faenza Codex: Music for Organ or for Lute Duet?" *EM* 20 (1992): 461–466, and Timothy J. McGee, "Once again, the Faenza Codex, a Reply to Roland Eberlein," *EM* 20 (1992): 466–468.

34. Discussed in chap. 6.

35. A. Chybinski, "Polnische Musik und Musikkultur des 16. Jahrhunderts in ihren Beziehungen zu Deutschland," *Sammelbände der Internationalen Musikgesellschaft* 13 (1911–1912): 486–490. The music in the organ book and some of the examples in the treatise have been transcribed in Johannes of Lublin, *Tablature of Keyboard Music*, ed. John R. White, CEKM 6 (American Institute of Musicology, 1967). There is a facsimile of the manuscript: *Tablatura organowa Jana z Lublina*, Monumenta musicae in Polonia, Seria B., vol. 1, ed. Krystyna Wiłkowska-Chomińska (Warsaw, 1964).

Extat autem non inutile inventum, quod multo nos levat labore, si diversas voces in unam compaginem redegerimus: Tabulaturam nostrates appellant eiusmodi contextum, quo loco notularum, quibus cantus describitur inrta [*recte* intra] lineas, simplicibus utimur elementis, iuxta vulgatam Guidonis Musici institutionem.	But there is a very useful discovery that relieves us of much labor, if we lay out the various voices in a single framework: our compatriots give the name "tablature" to such an arrangement, whereby, instead of the notes by which a song is written down between lines, we use simple letters, according to the standard system of Guido the Musician.[36]

Nearly a century later, Joachim Burmeister used a form of letter notation related to German organ tablature for the music examples in his treatise *Musica poetica*[37] (see plate 3.6). Despite the advantages of tablature, there are few examples where it was used illustrate vocal music.

READING IN PARTS

The most striking conclusion to be drawn from this discussion of formats is the fact that most of the examples were notated in separate parts, in one form or another. The ubiquitousness of this format suggests that reading in parts must have been a common skill. Although some scholars have doubted the ability of sixteenth-century musicians to read in parts, there is strong evidence—beyond the prevalence of notation in separate parts—that they could.[38]

Evidence concerning competitions for vacant positions suggests that organists had to be able to read in separate parts.[39] Robert Stevenson cited Bernardo Clavijo del Castillo's examination for a professorship at the University of Salamanca: "Next, a *monachordio* (spinet) was brought into the examination room. The partbooks of Clavijo's own *Motecta* published at Rome five years earlier were brought out, whereupon he was asked to sing and play one of his six-part motets."[40] He also cited the 1552 competition for the organist's position at Málaga Cathedral:

36. *Musurgia seu praxis musicae* (Strassburg, 1536), 35–36. Luscinius had probably completed a loose translation into Latin of portions of Sebastian Virdung's *Musica getutscht* (Basel, 1511) by about 1518. See *Musica getutscht: A treatise on Musical Instruments (1511) by Sebastian Virdung*, trans. and ed. Beth Bullard (Cambridge, 1993), 32–33; 61–72.

37. Joachim Burmeister, *Musica poetica* (Rostock, 1606; repr. Kassel, 1955), trans. Benito Rivera under the title *Musical Poetics* (New Haven, 1993).

38. There is evidence for a later period. For example, J. N. Forkel (*Über Johann Sebastian Bachs Leben, Kunst und Kunstwerk* [Leipzig, 1802]) described Bach's ability to read in parts: "He even saw so easily through parts laid side by side that he could immediately play them. This he often did when a friend had received a new trio or quartet for stringed instruments and wished to hear how it sounded." See Hans T. David and Arthur Mendel, eds., *The Bach Reader* (New York, 1945; rev. ed., 1966), 311.

39. The evidence often cited, concerning San Marco in Venice, actually refers to the skill of improvisation. See the discussion by Judd, "The Use of Notational Formats," 86.

40. Robert Stevenson, *Spanish Cathedral Music in the Golden Age* (Berkeley, 1961), 307–309.

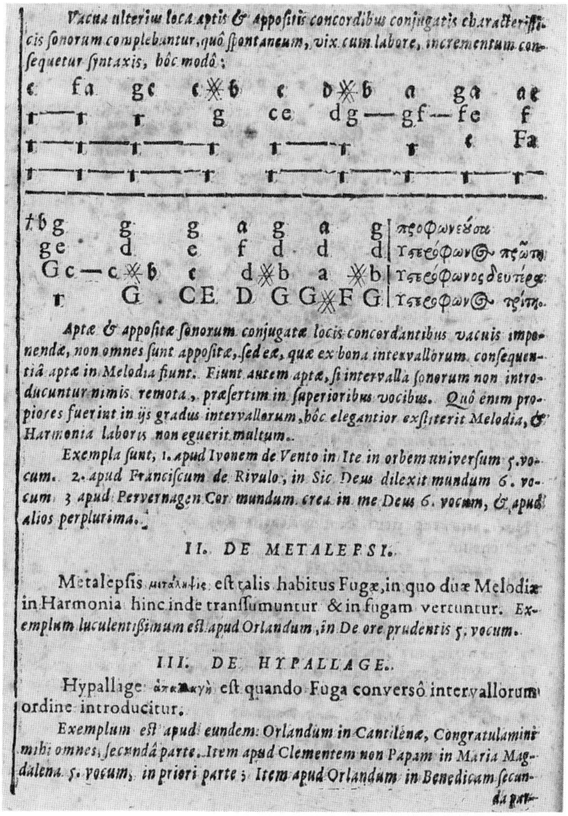

Vacua ulterius loca aptis & appofitis concordibus conjugatis characteri-
ficis fonorum complebuntur, quô fpontaneum, vix cum labore, incrementum con-
fequetur fyntaxis, hôc modô:

Aptæ & appofitæ fonorum conjugatæ locis concordantibus vacuis impo-
nendæ, non omnes funt appofitæ, fed eæ, quæ ex bona intervallorum. confequen-
tiâ aptæ in Melodia fiunt. Fiunt autem aptæ, fi intervalla fonorum non intro-
ducuntur nimis. remota., præfertim in fuperioribus vocibus. Quô enim pro-
piores fuerint in ijs gradus intervallorum, hôc elegantior exftiterit Melodia, &
Harmonia laboris non eguerit multum.

Exempla funt, 1. apud Ivonem de Vento in Ite in orbem univerfum 5. vocum. 2. apud Francifcum de Rivulo, in Sic Deus dilexit mundum 6. vocum 3 apud Pervernagen Cor mundum crea in me Deus 6. vocum, & apud
alios perplurima.

II. DE METALEPSI.

Metalepfis μετάληψις eft talis habitus Fugæ, in quo duæ Melodiæ
in Harmonia hinc inde tranffumuntur & in fugam vertuntur. Exemplum luculentifsimum eft apud Orlandum, in De ore prudentis 5. vocum.

III. DE HYPALLAGE.

Hypallage ἀπαλλαγὴ eft quando Fuga converfô intervallorum
ordine introducitur.

Exemplum eft apud eundem Orlandum in Cantilêna, Congratulamini
mihi omnes, fecundâ parte. Item apud Clementem non Papam in Maria Mag-
dalena 5. vocum, in priori parte; Item apud Orlandum in Benedicam fecundâ par-

PLATE 3.6   Burmeister,
Musica poetica (1606),
p. 58

"After vespers a choirbook was placed before each, opened at random, and the sight- and score-reading ability of each was tested."[41] Iconographical evidence in support of this view comes from Johann Sadeler's engraving of *St. Cecilia at Prayer*, which shows an angel seated at an organ reading from a choirbook.[42]

Another witness to the skill of reading from separate parts is the Spanish theorist Juan Bermudo. In his *Declaración de instrumentos musicales* he gave similar advice first to keyboard players, then to vihuelists, and finally to harpists.[43] The passage that has been cited most frequently concerns the advice for keyboard players, which contains a verb, *poner*, that is open to several interpretations. Its basic meaning is "to set."[44]

41. Stevenson, *Spanish Cathedral Music*, 123. Málaga AC 1550–1554, fol. 83ʳ. The references taken from Stevenson were cited by Judd, "The Use of Notational Formats," 30.

42. *Musik in Bayern. II. Ausstellungskatalog* (Tutzing, 1972), catalog number 131, plate 14.

43. *Declaración de instrumentos musicales* (Osuna, 1549; 2d ed. 1555; repr. of the 1555 edition, Kassel, 1977). For an important new account of Bermudo, see Wolfgang Freis, "Becoming a Theorist: The Growth of Juan Bermudo's *Declaración de instrumentos musicales*" (forthcoming).

44. I am quoting Wolfgang Freis's forthcoming translation (with slight modifications).

Todo quanto avemos dicho hasta ahora es para venir a este fin, de poner canto de organo en el monachordio. No se puede uno llamar tañedor: sino sabe poner musica suya, o agena. Tres maneras de poner se offrecen al presente: y todas las demas se reduzen a estas tres.

La primera es teniendo el libro de canto de organo delante. El que tañedor quisiere ser, si es buen cantor, que sabe de composicion: con estudiar lo ya dicho en este libro, y entender el monachordio: puede poner en el obras, con solamente tener delante el libro. Esta manera de poner es muy trabajosa, porque llevan mucha cuenta mirando todas las bozes: pero es gananciosa. Hazen con ella gran caudal de Musica.

Si de composicion no sabe, y no esta exercitando en poner, sino que comiença, o no quiere trabaxar tanto: ha primero de virgular el canto de organo, a la forma de lo que yo dexo encima de las cifras, en el capitulo siguiente: y assi repartido por sus compases, puesto delante sobre el monachordio, de manera que no impida las cuerdas, lo puede poner. Estas dos formas de poner en el monachordio son comunes, y buenas para los ya señalados.

La tercera manera es poner por cifras.

All we have said until now is to come to this end: to *poner* [set] polyphony on the keyboard. No one can call himself a performer unless he knows how to *poner* [set] his own music or that by others. Three ways of *poner* [setting] are offered at present, and all the others are reduced to these three.

The first one is having a book of polyphony in front of one. He who wants to be a performer—if he is a good singer who knows about composition—by studying what is in this book and understanding the keyboard can *poner* [set] works on it [i.e., the keyboard] with only having the book in front of him. This way of *poner* [setting] is very laborious, for there is a lot of keeping track [literally, counting] when looking at all the parts, but it is very profitable; one can make a lot of music this way.

If he does not know composition and is not practiced in *poner* [setting] but is just beginning or does not want to work so much, he must first score the polyphony in the way I show above the ciphers [i.e., the tablature] in the [example in the] following chapter. Thus, having divided the music into its measures and placed it in front on the keyboard in a way that it does not interfere with the strings, he can *poner* [set] it. These two ways of *poner* [setting] for the keyboard are common and good for those who are already accomplished performers.

The third way of *poner* [setting] is by ciphers [i.e., tablatures].[45]

45. From book 4, chap. 41: "como se porna en el monachordio," *Declaración de instrumentos musicales*, fol. lxxxiiⱽ. Bermudo first published the recommendations in 1550 in *El arte tripharia*, most of which was subsequently incorporated into the 1555 *Declaración*. See Robert Stevenson, *Juan Bermudo* (The Hague, 1960) and Freis's forthcoming study. The recommendations appear in different orders in the two versions. In the 1550 version, the order goes from the most elementary to the

The passage has been interpreted in two sharply different ways according to the meaning ascribed to *poner*. In one interpretation, which I believe to be the correct one, *poner* means "to play" (i.e., to perform) in the sense of translating vocal music into an instrumental performance.[46] As Judd explained: "*Poner en el monachordio* (literally,'to place on the keyboard') is the regular phrase encountered for the process of playing vocal music at the keyboard. The meaning of the phrase is akin to arranging, intabulating or transcribing, and always refers to playing mensurally notated vocal music at the keyboard, but it is not specific regarding notation employed."[47] This interpretation of Bermudo's advice essentially means that keyboard players can perform vocal music from three different formats appropriate to their level of skill or experience: choirbook, score, or tablature.[48]

The competing interpretion translates *poner* as "to intabulate." At the heart of this interpretation is the strong conviction that it was impossible for performers to read from separate parts.[49] Lowinsky, for example, interpreted the difficulties encountered in the first method to mean the difficulties of making a tablature from four separate parts:

> Likewise, we should not regard Bermudo's admission of the difficulties inherent in drawing a tablature from the choirbook as strictly limited to this process—for obviously it is more laborious to write a tablature from the choirbook in which each part stands in its own field without any visual relation to the others—rather than understand it to mean that a player is supposed to perform from a choirbook. *Tañer* means to play. The term used here, however, is *poner* . . . .[50]

He then cited two other passages where he believed that *poner* meant to intabulate. According to this interpretation, the gist of the above passage would be: there are three ways to intabulate music, directly from choirbook, from score, from ciphers. But this interpretation makes little sense: what form would the intabulation from tablature take?[51]

---

most advanced: using a number tablature (prepared from a score), using a score, and playing directly from the choirbook. In the 1555 version, the order is reversed.

46. Robert Stevenson (*Juan Bermudo*, 54) paraphrased the passage as follows: "Since so little of value is available in Spain, each player must work out his own salvation. He needs to do one of three things (ch. 41): (1) learn how to combine at sight all the various parts copied into a choirbook—a hard thing to do; (2) prepare for himself barred vocal scores; or, (3) learn how to intabulate." Judd ("The Use of Notational Formats," 27–30) also followed this interpretation.

47. Judd, "The Use of Notational Formats," 27n.

48. The idea of format as a function of skill level is an important part of Judd's argument.

49. This view was first articulated by Schwartz ("Zur Partitur," 73–74), who challenged Kinkeldey's interpretation of *libro* (translated by Kinkeldey as *Notenbuch*) to mean choirbook. According to Schwartz, if *Notenbuch* referred to printed books, the repertory would be small indeed. That there were many manuscript choirbooks did not help Kinkeldey's case since choirbook format and solo performance were mutually exclusive. Choirbook format was appropriate for many people to read from a single book but the disposition (soprano in the upper left, bass in the lower right) was poor for keyboard performance.

50. Lowinsky, "Early Scores," *Music in the Culture*, 822–823, n. 50.

51. Klaus Haller, *Partituranordnung und musikalischer Satz* (Tutzing, 1972) and "Partitur," *Handwörterbuch der musikalischen Terminologie* (Wiesbaden, 1976), while agreeing with Lowinsky's interpretation of *poner*, attempted to make somewhat clearer distinctions in three methods. In the first

Convincing evidence to refute this interpretation can be found by comparing Bermudo's advice to vihuelists and harpists with that for keyboard players: in the parallel passages the meaning of *poner* becomes absolutely clear.[52] In the section on the vihuela, Bermudo actually used the verb *tañer*: the very skilled musician can *play* with the music book in front of him:

Los exercitados en cifrar, y los buenos musicos, y los que quieren tomar un poco de trabajo con gran provecho: basta les el libro delante para de puntos hazer cifras. El tañedor que sin virgular la musica hiziesse cifras: seria cosa mas prima, y le daria gran ser en el arte de tañer. Possible es, que el musico exercitando se a cifrar por el libro: viniesse a tanta perfection en la intelligencia y uso dela vihela: que tañesse puesto el libro de canto de organo delante de si.	For those experienced in intabulating, the good musicians, and those who want to take on a little bit of work to great advantage, it suffices for them to have the book in front in order to turn notated music into tablature. A player who could make tablatures without scoring the music would be a most excellent thing and it would give him great stature in the art of playing. It is possible that a musician, in practicing making tablatures from the book, may reach such perfection in the knowledge and use of the vihuela that he would play (*tañesse*) from the book of polyphony placed before him.[53]

The section on the harp makes clear that there are no numbers, that is, tablature, involved in the technique of reading from the book.

El que pusiere canto de organo en la harpa sin cifrar, con solamente tener il libro de canto de organo delante: gran trabajo seria, mayormente sino fuesse muy exercitado en composicion, o en exercicio de poner en instrumentos: pero seria grande el provecho y abilidad que gran searia.	He who would *poner* [set] polyphony on the harp without intabulation, only by having the book of polyphony in front of him: it would be a great deal of work, especially if he were not very experienced in composition or in the practice of *poner* [setting] on instruments, but the profit would be great, and what a skill it would be.[54]

method, the experienced musician can go directly from choirbook to tablature. In the second method, the inexperienced musician must first make a score and then a tablature. The third method employs barlines extending through tablature. Haller assumed that the end result of all three methods was tablature; the difference lies in what was done as a way of preparing to make the tablature. The problem with this reading, as with Lowinsky's, is that Bermudo did not mention ciphers until the discussion of the third method.

52. Judd ("The Use of Notational Formats," 30) cited these two passages.

53. *Declaración de instrumentos musicales*, fol. xcviii[v].

54. *Declaración de instrumentos musicales*, fol. cxii[v].

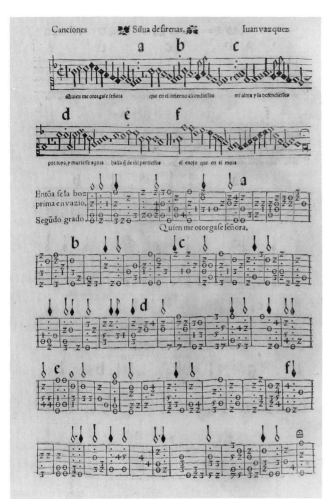

PLATE 3.7
Valderrábano, *Libro
de musica de vihuela,
intitulado silva de sirenas*
(1547), fol. 42ᵛ

It is difficult for us to imagine how musicians managed to keep track of the separate parts. In some instances, they may have added lines to segment the music into sections. The German schoolteacher Johann Frosch included two motets notated in choirbook format in his textbook, *Rerum musicarum opusculum*. He used vertical lines to mark off segments of music in each of the parts and labeled the segments with Roman numerals (see plates 7.25–26).[55] The Spanish composer and vihuelist Enríquez de Valderrábano used letters resembling our rehearsal letters to connect the instrumental and vocal parts in his mid-sixteenth-century intabulations of vocal music (see plate 3.7). It also seems likely that faint markings that functioned like rehearsal letters may have been

55. *Rerum musicarum opusculum rarum ac insigne, totius eius negotii rationem mira industria & brevitate complectens*, sig. E ivᵛ–iiiʳ (Strassburg, 1535; repr. New York, 1967).

added to sources. In some instances the actual spacing on the page may have been helpful.[56]

The text could be used to provide an approximate location. In the theoretical correspondence preserved in VatV 5318, writers usually identified the passages they discussed by means of the text (e.g., "the passage where the tenor has the words . . .") or by counting (e.g., "at the seventeenth breve").[57] We know, too, that musicians could use rests to help them keep their place in the tactus.[58]

The issue goes beyond technique, however. We need to assume a different sort of musical memory from ours.[59] A passage in Thomas de Sancta María's *Libro llamado Arte de tañer Fantasia* is suggestive. In book 1, chapter 21, the student is offered:

De avisos breve para que los nuevos subieten presto qualquier obra. La primera, es tañer a compas. . . . La segunda cosa, es cantar cada boz por si, entendiendola Solfa de rayz. La tercera cosa, es entender todas las Consonancias y Disonancias que llevare la obra, assi las que fueren a duo, como los que fuere a tres y a quatro.	Some brief instructions by which the beginner may quickly master any work. The first is to play in accordance with the tactus. . . . The second thing is to sing each voice by itself, and to achieve a fundamental comprehension of its melodic line. The third thing is to comprehend all the consonances and dissonances contained in the work, those formed in two [voices] as well as in three or four.[60]

The next chapter, on how to derive benefit from compositions, advises the student to see how the imitation works, to study the entrances of the individual voices and their placement relative to cadences, to study and remember all the cadences, to note all the consonances and dissonances, and to study the variety in the imitation of subjects. The impression is of careful study, one line at a time, and then line against line. The student is to keep in his memory the cadences

56. An example of spacing in a manuscript is discussed by Bloxam, "Newly-discovered Fragments" (BrugS 538); another is discussed by Kmetz, "The Drafts of Jodocus Fabri." Leech-Wilkinson, *Compositional Techniques*, 200–201, discussed an interesting instance of an isorhythmic motet whose two lower voices were laid out in a version of quasi-score to show missing notes in each *talea* (four staves, in the order F3F3c4c4). If a scribe could notate the piece this way in an attempt to correct what he thought was a corrupt reading, surely a composer could have done so as well.

57. Blackburn et al., *A Correspondence*, 119–120.

58. For example, consecutive semibreve rests that occur in different *tempora* would usually be notated as two semibreves and not combined into a single breve. See the discussion in Owens, "The Milan Partbooks," 93.

59. See the illuminating study by Mary Carruthers, *The Book of Memory: A Study of Memory in Medieval Culture* (Cambridge, 1990). For an investigation of one aspect of musical memory, see Virginia Newes, "Writing, Reading and Memorizing: The Transmission and Resolution of Retrograde Canons from the 14th and Early 15th Centuries," *EM* 18 (1990), 218–234.

60. (Valladolid, 1565; repr. Geneva, 1973), 1, fol. 57^{r-v}; trans. Almonte C. Howell, Jr. and Warren E. Hultberg under the title *The Art of Playing the Fantasia* (Pittsburgh, 1991), 154.

and the melodic progressions so he may use them in his own improvisations (*fantasie*). We can assume from passages like this one that musicians must have had aural memories or habits of reading (perhaps voice by voice) quite different from ours; perhaps a sixteenth-century musician would be equally amazed at the ability of today's musicians to read a complicated orchestral score.

In suggesting a greater facility for reading or reading/memorizing in parts than has generally been assumed, I do not wish to make the process seem anything but cumbersome. Once a piece was notated in separate parts, it was difficult to catch mistakes without having it sung or checking one voice against another.[61] Perhaps as a result of these difficulties, during the second half of the century musicians began to employ scores to help them study polyphonic music.[62]

It is important to remember how much composers and performers relied on performance for their work with music notated in separate parts. An interesting example concerns two little-known composers, Andrea Festa and Benedetto Spinone, who made a bet in 1555 about who had composed a better sixth voice for Adrian Willaert's *Qual anima ignorante* and Cipriano de Rore's *Per mezzo i boschi*. Which was "more beautiful, artful, and observant of the rules" ("et pulchriorem et artificiorem ac conformiorem regule")? The sixth parts, identified only by the marks '+' and '#', were sent to Gottardo Occagna in Venice, who presented them to Willaert. Willaert, not wanting to judge the music, finally (to quote Occagna) "agreed and had them sung several times by those singers who are held in great esteem in these parts; and so everyone, being of one mind, signed the part with their signatures, as your lordship can see."[63] Willaert and seven singers, all from San Marco, judged the two parts marked '+' to be better. It is certainly suggestive—though not really surprising—that Willaert chose to judge the merits of two added sixth voices not by reading the music (notated in separate parts) but by having it performed.[64] There is other evidence that suggests that once music was notated in separate parts even the composer could not readily imagine what it sounded like by just looking at it; he needed to hear it performed. For example, Giovan Tomaso Cimello sent music to Cardinal Sirleto, without having it performed first because there were no singers, and he asked the singers to try out a motet and change it as necessary.[65] Another example

---

61. See Blackburn et al., *A Correspondence*, 119–124.

62. The well-known letter from Giovanni Pierluigi da Palestrina to his patron, Duke Guglielmo Gonzaga, reveals that Palestrina scored a motet by Guglielmo so that he could study it better ("per meglio contemplarlo ho partito il Mottetto"); see the discussion in chap. 11. For further discussion of the use of scores for study, see below.

63. ". . . si redusse più e più volte a farli cantar da quelli cantori che qui sono in più stima, e così tuti d'acordo hanno sotoscritto quella parte che vostra signoria vedrà de lor pugno"; see Maurizio Tarrini, "Una gara musicale a Genova nel 1555," *Note d'archivio per la storia musicale*, nuova serie, 3 (1985): 166.

64. There is an interesting wrinkle: in 1559 Andrea Festa alleged that these signatures were obtained by fraud and that the bet had never been resolved, and he cited supporting testimony by Willaert that is not extant. Occagna had not questioned the authenticity of the signatures or the validity of the competition.

65. ". . . l'ho voluto fare non curando che qui non sian cantori, da provare prima i Canti . . .

comes from Machaut's *Le Voir Dit*, letter XXXIII: "My very sweet-heart, I've made the rondeau where your name is, and I would have sent it to you with this message: but by my soul I've never heard it and I'm not at all accustomed to part with anything which I've made unless I've heard it."[66]

WRITING MUSIC

The variety of formats used gives an indication of what musicians could read, and possibly could employ for writing. The actual recommendations made by teachers and the authors of the music treatises, however, were far more limited, and depended on different factors, such as the skill of the student, and on the geographical region.

Most of the explicit advice about formats comes from the German theoretical tradition.[67] The theorists often advocated at least two different formats, depending on the level of skill. One format—the ten-line staff—is quite unambiguous, but the alternative formats are not as clear. For example, Cochlaeus offered the following recommendation in his chapter concerning general rules for composing:

Possunt autem omnes partes simul componi et quelibet item primum ac seorsum. Frequentius tamen tenor ceteris prior poni solet. Etenim exercitatus cantilenarum compositor singulas partes seorsum facere potest, rudimenta vero addiscentes (quum vocum concordantie atque clausule animo nondum insident) per decem lineas omnes certe partes simul componere opere pretium est.	Moreover, all the parts can be composed together/at once (*simul*), and also any of them first and separately (*seorsum*). More frequently, however, the tenor is laid down before the others. And indeed the practiced composer of songs can write (*facere*) the individual parts separately (*seorsum*), while it is worthwhile for those learning the rudiments (since the concords of the voices and the cadences (*clausulae*) are not yet fixed in the mind) to compose all the parts together on the ten-line [staff].[68]

Invoco ms. Alessandro à far provar il motetto da qualch'amico [four singers listed], e lor sia licito, mutare, mancar, aggiunger e rinovare et habbianmi compassione che stò in questo Morrone dove non si conosce l'Antifonario etc."; Raffaele Casimiri, "Lettere di musicisti (1579–1585) al Cardinal Sirleto," *Note d'archivio* 9 (1932): 104.

66. "Mon tresdous cuer iay fait le rondel ou vostres noms est et le vous heusse envoie par ce message mais par mame ie ne loy onques et nay mie acoustume de bailler chose que ie face tant que ie laie oy"; Leech-Wilkinson, "*Le Voir Dit* and *La Messe de Nostre Dame*," 54.

67. Willibald Gurlitt, "Die Kompositionslehre des deutschen 16. und 17. Jahrhunderts," in *Bericht über den Internationalen Musikwissenschaftlichen Kongress Bamberg 1953* (Kassel, 1954), 103–113, and Klaus Wolfgang Niemöller, "Zum Einfluss des Humanismus auf Position und Konzeption von Musik im deutschen Bildungssystem der ersten Hälfte des 16. Jahrhunderts," in *Musik in Humanismus und Renaissance*, ed. Walter Rüegg and Annegrit Schmidt (Weinheim, 1983), 77–97, provide a useful context for many of the writers considered here. Also helpful is Rivera, *German Music Theory*.

68. *Musica activa*, fol. 28ʳ.

Cochlaeus distinguishes between beginners, who should use ten-line staves, and experienced composers, who can work *seorsum*. It is not clear just what format the term *seorsum* implies. Hermelink cited this passage as part of the evidence for the two formats he believed were in common use: score format and the ten-line staff. He attacked Kinkeldey's "superficial" reading of the passage, namely, that composers could have worked directly in separate parts.[69] I am skeptical that Cochlaeus meant score format. *Simul* can mean together or at the same time, which in musical terms are two quite different things. But it seems likely that in this passage it is intended to be seen in opposition to *seorsum*—*simul* (together) and *seorsum* (separately)—and that both are used in a spatial rather than temporal sense. *Seorsum* probably implies a format using separate parts such as quasi-score or a choirbook format. In any case, the main point is clear: beginners will have an easier time working with the voices all together on a ten-line staff rather than written out separately.

Like Cochlaeus, Ornithoparcus also suggested or at least implied that different formats were in use. He preferred that the "schala decemlinealis" *not* be used, without explaining what he recommended in its place, but acknowledged that it was necessary for beginners:

Necessarium erit artis huius Tyronibus: schalam decemlinealem ut forment, formatam, cancellis distinguant: Ita ut singula tempora, singulis cancellis, clavibus rite signatis: ne confusa notarum commixtione impediantur: inscribere valeant. Prestantius tamen est absque schala condere, quod cum difficile sit, a scala incipiant adulescentes, hoc modo.	It is necessary for yong beginners to make a Scale of ten lines, then to distinguish it by bounds, so that they may write each time within each bound, by keyes truly marked, least the confused mingling together of the Notes hinder them; yet is it better to compose without a Scale, but because it is hard, let yong men begin with a Scale.[70]

The anonymous author of "Juxta artem conficiendi," whom Dahlhaus believed to have worked ca. 1520, listed as part of his advice about how to compose three rules that explain how to transfer music from the ten-line staff to five-line staves.[71] He was specifically concerned with which clefs to use for particular vocal ranges. Clearly, he took for granted the use of the ten-line staff as the place where the actual composing—that is, the writing down of music or of musical exercises—occurred; the next stage was to copy each part onto its own five-line staff. Unfortunately, he provided no indication of how these five-line staves were arranged.[72]

Even after mid-century the evidence about format remains ambiguous. Dressler explained:

---

69. Hermelink, "Die Tabula compositoria," 224. Hermelink discussed all of the theorists considered here, but drew different conclusions about format.

70. *Musice active micrologus*, Dowland translation: *Andreas Ornithoparcus His Micrologus*, 83.

71. Anonymous, "Juxta artem conficiendi," in Dahlhaus, "Eine deutsche Kompositionslehre," 42.

72. As we saw in the previous chapter, Lampadius showed a musical example in two formats: first on a ten-line staff, and then on separate five-line staves in quasi-score (plates 2.3–4).

Quot lineis utuntur poetae, supra quas componunt? Exercitati supra quinque lineas componunt quae res cum incipientibus numerandi pareat [*recte* paret] difficultatem concedimus ut 10 lineis utantur, et hoc a bonis et candidis non reprehendi potest, quia cum intra scalam, quae ex 10 lineis constat totum harmoniae corpus includatur, nemo non videt incipientibus facilius esse de conjunctis consonantiis quasi in tabula positis iudicare in hoc genere mediocriter exercitati si ad quinque lineas se assuefacere voluerunt, liberum erit.	How many lines do *poetae* use on which they compose? Those who are experienced compose on five lines, which, since it poses difficulty in counting for beginners, we grant that they may use ten lines, and this cannot be criticized by good and honest men, since within the scale, which consists of ten lines, is included the whole body of harmony; anyone can see that it is easier for beginners to judge in this way the conjunct consonances placed as if in a chart (*tabula*). If those who are moderately experienced in such matters want to accustom themselves to five lines, so they may.[73]

Dressler distinguished between five- and ten-line staves, but unfortunately did not describe the layout for the five-line staves; nothing in this particular description suggests that they were deployed in score format.[74]

Toward the end of the century, however, the use of score became explicit. Calvisius, in his draft for *Melopoiia*, explained that composers used separate five-line staves, written close together and joined by vertical lines:

(226) Prima et antiquissima ratio componendi est: per systemata, hoc est, si quaelibet harmoniae pars vel vox quinque lineis, si res peragatur per characteres, notulas et pausas etc., scribatur, quemadmodum cantilenae alias solent, hoc tantum observetur, quod tot sint systemata quot partes vel voces harmonia contineat, et quod systemata haec arctius scribantur, et per lineas parallelas tactum unum vel	The first and most ancient way of composing is this: by staves (*systemata*), that is, if each part of the harmony or voice is written on five lines, with signs, notes, and rests, etc., as songs are usually written elsewhere, this only must be observed, that there be as many staves as there are parts or voices in the harmony and that these staves be written very close together and be evenly divided

73. "Praecepta musicae poeticae," chap. 6. While Dressler thought of the alignment in terms of a table or chart, other writers (for example, Johannes Nucius, *Musices poeticae sive de compositione cantus praeceptiones* (Neisse, 1613; repr. Leipzig, 1976) or Friedrich Beurhaus, *Erotematum musicae libri duo* (Dortmund, 1573; repr. of 1580 edition, Cologne, 1961), often used the metaphor of soldiers lined up in battle formation. Galliculus (*Isagoge de composicione cantus*, sig. D iiiᵛ) described the clefs in a ten-line staff as placed "as if in a nest."

74. Rivera (*German Music Theory*, p. 62) makes the same point, but concludes, on the basis of the passage in Lampadius as well as those in Calvisius and Lippius to be discussed below, that Dressler meant score format. Another ambiguous passage can be found in Beurhaus, *Erotematum musicae*, sig. G viiiʳ. See Walter Thoene, *Friedrich Beurhusius und seine Musiktraktate*, Beiträge zur rheinischen Musikgeschichte 31 (Cologne, 1959).

duos enim continentes aequaliter dis-
tinguantur. Hoc modo cavetur quidem ne notulae et reliqua signa inter
se confundantur, sed cum quodlibet
systema suas habet peculiares claves,
sic quidem diversas, in diversis lineis
signatas, diversas etiam notulas quan-
titate inter se discrepantes. Si praeterea partes vel voces harmoniae mul-
tae sint, puta vel quinque vel sex vel
plures, quae uno intuitu comprehendi
non possunt, sicut mens melopoei ad
singula systemata attendens mire fa-
tigetur, tanta rerum diversitate per-
turbetur et tandem mole rerum ob-
ruatur, ideo sunt, qui omnia haec
strictius coarctant et sub unum intui-
tum conjiciunt, omnia systemata in
unum contrahendo, quod conse-
quuntur in decem vel undecim lineis,
quibus claves signatas suis locis prae-
figunt, quas similiter transversis lineis
distinguunt, ad capacitatem tactus unius vel duorum, et partes seu voces ita
inscribunt. Fit hoc modo, quando
partes vel voces inter se miscentur et
altera in alterius locum succedit, ut
notulae variis modis confundantur.
Cui remedium hoc inventum est, ut
unius partis notulae rotundo, alterius
quadrato, alterius item triangulorum
corpore scribantur. Aut etiam, ut notulae diversarum partium colore dis-
tinguantur, ut quaedam atro, quaedam
robore [sic; recte rubro?], quaedam
viridi colore scribantur.

by parallel lines containing one or two
tactus. In this way one takes care lest
the notes and other signs become confused, since each staff has its own particular pitches (*claves*), indeed signed
differently on different lines, and also
different note-shapes (*notulas*), differing
from one another in length. If, moreover, the parts or voices of the harmony are many, say five or six or more,
which cannot be comprehended at a
glance, just as the mind of the composer considering all the individual
staves one at a time will be exceedingly
fatigued, perturbed by such diversity,
and finally overwhelmed by the mass
of material, there are those, therefore,
who compress everything more tightly
and join it together in one view, drawing together all staves into one large
staff comprised of ten or eleven lines,
to which they prefix the signed clefs in
their appropriate places, and which
they similarly divide by vertical lines at
the space of every one or two *tactus,*
and on this basis they write out the
voices or parts. It can happen, using this
method, when the parts or voices are
mixed or one takes over in place of
another in the same place, that notes
can be confused in various ways. The
solution for this problem is that the
notes of one part are written with
round, for another with square, and for
a third with triangular shapes. Or else
the notes of the different parts are distinguished by color, one black, another
red, a third green.[75]

Calvisius wrote that the format that we recognize today as a score was a very
ancient way of composing.[76] He seems not to have made a distinction on the

---

75. The text is taken from Dahlhaus, "Musiktheoretisches," 133–134. See also the discussions by
Hermelink, "Tabula compositoria," 225–226 and Rivera, *German Music Theory,* 61–62.

76. As one of the first to write a history of music (*Exercitationes musicae duae* [Leipzig, 1600; repr.
Hildesheim, 1973], 124–135), he had an unusual interest in and knowledge of the past; it would be

basis of skill level (though given the didactic intent of his treatise it is possible that he was addressing only beginners), but rather on the number of voices. It is interesting that he found the score a difficult format (or thought that his readers might) to use when there were more than four voices, and he recommended the use of the ten- or eleven-line staff instead.

Johannes Lippius, a student of Calvisius, offered somewhat different evidence. He divided the musical scale into two types, conjunct and disjunct (a distinction similar to that made by Beurhaus):

Sedes est systema musicum.

Quod vel maius est totius scalae et coniunctum ex pluribus lineis longis et spatiis utrisque inferioribus et superioribus per lineas perpendiculares brevis, □. duorum tactuum distantia sectis, repraesentans praesertim cantilenam harmonicam compositam. [figure of an empty ten-line staff, with barlines]

Vel est minus partis scalae et disiunctum ac simplex ex paucioribus lineis et spatiis per lineas perpendiculares non semper actu distinctis confectum, inserviens comprimis melodiae extrahendae et notandae. [figure of an empty five-line staff with partial ledger lines above and below, no barlines]

Ambo ponenda sunt in mappa et palimpsesto compositorio seu melopoetico: prius quidem incipienti maxime, posterius perfectiori, ita tamen ut aliquot systemata simplicia iisdem lineis perpendicularibus dispescantur. [figure of two empty five-line staves, with barlines]

A staff (*systema*) is the seat of musical notes.

Which can be either greater, of the whole scale, conjunct, made from many long lines and the spaces above and below them, divided by perpendicular lines at the distance of a breve of two *tactus*, showing especially the composed harmonic song,

or lesser, of part of the scale, disjunct and simple, made from fewer lines and their spaces, not always divided by barlines, serving especially for drawing out and notating melodies.

Both can be placed on the *mappa* and *palimpsestus compositorius seu melopoeticus* [composer's tablet].[77] The first, however, is especially for beginners, the second for the more experienced, however in such a way that several simple staves are divided by the same perpendicular lines.[78]

Lippius distinguished between five-line staves used without barlines for individual lines, presumably for performance or for the final notated version, and five-line staves lined up one on top of the other, with barlines (i.e., in score format), for use by experienced composers.

Well into the seventeenth century, writers in the German sphere continued

---

interesting to know just how old he meant "very ancient" to be. Apart from what he learned in treatises, the oldest repertory he seems to have known (or at least the oldest composer he knew by name) was that of Josquin.

77. See the discussion in chap. 4.

78. Lippius, *Synopsis musicae novae*, sig. D 5ᵛ–6. See Rivera, *German Music Theory*, 60–61.

to describe a variety of different formats. In 1631 Schonsleder explained that there were three methods for composing: ten-line staff, score, and tablature.

Caput II. Modi componendi	*Chapter II. Methods of Composing*
Tres sunt. Primus Belgarum & quorumdam aliorum est, constans decem lineis, in quibus duae tantum claves ponuntur, Discanti & Bassi. Notae inter sese sunt implicatissimae propter vicinitatem & angustias spatiorum. Labor est discernere. Proinde aliqui discernunt diverso colore, aut aliis characteribus vel punctis. . . . Modus iste familiaris est organistis, quibus notae in suis spatiis ita visae facilius veniunt in digitos.	There are three. The first is used by Belgians and others, consisting of ten lines on which two clefs are placed, of the discantus and bassus. The notes are very entangled because of the closeness and the narrowness of the space. It is hard work to distinguish them. As a result, some distinguish them with different colors, or with different shapes or notes. . . . The method is familiar to organists, for whom notes seen this way in their places come more easily to the fingers.
Secundus modus est facilior quia distinctior & usitatissimus: cum singulae voces suas quinas lineas discrete habent: & compositio in tempora ductis per omnes voces lineis distinguitur.	The second way is easier because it is clearer and it is used very frequently, namely, when individual voices each have their own five-line staff, and the composition is divided into measures by lines drawn through all the voices.
Tertius modus est per litteras, hoc est, notas ipsarum clavium, quae singulae suis litteris noscendae proponuntur. Modus superiori aetate usitatissimus: iam tantum non contemptus & vilis. Tamen commoda haec habet. Primum non est opus cartella, seu deletili tabula (quae ad secundum modum pertinet), sed quaevis chartula sufficiet, cui tua cogitata illinas. Deinde quod hic angusto brevique spatio scribis, ibi (in notis) tertio aut quarto tanto spatio opus erit, plurimumque loci capiendum. Praeterea vicinitas & distinctio clavium magnam lucem facilitatemque affert scribenti. Ad haec facilius citiusque videbis si quid aberraveris. Unicum incommodum est, quod puerum describendo allegare non potes (ut in secundo modo) auctorique ipsi labor ille suscipiendus. Hunc modum ad finem libri trademus. Nos in docendo	The third way is with letters, that is, with the notes of the keys themselves, which are displayed with letters. This method was very often used in past times, and even now is not despised. For it is convenient for several reasons. First, there is no need for the *cartella* or erasable tablet (which the second method uses), but any scrap of paper suffices on which to write out what you have thought up. The next reason is that here [with this method] you can write in a narrow or small space, there (with notes) you need three or four times as much space. Furthermore, the closeness and differences in the clefs offers clarity and facility to the writer. You will be able to see more quickly and easily if you make a mistake. The only inconvenience is that you cannot send a stu-

iam utemur secondo modo tamquam usitatissimo, oculisque magis patente: quoniam contra torrentem niti irritus labor est. Qui tertio velit insuescere, iisdem huius tractatus praeceptis utetur & adiuvabitur.

dent to transcribe it (as in the second method) and that task must be undertaken by the composer himself. We explain this method at the end of the book. In teaching we use the second method since it is the most customary and lies more clearly before the eyes since work without effect goes against the stream of elegance. Whoever wishes to follow the third may use and benefit from the rules in this treatise.[79]

Schonsleder described the practice of composing in tablature as venerable, but in fact there is surprisingly little surviving evidence of its use.[80]

Only one writer working outside the German tradition made a recommendation about format. Juan Bermudo advised beginners to use a score for composing:

Algunos que no saben contrapunto, y quieren començar a componer con sola cuenta de consonancias: suelen virgular el papel pautado per no perderse en la cuenta. Y aunque este modo sea barbaro: porne exemplo del para los que tuvieren necessidad, y quisieren seguirlo.

Some who do not know counterpoint and want to begin to compose by only counting [i.e., calculating] the consonances are accustomed to bar the music paper so as not to lose themselves in the counting. And although this method is crude, I give an example for those who need it and wish to follow it.[81]

---

79. Schonsleder, *Architectonice musices*, 1–2; discussed by Apfel, *Geschichte*, 494–510. Herbst (*Musica poetica*, 33) essentially translated Schonsleder's recommendations, but made a few significant changes. Like Schonsleder, he associated the ten-line staff with the Netherlanders. Unlike Schonsleder, he linked organists not with the ten-line staff but rather with tablature. It is not clear, either in Schonsleder or in Herbst, that the ten-line staff is the classic form encountered in the sixteenth century. It is striking, for example, that only two clefs are notated, soprano and bass, while in most sixteenth-century ten-line staves three clefs (and sometimes more) were drawn. This first method may perhaps be a form of keyboard intavolatura, for example, like that found in some English sources, where there is no break between the staves for the left and right hands. On the other hand, the references to the use of color and shape to distinguish the voices is certainly reminiscent of sixteenth-century practices. The passage from Herbst was quoted by Hermelink, "Die Tabula," 226 and *Dispositiones modorum*, 49; Hermelink and Apfel were both unaware of Herbst's use of Schonsleder.

80. Michael Praetorius (*Syntagma musicum*, 3 [Wolfenbüttel, 1619], 46) indicated that German organists used tablature not only for performance but also for composition. See the discussion in chap. 6.

81. *Declaración*, fol. cxxxiiii[r]. This passage has been translated also by, among others, Lowinsky ("Early Scores," *Music in the Culture*, 822) and Stevenson (*Juan Bermudo*, 68: "It is the habit of some who know no counterpoint—but who wish to start composing simply by counting up consonances—to draw bar-lines through the staves on a sheet of music paper in order that they will not lose themselves in their count. Although this is a barbarous habit, I give an example for the benefit of those who are addicted to it"). See the discussion by Kinkeldey, *Orgel und Klavier*, 188–189.

PLATE 3.8   Bermudo, *Declaración* (1555), fol. 134ᵛ

His example (see plate 3.8) shows three voices (tiple, tenor, contra), with the cleffing c2c3F4; it is barred every breve except for the final measure, which contains three breves. Bermudo clearly condemned the practice, thereby implying that skilled composers worked in a different way. Unfortunately, he provided no description of the format they used.

The theorists, then, do offer some direct advice, but far less than we might hope. Their indirect advice—in the form of the examples in the treatises—offers perhaps a more accurate picture of the possibilities. Taken together, the two kinds of evidence suggest the use of ten-line staves (at least in the German-speaking realm) by beginners. Only during the final decades of the century did the score become a recommended method. Outside of Germany, the only witness to the use of score was Bermudo, and he reluctantly approved its use by beginners.

To see how composers used these possible formats, we will need to consider the written evidence they have left behind—tablets and autograph manuscripts. But first we should explore—as best we can—the aspects of composition that took place independent of writing.

CHAPTER FOUR

COMPOSING WITHOUT
WRITING

It may be useful to think of the process of composition as divided into two main phases. One consists of all that the composer may have thought and conceived before writing anything down (the subject of this chapter). The other (discussed in chapters 5, 6, and 7) concerns the shaping of a composition once it began to take on written form, either on an erasable surface such as slate or on paper.

Invoking the notion of phases helps to describe different kinds of activities: thinking versus writing. But we should be careful not to assume that the phases were necessarily sequential—first the unwritten, then the written—or that the activities were separate. The reality was certainly more complex.

COMPOSING "IN THE MIND"

Perhaps the most intangible and elusive of all aspects of compositional activity are the stages where the composer was thinking about the music without writing it down. Simple intuition suggests that composers working before 1600, like those of later times, must have been able to work "in the mind." We will obviously never capture their thoughts, but we can at least document this phase of their activity.

One example concerns the Flemish madrigal composer Cipriano de Rore, whose autograph manuscript we will consider in chapter 9. Luzzasco Luzzaschi, a Ferrarese composer and organist who studied with Rore, described Rore's working methods in a 1606 affidavit that attested to the authenticity of a Rore autograph manuscript (now preserved in Milan, Biblioteca Ambrosiana: MilA 10) and a *cartella* or tablet (no longer extant) that he had used for composing. Luzzaschi was giving both objects to Cardinal Federico Borromeo, who was collecting manuscripts and printed books for the Biblioteca Ambrosiana,[1] which opened to the public in 1609:

---

1. On Borromeo's patronage, see Pamela M. Jones, *Federico Borromeo and the Ambrosiana: Art Patronage and Reform in Seventeenth-Century Milan* (Cambridge, 1993), esp. 40–45 (concerning the library); and Robert L. Kendrick, "Musical Self-Expression in Federico Borromeo's Milan," paper read at the annual meeting of the Renaissance Society of America in 1995.

Io Luzzascho Luzzaschi Cittadino Ferrarese, faccio fede che questa Cartella fù del famosissimo, et Eccellentissimo Cipriano Rore Fiammengo Musico, et Maestro di Cappella del già Eccellentissimo Signor Duca Ercole d'Este secondo di Ferrara. Sopra la qual Cartella scriveva le compositioni fatte prima da lui a mente, com'era sempre suo costume. Io in quel tempo essendo suo discepolo lo vidi à scrivere sopra detta Cartella la Gloria d'una Messa che fece in Ferrara et altre sue compositioni fatte in diversi tempi. Et detta Cartella donò à me quando parti di qui, che fù l'Anno 1557 insieme con l'annesso Miserere composto da lui in Fiandra quando era giovine, et scritto di sua mano, et hora ne facc'io presente all'Illustrissimo et Reverendissimo Signor Cardinale Borromeo mio Signore et patrone Colendissimo affermando quanto hò detto di sopra esser' la verità.

Io Luzzasco Luzzaschi hò scritto di mia propria mano la presente fede, in Ferrara alli 29 Settembre 1606

I, Luzzasco Luzzaschi, Ferrarese citizen, swear that this *cartella* belonged to the most famous and most excellent Cipriano Rore, Flemish composer and *maestro di cappella* of the late most excellent Lord, Duke Ercole II d'Este of Ferrara, on which *cartella* he used to write the compositions made first by him in his mind, as was always his custom. I, being at that time his student, saw him write on the aforementioned *cartella* the Gloria of a Mass that he made in Ferrara and others of his compositions made at various times. And he gave the aforementioned *cartella* to me when he left here, which was in 1557, together with the attached *Miserere*, composed by him in Flanders when he was young, and written in his hand, and now I make this known to the most illustrious and most reverend Lord Cardinal Borromeo, my lord and most cherished patron, affirming that what I have said above is the truth.

I, Luzzasco Luzzaschi, wrote the present affidavit with my own hand, in Ferrara on September 29, 1606.[2]

According to Luzzaschi, Cipriano's process had at least three stages: one in the mind, one written on the *cartella*, and one written on paper. Unfortunately, beyond this description and anything we can deduce from the music itself, we know nothing about the first, unwritten phase.

A second composer, Claudio Monteverdi, described a similar phase of mental composition in a letter that he wrote in 1607:

. . . così visto il comandamento di S.A.S. di longa mi posi a comporre in musica il sonetto, et vi sono statto dietro sei giorni, et duoi altri tra provarlo e rescriverlo. . . .

. . . and so on seeing His Highness's [=Vincenzo, fourth Duke of Mantua] commission, I straightway began setting the sonnet to music, and was engaged in doing this for six days, then two more what with trying it out and rewriting it. . . .

---

2. Owens, "The Milan Partbooks," 276.

| L'altro sonetto lo manderò in musica composto a V.S. Ill.ma quanto prima poichè nella mente mia nella sua orditura è da me fatto, ma caso che niente dilongassi il tempo secondo il volere di S.A.S. mi farà gratia d'un minimo cenno che di longo lo manderò. | I shall send Your Lordship the other sonnet, set to music, as soon as possible—since it is already clearly shaped in my mind—but if I should spin out the time even a little, in His Highness's opinion, please be good enough to let me know and I shall send it at once.[3] |

Monteverdi's language ("nella mente mia nella sua orditura è da me fatto") invokes the rich imagery of weaving. "Orditura" is the pattern of warp lines laid down initially on the loom. By extension it means the essential lines of an intellectual work.[4] The implication is that the composition, at least in its essence, existed virtually complete in Monteverdi's mind: all that remained was to write it down—and then, of course, to follow the process he used for the other sonnet, namely, to try it out and to rewrite it. If we take Monteverdi's words literally—and we must remember that he could be making empty claims—then composing and writing out were quite different activities. The first piece had taken six days to compose and write down, then two more to perform, revise, and rewrite. The second piece was nearly composed, that is, Monteverdi knew its main outline, its *orditura*, despite the fact that it was not yet written down.

Theorists also suggest a stage in the process where the work takes place essentially in the mind. Lampadius distinguished between a mental and a written stage in composing:

| Quemadmodum enim Poetae naturali quodam impetu, ad condenda Carmina, excitantur, habentes in animo res, quas descripturi sint, inclusas etc. Sic etiam oportet Componistam prius quasdam, in animo, clausulas, sed optimas, excogitare, & quodam iuditio easdem perpendere, ne aliqua nota totam vitiet clausulam, et auditorum aures taediosas faciat. Deinde, ad exercitationem accedere, hoc est, excogitatas clausulas, in ordinem quendam distri- | For just as poets are stirred by a certain natural impulse to write their verses, having in their minds the subjects that are to be described, so also the composer ought first to think out in his mind musical phrases, indeed very good ones, and to consider them carefully with good judgment lest one note ruin the whole phrase and tire the ears of the listener, and then proceed to the working out, that is, to distribute in a certain order the phrases that have been thought out |

3. Claudio Monteverdi, *Lettere*, ed. Éva Lax (Florence, 1994), 18–19: letter to Annibale Iberti, Cremona, 28 July 1607; translation: *The Letters of Claudio Monteverdi*, trans. Denis Stevens, rev. ed. (Oxford, 1995), 44. Stevens imagines that the two sonnets mentioned in the letter could be the two *a cappella* settings in the next book of madrigals to be published (Book VI, 1614): *Zefiro torna* and *Ohimè il bel viso* (both by Petrarch).

4. G. DeVoto and G. C. Oli, *Dizionario della lingua italiana* (Florence, 1971). John Florio (*A Worlde of Wordes* [London, 1598; repr. New York, 1972], 248) defines *orditura, ordimento* as "a warping, a weaving, a devise, a complotting, a contriving."

buere, & eas, quae videntur aptiores servare.

and to save those phrases that seem more suitable.[5]

Being able to keep music in one's mind is one of the skills that distinguishes the experienced composer from the beginner. Thus, the German writer Johannes Avianius, recognizing that beginners have a hard time working "in the mind," recommended that they write down their *fugae* (points of imitation).[6]

Composing "in the mind" is related to other kinds of unwritten musical activities. Musical instruction involved training in improvised counterpoint. Coclico's description of a course of study was probably typical:

Cognitis his spetiebus & doctrina, quomodo his uti debeamus: Comparet sibi puer, tabulam lapideam, in qua facile scribitur, & deletur, ac sumat Tenorem ex cantu Chorali, & ita per speties primo faciat notam contra notam.

Cum autem utcunque fuerit assuetus notam contra notam ex tempore facere, & practicus fuerit, tunc poterit ad contrapunctum fractum accedere. In hoc ubi etiam exercitatus fuerit, reliquat tabulam lapideam, & discat ex tempore canere, super Choralem cantum, aut figuralem ex libro aut scedula. Sed hic continua exercitatione opus est.

Having learned these species [of intervals] and the method, here is how we ought to use them. The boy should provide himself with a slate on which one may easily write and erase; he should take a Tenor from plainchant and begin to write note against note, through the intervals.

Whenever he has gotten used to making note against note by improvisation and has become practiced in it, then he can go on to florid counterpoint. When he has become trained in this too, he should put aside the slate and learn to sing in improvising on plainchant or on figured music from a book or a sheet of paper. But in this there is need for continual exercise.[7]

Zacconi criticized several methods for learning improvised counterpoint that he had encountered:

Per molto e molto ch'io col tempo m'habbia pratticato e conversato con Musici valent'huomini maturi e buoni, e veduto lo stile che loro tene-

For all the many times that I over the years have worked with and conversed with good musicians who were talented and experienced, and

5. *Compendium musices*, sig. G v[v]. This translation (which I published in "The Milan Partbooks," 296) is an adaptation of one by Lowinsky, "On the Use of Scores," in *Music in the Culture*, 798.

6. *Isagoge in libros musicae poeticae* (Erfurt, 1581) sig. D i[v]: "ut autem Tyrones qui fugas in mente nondum possunt instituere, adiuventur aliquantulum, asscribere placet modum fugas utcunque per necessitatem efficiendi." See Benito Rivera, "The *Isagoge* (1581) of Johannes Avianius: An Early Formulation of Triadic Theory," *Journal of Music Theory* 22 (1978): 43–64; and Rivera, *German Music Theory*.

7. Coclico, *Compendium musices*, sig. K i[v]; trans. Albert Seay, *Musical Compendium* (Colorado Springs, 1973), 23 (with revisions).

ano in insegnar di Contrapunto à i loro Scolari, non hò mai veduto c'habbino tenuta maniera lodevole e facile in insegnare à i Scolari loro di far Contrapunto alla mente: ma tenendolo diverso; chi non gli l'hà insegnato se non con dirgli "impara da te stesso col imaginarti prima quello che tu vuoi estendere su la Cartella, che pigliandone tu pratica, ne diverai patrone e possessore." E chi gli l'ha mostrato nella persona sua, intanto che facendo allo Scolare cantar il canto fermo, eglino stessi contrapuntizandovi sopra, diceano: "senti, si fa cosi, e si fa colà." Altri anco interrogendo lo scolare con dirgli: "Che cosa fareste tu sopra queste quattro note; pensa bene nella tua mente quello che tu vi vuoi fare, e poi famelo sentire senza che quì in cartella tu me ne facci mostra e nota alcuna." E ve ne debbano anco per mia fe esser dell'altre delle maniere ch'io non l'ho vedute ne pratticate; ma che giova, se questi tali non vanno per la diretta via che dovereb-bono andare?

seen the methods they used in teach-ing counterpoint to their students, I have never seen one who has a good and straightforward technique for teaching their students to do counter-point "alla mente," but just the oppo-site: one tells the student "learn by yourself by imagining first that which you would write out on the *cartella*, so that with practice, you will become accomplished"; someone else shows how he would do it himself, making the student sing the cantus firmus, while he himself sings a counterpoint above it and says, "listen, do it this way, do it that way." Yet others again ask the students, "What would you do above these four notes, think carefully in your mind what you want to do and then let me hear it without showing me any of the notes on the *cartella*." And there are doubtless other ways that I have neither seen nor experienced, but what good are they if they don't take the direct path to where they are going?[8]

Improvisation was important not only for learning but also for performing a variety of different repertories, both instrumental and vocal. Banchieri's barnyard *Contraponto alla mente* is a written-out example of what must have been a com-mon practice.[9] Composing first "alla mente" would not have been difficult for musicians who were trained to sing "alla mente."[10] While there are important differences between singing *alla mente* (singing an improvised counterpoint to a given line) and composing *alla mente* (conceiving the entire fabric of a new com-

8. Lodovico Zacconi, *Prattica di musica seconda parte* (Venice, 1622; repr. Bologna, 1983), 84.

9. Adriano Banchieri, *Contraponto bestiale alla mente,* in *Festino nella sera del giovedi grasso* (Venice, 1608).

10. Concerning improvisation, see, among others, Ernest Ferand, "Improvised Vocal Counter-point in the Late Renaissance and Early Baroque," *Annales musicologiques* 4 (1956): 129–174; Klaus-Jürgen Sachs, "Arten improvisierter Mehrstimmigkeit nach Lehrtexten des 14. bis 16. Jahrhunderts," *Basler Jahrbuch für historische Musikpraxis* 7 (1983): 166–183. Keith Polk, *German Instrumental Music of the Late Middle Ages* (Cambridge, 1992), 167–213, presents a possible course of study, based on Johannes Tinctoris and Conrad Paumann, by which instrumentalists may have learned to improvise.

position), both reflect a world in which the distinctions between improvised and written music were not great.[11]

One major component of the work that may have happened primarily "in the mind" can be described by Christopher Reynolds's useful term "compositional planning."[12] In the absence of a sketch, for example showing a poem divided into segments, or a chart with cadence points, we can only capture these aspects of composition by studying the end product and imagining the composer's choices. The evidence for planning is the music itself.

"Compositional planning" could encompass every aspect of the music—from the use of pre-existent material to decisions about musical structure, from the choice of clefs to decisions about cadence points. The "theorists" (music teachers) gave beginners advice about choices they needed to make; composers presumably faced many of the same decisions. Some were matters of convention, while others were determined by the terms of the particular commission that led to the composition of a particular piece of music.[13] At the core were the choices about setting the text.[14] Hermann Finck's advice is illustrative:

Etenim Componista artificiosus compositurus aliquam cantilenam, ante omnia textus rationem habet, hunc diligenter ex omni parte perpendit, considerans qualis illi melodia addi possit, quae apposite ad ipsum textum quadret, sensumque eius & singulos affectus orationis quam propriissime exprimat. Et quia in uno eodemque textu, diversae materiae tractantur, variae etiam fugae & clausulae excogitandae sunt, quae affectus in textu	Indeed the composer who wants to compose a composition must above all take the text into account, diligently examine all its parts, considering what kind of melody can be added to it, which would go with it suitably and express most properly its meaning and the affection of the individual words. And since different subjects are treated in one and the same text, various fugues and clausulas are to be invented, which express

11. For recent debates about the meaning of Tinctoris's term *res facta* in relation to this distinction, see Margaret Bent, "*Res facta* and *Cantare Super Librum*," *JAMS* 36 (1983): 371-391; Blackburn, "On Compositional Process"; David E. Cohen, "*Contrapunctus*, Improvisation, and *Res Facta*," paper read at the annual meeting of the American Musicological Society, 1989; and Peter Cahn, "Zur Vorgeschichte des 'Opus perfectum et absolutum' in der Musikauffassung um 1500," in *Zeichen und Struktur in der Musik der Renaissance*, ed. Klaus Hortschansky (Kassel, 1989), 11-26.

12. Christopher Reynolds, "Musical Evidence of Compositional Planning in the Renaissance: Josquin's *Plus nulz regretz*," *JAMS* 40 (1987): 53-81.

13. On convention, see, for example, Johannes Tinctoris, *Liber de arte contrapuncti*, bk. 3, chap. 8, *Opera theoretica*, ed. Albert Seay, CSM 22 (American Institute of Musicology, 1975), 2: 155; Nicola Vicentino, *L'antica musica ridotta alla moderna prattica* (Rome, 1555; repr. Kassel, 1959), fol. 84ᵛ; Pietro Pontio, *Ragionamento di musica* (Parma, 1588; repr. Kassel, 1959), 154 f.; Thomas Morley, *A Plaine and Easie Introduction to Practicall Musicke* (London, 1597; repr. Amsterdam, 1969). See James Armstrong, "How to Compose a Psalm: Ponzio and Cerone Compared," *Studi musicali* 7 (1978): 103-139.

14. For theoretical *dicta* on this subject, see Don Harrán, *Word–Tone Relations in Musical Thought from Antiquity to the Seventeenth Century*, MSD 40 (American Institute of Musicology, 1986).

| contentos propriis quasi coloribus depingant atque exprimant. | and depict as if with specific colors the affections found in the text.[15] |

If we work backward from the text, we can see the composer as reader and infer the choices he made.[16]

There are problems with working from the music to imagine what paths composers may have followed. Was the composer aware of everything that we may find in the music? Can we be sure that we are not imposing concepts foreign to the music? Nevertheless, the approach can be profitable because it helps us to see the process of composing as a series of discrete "problems" that needed solving.

COMPOSING WITH INSTRUMENTS

A second realm that may reflect composing without writing is the use of instruments. There is evidence that both amateurs and professional composers used instruments for the early stages of composing. Finck condemned composers who had to

| vel saltem tam diu Clavicordium sollicitant, donec habitu qualicunque acquisito, ex clavium tactu & digitorum articulatione concentum aliquem animadvertere, eumque in cartam inde transferre discant. Ac sic tandem cantilenam repletam pausis & vitiis nulla toni ratione habita proferunt. Huiusmodi Componistarum hodie magnus est numerus. | pound on the clavichord for a long time until having acquired a certain experience they learn how to recognize a certain harmony from the touch of the keys and the movement of the fingers and then transfer it to paper. And thus, finally, they produce a composition full of rests and mistakes, having no relation to any mode. The number of composers of this sort today is great.[17] |

Vincenzo Galilei divided composers into categories according to their skills. Some, like Annibale Padovano, Claudio Merulo, Giuseppe Guami, and Luzzasco Luzzaschi, were excellent both at performing and at notating their compositions in writing; others could do one or the other (play or write) but not both. He pointed out that to be truly excellent in both realms they had to follow a rigorous course:

15. Hermann Finck, *Practica musica* (Wittenberg, 1556), sig. Rr iv. The translation is by Frank E. Kirby, "Hermann Finck's Practica musica: A Comparative Study in 16th Century German Musical Theory," Ph.D. diss., Yale University, 1957, 278–279. I have added the final sentence in this paragraph, not translated by Kirby. The vividness of these remarks makes the loss of Finck's treatise on composition seem particularly regrettable.

16. My thinking on this subject was greatly influenced by Don Michael Randel, "Dufay the Reader," in *Music and Language*, Studies in the History of Music, 1 (New York, 1983), 38–78. See also my essay, "Music and Meaning in Cipriano de Rore's Setting of *Donec gratus eram tibi*," in the same volume, 95–117.

17. Finck, *Practica musica*, sig. Oo iiiv. Cited by Lowinsky, "On the Use of Scores," *Music in the Culture*, 799 n.

la cagione poiche questi sadisfacciano si con la penna & col sonar loro, è questa. Sono primamente stati piu & piu anni sotto la disciplina de primi huomini del mondo in quella professione, & con molte comodità; hanno vedute & diligentemente essaminate tutte le buone musiche de famosi Contrapuntisti; con i quali mezzi si sono acquistati un Contrapunto purgatissimo & squisito; hanno studiato in esso strumento tutto quel tempo con la maggiore diligenza & assiduità che imaginare si possa, & del continovo vanno studiando & imparando; sono stati in piu parti del mondo & pratticato con diversi valenti huomini della professione loro; sono di piu stati dotati dalla natura di bellissimo ingegno, di gran giuditio, di felice memoria, & di fiera & insieme leggiadra dispositione di mani: oltre all'havere (& meritamente) havuto occasioni di servire non solo Principi grandi & ricchissimi; ma intendentissimi & giuditiosi in particolare della musica, & di piu liberali.

The reason why these make a mark both with the pen and with their playing is this: first, they studied for many, many years with the best men in the business, and with great profit; they looked at and diligently studied all the good music of the most famous composers (*contrapuntisti*) through which means they acquired a refined understanding of counterpoint; they studied their instrument with the greatest diligence and devotion that can be imagined and continue studying and learning; they have been all over the world, playing with other skilled performers; they have been endowed by nature with a wonderful imagination, great judgment, an excellent [literally, happy] memory, and an at once spirited and graceful disposition of the hand; and, beyond all that (and rightly) they had the opportunity to serve princes who were not only great and rich but also very knowledgeable and judicious especially about music and, moreover, generous.[18]

Galilei also described performers whose skills did not include writing music down in notated form:

Altri che sono desiderosi & gli pare meritare d'essere tra questi numerati, per haver solo nel sonare una tal fierezza & dispositione di mani, che fanno maravigliare la piu parte di quelli che gli ascoltano; i quali nel mettersi à scrivere quel saper loro, vanno così à rilente à mettere in carta quello che hanno avanti sonato, che alcuni che vedono & essaminano poi gli scritti loro, gli giudicano di ciascuni altri che di essi.

Others who are desirous and who seem to merit being in this company for having only in their playing a certain confidence (*fierezza*) and disposition of the hands that make most of those who listen to them marvel, when they set themselves to writing down what they know go so slowly to put on paper that which they played earlier that some who look at and examine afterward what they have written judge it to be written by someone else.[19]

18. Vincenzo Galilei, *Dialogo della musica antica et della moderna* (Florence, 1581; repr. New York, 1967), 138–139.
19. Galilei, *Dialogo*, 139.

PLATE 4.1   Bálint Bakfark, *Intabulatura* (1553), title page

His account makes clear that composers of keyboard or lute music could compose at their instrument, and then either write down the music or not, depending in part on their skill. It is noteworthy that the Hungarian lutenist and composer Bálint Bakfark had himself portrayed in the woodcut on the title page of his first publication holding a lute while seated in front of a table that had a quill pen and an open music book: the image is of the composer playing and writing (see plate 4.1).[20]

The evidence that composers used instruments for composing vocal music is slight, but significant. A passage from a fifteenth-century French romance portrays the hero, Cleriadus, as composer and performer. According to Howard Mayer Brown's interpretation, Cleriadus has received a text to set, probably a rondeau. "He borrows a harp and asks his servant to bring him pen and paper, whereupon he sets the poem to music."[21] Cleriadus first set the text to music ("J'ay mis vostre chançon en chant") and then arranged it for the harp ("et si

20. *Intabulatura Valentini Bacfarc Transilvani Coronensis Liber Primus* (Lyons, 1553). See Walter Salmen, *Musiker im Porträt, 1: Von der Spätantike bis 1600* (Munich, 1982), 176–177.

21. Howard Mayer Brown, "Songs After Supper: How the Aristocracy Entertained Themselves in the Fifteenth Century," in *Musica Privata: Die Rolle der Musik im privaten Leben. Festschrift zum 65. Geburtstag von Walter Salmen*, ed. Monika Fink, Rainer Gstrein, and Günter Mössmer (Innsbruck, 1991), 44. Brown arrives at a different interpretation of this passage from the one offered by Christopher Page, "The Performance of Songs in Late Medieval France, A New Source," *EM* 19 (1982): 441–450, written before the publication of the modern edition. See *Cleriadus et Meliadice. Roman en prose du XVe siècle*, ed. Gaston Zink (Geneva, 1984). See also Howard Mayer Brown, "Cleriadus et Meliadice: A Fifteenth-Century Manual for Courtly Behavior," in *Iconography at the Crossroads*, ed. Brendan Cassidy (Princeton, 1993), 215–225.

est desja mise sur la harpe"). The harp was used both for composing and for performing.

There is also evidence that Palestrina may have used the lute in composing. A letter from a Mantuan court official, Annibale Capello, describes Palestrina's composition of a Mass for Duke Guglielmo Gonzaga: "Palestrina has begun to set the Kyrie and Gloria of the first mass on the lute."[22] Given the fact that many composers were accomplished organists or lutenists (including William Byrd, Adrian Willaert, and Palestrina himself) it is quite likely that further evidence will turn up.

———

It should be no surprise that a chapter about composing without writing should be so brief: by definition all the evidence allows us to do is to speculate about the methods. It is to the parts of the process that involved writing that we must direct our attention.

22. See chap. 11.

CHAPTER FIVE

ERASABLE TABLETS

While composers were certainly able to hear and work out music in their minds without recourse to writing, at some point the music had to assume a graphic form so that it could be preserved, transmitted, and performed. The evidence suggests that composers employed two different kinds of surfaces for writing down their music: (1) an erasable surface such as slate that could be used many times and (2) paper. In the period we are considering, the pencil had not yet been invented, so writing on paper meant using pen and ink; "erasure" could be achieved only by scraping the ink from the surface of the paper (often resulting in holes in the paper).[1] Paper could therefore be used only once. Despite the differences in the properties of the two kinds of writing surfaces, composers seem to have used them both in much the same way, for all the written stages of a composition, from the earliest sketches to the final version.

Suzanne Clercx first drew attention to the existence of the erasable tablet as a tool in composition when she reported the discovery of a slate containing six staves on front and back.[2] Siegfried Hermelink offered a thorough account of what he called the *tabula compositoria* by bringing together references in music treatises as well as documents.[3] He showed that the tablets, made of wood, stone, or some other erasable surface, were incised with either ten-line or five-line staves, and he traced their use, particularly in the realm of music education, well into the nineteenth century.

A number of recent discoveries invite a fresh consideration of tablets and their use. Several more tablets have been unearthed in archeological excavations, and newly discovered documents give a better idea of how they were used. For example, the rich cache of letters preserved primarily in the manuscript miscellany VatV 5318, now available in an excellent critical edition, offers interesting

---

1. For a discussion of the technology of writing with paper, pen and ink, see chap. 6.
2. Clercx, "D'une ardoise," 157–170, based on the archeological report by J. Mertens, "Recherches archéologiques dans la collégiale Saint-Feuillen," in *Bulletin de la Commission Royale des Monuments et des Sites* 4 (1953): 160.
3. Hermelink, "Die Tabula compositoria," 221–230.

details about the acquisition and use of tablets by Italian composers and theorists in the 1520s and 1530s.[4] My discovery that a composer as important as Cipriano de Rore used an erasable tablet—*cartella*—as part of the second phase of his compositional process (after working the music out in his mind and before writing it out on paper) suggests that a thorough understanding of the tablet is of crucial importance for understanding compositional process.[5]

Let us begin with the tablets themselves. What were they made of? How big were they? How were they used? The evidence to answer these questions comes from documents, descriptions in theoretical treatises, representations in paintings and engravings, and surviving exemplars.

A working definition of a tablet is an object with a smooth surface on which something can be written and then erased. The terms for the tablets give valuable clues about their appearance (see table 5.1).[6] While some are simply called tablets (*tabletes, tabella, tavola, tabula*), others are known by their substance (*ardoyse, schiffer stein,* slate) or by the property of erasability. Lippius' term (later used also by Walther) was *palimpsestus compositorius*; a palimpsest is a surface from which the original writing has been erased and new writing added.

By far the most common name for these tablets was *cartella* (Italian and also Latin) and its cognates. The fact that *cartella* has as its root *carta,* or paper, has made it difficult for scholars to accept that *cartella* could mean an erasable tablet made of something other than paper.[7] Yet a number of documents make clear that a *cartella* was an erasable tablet. The English lexicographer John Florio defined *cartelle*—the plural form of *cartella*—as "a paire of tablets, writing tables. Also the side postes of a doore."[8] Schonsleder, writing in 1631, referred to the "cartella seu deletili tabula" in his account of the methods of composing; Herbst's 1643 German translation of the passage refers to the *cartella* as "Cartell oder Lösch-Tabell." In 1529 the Italian choirmaster and composer Giovanni Spataro requested a "cartella, o vero una tabula de abaco."[9] *Abbaco* is a branch of mathematics dealing with the practical problem-solving needed by merchants (currency conversion, for example).[10] A *tabula de abbaco* or slate for doing computations can be seen in representations

4. Blackburn et al., *A Correspondence.*

5. Discussed below and also in chaps. 4 and 9.

6. The texts of many of the documents or passages referred to on the table are given at the end of this chapter.

7. See, for example, the comment by Culley, *Jesuits and Music,* 74: "The *cartella* mentioned in the preceding quotation refers to a folder or case in which books and assignments for class were carried. Hence, to 'show the *cartella,*' or 'to give an account of the *cartella,*' was to present one's written exercises in music."

8. John Florio, *A Worlde of Wordes,* 62. On Florio, see Gunnar Tancke, *Die italienischen Wörterbücher von den Anfängen bis zum Erscheinen des Vocabolario degli Accademici della Crusca (1612)* (Tübingen, 1984), 72–75, 242. The term does not appear in the first edition of *Vocabolario degli Accademici della Crusca* (Venice, 1612). Later editions include a series of meanings that suggest an oversize object made from some sort of paper (such as a folder for maps) or a sign (bus signs, boards used for listing the hymns), but nothing related to writing music.

9. Blackburn et al., *A Correspondence,* Letter 18; appendix, doc. 3.

10. Paul Grendler, *Schooling in Renaissance Italy: Literacy and Learning, 1300–1600* (Baltimore, 1989), 306 ff.; see also Blackburn et al., *A Correspondence,* 121.

TABLE 5.1 Terminology for Erasable Tablets

Term (alphabetical order)	Source	Document [a]	Date
ardoyse (French)	Cretin, "Plainte sur le trepas de . . . Bracconier"	2	1512
cartella (Italian)	Spataro correspondence (see Table 5.3)	3 – 10	1529 – 1533
cartella	Verona: inventory (Turrini)		1559
cartella	Bergamo, MIA: testimony against Pietro Pontio	12	1566
cartella	Mantua: Merulo letters	13	1566
cartella	Rome, Collegio Germanico: rules	16	1587
cartella	Florence, Santa Maria Novella: pay documents	17	1592 – 1596
cartella	Rome, San Luigi dei Francesi: pay documents	18	1593 – 1596
cartella	Florio, *Worlde of Wordes*		1598
cartella	MilA10: letter of Luzzaschi [b]		1606
cartella	Diruta, *Seconda parte del Transilvano*	19	1609
cartella	Florio, *Queen Anna's New World of Words*		1611
cartella	Banchieri, *Cartella musicale*	20	1614
cartella	Scaletta, *Primo scalino*		1622
cartella	Zacconi, *Prattica di musica seconda parte*	21	1622
cartella	Doni, *Lyra barberina*	22	1632 (publ. 1763)
cartella	Padua, Sant'Antonio: inventory (Sartori)		1662
cartella	Bontempi, *Historia musica*		1695
cartella seu deletili tabula (Latin)	Schonsleder, *Architectonice musices* [c]		1631
cartell (Catalan)	anon., *Curial e Güelfa* (Knighton)	I	mid-15th c.
Cartell (German)	Praetorius, *Syntagma musicum*		1619
Cartell oder Lösch-Tabell (German)	Herbst (translation of Schonsleder) [d]		1643
palierten schiffer stein (German)	Württemberg: purchase of Hemmel's slate	14	1568
palimpsestus compositorius (Latin)	Lippius, *Synopsis musicae novae*		1612
palimpsestus compositorius	Walther, *Musicalisches Lexikon*		1732
slate (English)	Cocker, *England's Pen-man*		1703
tabella (Latin)	Puteanus, *Modulata Pallas*		1599
tabletes (French)	Bourges: pay document (Higgins)		1407
tabula (Latin)	Luscinius, *Musurgia*		1536
tabula (Latin)	Burmeister, *Musica poetica*		1606
tabula compositoria (Latin)	Lampadius, *Compendium musices*	11	1537

TABLE 5.1   *(continued)*

Term (alphabetical order)	Source	Document	Date
tabula lapidea (Latin)	Coclico, *Compendium musices*		1552
tabula o vero cartella (Italian)	Spataro correspondence, Letter 30	7	1531
cartella o vero una tabula de abaco (Italian)	Spataro correspondence, Letter 18	3	1529
tavola di pietra (Italian)	Florence: Corteccia's will	15	1571

[a] The documents are given at the end of this chapter.
[b] See above, p. 65.
[c] See above, p. 61.
[d] See above, p. 62.

of gambling (to keep the accounts) and of money changers.[11] Johann Sadeler's engraving of *Arithmetica* has a female allegorical figure seated at a table and writing with one hand on a large tablet that she holds with the other; in the background is a smaller tablet with a hole in the top leaning against a wall.[12]

WHAT WERE THE TABLETS MADE OF?

Some of the sixteenth-century documents describe the substance used for the tablets as stone.[13] In fact, all of the surviving tablets with either blank staves or musical notation are made of stone, specifically slate. They have been been discovered at archeological excavations associated with churches or schools in Ireland,[14] England,[15] France,[16] Belgium, and the Netherlands[17] (see table 5.2):

11. One example is Jan Steen's *Der Streit beim Spie* in Berlin, which shows a slate with chalk on a table to keep gambling records. Another example of tablets is Raphael's *A School of Athens*. A. S. Osley, *Scribes and Sources: Handbook of the Chancery Hand in the Sixteenth Century* (Boston, 1980), 223, cited a treatise published by Plantin in 1567 concerning the use of tablets in business: "This is still done in our time by people who have much to do and have business to transact in several places. In order not to forget anything, they carry tablets on which they write with a needle [Flemish: with a slate pencil]."

12. *Hollstein's Dutch and Flemish Etchings, Engravings, and Woodcuts ca. 1450–1700*, 21 (Amsterdam, 1980), no. 549; facsimile in *Una dinastia di incisori, i Sadeler*, ed. Caterina Limentani Virdis, Franca Pellegrini, and Gemme Piccin (Padua, 1992), no. 10.

13. For example, Coclico's *tabula lapidea*, Corteccia's *tavola di pietra*, Hemmel's *palirten schiffer stein*.

14. Bliss, "The Inscribed Slates at Smarmore," 33–60, especially 42–45; Derek Britton and Alan J. Fletcher, "Medieval Hiberno-English Inscriptions on the Inscribed Slates of Smarmore: Some Reconsiderations and Additions," *Irish University Record* 20 (1990): 71–72.

15. V. Pritchard, *English Medieval Graffiti* (Cambridge, 1967), 170–171; Blezzard, "The Wells Musical Slates," 26–30; R. S. Bate, "Musical Slates," *Notes and Queries from Somerset and Dorset* 31, no. 49 (1936): 50–51.

16. Chailley, "Tabulae Compositoriae," 51–54.

17. Concerning the slate from Fosse first reported by Clercx ("D'une ardoise") as well as two

Other kinds of surfaces were also used. Lampadius described tablets as made of wood or stone ("tabulis ligneis vel lapideis").[18] Philomathes used a term—*pluteus*, a board or plank—that suggests a wooden tablet.[19] Florio, in the second edition of his Italian–English dictionary, defined *cartella* as:

> a kind of sleeked pasteboord to write upon and may be blotted out againe. Also leaves of writing tables. Also an instrument full of holes used by Iewellers to measure pearles and of gunners to measure bullets.[20]

Documents from the account books of fra Tommaso Minerbetti, organist at Santa Maria Novella, describe the substance as plaster.[21] Other documents from sixteenth-century Florence show that the tablets could also be made from wax.[22]

Some of the iconographic and documentary evidence suggests that the tablets could have been a kind of stiff paper (perhaps an explanation for the name *cartella*). An early seventeenth-century portrait of Ruggiero Giovannelli shows the composer holding a curved sheet of heavy paper and a pen.[23] A much later witness, Johann Gottfried Walther, described a *palimpsestus* as made from donkey skin that had been treated with plaster and varnish.[24]

The documents do not always reveal the substance. The correspondence between the two music theorists Giovanni Spataro and Giovanni del Lago is a case in point (see table 5.3). In 1529 and again in 1533 Spataro, who was living in Bologna, asked Del Lago to buy him a *cartella* in Venice. Several of the 1529 letters refer to a "foglio rigato," which Bonnie Blackburn equated with the *cartella*: "By calling it 'foglio rigato' Spataro seems to indicate that is is made of heavy paper, perhaps pasteboard, and not stone."[25] It is possible, however, that the *cartella*

---

others found in Ghent and IJsselstein, see Eugeen Schreurs, *Anthologie van muziekfragmenten uit de Lage Landen* (Leuven, 1995) (facsimiles), which must be consulted in conjunction with *Bedreigde klanken? Muziekfragmenten uit de Lage Landen,* ed. Eugeen Schreurs and Bruno Bouckaert (Leuven, 1995) (brief descriptions with bibliography).

18. Lampadius, *Compendium musices*, sig. G v^v, discussed below.

19. Philomathes, *De nova domo*, discussed in chap. 2.

20. John Florio, *Queen Anna's New World of Words* (London, 1611, repr. Menston, 1968), 86.

21. Frank A. D'Accone, "Repertory and Performance Practice at Santa Maria Novella at the Turn of the 17th Century," in *A Festschrift for Albert Seay: Essays by his Friends and Colleagues*, ed. Michael D. Grace (Colorado Springs, 1982), 92. The documents are in Florence, Archivio di Stato, Corporazioni Religiose Soppresse N.o 102 Santa Maria Novella, vol. 457, Libro di spese dell'eredità Minerbetti, 1592–1609 (CRIA 6804), fols. 48^v–50^r. Cited by Frederick Hammond, *Girolamo Frescobaldi: A Guide to Research* (New York, 1988), 76; appendix, doc. 17.

22. Tim Carter, "Music-Selling in Late Sixteenth-Century Florence: The Bookshop of Piero di Giuliano Morosi," *Music & Letters* 70 (1989): 495. The documents (not yet published) are in Florence, Archivio di Stato, Libri di Commercio 553: 'Quaderno' of Piero di Giuliano Morosi libraio, begun 20 August 1588. For comments on various possible surfaces, see Osley, *Scribes and Sources*, 35, a reference made by Erasmus to unusual writing surfaces: "And today there are some who write with a bronze or silver stylus on plates smeared with dust."

23. Facsimile in Herman-Walther Frey, "Die Kapellmeister an der französischen Nationalkirche San Luigi dei Francesi in Rom im 16. Jahrhundert," *AfMw* 22 (1965), plate I, after p. 48.

24. *Musicalisches Lexikon oder Musicalische Bibliothec* (Leipzig, 1732); cited by Hermelink, "Die Tabula," 227.

25. Blackburn et al., *A Correspondence*, 121.

TABLE 5.2 Extant Tablets

Present location	Original site	Size (cm)	Staves	Notation	Possible date	Facsimile/transcription
[Beauvais (France)]	Cathedral St-Pierre					
1)		11.3x8.4	4	none	2/2 15th-ca. 1520	none
2)		9x7.5	4	mensural	2/2 15th-ca. 1520	Chailley
Dublin (Ireland), National Museum	Smarmore, church					
1) 1961:12		11.5x9.5	2	mensural	2/4 15th c.	plate 5.3
2) 1961:24		14.5x9.1	3	mensural (dance?)	2/4 15th c.	Bliss (Dart)
3) 1961:34		12.2x7.5	1	mensural (secular text?)	2/4 15th c.	Britton and Fletcher
4) 1961:41		6.2x3.4	unknown	unknown	2/4 15th c.	none
Ghent (Belgium), Dienst Stadsarcheologie SBW 93-4/156	Ghent	5.6x12.4	1	mensural (tenor cantus firmus?)	2/2 15th c.	Schreurs
IJsselstein (Netherlands), private collection R. Ooyevaar	IJsselstein, chapel of Lopiker	11.5x14	3, front and back	stroke	15th c.	Schreurs
Jambes (Belgium), Direction des Fouilles de la Région Vallonne, Fos 52/8	Fosse, St-Feuillien, well	15.5x31	6, front and back	none	15th–17th c.	Clercx; Schreurs
Wells (England), Wells Museum	Mudgley manor house					
1)		6x5 inches	4 (front)	mensural and stroke	15th c.?	Pritchard, fig. 222; Blezzard
2)		4x3.5 inches	2 (front)	mensural	15th c.?	plate 5.2; Pritchard, fig. 221; Blezzard

TABLE 5.3   References to a *Cartella* in the Spataro Correspondence

Letter	Date	Sender/Recipient	Synopsis
18	25 Jan. 1529	Spataro to Del Lago	requests a *cartella* or abacus tablet from Venice that is square and long on each side as this sheet or letter (ca. 32 cm square) for composing sometimes some piece of music
lost	25 Feb. 1529	Del Lago to Spataro	sent with "foglio rigato"; requests contra alto of *Deprecor te*
20	undated [13 – 28 Mar. 1529]	Spataro to Del Lago	received letter of 25 Feb. on 13 March; sends contra alto
lost	20 Mar. 1529	Del Lago to Spataro	sent with *cartella*
21	31 Mar. 1529	Spataro to Del Lago	(1) received letter of 20 March on 27 March, "from which I understood what you said concerning another letter of yours [=lost letter of 25 Feb.] sent to me with 'el foglio rigato,' about which I will not say anything more for having (before now) given you an answer and sent the contra alto you had requested"
			(2) received the *cartella*, which is just what I wanted; why didn't you tell me of the price?
22	5 Apr. 1529	Spataro to Del Lago	"from two of my letters sent to you, that is, one with that contra alto which you requested [=Letter 20], and the other in response to your letter to which the *cartella* was attached [=Letter 21]"
23	28 May 1529	Spataro to Del Lago	refers to the *fante* who had brought the *cartella* from Venice to Bologna
30	30 Jan. 1531	Spataro to Aaron	Spataro, replying to Aaron's criticism that a motet ended on the wrong beat (literally, the number of semibreves was incorrect), rechecked his "tablet or *cartella* where it was first composed" and discovered that he had written an "8" where he should have written a "9"

TABLE 5.3 *(continued)*

Letter	Date	Sender/Recipient	Synopsis
36	27 Nov. 1531	Spataro to Aaron	Spataro, replying to Aaron's criticism of a pitch in the manuscript copy of *Virgo prudentissima*, finds that he had written the correct pitch on the *cartella* where he had originally composed it and asks Aaron to make the change
49	2 Jan. 1533	Spataro to Aaron	Spataro explains some mistakes (there were notes missing in the tenor and canto) in the manuscript copy of *Ave gratia plena*: he had trusted himself too much and had copied the music directly from the *cartella* without having the music sung
54	4 June 1533	Spataro to Del Lago	requests a *cartella* as large as "half the size or perhaps a finger's width or two larger" than the page on which the letter was written (30.5×20 cm)
55	30 July 1533	Spataro to Aaron	received the *cartella* from Del Lago
56	30 July 1533	Spataro to Del Lago	thanks him for the *cartella* which is just right; wants to know the price, unless it is a gift

and the "foglio rigato" were two different objects, sent separately.[26] If that is the case, we are left in the dark both about the nature and purpose of the "foglio rigato" and about the substance from which this particular *cartella* was made.

The one property all *cartelle* had in common was erasability. We saw in the previous chapter that Coclico required his students to provide "a stone tablet, on which something may easily be written and erased.[27] Luzzaschi's testimony about Rore's *cartella* also focused on its repeated use. He wrote:

that this *cartella* belonged to the most famous and most excellent Cipriano Rore, Flemish composer and *maestro di cappella* of the late most excellent Lord, Duke

26. Letter 21 (appendix, doc. 4) refers to two separate letters from Del Lago: (1) a letter of 25 February, to which Spataro had already replied with his Letter 20, and (2) a letter of 20 March, received on 27 March, to which he was replying with his Letter 21. I think it likely that each letter accompanied a separate object, the "foglio rigato" with Del Lago's letter of 25 February and the *cartella* with the letter of 20 March. A possible corroboration of this view can be found in Letter 22 (appendix, doc. 5).

27. See chap. 4. On Coclico, see Guillaume de Van, "La Pédagogie musicale à la fin du moyen âge," *MD* 2 (1948): 94.

Ercole II d'Este of Ferrara, on which *cartella* he used to write the compositions made first by him in his mind, as was always his custom. I, being at that time his student, saw him write on the aforementioned *cartella* the Gloria of a Mass that he made in Ferrara and others of his compositions made at various times. And he gave the aforementioned *cartella* to me when he left here, which was in 1557.[28]

Zacconi, while not describing the material from which *cartelle* were made, was also explicit about erasability.

I said in the preceding chapter that the student, having provided himself with books suitable to a like profession, should score those examples and examine them very well. And then having written them out in score on the *cartella* he should not do what some do, who, having seen the way the music works, erase them and pay them no more heed. He who is eager to learn, having done all the exercises on the *cartella* just now mentioned and demonstrated above, will write all of them in a separate book.[29]

WHAT WERE THE SIZES OF THE TABLETS?

Tablets came in different sizes, appropriate to their various functions. The largest ones, known only from iconographical evidence, resemble blackboards still found in classrooms today: a large tablet affixed to a wall. One example is a woodcut of a music lesson printed by the Nuremberg printer Hieronymus Höltzel in *Latinum ideoma Magistri Pauli Niavis* (Nuremberg, 1501) (see plate 5.1).[30] Another representation of a large blackboard is found in the set of organ portals painted in 1512 for the church of St. Anna in Augsburg by Jörg Breu the Elder. There are two large, thick tablets resting on columns, on which are inscribed the six hexachord syllables *ut re mi fa sol la*.[31]

The other type of tablet was portable, and it too came in different sizes and shapes. The correspondence between Giovanni Spataro and Giovanni del Lago makes clear that various sizes were available. When Spataro requested *cartelle* from Del Lago, he specified what he was looking for in terms of the size of the paper he used for writing the request. One of them was to be "square and long on each side as this sheet or letter," that is, 32 cm (roughly 12 in.) square (Letter 18, doc.

---

28. See chap. 4.

29. Zacconi, *Prattica di musica seconda parte*, 162 (appendix, doc. 21d).

30. Nuremberg, Stadtbibliothek, 2 an Phil.600.4°/Rar., sig. a I[r]. Reproduced in Walter Salmen, *Musikleben im 16. Jahrhundert*, Musikgeschichte in Bildern 3/9 (Leipzig, 1976), pl. 93, with detailed commentary. Other examples include: the woodcut from 1592 by Master "AE" showing an even larger blackboard with six staves, three of which have music, reproduced in Wéber, "L'Enseignement de la musique," 109 and in *Die Musik des 15. und 16. Jahrhunderts*, ed. Ludwig Finscher, Neues Handbuch der Musikwissenschaft 3, (Laaber 1990), 80; a historical initial from a 1564 print showing a classroom with a blackboard, reproduced by Salmen as pl. 95; and the three additional examples cited by Flynn, "The Education of Choristers," 183.

31. A facsimile of the portals and of two later drawings can be found in Martin Staehelin, *Die Messen Heinrich Isaacs* (Bern and Stuttgart, 1977), 2, plates Ia–c. Staehelin discusses the plausibility of the hypothesis advanced by Moser that the bearded figure writing on the blackboard was Isaac; the later copies identify him as Tubal.

Latinum ideoma Magistri Pauli Niauis Pro paruulis editum.

PLATE 5.1   Anonymous, *Music Lesson* in *Latinum ideoma
Magistri Pauli Niavis* (1501)

3). The other was to be "half the size or perhaps a finger's width or a little larger"
than the page on which the letter was written (Letter 54, doc. 10). Since the page
measures 30.5 × 20 cm, Blackburn concluded that the *cartella* would have mea-
sured approximately 6 × 9 inches.[32] The only other documentary evidence about
size comes from the Minerbetti account books, cited above, which describe one
of the *cartelle* as "tre quarti grande et per ogni verso" (three-quarter size, written
front and back).[33]

   All of the extant slates are rather small. The largest, from Fosse, is oblong, about
the size of a partbook (6 × 12 in.), similar in size and format to one of Spataro's
cartelle. The rest are very uneven in size, either upright or square in format (see
plates 5.2 – 3).

   The best indication of what these portable tablets looked like comes from

---

   32. Blackburn et al., *A Correspondence*, 123: "The advantage of having a *cartella* that is wider than
it is tall is that more music can fit on one line. A *cartella* this size would probably have six staves,
allowing for the composition of a six-voice work." This interpretation seems to me to go beyond
what Spataro's letter actually says.
   33. Appendix, doc. 17.

PLATE 5.2   Slate: Wells

PLATE 5.3   Slate: Smarmore

PLATE 5.4   Dirck Volkertszoon Coornhert (after Maarten van Heemskerck, *Allegory of Good and Bad Music* (detail)

iconographic evidence. There seem to be two sizes: a large tablet that is usually taller than it is wide, and a smaller one in either upright or oblong format.

A good example of a large tablet is found in an engraving of Maarten van Heemskerck's *Allegory of Good and Bad Music* (1554) (see plate 5.4).[34] The figure of Industria (Diligence) holds a large tablet that contains ten five-line staves. She is writing on the tablet with an implement attached to it with a string. The tablet is large—about the size of her torso from waist to shoulder—and quite thick. Like many portable tablets, both the larger and smaller ones, it has a square handle at the top with a hole in it, perhaps used for hanging the tablet on a wall. Another example is found in Johann Sadeler's engraving of the *Annunciation to the Shepherds* (1587, after Martin de Vos) (see plate 5.5). The nine angels of a heavenly choir each hold the music for one of the voices of Andreas Pevernage's *Gloria in excelsis Deo* (according to the identification on the ninth voice). Three of them have tablets similar to the one held by Industria, though without a hole at the top; each tablet has five

34. Owens, "The Milan Partbooks," 282. Ilja M. Veldman (*Maarten van Heemskerck and Dutch Humanism in the Sixteenth Century* [Amsterdam, 1977], 74–76) identified the engraver of this version as Dirck Volkertszoon Coornhert. Veldman's interpretation of the allegory needs to be modified in light of H. Colin Slim's identification of the music in Segment 1 of the engraving ("Images of Music in Three Prints after Maarten van Heemskerck," in *Iconography at the Crossroads*, edited by Brendan Cassidy [Princeton, 1993]), 232–239).

PLATE 5.5   Johann Sadeler (after Martin de Vos), *Annunciation to the Shepherds*

staves.[35] Yet another example, also without a hole, is found in Gregor Reisch, *Margarita philosophica* (Basel, 1508 and many other editions) (see plate 5.6). A woodcut at the beginning of the section on music includes a female figure holding a square tablet with two staves, one containing mensural notation, the other Hufnagel chant notation. It may well be indicative of the strong association of music and tablets that Dosso Dossi included two large stone tablets, each inscribed with a musical canon, in his *Allegory of Music* (ca. 1524–34).[36]

The second, smaller type can be seen on the title page of Ornithoparcus' *Musice active micrologus* (1517) (see plate 5.7). Two figures, identified as Orpheus

35. *Hollstein's Dutch and Flemish Etchings*, 21, no. 181. Facsimile in *Die Singenden in der graphischen Kunst 1500–1900*, Kunstsammlung der Veste Coburg (Essen, 1962), plate 3.

36. Facsimile and discussion in H. Colin Slim, "Dosso Dossi's Allegory at Florence about Music," *JAMS* 43 (1990), especially 66–69. Tablets (without music) do occur in a number of Dosso's paintings. See Felton Gibbons, *Dosso and Battista Dossi: Court Painters at Ferrara* (Princeton, 1968), plates 28, 34, 67, 73, 87, 96, and 106.

PLATE 5.6   Gregor Reisch,
Margarita philosophica (1508),
sig. n ii[r]

and Euridice, hold a tablet on which is written a four-measure phrase of discantus and tenor, in quasi-score format, cadencing on F. It is obviously impossible to judge the actual size because the tablet is out of proportion to the human
figures; the representation is otherwise entirely characteristic of this type of
table.[37] Another example, this time drawn to scale and in upright rather than
oblong format, can be found in the portrait of Adam Gumpelzhaimer, discussed
below (see plate 5.11).

The variety in size and shape of tablets raises questions about their cost and
where they might be acquired. Information is sketchy, but it is clear that tablets
were objects valuable enough to be listed in inventories[38] and included in wills.[39]
It is telling that Luzzaschi valued Cipriano's *cartella* enough to keep it for forty
years and then give it to Borromeo, with a formal affidavit of its authenticity; of
course, in this case, the *cartella*'s worth may reflect Cipriano's status rather than its
absolute value.

37. Another small tablet is found in Niccolò Il Giolfino, *La Musa Tersicore*, discussed by Ben-
venuto Disertori, *La musica nei quadri antichi* (Calliano, 1978), 33–35. The tablet hangs from the
branch of a tree, tied with a ribbon; its shape is more ornate. It has two staves containing music.

38. For example, Padua, Archivio di Stato, S. Antonio Confessore, b. 70, fol. 103[r], 11 May 1662:
"diversi libri di Theorica di musica, cartelle da comporre." The inventory has been published by
Antonio Sartori, *Documenti per la storia della musica al Santo e nel Veneto*, ed. E. Grossato (Vicenza,
1977), 46.

39. One example is the 1571 will of the Florentine composer Francesco Corteccia, given in the
appendix, doc. 15 and discussed below.

PLATE 5.7
Ornithoparcus, *Musice active micrologus* (1517), title page

Despite the evidence of widespread use both for music education and for composition, tablets—at least those of high quality—were evidently not readily available, but had to be purchased from stores specializing in music. In fact, three documents record the purchase of *cartelle* in Venice, the most important Italian center of music printing. It is striking that Spataro, who was living in a university town and an important commercial center, Bologna, had to ask a colleague living in Venice to buy *cartelle* for him. In 1566, Guglielmo Gonzaga, Duke of Mantua and an avid amateur composer, requested that Claudio Merulo, the Italian organist and composer who was just at the beginning of a stint in the music printing and selling business in Venice, supply him with twelve *cartelle* that Merulo had had ruled ("ch'io facessi rigare"), at a total cost of two *scudi*.[40] At the

---

40. Antonino Bertolotti, *Musici alla corte dei Gonzaga in Mantova dal secolo XV al XVIII* (Milan, 1890), 56–57; appendix, doc. 13. The letters were discussed by Rebecca A. Edwards, "Claudio Merulo: Servant of the State and Musical Entrepreneur in Later Sixteenth Century Venice," Ph.D. diss., Princeton University, 1990, 189; she assumed that *cartelle* meant paper. The letters are in Mantua, Archivio di Stato, Archivio Gonzaga, Carteggio Diversi (di Venezia), B. 1498. A follow-up letter dated 4 January 1567 reveals that the *cartelle* had not yet arrived. Two *scudi* (which was worth approximately 8 *lire*) represented nearly half the annual salary of the "mastro de canto fermo" at Santa Barbara (18 *lire* in 1588). See Iain

end of the century, however, Minerbetti could buy his *cartelle* from music shops in Florence as well as Venice. Further research among the inventories of music shops may well yield additional information.

The tablets all had permanent staves, probably incised with a sharp object, or drawn with ink or paint.[41] The number and placement of staves, as well as the format, were appropriate to the various functions for which the tablets were employed.

HOW WERE THE TABLETS USED?

Tablets served at least three different functions. They played a role in music instruction, they helped instrumentalists make intabulations, and they offered an economical way for composers to work on their music.

The tablet served as a basic tool for learning music, and especially for counterpoint lessons. References to tablets are found in many counterpoint and *musica poetica* textbooks of the sixteenth century. Banchieri's decision to entitle a treatise *Cartella musicale* is telling: the treatise, like a tablet, was an aid to learning.[42] He used *cartella* also to refer to a page consisting entirely of music. For example, on pp. 12–13 are two *cartelle* that show how to mutate in the soprano clef, both with and without a flat in the signature: "First *cartella* with the mutations in the clef/key (*chiave*) of ♭ *molle* . . ." and "Second *cartella* of C with the mutations of ♮ *quadro*." Thus, the example or explanation is itself a *cartella* (see plate 5.8). The disposition of notes on the page may resemble the writing on an actual tablet.

The pedagogical function was probably the longest lived and most common of the functions, at least to judge from the extant evidence. The earliest document referring to tablets of which I am aware is associated with instruction. A payment from 1407 records six "tabletes [original reading: *tables*] pour faire le contrepoint" purchased for the choirboys in Bourges.[43] At the other end of the temporal spectrum, a music dictionary published in 1826 contains an entry for *cartella* emphasizing its pedagogical use.[44]

Fenlon, *Music and Patronage in Sixteenth-Century Mantua* (Cambridge, 1980), 166, 184. A set of partbooks of madrigals by Orlando di Lasso cost just less than a *lira* in 1556 ("Lire 0 soldi 16 denari 6"). See Giuseppe Turrini, *L'Accademia filarmonica di Verona* (Verona, 1941), 81. Turrini recorded "una cartella da notar canti di sfoglio" in a 1559 document (p. 134), but without indication of price.

41. Reinhard Strohm, *The Rise of European Music, 1380–1500* (Cambridge, 1993), 289, discovered a document (not yet published) recording payment for painting staves on a blackboard in Bolzano.

42. Adriano Banchieri, *Cartella musicale nel canto figurato fermo, & contrapunto . . . novamente in questa terza impressione ridotta dall'antica alla moderna pratica* (Venice, 1614; repr. Bologna, 1968).

43. Higgins, "Music and Musicians," 692. Bourges, Archives Départmentales du Cher, 8 G 1634, fol. 48ʳ, payment to Johannes Césaris, 1407. Other documents recording the purchase of *cartelle* for use by choirboys come from Rome: San Luigi dei Francesi, Archivio, Mandati, filza 41 (see A. Cametti, "La scuola dei pueri cantus di S. Luigi dei francesi in Roma e i suoi principali allievi (1591–1623)," *Rivista musicale italiana* 22 [1915]: 599, 610, and 622, given in the appendix, doc. 18) and Collegio Germanico (see Culley, *Jesuits and Music,* 70–74, 292–295), appendix, doc. 16.

44. Pietro Lichtenthal, *Dizionario e bibliografia della musica* (Milan, 1826), cited (with several other dictionary entries from the eighteenth and nineteenth centuries) by Hermelink, "Die Tabula," 227.

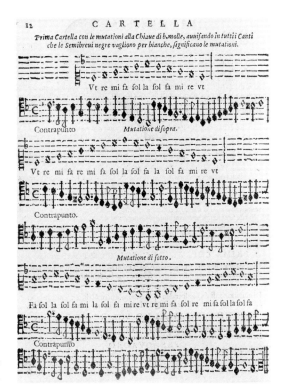

PLATE 5.8a   Banchieri, *Cartella*
              musicale (1614), p. 12

It seems likely that the extant slates were probably used either in teaching or
by beginners, though it has proven difficult to get meaningful transcriptions
from the surviving fragments. Most of the tablets have only single or unrelated
lines of music.[45] The slate from Beauvais is in quasi-score; Chailley's transcription shows a two-voice contrapuntal exercise with the tenor on top and the
soprano beneath it, as well as a third, unrelated voice consisting solely of semibreves.[46] None of the extant tablets is in score, perhaps not surprising given the
relatively early dates assigned to them.

Since the surviving slates provide little information about what was written
on them, we need to turn to descriptions in documents and textbooks. Sometimes the texts deploy the musical examples in the way they might have been
written on the tablet. For example, in his *Compendium musices* (1552), Coclico
provides an example of simple counterpoint (see plate 5.9).[47] He puts the tenor
cantus firmus (c4) at the top of the page and underneath it an "exemplum

45. Blezzard ("The Wells Musical Slates," 26–30) proposed an identification of some of the
music on the Wells slates as *Kyrie Pater cuncta* and *Ite cunctipotens missa est.* Dart (as quoted by Bliss,
"The Inscribed Slates") thought that the music on one of the Smarmore slates was a dance tune.

46. Chailley, "Tabulae compositoriae."

47. Coclico, *Compendium musices*, sig. K ii[r]: "Primum exemplum de contrapuncto simplici.
Addidi huic bono exemplo etiam & pravum, ut puer sciat quid vitare debeat in contrapuncto,
nempe ne faciat duas quintas, aut duas octavas immediate invicem sequentes."

PLATE 5.8b   Banchieri, *Cartella musicale* (1614), p. 13

bonum." After a brief statement about the prohibited motions in voice-leading, he provides a second, flawed counterpoint (his word is "pravus," deformed, misshaped), with the errors marked by numbers written under the offending notes (see example 5.1).

At least for the period before 1550 or 1575, the tablets used for counterpoint exercises probably looked like Coclico's example, using quasi-score format, not an actual score with barlines. It is not always easy to tell, however, what format was employed. For example, one of the witnesses called to testify against Pietro Pontio, Leonardus de Brixia, the organist at S. Maria, in alleging that Pontio had not used the methods employed by Willaert, Cambio, or Donato, provided an interesting account of what a teacher should do:

> Everyone whom I have seen teach singing and counterpoint both in this city and in Venice first makes the students sing one by one and then together until they have learned the music. And the same thing is done in counterpoint: one looks it over, corrects the *cartella* first with care, and then has it sung, and this is the true way of teaching. And it's necessary to be patient, but this master, as I understand from many of his students, rarely looks over the *cartelle, caselle,* and consonances (*consonantie*) of the counterpoint exercises but only makes them sing, and from this arise the mistakes because the ear can deceive.[48]

48. Murray, "The Voice of the Composer," 46–47; and Murray, "On the Teaching Duties," 115–128. BergBC 989, fol. 16ʳ; appendix, doc. 12.

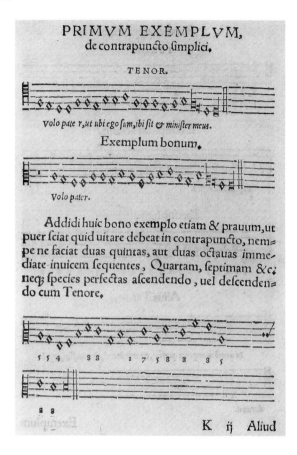

PLATE 5.9 Coclico,
Compendium musices (1552),
sig. K ii[r]

Consonantie suggest consonance tables or some sort of exercise involving vertical relations, perhaps, as in the Coclico example, noted with numbers. *Caselle* refers to the little boxes created by barlines, either measures—implying score—or brief phrases or segments, perhaps long enough to incorporate a musical example such as a cadence.[49]

Toward the end of the sixteenth century, the use of score for counterpoint exercises probably became common. The vivid testimony of the Italian theorist and composer Lodovico Zacconi leaves no doubt about either the centrality of the tablet in musical instruction or the use of score by the end of the century. Zacconi distinguished between improvised and written counterpoint; in its written or composed form, it is "laid out in books, on paper, and on the *cartella.*"[50] The two kinds of counterpoint are complementary: improvised coun-

---

49. The term *caselle* is used by Cimello, Diruta, Zacconi, and others. The manuscript in RomeSC G.384, which contains theoretical material mixed with musical exercises, has examples that look at first glance to be in score, but the barlines actually demarcate musical segments ("punti diversi"). See the discussion of formats in music treatises in chap. 3.

50. Zacconi, *Prattica di musica seconda parte*, 7; appendix, doc. 21a.

EXAMPLE 5.1   Coclico, *Compendium musices*: (a) good counterpoint; (b) bad
counterpoint

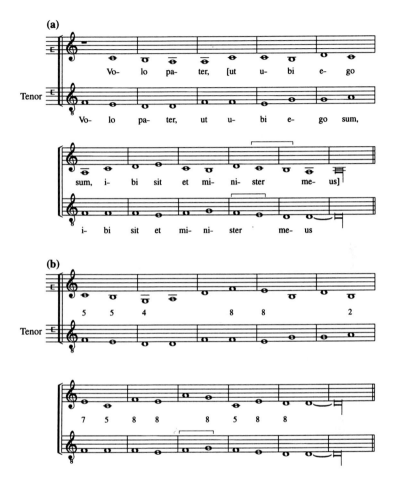

terpoint brings fame, wonderment; written counterpoint teaches perfection.[51]
Zacconi used a *cartella* in his own counterpoint studies. When he traveled to
Mantua on business, he brought his *cartella* with him. He sought out Hippolito
Baccusi, *maestro di cappella* at the Cathedral, and explained that he wanted to
learn counterpoint. Baccusi, having looked over two of his lessons on the *cartella*,
began to teach him *contrapunto alla mente*.[52] Zacconi was explicit about the use of
score, and he also provided a visual example:

51. Zacconi, *Prattica di musica seconda parte*, 131. Puteanus, *Modulata Pallas*, 41, makes the same
distinction. There are two sorts of harmony: that heard by the ear or thought in the mind and that
written on the *tabella*.

52. Zacconi, *Prattica di musica seconda parte*, 84; appendix, doc. 21c.

PLATE 5.10   Diruta, *Seconda parte del
Transilvano* (1609), p. 3

> The pupil who wants to begin to write counterpoint, having acquired a *cartella*
> divided into enough measures, and having selected a cantus firmus . . . will take the
> following course, namely, to set it out, two semibreves per measure, and place its
> final in such a way that the counterpoint can conclude with a consonance, and
> then beginning to dispose above it the consonances, he will write it out in the way
> that can be seen here.[53]

There follows a two-voice example in open score.[54] In another passage, Zacconi
suggested that students could copy out passages from other compositions in
score on the *cartella* for study.[55]

A second function that the *cartella* served was to aid in making keyboard
intabulations. Diruta recommended a *cartella* that is ruled and barred ("rigata, e
partita") in open score, except for the last two staves, of which one will have five
lines and the other eight (see plate 5.10).[56] He instructed the student to take the
soprano and to score it (i.e., write it out in score) two beats per measure ("due

53. Zacconi, *Prattica di musica seconda parte*, 68 – 69; appendix, doc. 21b.

54. Zacconi, *Prattica di musica seconda parte*, 69. A similar example is found in Horatio Scaletta,
Primo scalino della scala di contrapunto (Milan, 1622), 11. A three-voice score, barred every breve, has
the cantus firmus on the middle staff and numbers on the other two.

55. Zacconi, *Prattica di musica seconda parte*, 162, discussed above.

56. Girolamo Diruta, *Seconda parte del Transilvano* (Venice, 1609), trans. Murray C. Bradshaw and
Edward J. Soehnlen under the title *The Transylvanian* (Henryville, 1984); appendix, doc. 19. Discussed (among others) by Kinkeldey, *Orgel und Klavier*, 194, and Haller, "Partitur," 3.

battute per casella"). His examples show barlines both for the open score and for the intabulation. Once a student had thoroughly mastered the method for making an intabulation from a score, he would be able to make one without needing to write out the parts first in score.

Contemporary documents affirm Diruta's recommendations. The Florentine organist Minerbetti purchased three *cartelle* over a six-year period that were ruled for making intabulations ("da musica e intavolatura, rigata per intavolatura"). As D'Accone explained, "When fra Tommaso intabulated or arranged vocal music, he first did it on plaster writing pads lined with indelible staves; the record shows he purchased three of them on different occasions. These, as we know, were extraordinarily useful because mistakes could be easily corrected and because they could be erased after the music on them was transferred to paper."[57]

For our purposes, the most important function of the tablet was for composing. The earliest evidence of its use in composition comes from a mid-fifteenth-century Catalan novel, *Curial e Güelfa*:

> Next to that was another Queen, dressed in many colours and very richly, and she was so happily engaged in singing that it was a marvel to see. And in her hand she had a *cartell* notated with music, at which she looked continuously and which she corrected with a pen.[58]

The figure here is allegorical, not linked explicitly with an actual composer; still, the association with writing on the slate and making corrections is noteworthy. The earliest testimony linked unequivocally to composition, Cretin's lament for Braconnier (1512), is an exhortation to the composer Johannes Prioris to take up his slate and compose a *Ne recorderis*.[59]

A number of documents link composers to the use of tablets in composing. Luzzaschi recorded its use by Cipriano de Rore. Giovanni Spataro left evidence in his correspondence. Francesco Corteccia bequeathed his "stone tablet for composing music" to his "creato" Michele Federighi, canon at San Lorenzo.[60] The German composer Sigmund Hemmel (d. 1564) used a "large polished slate stone for composing"; this slate was purchased from his widow for a substantial sum four years after his death by singers in the Hofkapelle.[61] Guglielmo Gon-

57. Cited at n. 21. D'Accone, "Repertory," 92.

58. Anonymous, *Curial e Güelfa*, ed. A. Rubio y Lluch (Barcelona, 1901), 459; trans. P. Waley under the title *Curial and Guelfa* (London, 1982). Cited by Tess Knighton, "The *a cappella* Heresy in Spain: An Inquisition into the Performance of the *Cancionero* Repertory," *EM* 20 (1992): 569; appendix, doc. 1.

59. Guillaume Cretin, "Plainte sur le trespas de feu maistre Jehan Braconnier, dit Lourdault, chantre." First cited in this context by Clercx, "D'une ardoise," 163. See de Van, "La Pédagogie musicale," 94, and Guillaume Cretin, *Oeuvres poétiques*, ed. Kathleen Chesney (Paris, 1932), 215. See appendix, doc. 2.

60. Mario Fabbri, "La vita e l'ignota opera-prima di F. Corteccia," *Chigiana* 22 (1965): 202, published portions of Francesco Corteccia's will (Florence, Biblioteca Medicea Laurenziana, Archivio San Lorenzo, MS 2344, Filza 3a di Testamenti, fols. 163ʳ– 165ʳ). See appendix, doc. 15.

61. Hermelink (*Dispositiones modorum*, 33 and "Die Tabula compositoria," 224) cited a payment that recorded the purchase of Hemmel's slate for 1½ *Gulden* in 1568. W. Brennecke, "S. Hemmel," *MGG* and *NG*, cited the date of purchase as 8 January 1565. See appendix, doc. 14.

PLATE 5.11
Gumpelzhaimer,
Compendium musicae
(1625), portrait (wood-
cut by Lucas Kilian,
1622)

De Virtute Musica A. Gumpelzhaimeri.
Qvid forma melius? qvid fulvo carius auro?
Qvid toto regnis majus in orbe datur?
Iaspide qvid pulchrum magis est? qvid melle tenaci
Dulcius? Hylaeis candidatusq́ rosis?
Dulcior est virtus sed Musica, pulchrior una
Forma, auro, regnis, jaspide, melle, rosis.
E. Ehinger. Primarius.

zaga's name should probably be included; his purchase of twelve *cartelle* could have been for the use of other composers working in Mantua as well as for himself.[62] A portrait of Adam Gumpelzhaimer, a German composer and author of one of the most popular music textbooks of his day, included a tablet with music for four voices notated in quasi-score (see plate 5.11).[63] The tablet was evidently regarded as one of the attributes or iconographical symbols for identifying a composer—like the ubiquitous quill pen and music paper. Still another instance is the account of Orfeo Vecchi found in Borsieri's dictionary of famous Milanese:

> Orfeo Vecchi, late *maestro di cappella* at the Scala, was a musician and composer of such skill that working with just the *cartella* he could write a motet even for several choirs in the same time as it would take a very experienced writer to write a letter.[64]

62. See n. 40.

63. The portrait, engraved by Lucas Kilian in 1622, appears in the 1625 edition of *Compendium musicae* (VienNB, Musiksammlung, S.A.73.B.59). Salmen, *Musiker im Porträt*, 1: 176–177.

64. Girolamo Borsieri, *Il supplimento della nobiltà di Milano* (Milan, 1619), 54–55.

Borsieri also described Gioseffo Caimo and Girolamo Casati as musicians "di molto prattica sopra la cartella."

One other important witness to the use of tablets needs to be discussed in this context. The German theorist Auctor Lampadius, writing in 1537, provided contradictory testimony about the use of wooden or stone tablets by composers.

> *What sort of* tabula compositoria *did the ancient composers use?*
>
> No one can give either a description or an example of the *tabula* that Josquin, Isaac, and other learned composers used. The reason for this is that those ancients were not satisfied with tablets of wood or stone—not that they did not use them, but that they applied themselves more to theory than to practice, on account of which whoever is ignorant of this art will never compose securely but only labor in vain. . . .
>
> Here follows the order for distributing the voices or the parts of the song which the older composers used instead of tablets.
>
> [four-voice open score][65]

On the one hand, he wrote that the older composers (i.e., Josquin, Isaac, and other learned composers) did use tablets, although he could not describe them because, as he explained, the composers were more concerned with theory than with practice and worked the music out first in their minds.[66] On the other hand, he concluded the section by giving an example of how to lay out the voices of a composition, namely, in open score, a method which he said the older composers used *instead of* tablets. Perhaps he associated the *tabula compositoria* with the *scala compositoria*, which in turn could mean either a ten-line staff or the range of the gamut. The passage is certainly difficult to interpret.[67] Lampadius clearly associated the use of tablets with musical composition. Yet without a better understanding of his biography and writings we should be cautious about drawing conclusions about how Josquin and Isaac used tablets and what sort of format they or composers contemporary with Lampadius may have used.

The use of tablets for composition extended well past the sixteenth century. Banchieri, writing at the beginning of the seventeenth century, assumed the use of the *cartella* to be standard in composition; in making a distinction between the new and the old styles, he explained that the older composers used to fill up their *cartelle* first with notes and then later add the words. In the modern style, the words came first.[68] The continued use of tablets by composers in the ensu-

---

65. Lampadius, *Compendium musices*, sig. G v^v; appendix, doc. 11. For a translation of the entire passage, see Lowinsky, "On the Use of Scores," 798. See also the discussion in chap. 4.

66. Bush, "The Recognition of Chordal Formation," offered the interesting suggestion that Lampadius' *tabula compositoria* could refer to consonance tables. Aaron's chord table (see chap. 2) is called "Tavola del contrapunto."

67. A partial list of interpretations includes: Lowinsky, "On the Use of Scores"; Bush, "The Recognition of Chordal Formation"; Hermelink, "Die Tabula compositoria"; Chailley, "Tabulae Compositoriae"; Owens, "The Milan Partbooks"; and Reynolds, "Compositional Planning."

68. Banchieri, *Cartella musicale*, 165; appendix, doc. 20. Giovanni Battista Doni, *Lyra barberina* (completed in 1632, first published in Florence, 1763), 2: 73, did as well; he noted that to set words like "heaven," composers tried to use the highest notes of the *cartella*. See appendix, doc. 22.

ing centuries can be inferred, although documentation linked to actual composers is scanty.[69] Documents recently published by Ulrich Konrad show that composers were still using tablets as late as the mid-nineteenth century; he has found evidence of their use by Johann Joachim Quantz, Wolfgang Amadeus Mozart, and Clara Wieck.[70]

WHAT DID COMPOSERS WRITE ON THE TABLETS?

In trying to understand how sixteenth-century composers used tablets, we need to consider three interrelated questions. What format did they use? How much music did they write at a time—a whole composition or just part of a composition? How long did they keep the material on the tablet before erasing it?

The answer to the first question was probably determined in part by the length of the music and by the size of the tablet. The evidence suggests that composers' tablets probably resembled students' tablets in some ways, although they were probably bigger and of a better quality, and certainly more valuable than the crude pieces of slate that have survived. The earliest evidence suggests that composers wrote in separate parts, but by the second half of the century they had begun to use score.[71]

Spataro's letters clearly show that he was not writing in score on his *cartella*.[72] In a letter to Pietro Aaron, Spataro defended himself against Aaron's criticism that he had committed the error of having an uneven number of semibreves, so that the piece, in effect, ended on the upbeat.

> But where you say that the number is not correct, I realized this just now, looking at the tablet or *cartella* where I had first composed it, because (for my clarification) I wrote the figure eight where I meant it to be nine.[73]

Blackburn's interpretation of the passage is surely correct:

> Aaron remarked that Spataro's motet came out with an uneven number of semibreves . . . Spataro must have composed a passage and marked the end with the figure 8 to remind himself that it was eight semibreves long and that he would have to start the next passage at the beginning of the measure. But he had miscounted;

---

69. The best account is Hermelink, "Die Tabula compositoria."

70. Ulrich Konrad, *Mozarts Schaffensweise: Studien zu den Werkautographen, Skizzen und Entwürfen* (Göttingen, 1992), 101–102.

71. I disagree with Hermelink's conclusion that the format was either the ten-line staff or score ("Die Tabula compositoria").

72. I take issue with Blackburn's and Lowinsky's translation of *cartella* as score in my review of Blackburn et al., *A Correspondence* in *JAMS* 46 (1993): 317–318.

73. A Correspondence, 122, Letter 30; appendix, doc. 7. The translation is by Blackburn. A more literal translation is: "But where you say that it is not in its proper number, I realized this now, looking at the tablet or rather *cartella* where it was first composed by me, because (for purposes of clarity) I wrote the number 8 where 9 should have been written. But of this I care little because this responsory is signed with the sign ₵, which in singing one beats the semibreve. If it had been signed with ₵, it would have been a very obvious error because there would not be the full measure of the tempus given in the breve, as that diminished sign indicates." In the synopsis of the letter, Blackburn translated *cartella* as score (p. 423).

there were really nine semibreves, and so his motet ended in the middle of a measure. If the whole motet had been composed in a score with barlines, this could not
have happened without the composer's being immediately aware of it.[74]

A second statement reinforces the point: "It is not necessary to believe that the
music [on the *cartella*] had to be barred; if Spataro made a mistake in counting
semibreves, it shows that the work was not barred; the voices were probably simply aligned under each other."[75]

Another letter, written to Aaron on 2 January 1533 (Letter 49), adds further
weight to the view that composers—at least of this period—did not write
music in score on the *cartella*. Spataro, again defending himself against Aaron's
criticisms, writes:

> And continuing you say that in two or three other places you found two [i.e., par-
> allel] fifths, one perfect and the other imperfect, etc., which were used by me
> because I believe that they are not against the art of harmonic faculty. Concern-
> ing the notes which were missing in the tenor and in the cantus, you did well to
> place them, as you said, in their proper places. And I thank Your Excellency very
> much that you have deigned to make careful observations about my poorly
> ordered compositions, the poor ordering of which arose from trusting myself too
> much because without otherwise having them sung I notated them from the
> *cartella* and sent them to you. But afterward I became aware of some of those errors
> and some were emended by me, for which I was certain that I would be admon-
> ished by Your Excellency, which admonitions are accepted by me like those from
> a father, and so I offer my unending thanks.[76]

This passage, as I have argued elsewhere, is open to more than one interpretation,
depending on how much music was encompassed by Spataro's reference to "tali
mei male ordinati concenti."[77] Spataro's excuse that he had copied the music
from the *cartella* and sent it off without having performed it first could refer to
the mistakes that Aaron had found in all three motets he commented on in his
letter or only to the notes missing in the tenor and cantus of one of the pieces.
At the very least, the passage indicates that it was not easy to spot an error at
sight; one had to sing the music to find the mistakes, perhaps one part against
another, as mentioned elsewhere in the correspondence. But it is not unreasonable to conclude that the music on the *cartella* was not in score: Spataro was
unlikely to have overlooked missing notes if the music had been in score.

It is hard to say when composers began to use score in composing either on
paper or on tablets. By the beginning of the seventeenth century, several German
theorists explicitly linked scores to tablets.[78] Lippius (1612) described the staves
on the *palimpsestus* by the experienced composer as divided with perpendicular
lines. Schonsleder (1631) and his translator Herbst (1643) made clear that the

74. *A Correspondence*, 122.
75. *A Correspondence*, 123.
76. *A Correspondence*, Letter 49 (my literal translation). See appendix, doc. 9; I give a literal transcription of the text, showing the original punctuation, but expanding the abbreviations.
77. See my review of *A Correspondence*.
78. See the discussion in chap. 3.

tablets composers used for composition were in score. Both writers, in describing methods for composing, listed three: ten-line staff, score, and tablature. According to Schonsleder, *cartelle* were used for the second method, while Herbst wrote that *cartelle* were used for both the first and the second.

In some cases composers may simply have sketched portions of a composition on a *cartella*, erasing them once they had been copied out on paper. But in others, it is clear that the *cartella* could hold entire compositions. The small size of the extant slates—preserved, to be sure, in fragmentary condition—would hardly have permitted more than a phrase or so of music. Yet the documentary evidence suggests that slates could have been much larger—the 12-inch square tablet of Spataro comes to mind—and the iconographic evidence suggests an even larger size.

There is evidence that composers might well have fitted an entire composition on a *cartella*, and that the *cartella* served in this instance not as a place for sketching a phrase but as a place for drafting the entire composition. In a letter to Aaron, Spataro wrote that he had looked over his *cartella* to check on a possible error:

> Your Excellency, to win me over with generosity, advises me about five of what you call errors found in my composition called *Virgo prudentissima*, concerning which wanting to show with valid explanations that what you call my errors are not errors would require not a letter but a whole treatise. . . . Of the five aforementioned errors I concede only one, that is, that which falls in the tenor with the contra alto at the word "genetrix," as here [example], in which tenor you should make the second minim be E *la mi grave*, which is how I found it on my *cartella* where I had originally composed it.[79]

In this case, the composition could have remained on the *cartella* for a relatively long period. We know that Spataro sent the motet to Aaron on 24 October 1531 (Letter 35) and that the music was still on the *cartella* a month later (27 November 1531, Letter 36), thereby allowing him to defend himself against Aaron's criticisms. Perhaps a composition stayed on the *cartella* long enough to be checked by the various means Blackburn outlined, by performance and by sending it to colleagues for their opinions. Once the trial period was over, the piece could be copied into the choirbooks of San Petronio. Another instance is the *Ave gratia plena*, sent in a letter written in Autumn 1532 (Letter 46), and defended in the letter of 2 January 1533 (Letter 49), quoted above; the motet was subsequently emended and entered into the San Petronio choirbook BolSP 45.[80] In each of these instances, the fact that Spataro was able to defend himself suggests not only that the music was still on the *cartella* but also that all of the music for the composition was on the *cartella*.[81] Spataro evidently did not immediately erase a composition from the *cartella* even after copying it on paper; he could look back at his working draft.

79. *A Correspondence*, Letter 36 (my literal translation). See appendix, doc. 8.
80. See the discussion in chap. 6.
81. For a somewhat different interpretation, see Blackburn, *A Correspondence*, 122–123.

Other evidence for keeping a complete composition on a *cartella* comes from the *processo* against Pietro Pontio. One of the witnesses, Leonardus de Brixia, told of performing a Magnificat by Francesco Bordogna:

> I sang in my academy of singers a Magnificat composed by Francesco Bordogna last Sunday and in singing I told him there were errors in it. And he answered me, "But the reverend *maestro di cappella* [Pontio] had looked it over and made me sing it and told me that it was fine." And I told him, "If you show me the original, I will find the problem for you." And so he showed me the *cartella* and I found two octaves, one after the other, which are prohibited.[82]

In this instance, Bordogna used the *cartella* to preserve a complete draft of the music; the account does not make clear whether he had used it also for working out individual phrases. The *cartella* was the original; the performers presumably sang from a copy made from the *cartella*, not from the *cartella* itself.[83]

In the absence of *cartelle* that preserve either drafts or sketches of compositions, we can only speculate about their use. Luzzaschi's account of Rore's *cartella* does not specify how much music was written on it: "I, being at that time his student, saw him write on the aforementioned *cartella* the Gloria of a Mass that he made in Ferrara and others of his compositions made at various times."[84] We might infer from the letter that it was large enough to hold an entire Gloria, but it is also possible that Luzzaschi had watched as Rore worked on the Gloria, one phrase at a time.

The evidence concerning tablets clearly indicates their widespread use by composers as well as by students. I think it likely that composers could have used the *cartella* at various times during their work, for sketches, more extended drafts, and even fair copies of entire compositions. In this case, the *cartella* would parallel paper in function, except that it could be used many times. Burmeister's reference to writing down the voices of a fugue "on paper or a tablet or some other material" ("papyro vel tabula aliave materia") suggests a sense of equivalence.[85]

Clearly, the lack of evidence makes it impossible to say any more about how composers used the *cartella*. To learn more about how composers worked on their music once it began to be written down, we need to turn to the only evidence that has survived, their autograph manuscripts.

APPENDIX: SELECTED DOCUMENTS CONCERNING ERASABLE TABLETS (*CARTELLE*)

1. Mid-15th century: Anonymous, *Curial e Güelfa*
   (Text: Knighton)
   Tantost prop daquesta staua una altra Reyna, de varies colors vestida, empero molt ricament abillada, e staua tan alegre cantant que aço era una gran me-

---

82. Murray, "The Voice of the Composer," 46–47; BergBC 989. See appendix, doc. 12.

83. Just what Bordogna was singing from when he showed it to Pontio, and whether he sang with others or by himself one voice at a time is unclear.

84. See chap. 4.

85. *Musica poetica*, 66.

rauella. E tenia en la ma un cartell scrit e notat a nota de cant, en lo qual
miraua continuament e ab una ploma esmenaua . . .

2. 1512: Cretin
(Text: de Van)
Nostre bon pere et maistre Prioris
prenez l'ardoyse et de vostre faczon
composez cy ung "ne recorderis."

3. 25 January 1529: Spataro, Letter 18
(Text: Blackburn)
. . . Item prego V. E. me mandi una cartella, o vero una tabula de abaco, la quale
sia quadra et longa per ciascuno lato, o verso quanto è longo questo foglio o
vero littera [32 cm], la quale tabula o vero cartella voglio per componere
alcuna volta qualche concento, et del pretio daritime adviso, che satisfarò del
tuto.

4. 31 March 1529: Spataro, Letter 21
(Text: Blackburn)
. . . A li dì 27 del presente ho receputo una vostra de dì 20 signata a me gratis-
sima, per la quale ho inteso quanto diceti circa un'altra vostra a me missa con
el foglio rigato, circa la quale altro non dico per havere (prima che hora)
datovi resposta et mandate el contra alto, el quale V. E. chiedeva.
    . . . Ho havuto la cartella, la quale è molto al proposito mio, ma me sono
maravegliato che non dati aviso del pretio, perché ve haria mandato la valuta,
perché la mia natura è che lo amico non habia danno. Sì che fati vui, et asai
ve rengratio.

5. 5 April 1529: Spataro, Letter 22
(Text: Blackburn)
. . . Per due mie a V. E. misse, cioè una con quello contra alto, el quale chiedeva
V. E. [no. 20], et l'altra in responsione de quella con la quale era ligata la
cartella [no. 21], haveti potuto intendere . . .

6. 28 May 1529: Spataro, Letter 23
(Text: Blackburn)
Ma siati certo che haveva ligato tale tractato et posto in ordine per mandarlo
qua a V.E., ma per essere el volumine alquanto grande, a me non pareva cosa
da mandare per via de banco o vero mercatante. Pertanto aspectava che el tor-
nasse a Bologna quello fante el quale me portò la cartella . . .

7. 30 January 1531: Spataro, Letter 30
(Text: Blackburn)
. . . Ma dove diceti che non gli è el suo numero, de questo hora me sono
acorto, guardando sopra la tabula o vero cartella dove prima fu da me composto, perché (per certa mia chiareza) segnai el numero octonario dove voleva

essere signato el novenario. Ma de questo poco curo, perché esso responso è signato con questo segno ¢, nel quale cantando se bate la [semibreve]. Se fusse segnato con questo ¢, seria errore evidentissimo, perché non gli seria la mensura integra del tempo dato in la breve, come vale tale segno diminuto.

8. 27 November 1531: Spataro, Letter 36
    (Text: Blackburn)
    . . .V. E. (per vincermi de liberalità) me advisa de cinque (che vui chiamati errori) trovati in quello mio canto, "Virgo prudentissima" chiamato, de li quali errori, volendo demonstrare con rasone valide che tali da vui chiamati mei errori non sono errori, non bastaria una epistola ma seria quasi uno condecente trattato. . . . Pertanto de li predecti cinque errori solo uno ve concedo, cioè quello che cade nel tenore con el contra alto soto la parola 'genetrix', ut hic: [example] nel quale tenore ponereti la seconda minima in E *la mi* grave, et per tale modo l'ho trovato stare in la mia cartella dove primamente fu composito.

9. 2 January 1533: Spataro, Letter 49
    (Text: Owens)
    Et seguitando diceti, che in dui, o, tri altri lochi, haveti trovato doe quinte, una perfecta: et l'altra imperfecta etc le quale da me sono usitate perche credo, che non siano contra l'arte, de la harmonica faculta: circa le note: le quale mancavano in lo tenore: et nel canto haveti facto bene ponerle, come diceti a li soi lochi debiti: et molto rengratio vostra excellentia che s'è dignato fare deligente discorso circa tali mei male ordinati concenti, el quale male ordine, è nato per tropo fidarmi da mi medesimo: perche senza altramente farli cantare li notai de la cartella, e, a vostra excellentia li mandai: ma dapoi de alquanti de tali errori me acorsi, et alcuni furno da me, emendati: per tanto io teneva per firmo, che da vostra excellentia seria admonito: le quale admonitione sono da me aceptate come paterne, per tanto ve rendo gratie senza fine.

10. 4 June 1533: Spataro, Letter 54
    (Text: Blackburn)
    . . . Altro circa questo al presente non se dirà perché el portatore de la presente me acelera et vole partirse. Ma prego V. E. me voglia mandare una cartella come già facesti, la quale sia grande quanto è la medietà de tuto questo foglio, ma sia uno digito, o poco più, più largha [30.5 × 20 cm]. Et datime adviso del costo, che subito ve remeterò el pretio . . .

11. 1537 (1554 edition): Lampadius, *Compendium musices*
    Da tabulam compositoriam, quam veteres illi Musici usurparunt? Tabulam qua usus Iosquinus & Isaac & reliqui eruditissimi, nemo verbis neque exemplis tradere potest. Eius ratio est, quod veteres illi, tabulis ligneis vel lapideis non contenti fuerunt, non qui iis non usi fuerint, verum magis se ad Theoricam quam ad practicam applicarunt, quare qui hanc artem ignorant, nihil certi component, sed plane operam luserint.

Quomodo haec deprehendam? obscura quidem res est, praecipue The-
oricam ignorantibus, natura enim. in hac arte componendi cantilenas, red-
dimur eruditiores certioresque. Quemadmodum ... [passage cited on p. 66]
Deinde, ad exercitationem accedere, hoc est, excogitatas clausulas, in
ordinem quendam distribuere, & eas, quae videntur aptiores servare.

Quis est iste ordo distribuendi voces? Est qui antiquitus, & ab ipso
Iosquino, servatus & traditus est, quam quoque instructissimi quidam Musici
nostro tempore discipulis suis tradidere.

Sequitur ordo distribuendi voces sive cantilenarum partes, quem prisci
tabularum vice usuparunt.

[open score, four voices]

12. 3 August 1566: Pontio *processo*, testimony of Leonardus de Brixia
(Text: Murray, 46–47, with minor emendations)
Ho poi anchor nella mia Academia de cantori cantato uno Magnificat composto da messer pre Francesco Bordogna et fu Dominica passata et nel cantar gli disse era dentro errori. Et lui mi rispondeva "l'ha pur visto il reverendo Maistro di Capella et me la fatto cantare e disse stava bene." Et io
gli disse "se me mostrareti lo originale vi ritrovaro il diffetto." Et cosi mi a
poi monstrato la cartella et ho ritrovato doi ottave, una drio a l'altra quale
sono prohibite. Et percio se cosi e vero come esso Bordogna me a detto, se
conossaria uno manifesto errore che mo sia cosi la verita che l'habba fatto
cantare esso reverendo Maistro questo non lo scio. Et ne ho visto anche del
Tenorino et altri clerici quali me affermavano che esso reverendo Maestro
gl'havea fatti cantare et detto che stavano bene. Et pur vedendoli, io gli facea
conoscer gl'errori che erano dentro, et se detti clerici havesse anchora detti
contraponti monstraria a ciaschuno tali espressi errori che mo lo maiestro
la facia a malitia overo per ignorantia, o per non voler la fatica questo no lo
scio, ma ben vi dicco, che ciaschuno qual ho visto a insegnare canto et contraponcto si in questa cita come in Venetia fanno prima cantar gli scolari ad
uno ad uno et poi in compagnia sin tanto che hanno imparato. Et il
medemo si fa del contraponcto si vede, et giusta prima la cartella con dili-
gentia, et poi si fa cantare, et questo e il vero modo di insegnare. Et bisogna
haver patientia, ma di questo Maestro intendo da molti de suoi scolari che
il detto Maestro rare volte gli viede le cartelle, caselle et consonantie del
contraponcto ma solum ge li fa cantare, et da questo perveniene poi gl'errori che l'orechia si ingana ...

13. 1566: Merulo letter
(Text: Bertolotti)
Io mando a V. Ecc.za Ill.ma le diece cartelle che mi ordinò ch'io facessi
rigare per le quali con l'altre due che portò seco, ho fatto sborsare a M.
Bartholomeo Merzaro del Calice N.o ii scudi i quali sono il pagamento
intiero di esse.

14. 1568: Hemmel
     (Text: Hermelink)
     Aussgeben Gelt uff die Cantorei und Hoff Capell in gemain den vij Januarij
     Sigmund Hemmels nachgelassner wittib umb ain grossen Palirten schiffer
     stein zu dem Componirn laut Zedels j gld xxx k.

15. 1571: Corteccia
     (Text: Fabbri)
     Item, lascio, do et dono a Ms. Michele di Bartolomeo Federichi, canonico
     di San Lorenzo et mio creato, le infrascritte cose, cioè: una tavola di pietra da
     comporre musica ... Item, tutti i volumi stampati di musica et da stamparsi,
     cioè Canzoni, mottecti et responsi, et tutti li mia [sic] spartiti.

16. 1587: Collegio Germanico
     (Text: Culley, 295)
     La mattina dopo la messa nel tempo della prima tavola vanno li Soprani in
     camera del Mastro di Capella dove secondo la capacità di ciascuno, che
     canta, e che rende conto della cartella.
        L'estate finito il detto esercitio li Soprani tornano in cameral del Maestro
     di Cappella, dove per qualche tempo li uni pigliano Lettione di sonare, gli
     altri s'esercitano chi in cantare chi nella cartella ciascuno secondo la sua
     capacità.
        L'inverno non vi essendo tempo per detti essercitii dopo il pranzo vanno
     li Soprani alla Camera del Maestro di Cappella un'hora incirca avanti la prima
     tavola, dove stanno sin che suoni alla seconda tavola, esercitandosi ciascuno
     secondo il suo bisogno in sonare, cantare, mostrare la cartella, e cose simili.

17. 1592 – 1596: Minerbetti
     (Text: D'Accone)
     E prima. Addì di Dicembre [1592] per una cartella da musica e intavolatura
     lire sette e soldi dieci pagati a Michael Angelo Sermartelli libraio con licen-
     tia del Reverendo Padre Priore, L.7.10

        E addì 8 di Agosto [1594] per una cartella di gesso da musica e
     intavolatura fatta venire di Venetia per via del signor Simone Fioravanti lire
     otto portò contanti per sua commissione il signor Hieronimo Amadori
     quale era tre quarti grande e per ogni verso, L. 8

        E addì 3 di Dicembre [1596] a una cartella ingessata rigata per intavo-
     latura lire sei portò contanti Giorgio Marescotti, L. 6

18. 1593 – 1596: San Luigi dei Francesi
     (Text: Cametti)
     a) 4 cartelle da componere musica [bought 13 August 1593 for 1 scudo 75
     baiocchi; paid 29 October 1593]

b) tre cartelle rigate da componere musica [bought July 1594]

c) una cartella da componere [bought 20 February 1596 for 35 baiocchi; paid 29 March 1596]

19. 1609: Diruta, *Seconda parte del Transilvano*
Primieramente in due modi vi voglio dimostrare lo stile c'havete da tenere ad intavolare semplicemente senza diminutione. Prima dovete haver la cartella rigata, e partita, eccetto le due ultime poste, delle quali una sarà di cinque righe, e l'altra di otto, come trovarete in diversi luoghi: e poi pigliarete la parte del Soprano, e lo partirete à due battute per casella. Nella seguente posta il Contr'alto, seguitando poi con l'istesso ordine il Tenore, & il Basso, come per gli essempi più chiaramente interederete. Divise c'haverete tutte le parti, incominciarete ad intavolare il Soprano nelle cinque righe à due battute per casella; . . . Et per facilitarvi, incominciarò à partire un Canto à due voci, à tre, e à quattro. Inteso c'haverete il modo di partire, & intavolare a quattro, potrete poi anco intavolare à cinque, à sei, à sette, & anco à otto, osservando il medesimo ordine . . .

20. 1614: Banchieri, *Cartella musicale*, 165
. . . la onde la maniera de gl'antichi fu questa, empievano la Cartella di note in Contrapunti osservatissimi, & poi sottoponevangli l'Oratione, quivi al Concerto sentivasi soavissima Armonia, ma tal armonia non solo era contraria all'Oratione, ma spesse fiate alle parole dolorose udivasi allegrezza, & alle parole baldanzose udivasi languidezza.

21. 1622: Zacconi, *Prattica di musica seconda parte*
(a) p. 7: noi n'habbiamo la Musica in compositione, distesa in libri, carte, e cartella.

(b) pp. 68–69: Lo scolare, che vorrà dar principio al far contrapunto, provistosi di cartella divisa à caselle à sufficienza, formatosi un canto fermo; ò secondo ch'egli vuole, ò cavato da un libro chorale, haverà questa particolar avertenza, di disporre due semibreve per casella, con darli il suo finale in maniera tale, che per consonanza il suo contrapunto vi possa concludere; e cominciando à disponervi sopra le consonanze, ve le compartirà nella maniera, ch'egli qui vede.
[example in open score, 2v]
E quando ch'egli vi haverà fatto un contrapunto tale, l'essamini bene, e vegga se vi hà fatto veruna cosa di cattivo; e veduto che stà bene secondo il suo parere, lo mostri à chi ne sà piu di lui; e sentitone il parer altrui, lasciando quell'essempio per rivederlo altre volte ancora, vederà di formarne un'altro, che sia vario da quel c'ha fatto; e facendo . . .

(c) p. 84: Onde per un mio negocio convenendomi andar à Mantova, ov'era Maestro di Capella Hippolito Baccusi, andando da lui, e narrandoli il desiderio mio, e quanto ch'io bramavo, veduto c'hebbe prima due mie let-

tioni in Cartella, un giorno mi menò da un suo scolare, al quale egli inse-
gnava di contrapunto alla mente . . .

(d) p. 162: Ho detto nel capitolo precedente che lo scolare provistosi de libri
atti à simil professione, partischi quegl'essempii, e gl'essamini ben bene. E
perche partitoli in cartella non facesse come fanno alcuni, che vedutone
gl'andamenti e le maniere, li cancellano, e non ne fanno più conto; questo
tale che bramarà d'imparare, fattone in cartella tutte le sudette prove poco fa
accennate, e dimostrate di sopra, ne li noterà tutti in un libro appartato, e la-
sciandovi spatii sufficienti, d'aggiongervi qualch'altra cosa.

22. 1763: Doni, *La Lyra Barberina*, 2: 73
Se vi sarà qualche parola, che dinoti altezza &c. o si parli di Cielo, stelle, e
cose simili, subito fanno una ricercata delle più acute, e più alte note della
cartella . . .

CHAPTER SIX

AUTOGRAPH COMPOSING

MANUSCRIPTS

We know that composers used a variety of different kinds of surfaces for writing down their music. But for the period from 1450 on, all surviving autograph documents that I am aware of were written on paper.[1] A surprising number have survived, more than anyone had suspected, and others will surely be discovered as we learn more about where to look for them.[2]

The main focus of this study is on those autograph manuscripts that present clear evidence of compositional activity.[3] I present a provisional list of such manuscripts at the end of this chapter (see table 6.1). In some cases the composer's name is unknown, but his (or her) identity as a composer is clear from the kinds of writing found in the manuscript. Knowing the name of the actual composer is important and helpful, but not crucial: any manuscript that contains evidence about working methods is valuable, regardless of whether it can be associated with a particular composer.

The task of arriving at an authoritative and comprehensive list of autograph

1. Before 1450, the written record appears to be too meager to permit well-substantiated conclusions about process, at least based on evidence from manuscripts, though I have not done a systematic search. For earlier autographs, see James Grier, "*Ecce sanctum qui deus elegit Marcialem apostolum*: Adémar de Chabannes and the Tropes for the Feast of Saint Martial," in *Beyond the Moon: Festschrift Luther Dittmer*, ed. Bryan Gillingham and Paul Merkley, Wissenschaftliche Abhandlungen 53 (Ottawa, 1990), 28–74; Margot Fassler, *Gothic Song: Victorine Sequences and Augustinian Reform in Twelfth-Century Paris* (Cambridge, 1993), 119; Lawrence Gushee, "New Sources for the Biography of Johannes de Muris," *JAMS* 22 (1969): 26 and plate II.

2. One category that I do not include and that deserves systematic investigation is "archaic" or "primitive" polyphony. For example, Peter Jeffery, "Music Manuscripts on Microfilm in the Hill Monastic Library at St. John's Abbey and University," *MLA Notes* 35 [1978–1979]: 21, identified what he called an "arranger's draft" in a manuscript now preserved in Schlägl, Stiftsbibliothek, MS 10.

3. The evidence concerning the methods used for subsequent adaptations and arrangements of a composition by scribes, performers, and arrangers, as well as by other composers, deserves its own investigation. See, for example, Margaret Bent's study of the role played by a scribe in shaping a composition to suit local needs, "A Contemporary Perception of Early Fifteenth-Century Style: Bologna Q15 as a Document of Scribal Editorial Initiative," *MD* 41 (1987): 183–201.

manuscripts is far from complete.[4] Identifying manuscripts or even brief entries in manuscripts as "compositional" is difficult: much of the music either is or appears at first glance to be anonymous; some of it is fragmentary and of apparently little significance; some of it is so messy as to be virtually impossible to decipher. These kinds of entries in manuscripts tend to be overlooked in inventories and catalogs, nor are they easily retrieved through traditional bibliographical tools. The manuscripts presented here are those that I know of or have identified myself; while I hope that they are a reasonable reflection of the source situation as a whole, I know that many more will be found.

Establishing the authenticity of manuscripts as autographs remains a major problem. While identifying writing as "compositional" depends on being able to transcribe and interpret it, the task of associating a manuscript with a particular composer requires the existence of other authenticated autograph documents or dependable documentary evidence. In his study of Cavalli autographs, Peter Jeffery observed that in many instances scholars left unstated the reasoning behind the assertion that a particular manuscript was a composer autograph; in other cases they relied on such dubious criteria as the presence of corrections or the irregularity of the hand.[5] His own work on Cavalli, based on careful examination of details of script and on comparison with authenticated exemplars such as notarial documents or letters, can serve as a model for authenticating autograph manuscripts. The problem in dealing with manuscripts from the sixteenth century and earlier, however, is that there is often relatively little opportunity for establishing authenticity. Although in some cases composers' autograph letters or documents in their hand do survive, it is rare to have a series of documents such as Jeffery had for Cavalli to show the development of a script over time.[6]

Table 6.2 (at the end of this chapter) contains a list of composers whose names have been linked—rightly or wrongly—with particular manuscripts. Some of these manuscripts were used for composition and thus are listed in table 6.1 as well, while others were not. The process of establishing a convincing list of autograph manuscripts proceeds by both addition and subtraction. The number grows as scholars succeed in identifying composers' hands.[7] But more thor-

4. For discussions of composer's autographs for the period before 1600, see Jeffery, "The Autograph Manuscripts of Francesco Cavalli," 1–2; Besseler and Gülke, *Schriftbild der mehrstimmigen Musik*, 152–155; Luther, "Autograph."

5. Jeffery, "The Autograph Manuscripts of Francesco Cavalli," 1–2. Jeffery lists among the scholars who rely on the presence of corrections Benvenuti, Lesure, Sherr, and Boetticher, and those who rely on the irregularity of the hand Rifkin, Steude, Bente, van den Borren, Jeppesen, Osthoff, Frati, and Vollhard.

6. For a good example of the results possible with a careful examination of letters and documents, see Kmetz's identification of a number of the hands among the Basel music manuscripts (*Die Handschriften*, 21, 341–346). Helmut Hell's study of Senfl's text hand, "Senfls Hand in den Chorbüchern der Bayerischen Staatsbibliothek," *Augsburger Jahrbuch für Musikwissenschaft* (1987): 65–137, is also exemplary.

7. Among recent examples, Owen Rees, "Newly Identified Holograph Manuscripts from Late-Renaissance Portugal," *EM* 22 (1994): 261–277, has identified manuscripts of Pedro de Cristo; and Robert Snow (Gaspar Fernandes, *Obras sacras*, Portugaliae Musica 49 [Lisbon, 1990]) has found a sketchbook used by Fernandes.

ough research can yield the opposite results as well. Manuscripts once attributed to such composers as Hofhaimer, Taverner, Lasso, Porta, Obrecht, and Monteverdi are no longer considered authentic.[8]

Even though more work remains to be done to identify autograph manuscripts, there is much to be gained from considering *as a group* those manuscripts that can reasonably be claimed as autographs. They have never before been studied systematically in this way, yet they can yield valuable information about compositional process. In the following chapter I will consider in some detail the music preserved in the manuscripts; the focus of this chapter is on the manuscripts themselves. My goal is to offer a typology of autograph composing manuscripts, in part to explain patterns of survival, in part to understand their function in a composer's work.

Before beginning the discussion of the manuscripts, I need to explain the terminology I employ to describe their contents. The music ranges from rough scribbles to neatly written copies; it reflects different stages of work. I use the terms "sketch," "draft," and "fair copy" to represent these early, middle, and late stages.[9]

Sketches capture in writing some parts of the first stages of work on a composition. They usually consist of brief segments of a composition, sometimes for just one or two voices, sometimes for the entire sonority. They are generally written quite roughly, with changes made by cancellation (lines drawn through notes) rather than by erasure or overwriting. The revision often comes directly after the original version. Sketches usually have no indications of text.

Drafts typically contain the entire composition or a substantial portion of it. They can range from being very rough in appearance—virtually indistinguishable from a sketch—to quite neat. Rough drafts share many of the characteristics of sketches (absence of text, changes made by cancellation, etc.), while more polished drafts sometimes have the text, perhaps in an abbreviated form. Both sketches and drafts are essentially private documents intended primarily for the use of the composer.[10]

Fair copies, in contrast, are neatly written, with full text. They are usually intended to be public documents, for use in transmission or performance, but they can also be part of a composer's personal library. Fair copies sometimes contain indications of revision, but the general impression is one of neatness.

By setting up these three stages I do not mean to imply that all compositions necessarily passed through every stage, although some probably did. The use of various stages reflects partly a composer's methods, partly the preservation of evidence. In many cases, only a fraction of the written evidence has survived, making it difficult to know whether all three stages were employed.

---

8. Jeffery, "The Autograph Manuscripts of Francesco Cavalli," 1–2, and the bibliography listed in table 6.2.

9. My thinking on this topic has been influenced by the work of my colleague, Robert L. Marshall, in *The Compositional Process of J. S. Bach: A Study of the Autograph Scores of the Vocal Works* (Princeton, 1972).

10. Kmetz ("The Drafts of Jodocus Fabri") makes the useful distinction between private and public.

Some autograph manuscripts contain little or no information about compositional process. The composer, who was often the *maestro di cappella*, functioned at times as scribe, preparing fair copies for performance. These autograph manuscripts are usually in choirbook format, though some are in partbooks. Examples include the choirbooks of Spataro in Bologna, Gaspar de Albertis in Bergamo, and Pedro de Cristo in Coimbra, as well as the partbooks of an unidentified composer in Castell'Arquato.[11] It is likely that other such examples will never be recognized simply because we are unable to link a particular scribal hand with a known composer. Senfl, for example, copied music as part of his instruction with Isaac, and he also copied sixteen choirbooks during his service at the court of Maximilian I, none of which has yet been identified.[12]

Another group of autograph fair copies consists of the manuscripts that composers prepared for transmission. For example, it is possible that the set of partbooks ParA 75/2 that contain a Mass based on Crecquillon's *Alles soubdain mon desir* was prepared by the composer, rather than by a scribe.[13] Manuscripts that consist of collections of fascicles are particularly likely candidates to contain composer autographs.[14]

A third category consists of manuscript anthologies that composers kept as a kind of personal library. Examples include the manuscripts of Ludwig Senfl (MunBS 3155) and Vincenzo Galilei (FlorBN AG 9).[15] Closely related would be manuscripts that composers kept for their own use as performers, including those belonging to Adam Gumpelzhaimer and Cosimo Bottegari.[16]

The autograph manuscripts of greatest interest for this study are the ones that composers actually used for composing. The music in these autographs ranges from the scribbles of amateurs to the sketches and drafts of experienced composers; it is written in a wide array of musical genres and in many different for-

11. Frank Tirro, *Renaissance Musical Sources in the Archive of San Petronio in Bologna*, Renaissance Manuscript Studies 4, 1: *Giovanni Spataro's Choirbooks* (American Institute of Musicology, 1986), with reproductions of Spataro's music and text hand in plates 2–6; David Crawford and Scott Messing, *Gaspar de Albertis' Sixteenth-Century Choirbooks at Bergamo*, Renaissance Manuscript Studies 6, (American Institute of Musicology, Stuttgart, 1994). For speculation about the identity of the Castell'Arquato composer, see below.

12. Hell, "Senfls Hand."

13. Roy Rudolph, in an unpublished seminar paper at Brandeis University, confirmed Lawrence Bernstein's suggestion that the model might be the Crecquillon chanson. The manuscript contains a few small-scale revisions; it is unclear whether they represent the efforts of a composer, copyist, or performer. The composer has yet to be identified.

14. For example, VienNB 11883 or BolC Q25.

15. Reproduction of FlorBN AG 9, fol. 3ʳ in Lowinsky, "Early Scores," *Music in the Culture*, 822.

16. On Gumpelzhaimer's autograph manuscripts, see Richard Charteris and Gertraut Haberkamp, "Regensburg, Bischöfliche Zentralbibliothek, Butsch 205–210: A Little-known Source of the Music of Giovanni Gabrieli and his Contemporaries," *MD* 43 (1989): 195–249. In addition to this set of partbooks, there are two scores, BerlS 40027 and 40028 (copied 1599–1603). See Lowinsky, "Early Scores," *Music in the Culture*, 820–821, including a reproduction of BerlS 40028, fol. 91ʳ. On Bottegari's lute manuscript (ModE C.311), see Carol MacClintock, "A Court Musician's Songbook: Modena MS C 311," *JAMS* 9 (1956): 177–192; *The Bottegari Lutebook*, edited by Carol MacClintock, The Wellesley Edition 8 (Wellesley, Mass., 1965), and Warren Kirkendale, *The Court Musicians in Florence during the Principate of the Medici* (Florence, 1993), 255.

mats. The revisions and changes help to show both the genesis of a musical composition and the composer's working methods.

Composers left traces of their work in many different kinds of manuscripts. Some are the large, formal sources, such as choirbooks, that were used for performing; on occasion these manuscripts contain revisions that show the composer achieving the final version of the composition. Others are rough sketches and drafts often scribbled on the blank staves of manuscripts that had other primary functions. A few of the sources are simply scraps of paper or small fascicles that composers used for the early stages of work. Most of these manuscripts were probably thrown away soon after the composition was completed; hastily scribbled and filled with erasures or cancellations, they had little aesthetic value and no reason to be saved.

The variety in the kinds of manuscript may reflect the availability and price of paper. Paper had come into common use in Europe only after the middle of the fifteenth century, gradually replacing vellum as the paper-making industry spread from Spain to Italy and Germany.[17] Paper was a valuable commodity. In the economics of book printing, for example, the cost of paper usually exceeded all the other expenses combined.[18] Another calculation equated the price of a quire (twenty-four sheets) in 1600 with a worker's daily wage; in today's terms the same amount might represent just ten minutes of labor.[19]

Music paper, already lined with the aid of a rastrum, was a specialty item stocked by music booksellers and by some stationers.[20] For example, the Milanese stationer Giovanni Battista Bosso sold music paper ruled for lute tablature.[21] In some areas it was possible to buy blank music paper with printed staves.[22] But composers (and scribes) also drew staves on paper themselves, either with a rastrum or by drawing individual lines.[23] A miniature from a sixteenth-century

---

17. For a brief sketch of the history of the development of paper, see Henri-Jean Martin, *The History and Power of Writing*, trans. Lydia G. Cochrane (Chicago, 1994), 207–210; originally published under the title *L'Histoire et pouvoirs de l'écrit* (Paris, 1988).

18. Lucien Febvre and Henri-Jean Martin, *The Coming of the Book: The Impact of Printing 1450–1800*, trans. David Gerard (London, 1976; 1990), 112–115; originally published under the title *L'Apparition du livre* (Paris, 1958). Bonnie J. Blackburn, "The Printing Contract for the *Libro primo de musica de la salamandra* (Rome, 1526)," *Journal of Musicology* 12 (1994): 347, demonstrated that the paper for printing the now lost *Libro primo de musica de la salamandra* was approximately one-third of the total cost.

19. George Thomas Mandel, "Paper—Growth without Profit," *IPH Yearbook* 1 (1980): 77–88. There is no dearth of documents recording the purchase of paper, but studies that normalize the prices across geographical areas or over time and relate them to other staples of daily life are harder to come by.

20. See, for example, Carter, "Music-Selling in Late Sixteenth-Century Florence."

21. Kevin M. Stevens and Paul F. Gehl, "Giovanni Battista Bosso and the Paper Trade in Late Sixteenth-Century Milan," *La Bibliofilia* 91 (1994): 57.

22. Iain Fenlon and John Milsom, "'Ruled Paper Imprinted': Music Paper and Patents in Sixteenth-Century England," *JAMS* 37 (1984): 139–163, offer a richly documented introduction to this topic.

23. On the rastrum (though primarily for a later period), see Jean K. and Eugene Wolf, "Rastrology and its Use in Eighteenth-Century Manuscript Studies," in *Studies in Musical Sources and Style: Essays in Honor of Jan LaRue*, ed. Eugene K. Wolf and Edward H. Roesner (Madison, 1990), esp.

Czech gradual (HradKM 13) shows a scribe copying music; on the table next to the page being copied are two rastra, two pots of ink, and two quill pens (see plates 6.1–2).[24]

The surviving manuscripts used for composition mirror the musical repertories of the time. The greatest number thus far identified contains vocal music, but a significant portion has instrumental music, including vocal music arranged for instrumental performance. The differences between the two kinds of music are reflected in the formats employed and in the type of notation.[25] At root is the basic difference in the mode of performance: instrumental music generally requires a single player, such as an organist or lutenist, who plays the entire composition, while vocal music (and instrumental music intended for ensemble performance) requires an ensemble consisting of at least as many performers as there are parts. Vocal music was notated in mensural notation; the music for each part is notated separately. Instrumental music, on the other hand, was notated in one of the several different kinds of tablature; some forms, for example open score and keyboard score, used many of the features of mensural notation, while others employed various systems of letters, numbers, and signs. For keyboard music, composers employed three different kinds of notation: keyboard score (two staves), open score (one staff per part), and tablature.

The extant autographs reveal an important principle: composers generally employed the same kinds of notation and format for composing that they would use for preparing the final version for performance or transmission. Composers of vocal music composed from the start in mensural notation, typically in separate parts, while composers of instrumental music worked in the notation characteristic for their instrument.

Differences between manuscripts containing vocal music and those containing instrumental music involve only the appearance of the music—format and notation. In terms of the types of manuscripts that have survived, the similarities are striking. Both kinds contain the same kinds of stages: sketches and drafts, fair copies with revisions.

The manuscripts divide into two broad categories. One consists of the private or personal papers of composers or composer-performers. They functioned to help the composer as he worked through the stages a composition passed through until its completion. The other consists of fair copies intended for transmission or performance; they frequently contain revisions that the composer made in the very final stages of composition. The basic distinction between the two categories is one of audience. The first category was intended to be used, if not exclusively, then primarily by the composer. The second was a public document that only incidentally happened to contain subtle evidence of the composer's craft.

237–242. The authors identified the earliest reference to the rastrum as the German handwriting manual, Heinrich Holtzmüller, *Liber perutilis* (Basel, 1553).

24. Reproduced in Rudolf Quoika, *Das Positif in Geschichte und Gegenwart* (Kassel, 1957), pl. 7. According to *CC*, the manuscript dates from 1584 to 1604.

25. See chap. 3.

PLATE 6.1   Matous
Radous, *Music Scribe*,
HradKM 13

MANUSCRIPTS FOR PRIVATE USE

A significant proportion of all of the autograph manuscripts identified to date are entries by a composer into space left blank in the manuscripts: empty staves at the bottom of pages or the back side of fascicles. In a number of cases, a composer simply appropriated a manuscript that originally had had one function and then after passage of time fell into disuse and became valuable simply as a source of blank, ruled paper. Given the cost of paper, it is no surprise to find that they frequently used whatever staff paper lay close to hand. From among a number of such "second-hand" manuscripts, I cite six examples to indicate the range of possibilities.

FlorBN Magl. 117: The Florentine composer Francesco Corteccia appropriated the empty staves in this early sixteenth-century chansonnier for sketching portions of several madrigals and drafting a motet.[26] He probably

26. See chap. 8 for an extended discussion of Corteccia's use of the manuscript as a sketchbook.

PLATE 6.2 Radous, *Music Scribe* (detail)

gained access to the manuscript during the 1530s, some fifteen to twenty years after the final chansons were copied.[27] It is striking that he scribbled not only on blank openings but also on the empty staves of pages that already contained chansons.

LonBLR A74–76: The Lumley partbooks, originally a source of English liturgical music from the reign of Edward VI, also had a second life. Several composers, among them Derick Gerarde, simply turned the books upside down and backwards, and added sketches and drafts of instrumental music in the blank staves.[28] Peter Holman has recently established the context for these late additions; he identified the music as a repertory of ensemble dances used by the royal string consort.[29]

27. For an excellent account of the manuscript in its primary function as a chansonnier, see Lawrence Bernstein, "A Florentine Chansonnier of the Early Sixteenth Century: Florence, Biblioteca Nazionale Centrale, Ms. Magliabechi XIX 117," *Early Music History* 6 (1986): 1-107.

28. On the primary function of the manuscripts, see *The Tudor Church Music of the Lumley Books*, ed. Judith Blezzard, Recent Researches in the Music of the Renaissance 65 (Madison, 1985); the later additions have been published in *Elizabethan Consort Music* I, ed. Paul Doe, Musica Britannica 44 (London, 1979).

29. Peter Holman, *Four and Twenty Fiddlers: The Violin at the English Court 1540–1690* (Oxford, 1993), 90–103. Daniel Page (Brandeis University) discussed aspects of compositional process in his paper "Composition at Nonesuch: The Consort Dances of British Library, MSS Royal Appendix 74–76," presented at the symposium "Creative Process in Renaissance Music," Brandeis University, 1992. On Gerarde's activities as a composer, see chap. 7.

UppsU 76b: Another manuscript that changed its function quite radically, UppsU 76b is a choirbook of French provenance containing Masses and motets dating from roughly 1515 to 1535.[30] During the middle decades of the sixteenth century, the manuscript became a lutenist's commonplace book. Jean-Michel and Nathalie Vaccaro have recently argued that the additions are in the hand of Guillaume Morlaye, a French lutenist and composer.[31] The Vaccaros base their identification both on the presence of Morlaye's name written in smudged ink upside down at the back of the volume and on the musical repertory. Whether the manuscript can be confirmed as Morlaye's—the latest known document for him is 1558—it is clearly a composer's workbook. It contains some original lute pieces as well as many intabulations of pieces published between 1570 and 1578. There are also a number of fragments and jottings, including two sketches in French lute tablature of an unidentified chanson, *Nul n'est*; a draft of the complete superius and the beginnings of the other voices are on the facing page.[32]

CastellC: This is one of the most striking examples of "second-hand" manuscripts. The numerous sketches were added by an unidentified composer whose hand (and music) dominates the collection of vocal and instrumental music from the second half of the sixteenth century preserved at the Chiesa Collegiata in Castell'Arquato.[33] He may be the "J. R." listed in CastellC 22, possibly Jacomo Rosso (Giacomo Rossi) *cantor*, whose name appears in several registers.[34] This composer, presumably the *maestro di cappella*, prepared fair copies for performances, using partbook format (some of the manuscripts are single sheets, others small fascicles, and still others substantial partbooks). A compulsive scribbler, he filled many of the blank staves and the backs of pages with sketches and drafts of his own music.[35] For example, he added sketches for a Magnificat and for several other unidentified pieces at the bottom of the first page of five of the seven

30. Thomas G. McCracken, "The Manuscript Uppsala, Universitetsbiblioteket, Vokalmusik I Handskrift 76b," Ph.D. diss., University of Chicago, 1985; *Uppsala, Universitetsbiblioteket, Vokalmusik i handskrift 76b*, ed. Thomas MacCracken, Renaissance Music in Facsimile 20 (New York, 1986).

31. Guillaume Morlaye, *Oeuvres pour le luth*, 2: *Manuscrits d'Uppsala*, ed. Jean-Michel and Nathalie Vaccaro (Paris, 1989).

32. Discussed in chap. 7.

33. A summary catalogue of the manuscripts, with a partial listing of their contents, has recently been published: Mario Genesi, *Castell'Arquato, Archivio della Chiesa Collegiata, Catalogo dei manoscritti musicali*, I Quaderni musicali di Castell'Arquato, 1 (Piacenza, [1987]).

34. Castell'Arquato, Archivio della Chiesa Collegiata, Exactiones et expensae 2 (1541–1578), b. 282, payments from 1559 until 1563; and Castell'Arquato, Archivio Communale, unidentified register (1435–1799), p. 131, payment on 5 January 1560 (courtesy of Prof. Lina Pagani). Genesi, *Castell'Arquato*, 29, interprets the initials as "J. R(oselli)."

35. In a quick perusal of the manuscripts of vocal music, described as "fascicoli n. 12–54" (fascicle is a misnomer: some of the manuscripts are indeed fascicles, but others are single sheets containing the music for one part, or substantial manuscript partbooks), I found sketches and drafts in nos. 12a, 22, 23, 24, 25, 30, 32a–f, 33, 35, 36, 37, 39, 42, 43, 45, 47, and 48, as well as on the covers of some of the prints (e.g., nos. 1a–f, 10a and c, and 20). Access to the collection is very limited. Study of the sketches will be possible only once the entire collection has been filmed and the music of this composer transcribed.

extant fascicles containing Claudio Veggio's vespers psalms (CastellC 47). I believe that he was also the musician whom H. Colin Slim identified as the principal hand of several keyboard fascicles.[36] While it is not possible to date his work securely, we know that he made keyboard arrangements of music available in print from the 1540s through the 1580s.[37]

BerlS 40021, fol. 257a: One instance of using all available paper is the gathering from BerlS 40021, fols. 257–260. The main corpus of the manuscript, a large choirbook of German provenance compiled ca. 1485–1500, contains Masses, motets, Magnificats, and other compositions by local German and more widely disseminated "European" composers such as Josquin.[38] There is in addition a series of bifolios of various paper types that Martin Just believes were probably sent by courier or by some other means to the anonymous scribe (whom he identified as Scribe Y) who came into the possession of the manuscript in about 1498; Scribe Y added them to the manuscript shortly thereafter as the final stage in its complex genesis. The fascicle in question contains an anonymous four-voice setting of the antiphon *Salve regina*, written by a scribe whom Just called "L," whose hand does not appear elsewhere in the manuscript. The compiler attached it to the manuscript by gluing the first page of the fascicle to fol. 257, thereby covering up some music that was of no importance to him. The folio, now detached and given the modern designation 257a, in fact contains sketches and a draft of a Christmas cantio, *In grandi cenaculo*, discussed in chapter 7. Scribe L was evidently taking advantage of the empty page at the beginning of the gathering to work on one of his own compositions.[39]

LilleA 1081: In some cases, a composer availed himself of paper whether it was lined or not. Guillaume Bouchel, a notary active at the Cathedral of Cambrai from 1437 until his death in 1476 and a friend of Dufay's, drafted a three-voice chanson, *A quoi passerai*, on the final, blank page of this bifolio. The bifolio, discovered by Craig Wright, is one of a sheaf of legal documents, many of them also in Bouchel's hand, from the Cathedral of Cambrai, containing transactions from 1440 to 1457.[40]

36. Slim IVa (=CastellC 4), Slim IVb (=CastellC 9), and Slim VI (=CastellC 8). H. Colin Slim, "Some Puzzling Intabulations of Vocal Music for Keyboard, C. 1600, at Castell'Arquato," in *Five Centuries of Choral Music: Essays in Honor of Howard Swan*, ed. Gordon Paine (Stuyvesant, N.Y., 1989), 127–151; and *Keyboard Music at Castell'Arquato*, ed. H. Colin Slim, Corpus of Early Keyboard Music 37 (American Institute of Musicology, 1975–).

37. Slim, "Some Puzzling Intabulations." Slim wondered about the presence of these fascicles in the Castell'Arquato collection; the proposed identification of the hand as a composer of vocal as well as instrumental music and as a musician responsible for the performing parts for sacred music used in the liturgy may answer a few of the questions.

38. Martin Just, *Der Mensuralkodex Mus. ms. 40021 der Staatsbibliothek Preußischer Kulturbesitz Berlin*, 2 vols. (Tutzing, 1975); *Der Kodex Berlin 40021*, ed. Martin Just, Das Erbe deutscher Musik 76–78 (Kassel, 1990-1991).

39. He could be the composer of the *Salve regina* as well.

40. Craig Wright, "An Example of Musical Inversion from the Circle of Dufay," in *Dufay Quincentenary Conference*, ed. Allan Atlas (Brooklyn, 1976), 144–148, 182. See also Blackburn, "On Compositional Process," 268.

PLATE 6.3   BrugS
538, leaf Cʳ: anony-
mous, chansons,
sketches and
drafts

Of course, not all sketches and drafts are to be found in "second-hand" manuscripts. Composers also worked with "dedicated" manuscripts that they used
exclusively for composing. The documents range in size from single pages to
small fascicles, even to entire volumes.

Single Pages

Composers must have frequently used loose pieces of paper that were not part
of any manuscript. A number of such examples have survived.

BrugS 538: These newly discovered leaves in Bruges, written by four different scribes, are datable from as early as the final decade of the fifteenth century
into the middle decades of the sixteenth.[41] In addition to fair copies of chansons
and a hymn, there are sketches and drafts of four other chansons and a large, six-
voice piece in choirbook format without text. Three as yet unidentified com-

41. Bloxam, "Newly-discovered Fragments." Facsimiles are given in Schreurs, *Anthologie van
muziekfragmenten.*

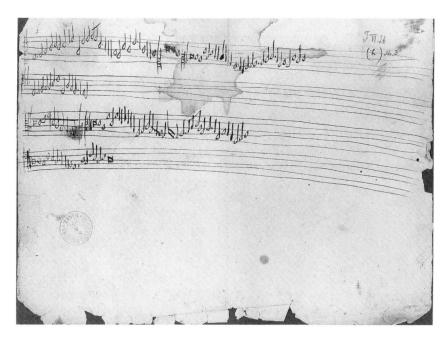

PLATE 6.4   BasU F.VI.26h, fol. 4ʳ: Fabri, unidentified compositions, sketches

posers used these leaves for composing. According to Jennifer Bloxam, Scribe 1, who worked on leaves A, B, and C, sketched the tenor (staves 1–2) and bass (staff 3) of a textless composition (Bloxam suggests that it might be a draft of *L'amy complais*) and three versions of the bass for *Mère de Dieu* on leaf Cʳ (see plate 6.3), and he sketched two voices for *L'amy complais* in choirbook format on leaf Bᵛ. Scribe 3 drafted a six-voice chanson, identified by Bloxam from the incipit on staff 11 as *Jamais de ma femme*, in choirbook format on leaves Dᵛ and Eʳ. She noted that the composer, as he worked out one particularly tricky passage, turned over the page (to leaf Eᵛ) and sketched out four of the voices in pseudo-score (c1c4c4F4). Scribe 4 drafted a six-voice composition in choirbook format on leaf F. The music has yet to be identified and analyzed.

BasU F.VI.26h, Nr. 3–4: This is another example of a composer working on loose pages, here two single sheets with hand-drawn staves.[42] No. 3, in oblong format, contains sketches in quasi-score for two compositions: on the left, one for four voices, ♭ c1c4c3F4; on the right, in darker ink, one for three voices, ♭ c2c3F4 (see plate 6.4).[43] No. 4, in upright format, contains a fair copy (with revisions) of a four-voice textless piece that John Kmetz believes to be a tenor Lied (the voices are in the order discantus, barritonans, contratenor, tenor) and

42. Kmetz, *Die Handschriften*, 65–66; Kmetz, "The Drafts of Jodocus Fabri." In his catalogue of the Basel collection, Kmetz suggested that Fabri may have been responsible for the sketches and draft in fascicle h as well as for those in fascicle d; in his more recent work, he considers the composer of fascicle h anonymous. I would support his earlier interpretation.

43. Kmetz offers a different interpretation, seeing the music as continuous.

on the other side, a sketch in quasi-score of an unidentified three-voice composition (c1c4F4).

Fascicles or Gatherings

It was probably even more common for composers to work with fascicles or small gatherings of paper, as in the following examples.

MunBS 267: The lutenist-composer of the "Recercata a Joan Henrico Herwart" used a group of bifolios now bound into this manuscript for sketching, drafting, and ultimately producing a fair copy of his ricercar.[44] The manuscript, like others in the rich cache of lute manuscripts owned by the Herwart family in Augsburg, is a miscellany created in the nineteenth century from loose bifolios and fascicles written by different hands on many different kinds of paper.[45] The arrangement was apparently quite haphazard (papers of like size were bound together), making it difficult to reconstruct the original state of the papers. The bifolio 32–33 (which measures 210 × 270 and has red ink on its edges) bears an original foliation (or piece number), "34," indicating that it once belonged to quite a substantial manuscript. On the other hand, it contains music at two different stages: the fair copy of the ricercar and one of an unidentified and incomplete composition, and sketches both for the ricercar and for another composition.[46] It is possible that the bifolio was removed from a manuscript and turned into scrap paper. The composer used the folios now numbered 34 to 49 (all of the same size and combining similar paper with two different marks) both for fair copies of intabulations and for sketches. The contents suggest that he was working with bifolios or pairs of bifolios. Thus, the pairs of bifolios 34–37 contain both the sketches for and the intabulation of Janequin's *La guerre*; fols. 38–41 contain fair copies of intabulations. The sketches and drafts for the ricercar are concentrated in the bifolios 42–43 and 44–45 (not originally contiguous) and

44. See the fundamental study by Arthur J. Ness, "The Herwarth Lute Manuscripts at the Bavarian State Library, Munich: A Bibliographical Study with Emphasis on the Works of Marco dall'Aquila and Melchior Newsidler," Ph.D. diss., New York University, 1984. For a list of the contents, concordances, and description see *Tabulaturen und Stimmbücher bis zur Mitte des 17. Jahrhunderts*, ed. Marie Louise Göllner, Bayerische Staatsbibliothek, Katalog der Musikhandschriften 2 (Munich, 1979), 38–41. The present foliation and numbering of the contents differs from that employed by Ness. The bifolio originally fols. 40–41 is now fols. 32–33; the bifolio originally fols. 45–44 is now fols. 44–45.

45. On the Herwart collection, see, in addition to Ness's study cited above, Marie Louise Martinez-Göllner, "Die Augsburger Bibliothek Herwart und ihre Lautentabulaturen: Eine Musikbestand der Bayerischen Staatsbibliothek aus dem 16. Jahrhundert," *Fontes Artis Musicae* 16 (1969): 29–48; Göllner, "On the Process of Lute Intabulation in the Sixteenth Century," in *Ars Iocundissima: Festschrift für Kurt Dorfmüller zum 60. Geburtstag*, ed. Horst Leuchtmann and Robert Münster (Tutzing, 1984), 83–96; H. Colin Slim, "The Music Library of the Augsburg Patrician, Hans Heinrich Herwart (1520–1583)," *Annales musicologiques* 7 (1964–1977): 67–109; and JoAnn Taricani, "A Renaissance Bibliophile as Musical Patron: The Evidence of the Herwart Sketchbooks," *MLA Notes* 49 (1993): 1357–1389.

46. Ness, "The Herwarth Lute Manuscripts," edition, no. 135, pp. 313–314; and Göllner, "On the Process of Lute Intabulation," 93–94; facsimile of MunBS 267, fol. 32r.

in the free space at the end of another pair of bifolios (46 – 49) that had been used by a different hand. The point is that composers then, like many of us today, kept sheafs of papers which they shuffled around and used for various projects.

FlorBN II.I.295, fols. 51 – 54: This example is a pair of bifolios containing sketches, drafts, and fair copies of keyboard music in open score, now bound into an otherwise unrelated manuscript of ensemble ricercars.[47] The bifolios contain five compositions: the middle portion of an unidentified ricercar, the beginning of an unidentified canzona, a sketch for another ricercar, and fair copies of two Frescobaldi *fantasie* (1608, nos. 6 and 11).[48] From the music that is missing it is clear that the surviving bifolios were part of a larger gathering; additional folios must have preceded and followed fol. 51 and an unknown number of folios are also missing after fol. 52.[49] The bifolios are probably in the same hand that wrote FlorBN Magl. 106bis, a manuscript that contains three anonymous keyboard compositions, a set of ricercars by Macque (fols. 9v– 34r), madrigals by Pomponio Nenna (fols. 34v– 41r), and a fragment of an unidentified six-voice sacred composition (fols. 41 – 42, ending "gloria qui natus es de virgine, cum patre et almo spiritu in secula").[50] It is possible that both manuscripts were written by the Flemish composer Carlo del Rio, whose name appears on the front of FlorBN Magl. 106bis; the presence of compositional revisions (for example, on fol. 8v and elsewhere) suggests that the scribe—whether Del Rio or someone else—was the composer of the keyboard pieces. It is interesting that the fascicle now represented by the two bifolios in FlorBN II.I.295 contains both the composer's music and copies of music by Frescobaldi. The character of the manuscript as a kind of miscellany is typical of many of the small manuscripts that composers used for their work.

MilA 10: Cipriano de Rore used a set of five small fascicles, each consisting of four folios, for drafting two compositions and preparing a fair copy of a third.[51] Now bound together as a single small volume, they were separate partbooks when he was using them for composition.

47. When I first examined the manuscript in 1990, the bifolios were out of order and stuck into the back of the volume; I figured out the correct order and left them in that order. When I consulted the manuscript again in 1994, it had been rebound and foliated; the added folios, now bound into the manuscript, are foliated 51 – 54. The main manuscript contains ensemble ricercars by Padovano (1556), Buus (1547), and Malvezzi (1577), copied from prints. See *Ensemble Ricercars. Cristofano Malvezzi, Annibale Padovano*, ed. Milton A. Swenson, Recent Researches in the Music of the Renaissance 27 (Madison, 1978).

48. Professor James Ladewig identified the music. We plan a joint study of the keyboard music in FlorBN II.I.295 and FlorBN Magl. 106bis.

49. The two bifolios are 51 – 54, 52 – 53.

50. Lowinsky, "Early Scores," in *Music in the Culture*, 810 – 811, figure 35.9 (where fols. 1v–2r are mislabeled as p. 16), believed that the instrumental pieces were written "by a lively, forceful, and either later or else younger hand than that shown in the slower and more accurate writing found in the remainder of the MS." I belive that a careful comparison of the clefs and other features will show that the entire manuscript was written by one hand.

51. See chap. 9.

Notebooks and Larger Volumes

Composers also used bound manuscripts of different sizes. Some of them were small notebooks that functioned like commonplace books: a kind of workbook for jotting down ideas and working out compositions as well as for copying music.

BergBC 1143: One example, from the realm of keyboard music, is the Bergamo organ book, BergBC 1143. Discovered in 1965, the manuscript preserves a collection of organ versets for Vespers and Mass propers intended for the liturgy at Santa Maria Maggiore.[52] Written by a certain Joannes Baptista de Fogliaris, a student of Gaspar de Albertis, the book contains primarily two-voice settings in which one voice (usually the lower) presents the cantus firmus in semibreves and the other serves as a counterpoint. The music is notated on five-line staves, with barlines usually every breve.

In some respects, the book resembles a student's exercise book; Gary Towne has suggested that it may reflect Fogliaris's studies with Albertis.[53] For example, on fol. 2[r] the chant, "Alleluia post pascha," notated (with an F3 clef) in semibreves and barred every breve, is on the top staff; beneath it are three alternative counterpoints, all notated with the treble clef. Towne dated the manuscript ca. 1550 on the basis of its liturgical contents as well as on a scribbled copy of a payment. My sense, however, is that Fogliaris may have used the book over a longer period of time, perhaps as much as a decade. The writing in the manuscript changes from beginning to end, beginning with very crude, oversized noteheads, and shifting gradually to a more fluent notation.[54] Another difference is layout: all of the pieces in the first gathering are notated with the cantus firmus on top and the counterpoint beneath; after fol. 17 the cantus firmus is always on the bottom.

There is little doubt that Fogliaris was actually using the book for composition: many of the pages contain corrections and cancellations.[55] There are also multiple versions of many of the compositions. These could be a result of his studies (the compositions found unacceptable by his teacher would be written again), but it is not inconceivable that they reflect rewriting at a later time.

BarcOC 28: Another example of this type of manuscript is a lost Catalan manuscript, preserved in Barcelona as a set of photographs.[56] The manuscript may have belonged to a priest named Pujol, possibly a canon at the cathedral of Girona.[57] Between 1539 and 1546 he added a number of musical entries to the

---

52. Gary Towne, "Music and Liturgy in Sixteenth-Century Italy: The Bergamo Organ Book and its Liturgical Implications," *Journal of Musicology* 6 (1988): 472–509.

53. Towne, "Music and Liturgy," 485–487.

54. The contrast is particularly clear on fol. 3[r], staves 5–6.

55. See chap. 7.

56. *CC*; typescript inventory by Jerry Call and Robert Snow. Sergi Casademunt i Fiol, "Un manuscript català inèdit del segle XV [*sic, recte*: XVI]," *Recerca musicologica* 3 (1983): 39–58, provides an inventory, transcriptions of some of the music, and a facsimile of fols. 49[v]–50[r]. According to *CC*, the manuscript was sold in the 1930s by the Barcelona book dealer Josep Porté to a priest in nearby Villafranca del Panadés; though its present whereabouts are not known, I suspect that it is still in Spain.

57. Casademunt i Fiol advanced two possible candidates: the poet Juan Pujol and the canon from

first sixty-five folios (out of 252). These include counterpoint exercises, copies of music by other composers, and, most interestingly for our purposes, sketches, drafts, and fair copies of his own music. The notebook offers a fascinating glimpse of a composer at work. Many of the compositions go through two or more stages, and most bear an indication of where and when each particular movement or section was composed.[58]

CastellC: Another example is a sketchbook—now dismembered—kept by the anonymous Castell'Arquato composer discussed above. A preliminary investigation of the collection suggests that a number of pages that now are used as covers both for the music prints and for manuscript partbooks once belonged to a sketchbook (or sketchbooks?). Some of the original foliation is still visible, suggesting that a reconstruction may be possible.[59]

———————

Composers kept music in larger, more substantial manuscripts as well.

BasU F.26.VIa, b, d–f: Jodocus Fabri, a composer whose sketches, drafts, and fair copies are found among the music manuscripts now preserved in Basel, kept music in several fascicles. Now separate, they were once bound together.[60] The fascicles, made of rather sturdy paper in upright format, are in effect a miscellany in which Fabri kept copies of music by other composers, written out in a form ready for performance, as well as several sketches and drafts of his own music. He evidently ruled the paper only as he needed it; he left some pages blank and ruled others according to the repertory he was copying (choirbook or a form of separate parts).

CoimU 48: This manuscript is almost like a personal library used more for storing music than for composition. An anonymous composer and organist from the Santa Cruz monastery in Coimbra (Portugal) kept two rather hefty manuscripts (CoimU 48 and CoimU 242) in which he had written out a large number of compositions in score.[61] But he also used one of the manuscripts, 48, for sketching and drafting an eight-voice Magnificat, an instrumental piece, and a highly chromatic piece for keyboard.

———————

A final type of manuscript is the composer's personal copy of his music. This kind of manuscript can approach the status of a manuscript for public use since one of

---

Girona. The entry on fol. 14ʳ ("dixi missa(m) i(n) honore(m) s(an)c(t)i Cosmae et da(miani)" and other references (e.g., "Som a Sent Salvador de breya a xxiii de mar. 1546 a la abbadia ab m.o capell y. c.") make clear that Pujol was a priest, and lend support to the latter possibility.

58. See chap. 7.

59. For example, no. 32a: fol. [6ᵛ], "31" draft of a bass with text "Matris meae"; no. 32d: fol. [6ᵛ], "47" contains a textless draft of a canto (bc1 A); 32e: fol. [6ᵛ] "23" textless draft of an alto (bc3 D); cover of print, scatola 8, no. 1e, front cover: "32."

60. Kmetz, *Die Handschriften*, 45–73; Kmetz, "The Drafts of Jodocus Fabri." The fascicles were presumably bound together during the sixteenth century.

61. Owen Rees, "Sixteenth- and Early Seventeenth-century Polyphony from the Monastery of Santa Cruz, Coimbra, Portugal," Ph.D. diss., Cambridge University, 1991. I was able to consult only the pages that Dr. Rees was kind enough to send me (pp. 316–335). See chap. 7.

its functions may well have been to be a neat enough copy to serve for performance. But it differs in being a manuscript probably in the personal control of the composer, while manuscripts for public use have been given to someone else.

Gerarde partbooks: Derick Gerarde, a Flemish composer who worked in England, kept his music, as well as that of his contemporaries, in sets of partbooks, five of which have survived at least partially among the manuscripts of the Lumley collection in the British Library.[62] He revised his music extensively, often by pasting new staves over the old versions, so some of the manuscripts record two or more versions of his music.[63]

RomeSG 59: Another example is RomeSG 59, a choirbook largely in Palestrina's hand, the place where he kept completed versions of some of his music. The manuscript has minute revisions, usually of text placement or of counterpoint. Two of the pieces also bear the names of singers, indicating that Palestrina used the manuscript for performing. Its relatively small size, in contrast to the enormous choirbooks being written at the time, attests to its personal, rather than institutional, use.[64]

These sources differ from one another in size, but they all share the characteristic of being a composer's private means for composing.

MANUSCRIPTS FOR PUBLIC USE

In contrast, manuscripts for public use only incidentally preserve evidence of compositional process. They are fair copies, with small-scale revisions that do not hinder the main function.

Most of the manuscripts are in a format used for performance. For example, Giovanni Spataro made changes in some of the compositions he copied in the Bologna choirbooks.[65] There are also instances where composers added autograph corrections to music written by other scribes. Carpentras may have added the revisions to his *Salve Regina* in VatS 42, fols. 154^v–157^r; as Richard Sherr noted, "the alterations in CS 42, if not in Carpentras's hand, were at least the product of his mind."[66] Giaches de Wert copied portions of two masses directly into Santa Barbara partbooks (MilC 142 and 143).[67]

Others were intended for transmission. For example, several compositions sent in the mail (that is, by courier) have been preserved in the miscellany VatV 5318, the huge collection of letters written by Renaissance musicians.[68] One of the main correspondents, Giovanni Spataro, enclosed a fair copy—with revisions—of his motet *Ave gratia plena* in a letter to Pietro Aaron, written sometime

62. The manuscripts are listed in table 6.2. See Charles Warren, "The Music of Derick Gerarde," Ph.D. diss., Ohio State University, 1966; and Warren, "Gerarde, Derick," *NG*.

63. John Milsom plans a study of Gerarde's "recompositions."

64. See chap. 11.

65. For example, BolSP 38 and BolSP 46.

66. Richard Sherr, "Notes on Two Roman Manuscripts of the Early Sixteenth Century," *MQ* 63 (1977): 66–73. On Carpentras as a reviser, see Howard Mayer Brown, "Carpentras," *NG*.

67. See chap. 7.

68. Blackburn et al., *A Correspondence*. See chap. 5.

in the autumn of 1532.[69] The autograph actually preserves two versions of the motet and allows us to see the composer at work revising his music even as he was preparing a fair copy.[70] Another example, to be discussed in chapter 10, is Isaac's autograph of the sequence *Sanctissimae virginis votiva festa*, a bifolio preserved in BerlS 40021.

Even more than private scribbles and sketches, fair copies prepared for public use represent a category of manuscripts whose significance for compositional process remains substantially unstudied. Closer scrutiny of erasures in fair copies will not only help to identify additional composer autographs but may also yield variant versions of compositions.

———————

This chapter represents a first attempt to sort the surviving documents of compositional activity into types. The records of a composer's work-in-progress are found in unexpected places: in the blank staves of manuscripts, on scraps of paper that were usually thrown away, in personal workbooks, and even in fair copies. It is hard to imagine a more disparate group of sources. It is no wonder that scholars have been slow to recognize their existence or to examine them in systematic fashion.

In a preliminary account like this one, there should be concerns about the nature of the evidence, both quantity and quality. Despite the sizable number of composing manuscripts that has survived, it will be immediately obvious that the vast majority of such manuscripts has not. We have only to think of what a small fraction of all music composed during the period from 1450 to 1600 is contained in the manuscripts discussed here. Other composing manuscripts will be discovered, but even so the total number will likely remain relatively small, no more than a few percent of all extant manuscripts.

It is even difficult to estimate what portion of all extant composing manuscripts I have succeeded in identifying, or whether the manuscripts considered here are representative. Given the newness of this sort of investigation, the scope can hardly be comprehensive, but at best illustrative. Perhaps the considerable diversity in the extant sources—in time, place, music, and kind of manuscript—indicates a good sample and thus makes the account I have presented here plausible.

69. Letter 46. See chap. 7.
70. See chap. 7.

TABLE 6.1 Autograph Manuscripts Used for Composing (ca. 1450–1625)

Manuscript	Composer	Date	Description	Bibliography
BarcOC 28	Pujol and others	1539–46	sketches (in quasi-score), drafts, and fair copies (in choirbook) in a commonplace book (now lost, preserved in photographs)	CC; Casademunt i Fiol, "Un manuscrit català"; pl. 7.3–4; chaps. 6–7
BasU FVI.26d	Fabri	early 16th c.	fascicle (once bound with fascicles a, e, h)	CC; Kmetz, *Die Handschriften*; Kmetz, "The Drafts of Jodocus Fabri"
4ᵛ–5ʳ			fair copy (with revisions) of Magnificat (3v) in choirbook format; draft of unidentified composition in quasi-score	
4ʳ			sketch of Magnificat, verse 10, in parts	pl. 7.5, chaps. 6–7
BasU FVI.26h	anon. (Fabri?)	early 16th c.	two loose pages	
no. 3 (r)			sketch of two textless compositions (♭c1c4c3F4 and ♭c2c3) in quasi-score	pl. 6.4, chap. 6
no. 4 (r)			draft with revisions of a textless composition (4v) (Tenorlied?) in parts (D, A, B, T)	
no. 4 (v)			sketch of a textless composition (3v) in quasi-score	
BergBC 1143	Johannes de Fogliaris	mid-16th c.	organ book (workbook) with sketches, drafts, and fair copies of organ versets (2v) in keyboard score	Towne, "Music and Liturgy"; pl. 7.7, chaps. 6–7
BerlS 40021				
f. 257aʳ	anon., "Scribe L"	ca. 1500	sketches for tenor, draft in quasi-score of *In grandi cenaculo* (4v); first page of a fascicle added to the choirbook	*Der Kodex Berlin 40021*, ed. Just; pl. 7.23, ex. 7.6, chap. 7
f. 256ᵛ–257ᵛ	Isaac	ca. 1500	fair copy with revisions of *Sanctissimae virginis* (4v) in choirbook and quasi-score formats; bifolio added to choirbook	Just, "Ysaac de manu sua"; Owens, "An Isaac Autograph"; pl. 10.1–3; ex. 10.1–2, chap. 10

BolC Q25 tenor, f. 40	anon. (same hand as Mass)	2/4 16th c.	draft in quasi-score (CTAB) of a textless composition (*falsobordone?*), at end of fascicle containing *Missa Christus resurgens*	CC
BrugS 41	anon.	mid-16th c.	drafts in bass partbook of a chansonnier	Vanhulst, "Le Manuscrit 41"
BrugS 538			music fragments (loose pages)	Bloxam, "Newly-discovered Fragments"; facsimiles: Schreurs, *Anthologie*
Leaf B^v	Scribe 1	early 16th c.	incomplete draft (tenor and bass) in choirbook format of *Je ne complains amour* (3v)	pl. 6.3; chap. 6
Leaf C^r	Scribe 1	early 16th c.	incomplete draft in parts of a chanson (tenor and bass)	
Leaves D–E	Scribe 3	mid-16th c.	draft in choirbook format of *Jamais de ma femme* (6v); sketch in quasi-score	
Leaf F	Scribe 4	mid-16th c.	draft in choirbook format of a textless composition (6v)	
CambriU Bux.96	anon.	after 1535?	line of chant, sketch of *Lord, now let us* in quasi-score on verso of rotulus copied by a bass singer	Bowers in Fenlon, ed., *Cambridge Music Manuscripts*
CastellC (ca. 20 MSS)	"J.R." [Rosso?] and other hands	mid-16th c.	sketches, drafts, and fair copies of sacred and keyboard music in a variety of formats	pl. 7.6, pl. 7.14–19, chap. 7
CoimU 48	anon.	2/2 16th c.	sketch of a Magnificat (8v), drafts of keyboard compositions in open score in an organist's score anthology	Kastner, "Los manuscritos"; Rees, "Sixteenth- and Early Seventeenth-Century Polyphony"; pl. 7.9
ErlU 473/4, fols. 242^v–244^r	Othmayr	1545	incomplete fair copy of *Der Tag, der ist so freudenreich* (4v) in choirbook format added at the end of a choirbook	CC; Haase, "Komposition"; pl. 7.24, ex 7.7, chap. 7

(continued)

TABLE 6.1 (*continued*)

Manuscript	Composer	Date	Description	Bibliography
FlorBN Magl. 117	Corteccia	1530s	sketches and drafts of madrigals, a motet, and unidentified compositions in quasi-score and choirbook formats; late additions to a chansonnier	CC; Bernstein, "A Florentine Chansonnier"; pl. 8.2–9, ex. 8.1–8, table 8.1, chaps. 6–8
FlorBN II.I.295	Carlo del Rio?	early 17th c.	sketch of a ricercar (4v) in open score in a fascicle (2 loose bifolios) now bound in an unrelated manuscript	Ladewig and Owens (forthcoming); pl. 7.8, chaps. 6–7
Flor BN Magl. 106bis	Carlo del Rio?	early 17th c.	fair copy with revisions (incomplete) of a ricercar (4v) in open score, in a composer's miscellany	
FlorD 21	anon.	early 16th?	sketch, incomplete draft of a textless composition (2v) in separate parts, scribbles on flyleaves of a processional	Cattin, "Un processionale"
LilleA 1081	Bouchel?	1440–57	draft of *A quoi passerai* (3v) on a blank page among notarial documents, written in separate parts (tenor, superius, contratenor)	Wright, "An Example of Musical Inversion"; Blackburn, "On Compositional Process"; pl. 7.20, ex. 7.4, chap. 7
LonBLR A23	Gerarde	mid-16th c.	sketches in quasi-score of two unidentified compositions (4v)	pl. 7.1–3
LoBLR A74–76 (original)	anon.	1549–52	fair copy with revisions of *Lord, now let thy servant* (no. 26)	Blezzard, ed., *The Tudor Church Music*
LonBLR A74–76 (later additions)	Gerarde and others	2/2 16th c.	sketches, drafts, and arrangements of music for string band in quasi-score	*Elizabethan Consort Music*, ed. Doe; Holman, *Four and Twenty Fiddlers*; Page, "Composition at Nonesuch"
MilA 10	Rore	1540s–1550s	draft of *Miserere mei, Deus* (5v) and of an incomplete textless composition (5v); fair copy with revisions of *Sub tuum praesidium* (4v), in separate partbooks	Owens, "The Milan Partbooks"; pl. 9.1–3, ex. 9.1–5, chap. 9

Siglum	Composer	Date	Description	Reference
MilC 195/17	[Wert]	2/2 16th c.	fair copy with revisions of *Jesu redemptor omnium*, single leaves	
MilC 142	Wert	2/2 16th c.	fair copies (some with revisions) added to part-books containing *Missa in festis duplicibus maioribus*	MacClintock, *Giaches de Wert*
MilC 143	Wert	2/2 16th c.	fair copies (some with revisions) added to partbooks containing *Missa in festis B. M. Virginis*	
MunBS 267	anon. (Herwart?)	mid-16th c.	sketches and fair copy with revisions of a ricercar ("à Joan Enrico Herwart") in lute tablature	Göllner, ed., *Tabulaturen und Stimmbücher* pl. 7.10–11
MunBS 9437	Antonio di Frari dit il Campanaro	mid-16th c.	sketches and drafts (nos. 14b, 26, 32) in keyboard score and six-line staff in an organ book containing intabulations	Göllner, ed., *Eine neue Quelle*
ParA 75/2	anon.	mid-16th c.	fair copy with possible compositional revisions of *Missa Alles soubdain mon desir*, in partbooks	
RomeSC o.231	Palestrina	2/2 16th c.	fair copy with revisions (performing parts—single leaves) of *Beata es virgo Maria* (8v)	pl. 11.3, chap. 11
RomeSC o.232	Palestrina	2/2 16th c.	fair copy with revisions (performing parts—single leaves) of *Omnis pulchritudo domini* (8v)	pl. 11.2, chap. 11
RomeSG 59	Palestrina (and other hands)	ca. 1573–87	fair copy with revisions of hymns, Lamentations, and other sacred music in choirbook format; draft of two compositions in quasi-score; a composer's *originale*	Casimiri, *Il "Codice 59"*; pl. 11.4, chap. 11
Sib HA3	anon.	2/2 15th c.	drafts of a contratenor for *To iours*, page bound in legal register	Fallows (forthcoming)

(continued)

TABLE 6.1 (continued)

Manuscript	Composer	Date	Description	Bibliography
UppsU 76a	anon.	early 16th c.	later additions to chansonnier	facsimile: *Uppsala, Universitetsbiblioteket 76a*, ed. Brown
f. 57^v–58^r			fair copy with revisions of *Vivent vivent en payx* (3v) in choirbook format	Brown, "Emulation"
f. 58^v f. 77^v			heavily revised draft of *Bon temps vient* (cantus) draft of *En contemplant* (3v) written in separate parts (superius, tenor, contratenor)	Brown; pl. 7.21
f. 78bis^v			fair copy of *En contemplant* (fragment of superius and tenor)	Adams, "Communications"; pl. 7.22
UppsU 76b	additions: Morlaye?	2/2 16th c. (1570–77)	choirbook turned into a lutenist's commonplace book	facsimile: *Uppsala, Universitetsbiblioteket 76b*, ed. MacCracken; Morlaye, *Oeuvres pour le luth* 2, ed. Vaccaro
f. 145^v–146^r			sketch, draft of *Nul n'est* (6v) in mensural notation in quasi-score format and in lute tablature	pl. 7.12, chap. 7
UppsU 76c	additions: Morlaye?	2/2 16th c. (1570–77)	choirbook turned into a lutenist's commonplace book with sketches and drafts in tablature	Morlaye, *Oeuvres pour le luth*, 2, ed. Vaccaro (e.g., fol. 112^v, pl. 8)
VatV 5318	Spataro	1532	fair copy with revisions of *Ave gratia plena*, four half pages sent in a letter	Blackburn et al., *A Correspondence*; pl. 7.13, chap. 7
WolfA 499	anon.	15th c.	draft of a portion of a Gloria (2v)	Preece, "W3—Some Fragments"

TABLE 6.2 Composers Associated with Autograph Manuscripts
(Note: doubtful or incorrect attributions are indicated by brackets around the composer's name)

Composer	Manuscript	Description	Bibliography
Albertis	BergBC 1207, 1208, 1209	choirbooks	Crawford and Messing, *Gaspar de Albertis' Sixteenth-Century Choirbooks*
Bakfark	KönS Gen. 2. 150	lute album book of Achatius zu Dolma	B. Bakfark, *Opera omnia*, ed. I. Homolya and D. Benko
Bottegari	ModE C.311	manuscript of songs for voice and lute	*The Bottegari Lutebook*, ed. MacClintock
Bouchel	LilleA 1081	draft of a chanson	Table 6.1
Carpentras	VatS 42	corrections for *Salve Regina* entered in a choirbook	Sherr, "Notes on Two Roman Manuscripts"
Carver	EdinNL 5.1.15	draft with autograph revisions and autograph fair copy of *O bone Jesu*	Preece, "Cant Organe"
Contino	MilC 42	fair copy in partbooks for Santa Barbara, Mantua	Contino, *Cinque Messe Mantovane*, ed. Beretta
Corteccia	FlorBN Magl. 117 FlorSL N	sketchbook (additions to an earlier chansonnier) fair copy with revisions added to choirbook (f. iii^r) in quasi-score	Table 6.1; chap. 8
de Cristo	CoimU 8, 18, 33, 36	fair copies (some with revisions) in choirbooks for Santa Cruz monastery, Coimbra	Rees, "Newly-identified Holograph Manuscripts"
Dowland	WoodS	additions to the Board Lute Book (fair copy and additions associated with lessons)	facsimile: *The Board Lute Book*; Ward
	WashF V.b. 280	student notebook with additions by Dowland as teacher; fair copy of *What if a day* (mensural notation), variations (tablature), other compositions	Ward, "The So-called 'Dowland Lute Book'"
Fabri	BasU FVI.26 b, d, r, f, h (3–4)	sketches, drafts, and fair copies in a composer's miscellany	Table 6.1
Fernandes	OaxC s.s. GuatC 1	composer's notebook fair copies in a choirbook	Gaspar Fernandes, *Obras sacras*, ed. Snow

(continued)

TABLE 6.2 *(continued)*

(Note: doubtful or incorrect attributions are indicated by brackets around the composer's name)

Composer	Manuscript	Description	Bibliography
Fogliaris	BergBC 1143	organ book (workbook)	Towne, "Music and Liturgy"; Table 6.1
Galilei	FlorBN AG 1	treatise (tablature, f. 43ᵛ)	*Die Kontrapunkttraktate Vincenzo Galileis*, ed. Rempp; Beccherini
	FlorBN AG 6 FlorBN AG 9	lute tablature (with revisions) anthology of madrigals in score (tablature, f. 24)	Lowinsky, "Early Scores"
Gerarde	LonBLR A17–22, A23–25, A26–30, A31–35, A49–54	five sets of autograph partbooks, some with revised versions	Warren, "The Music of Derick Gerarde"
Gumpelzhaimer	BerlS 40027–8 RegB 205–210	manuscripts in score partbooks	Lowinsky, "Early Scores" Charteris and Haberkamp, "Regensburg, Bischöfliche Zentralbibliothek, Butsch 205–210"
[Hofhaimer]	BasU F.VI.26c	organ treatise	Kmetz, *Handschriften*
Isaac	BerlS 40021	pages added to choirbook: *In gottes namen fahren wir* (fair copy); *Sanctissimae virginis votiva festa* (fair copy with revisions)	Just, "Ysaac de manu sua" Table 6.1
[Lasso]	VienNB 18744	illuminated partbooks	written by Johannes Pollet: Owens, "An Illuminated Manuscript"; Hell, "Ist der Wiener Sibyllen-Codex"; facsimile: *Vienna, Österreichische Nationalbibliothek*, ed. Owens
[Lasso]	GdańPAN E. 2165	fair copy of *Ce faux amours*	facsimile in Besseler and Gülke, *Schriftbild der mehrstimmigen Musik*; Haar, "Lasso"
Morlaye	UppsU 76b, 76c, 87, 412	lutenist commonplace books	Morlaye, *Oeuvres pour le luth*, 2, ed. Vaccaro; Table 6.1
Newsidler	MunBS 1627, 266, 2987, ParBN 429	lute tablature	Ness, "A Letter from Melchior Newsidler"

[Obrecht]	SegC s.s.	choirbook (f. 117ᵛ)	facsimile in *Musica* 15 (1961), Table 12; Staehelin, "Obrechtiana"
Othmayr	ErlU 473/4	incomplete fair copy of *Der Tag, der ist so freudenreich* added to a choirbook	Table 6.1, chap. 7
Palestrina	RomeSC O.231, O.232 RomeSG 59	fair copies of performing parts for two motets (8v) composer's *originale* (personal copy of hymns, lamentations in choirbook format	Table 6.1, chap. 11 / Table 6.1, chap. 11; facsimile in Besseler and Gülke, *Schriftbild der mehrstimmigen Musik*
	VatV 10776	fair copy of psalm entered in a choirbook	Jeppesen, "Palestriniana: Ein unbekanntes Autogramm"; pl. 11.1, chap. 11
[Porta]	BolC B140	notes on counterpoint lessons; other entries concerning music	written by Tomaso Graziani; facsimile in Besseler and Gülke, *Schriftbild der mehrstimmigen Musik*; chap. 2
Pujol	BarcOC 28	commonplace book	Table 6.1; chap. 7
Del Rio	FlorBN II.I.295, ff. 51–54; FlorBN Magl. 106bis	keyboard sketches and drafts	Table 6.1; chap. 6
Rore	MilA 10	drafts and fair copy of three compositions in partbooks (small fascicles)	Table 6.1; chap. 9
	MunBS 1503f	fair copy with revisions of Donato, *Fiamma amorosa* (6v) on six loose sheets	
"J.R."=Rosso	CastellC	sketches, drafts, fair copies of music for the Chiesa Collegiata	Table 6.1; chap. 6
Senfl	MunBS 3155 additions to Munich Hofkapelle choirbooks	composer's personal collection of Lieder Munich Hofkapelle choirbooks	Hell, "Senfls Hand"

(continued)

TABLE 6.2 (*continued*)

(Note: doubtful or incorrect attributions are indicated by brackets around the composer's name)

Composer	Manuscript	Description	Bibliography
Spataro	BolSP 29, 31, 38, 40, 45, 46	fair copies (some with corrections) in the San Petronio choirbooks	Tirro, *Renaissance Musical Sources*
	VatV 5318	fair copy with revisions of *Ave gratia plena*, sent in a letter	Table 6.1, chap. 7
[Taverner]	OxfB MS e. 420–2	Wanley partbooks	Hughes, "Sixteenth-Century Service Music"
Veggio	CastellC 5	organ book	Slim, "Keyboard Music"; Slim, "Veggio"
Wert	MilC 142	fair copies (some with revisions) added to partbooks containing *Missa in festis duplicibus maioribus*	MacClintock, *Giaches de Wert*
	MilC 143	fair copies (some with revisions) added to partbooks containing *Missa in festis B. M. Virginis*	MacClintock
	MilC 195/17	fair copy or draft (with revisions) of *Jesu redemptor omnium*	
	MilC 195/18	fair copy of *Subite proni ianuas*	

CHAPTER SEVEN

SKETCHES, DRAFTS,
FAIR COPIES

In this chapter I focus on the written evidence that composers have left of their work in progress. My goal is to suggest a typology that may prove useful for interpreting autograph composing documents for this early period. I am taking two complementary approaches to the topic. In the first, I consider the appearance of the music on the page—including such features as the format and the kinds of changes—to identify characteristic features associated with each stage of work. In the second, I use selected examples to illustrate the range of methods that composers employed.

PHYSICAL CHARACTERISTICS

As we saw in the previous chapter, it is useful to divide autographs into three main categories: sketches, drafts, and fair copies. The categories reflect in a general way the stages of work on a composition—early, middle, late. Like most schemes for classifying material, these categories should be regarded as rough approximations. While it is possible to offer a set of general characteristics that accurately describes most of the examples, there are inevitably instances where the distinction between categories is blurred.

Each of the stages has certain characteristic features such as the format, the kinds of corrections, or the presence or absence of text. Factors such as the amount of space available and its location on the page, the number of voices, and the conventions associated with a particular genre also play a role.

It is important to keep in mind that technology also is involved. The implements for writing influenced how composers could work and affected the appearance of their autograph manuscripts.[1] Cocker's 1703 list names some of the many implements then in use:

> 1. A choice *Pen-knife* of Razor-metal. 2. A *Hone*, and *Sallet-Oil*, wherewith to renew the Edge of your *Knife*. 3. Store of *Quills*, round, hard and clear, the Seconds

---

1. Joyce Irene Whalley, *Writing Implements and Accessories* (Detroit, 1975); Joe Nickell, *Pen, Ink, & Evidence: A Study of Writing and Writing Materials for the Penman, Collector, and Document Detective* (Lexington, Ky., 1990).

in the Wings of Geese or Ravens. 4. Pure white, smooth grain'd, well gum'd Paper, or a Book made of such, well pressed. 5. The best *Ink* that you can possibly procure. 6. *Gum-sandrick* beaten into Powder, searched, and tyed up in a fine Linen-cloth, wherewith pounce your Paper. 7. A flat *Ruler* for certainty, and a round one for dispatch. 8. A small pair of *Compasses*, wherewith to Rule double Lines at the first, and to keep your Lines equi-distant. 9. A choice *Black-lead Pen.* 10. *Indian Black-dust*, or fine Sand, to throw on Letters written in haste. 11. A smooth *Black Slate*, whereon to exercise the command of Hand in the expeditious producing of great Letters and Flourishes.[2]

Several of the schoolmaster treatises on handwriting that became common during the sixteenth century provide illustrations of the tools and explanations of their use.[3]

The main instrument for writing in this period was the quill pen, the point of which had to be cut according to the kind of letters or shapes desired. The graphite pencil that is the ancestor of the pencil in use today was developed during the second half of the sixteenth century, following the discovery of a source of graphite in England, and it came into common use only after 1600.[4] Other kinds of pencils, made from lead or other metal, left quite fine and faint lines, not appropriate for musical composition. All of the extant manuscripts used for composing were written with pen and ink.

The use of ink meant that erasure was difficult. There were only four ways to correct a mistake: write over it, cross it out, smudge it before the ink dried, or scrape the ink from the surface of the paper with a small knife.[5] The autograph composing manuscripts show all four methods. The choice of method was determined by the stage of work and the requirements for neatness.

SKETCHES AND DRAFTS

Sketches are usually brief, limited to a phrase or two. As the first written thoughts about a piece, they are typically very rough in appearance, written quickly and sloppily. There is generally no text. Mistakes are corrected or changes made not by the laborious process of erasing (that is, scraping the ink off the paper) but by drawing a line through the music. The new music is usually written to the right of the old, with no attempt to save space.

Sketches are generally written in one of several characteristic formats, determined in part by the amount of space available, in part by the genre. Since many sketches are quite short, it is not surprising to find them tucked away in odd spaces. Composers scribbled on whatever staff paper was available to them, arranging the parts to fit the space. Francesco Corteccia's sketchbook, FlorBN

2. Edward Cocker, *England's Pen-man*; facsimile in Whalley, *Writing Implements*, 22.

3. For example, an illustration from Giovanni Battista Palatino, *Libro nuovo d'imparare a scrivere* (Rome, 1540), and one from Urban Wyss, *Libellus valde doctus* (1549), both reproduced by Whalley, *Writing Implements*, 23–25. On the treatises, see Osley, *Scribes and Sources*.

4. Henry Petroski, *The Pencil: A History of Design and Circumstance* (New York, 1990), 36, cites Konrad Gesner's *De rerum fossilium lapidum et gemmarum Mexime, Figuris et similitudinis liber* (1565) as having the earliest known illustration of a pencil. He also showed a booklet of wax tablets bound together, with a stylus.

5. Nickell, *Pen, Ink, & Evidence*, 64–66.

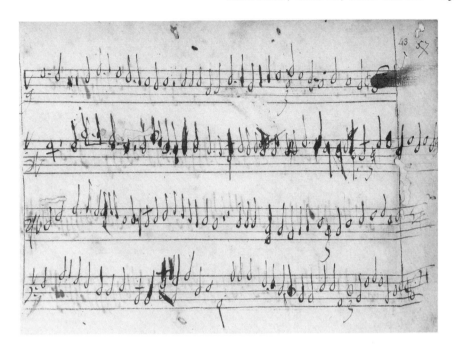

PLATE 7.1   LonBLR A23, fol. 43ʳ: Gerarde, unidentified composition, sketch

Magl. 117, is a striking example.[6] When there was little space, he simply squeezed voices rather haphazardly into the free space. One example is his sketch for part of *Con quel coltel* (see plate 8.8 and figure 8.2). Another, more orderly, example is his use of what might be called a "compact choirbook" arrangement, with the voices stacked in two columns, cantus and bassus on the left, tenor and altus on the right (see plate 8.4, staves 4–5).

Composers usually had more space available for their sketches. They generally used the format that I refer to as quasi-score. The voices are stacked one above the other, usually without any attempt at vertical alignment (and without barlines), often not even ordered high to low. This format was ideal for writing out a portion of a composition. The voices were in close physical proximity to one another. And because the segment was limited in size to the amount of music that could be fit on one line, it was not hard to see how the voices fit together (where they began and ended).[7]

A good example of this format is found among the manuscripts of Derick Gerarde. LonBLR A23 has three pages in quasi-score (fols. 43ʳ–44ʳ [*olim* 57–58]) containing sketches for portions of two unidentified compositions whose final version, so far as we know, has not survived.[8] The first of these (fol. 43ʳ; see plate 7.1) is the roughest in appearance: the four voices, ordered high to low (clefs

6. See chaps. 6 and 8.

7. When Corteccia had an entire page at his disposal, he frequently used this format (see, for example, plates 8.2 and 8.6).

8. I did not find them among any of Gerarde's partbooks.

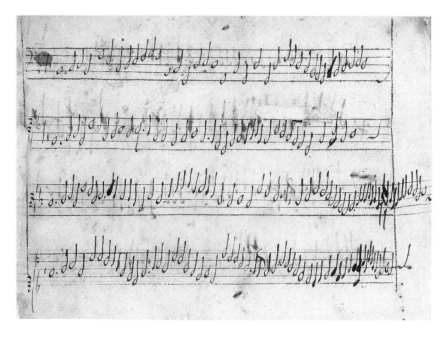

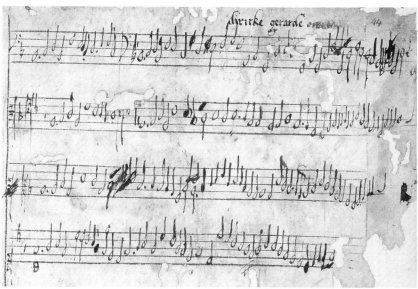

PLATE 7.2   LonBLR A23, fol. 43ᵛ (top) and 44ʳ (bottom): Gerarde, unidentified composition, sketch

g2c2c3F3), have many notes crossed out or drawn over, particularly the altus. The second composition—or more accurately, section of a composition—on fols. 43ᵛ–44ʳ is also for four voices (see plate 7.2). It exists in three separate sketches, two on fol. 44ʳ, one on fol. 43ᵛ. These sketches in turn contain revisions showing that the piece passed through at least five versions. Gerarde began with a two-voice imitative module (fol. 44ʳ, staves 1–2), for tenor and bassus, to judge by the clefs (see example 7.1). He abandoned this attempt after writing just two voices and possibly the clef for a third. In the next sketch, just to the right of this one, he began once again with a B♭ entry in the bassus but changed his mind. He squeezed in two and a half breve rests and wrote out the same contrapuntal module up an octave in cantus and altus (staves 4 and 3). He was making corrections as he was writing: for example, in the altus (m. 3) he crossed out a passage and wrote the final version immediately to the right of it. (The small staves are used to show the earlier versions.) He kept going until he reached a G cadence between tenor and bassus (m. 9), but he had run out of space for the upper two voices and made a real mess of the bass (the first version is illegible). So he wrote out what he had composed on fol. 44ʳ, including the corrections, on the facing page, fol. 43ᵛ. The first ten measures of fol. 43ᵛ are virtually the same as the latest version on fol. 44ʳ.[9] The new material occurs in measures 11–14: he had the space to finish (and revise) the top two voices. This example shows one way in which composing is additive. Gerarde arrived at a viable version of a good portion of a phrase, but left the end incomplete. He then wrote out what he had done and composed the portion that had been left incomplete in the earlier sketch.

In working with quasi-score format, composers sometimes added vertical marks to demarcate segments even within a single brace. For example, the Catalan composer Pujol sketched a four-voice composition in quasi-score in his commonplace book, BarcOC 28, on fol. 57b (see plate 7.3). From a later version of the piece, found on fol. 2 (see plate 7.4) we know that the composition is a Kyrie. Pujol worked in segments, drawing a line through each voice to mark the end of the particular segment. Each segment is identified by its own distinctively shaped line marker. These markers are not barlines: they occur at irregular intervals. Despite the fact that there was a relatively small amount of music on the page, Pujol needed phrase markers to help him keep his place, perhaps an indication of only elementary skills as a composer.[10]

There is little difference—at least conceptually—between squeezing parts haphazardly into a small and irregular space (as in the Corteccia examples cited above) and writing them in quasi-score format. In both cases, each part has its own line; furthermore, the parts for an entire segment stand in close proximity to one another. Either format works well for brief segments of music.

9. The only differences are: altus, m. 3₄ E written instead of D, crossed out and replaced by D; cantus, m. 9₁₋₃, turning figure added to cadence, sharp omitted.
10. For further discussion of Pujol's process, see p. 188.

EXAMPLE 7.1   [Gerarde], unidentified composition

fol. 44ʳ, staves 1-2 (left)

fol. 44ʳ, staves 1-4 (right)

fol. 44ʳ

EXAMPLE 7.1   (*continued*)

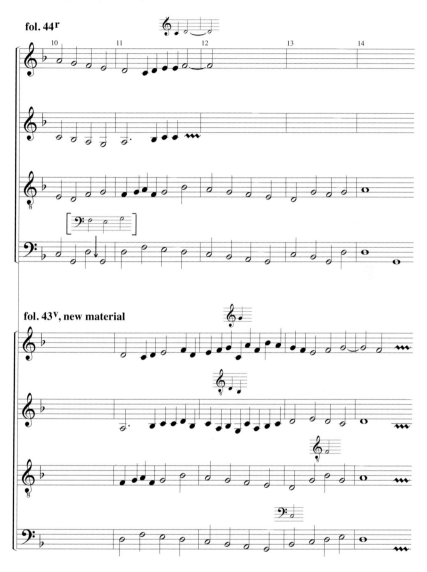

Drafts, in contrast to sketches, typically consist of longer portions of a composition or even the entire composition. Distinguishing sketches from drafts is not always easy: length is a somewhat arbitrary criterion. Either can be crudely written, with notes crossed out rather than erased, but drafts can also come close to a fair copy in appearance. The crucial difference, at least for vocal music, is the choice of format. Unlike sketches, which often use a quasi-score format suitable

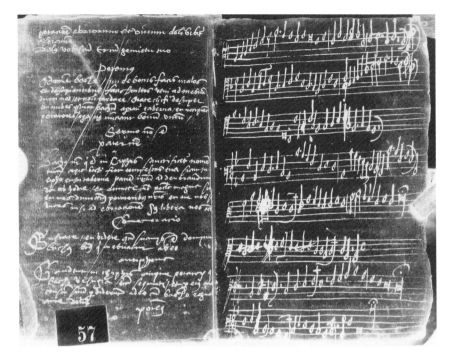

PLATE 7.3   BarcOC 28, fol. 57b: Pujol, Kyrie, sketch

PLATE 7.4   BarcOC 28, fol. 2: Pujol, Kyrie, draft

PLATE 7.5
BasU F.VI.26d,
fol. 4ʳ: Fabri,
Magnificat, draft

for brief segments, drafts of vocal music are typically written from the first in separate parts. Composers sometimes wrote each part in a separate partbook.[11] But they frequently used just one manuscript. If an entire opening or other comparably large space was available, they arrayed the voices in choirbook format, with each voice in its own quadrant. When space was more limited, they wrote the voices one after the other.

Corteccia's sketchbook contains a number of extended drafts written in choirbook format. For example, he wrote out a three-voice motet, *Domine non secundum*, on two consecutive openings.[12] He thought of the space as being divided into three areas (the top part in the upper left, middle part in the lower left, bottom part in the upper right). His work on fol. 38ᵛ-39ʳ is particularly

11. For example, Cipriano de Rore's drafts in the Milan partbooks, discussed in chap. 9.
12. FlorBN Magl. 117, fols. 26ᵛ–28ʳ.

revealing. He used choirbook format to work on three different four-voice compositions (see table 8.1, nos. 23–25), writing each one in succession within the
imaginary quadrants for the individual voices (see figure 8.3 and plate 8.9).
Another example is the opening (fols. 58ᵛ–59ʳ) on which he sketched the four
parts of the madrigal *Fammi pur guerr'Amor*: soprano and bass on the left, in two
versions, and the inner voices on the right (see plate 8.7).

Composers also drafted their music by writing out the parts one after the
other (I use "after" in this case in a spatial, not chronological, sense). For example, Jodocus Fabri drafted a portion of a three-voice Magnificat on fol. 4ʳ of
BasU F.VI.26d (see plate 7.5). A complete fair copy, with text incipits, is notated
in choirbook format on fols. 4ᵛ–5ʳ.[13] The draft, for verse 10, "Sicut locutus est,"
is laid out in parts: the top line (c1) on the first two staves and the beginning of
the sixth, the middle line (c4) on the third and fourth staves, and the bottom line
(c4) on the fifth staff. Fabri clearly did not know how much space he would
need for each part, nor had he worked the composition out elsewhere, at least
not completely. While the chronology of work on this page still needs to be
determined, it is possible, judging from the way the rests were squeezed into the
beginning of the bassus on staff 5, that the initial idea was for a tenor-bassus duet
in close imitation. When that did not pan out, Fabri needed to draw an additional staff freehand above the seven drawn with a rastrum to give him two staves
for the discantus; even so, he needed the beginning of the sixth staff to finish the
discantus. In this conception, the discantus and tenor were contrapuntal voices
working against the simpler, chant-based bassus.

Sketches and drafts for instrumental music, in contrast to those for vocal music,
were written in one of the forms of tablature notation idiomatic to the instrument.
The appearance is similar to the final version, except for the length of the passage
and the neatness of the writing; sometimes, however, the tablature is abbreviated,
for example by omitting designations of rhythm. Because the format is the same
for both sketches and drafts, distinctions between the two are more difficult to
make, and must be based on factors such as length, neatness, and possibly how
completely the music is notated (pitches only, for example, without rhythm).

A sketch in keyboard score in CastellC 2, fol. 2ᵛ is typical (see plate 7.6, staves
3–4).[14] The composition is in two voices, written on two seven-line staves. It is
not known whether it is the beginning of an intabulation of a vocal piece or of
an original composition for keyboard. The writing has the characteristic look of
a sketch: many of the notes are crossed out, others added. The piece breaks off
in the eighth measure.[15]

13. Kmetz, *Die Handschriften*, 54–56, 65–66, plates 6–7; and Kmetz, "The Drafts of Jodocus
Fabri." The discantus is on fol. 4ᵛ, staves 1–8, the middle voice on staves 9–12 and 1–2 of fol. 5ʳ,
and the bassus on staves 4–8.

14. On the keyboard fascicles, see H. Colin Slim, "The Keyboard Ricercar and Fantasia in Italy,
c. 1500–1550," Ph.D. diss., Harvard University, 1960; Slim, "Keyboard Music at Castell'Arquato";
and *Keyboard Music at Castell'Arquato*, ed. Slim.

15. This scribe/composer, whose name is not known, was probably also responsible for:
CastellC 2 [=Slim Fasc. I], fols. 1–2ᵛ, Arcadelt, *Occhi miei* [A]; fol. 2ᵛ, unidentified two-voice fragment [A]; fol. 3ʳ (st. 1–2), unidentified fragment (5 mm.) [x]; fol. 3ʳ (st. 3–4), unidentified fragment

PLATE 7.6   CastellC 2 [= Slim fasc. I], fol. 2ᵛ: anonymous, unidentified keyboard piece, sketch

The Bergamo organ book (BergBC 1143) reveals even more about an organ-ist's working methods. The composer, probably Joannes Baptista de Fogliaris, used the manuscript for sketching and drafting organ versets consisting of a contra-puntal line over a slow-moving chant cantus firmus.[16] Several different stages of work are evident. Most of the book contains drafts, many of them heavily revised, but there are also sketches. For example, the opening at fols. 37ᵛ–38ʳ has three dif-ferent compositions at various stages (see plate 7.7). On the top portion of both

(4 mm.) [x]; fol. 3ʳ, seven incipits labeled 'pavana' [x]; CastellC 6 [=Slim Fasc. III], fols. 1ʳ–26ᵛ, dances [D ≈ A]; CastellC 3 (lost, film at Isham Library) [=Slim Fasc. VIII], fol. 5ᵛ, Agnus dei (a few errors in pitches as well as overwritten notes may indicate that this is a composing draft); fol. 6ʳ, *Al car-moneso*; fol. 6ᵛ, *Pavana dela bataglia*; fol. 8ᵛ, *Todeschina*; and possibly a fascicle (described by Slim as a hand similar to x) that contains an eight-voice setting of *Domine adiuvandum me*, dated 1536, now lost. The letters in brackets are Slim's scribal identifications ("The Keyboard Ricercar"); he thought that several related hands were involved. There is an interesting connection between CastellC 2 and CastellC 6, however, that may suggest a single scribe. Fol. 3ʳ of CastellC 2 has on the left-hand side of the page the first five measures in staves 1–2 and the first four measures in staves 3–4 of two unidentified pieces in keyboard intabulation. In the blank space on the right-hand side of both pairs of staves the same hand has added a series of seven fragments of dances, each labeled 'pavana,' also in keyboard intabulation. The seven fragments are actually incipits of pavanes, four of which (nos. 4, 6, 7, and 8) are found in CastellC 6, in the same hand as the incipits. Along the top of the page the hand has written: "Notate che haverite mandarmi il presente libro et l'altro anchora." Could this be a communication between two musicians exchanging music, one providing a list of pieces?

16. Towne, "Music and Liturgy"; see also chap. 6.

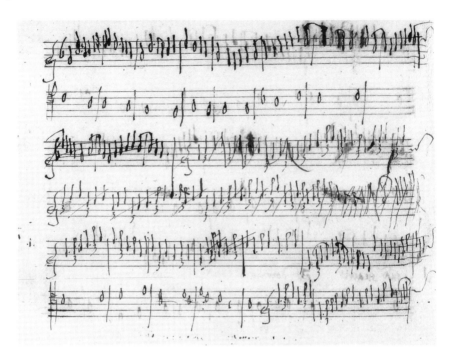

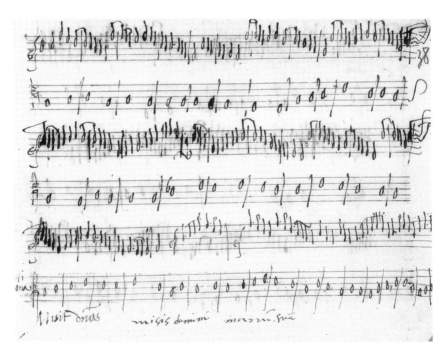

PLATE 7.7   BergBC 1143, fols. 37ᵛ (top) and 38ʳ (bottom): Fogliaris, organ versets, sketches and drafts

sides of the opening there are drafts, probably written close to the same time, to judge from the ink color and thickness of the notes, of *O quam suavis*, an antiphon for Corpus Christi. On fol. 37^v (staves 1–2 and the beginning of 3) is an incomplete draft of Version A, continued from fol. 37^r. It breaks off midway, with the upper voice continuing for a while without the cantus firmus. On the facing page (fol. 38^r) is another incomplete draft, this time of Version B, which breaks off just as Version A had. The final version begins on fol. 38^v. Probably at a later time, again judging from ink color and the kind of writing, Fogliaris used the empty staves for sketching two other compositions. Staves 3–4 on fol. 37^v have a sketch for the upper voice of *Sicut novelle* (without cantus firmus) that has been crossed out. The rest of the music on the opening relates to *Misit Dominus*. The composer began with both voices on the bottom two staves of fol. 37^v (the cantus firmus is notated with a c4 clef). After only a few measures, he stopped the cantus firmus and continued with the upper voice, jumping down to the last staff and then across the opening to staff 5. He wrote out the complete cantus firmus, this time notated with a c3 clef, on the bottom of fol. 38^r.[17] It is interesting that he could write counterpoints without the cantus firmus directly juxtaposed.

Some of the sketching and drafting of keyboard music took place in open score. While most of the extant manuscripts in score were used for performance or for study, a few show signs of being used for composition. A case in point are the sketches in FlorBN II.I.295 for the beginning of an otherwise unknown four-voice ricercar. The composer—possibly Carlo del Rio—tried several different versions of an opening on the second and third sets of staves (see plate 7.8).[18] The writing looks quick, with versions intermingled. It is also very messy: notes are crossed out, smudged, and overwritten.

CoimU 48, an organist's score anthology from the Santa Cruz monastery in Coimbra, Portugal, also contains several examples of composition in open score.[19] Fol. 119^r has a fair copy, with revisions of a four-voice textless composition; fol. 54^v has a heavily emended draft of a highly chromatic imitative piece;[20] and fols. 21^v-22^r have a messy draft of an eight-voice Magnificat (see plate 7.9). Owen Rees has identified all three as late additions to the manuscript not in the hand of the main scribe, but I think that they could all be the work of the same musician. The draft of the Magnificat, the text of which is partially entered under the lowest sounding voice, is the only instance known to me of the use

17. The complexity of work on this page indicates how valuable a complete edition of this source would be that takes into consideration all the sketches and drafts.

18. On the identity of the composer, see chap. 6.

19. On this manuscript, see Rees, "Sixteenth- and Early Seventeenth-century Polyphony," 316–335.

20. The piece is extremely unusual from the point of view of its notation; it uses, in addition to the customary ♭ and ♯, a *quadro* sign (our natural) to cancel the effect of a ♭ applied to B, and an "x," which Hoyle Carpenter ("Microtones in a Sixteenth Century Portuguese Manuscript," *Acta Musicologica* 32 [1960]: 23–28) has interpreted to mean "raise by a diesis" (roughly a quarter tone). There are a number of blotches, notes smudged out and overwritten, and three measures were crossed out between mm. 36 and 37. Rees ("Sixteenth- and Early Seventeenth-century Polyphony," 262) considers the piece to be a seventeenth-century addition to the manuscript.

PLATE 7.8   FlorBN
II.I.295, fol. 51ᵛ: Del
Rio(?), ricercar, sketch

of score for a vocal composition. It is no coincidence that we encounter it in an
organist's anthology, given the association of score format with keyboard music.
Of course, the decision to use the manuscript for the Magnificat in effect determined the format because the staves and barlines were already present.

I would also expect to find keyboard sketches in tablature, but no examples
have turned up yet.[21] The final composition in Jan of Lublin's organ book
(KrakPAN 1716), while possibly an unfinished draft written in German organ
tablature, is so neat in appearance that it may simply be an unfinished copy.[22]
But we know from the testimony of Michael Praetorius that organists, particularly in German-speaking realms, not only played but also composed in tabla-

21. Three possible examples of which I am aware all date from after 1600; see Cleveland Johnson, *Vocal Compositions in German Organ Tablatures 1550–1650: A Catalogue and Commentary* (New
York, 1989).

22. The manuscript, written ca. 1537–1548, contains a collection of organ compositions as well
as two treatises, one on how to set a chant melody and the other on how to make corrections. The
last piece in the collection, found on fols. 257ᵛ–258ʳ, is an untitled keyboard piece, the top line of
which continues for a page and a half to a cadence on F. The first measure contains music for a
middle voice and a bass, but then the bass stops and the middle voice continues until m. 15. See
Johannes of Lublin, *Tablature of Keyboard Music*, and *Tablatura organowa Jana z Lublina*.

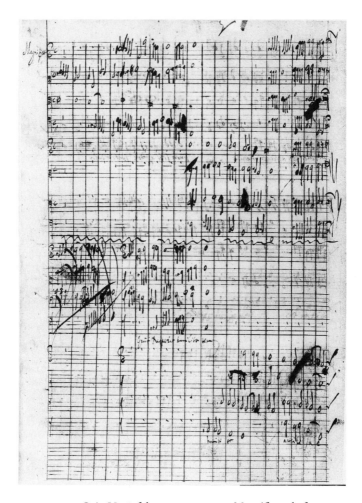

PLATE 7.9a   CoimU 48, fol. 21ᵛ: anonymous, Magnificat, draft

ture.[23] As late as the early eighteenth century, the young J. S. Bach still used tablature for composing some of his keyboard music; he also used snippets of tablature in the margins when space was tight.[24]

23. *Syntagma musicum,* 3: 46: "Dieweil aber die meisten Organisten in Deutschland, der
deutschen Buchstaben Tabulature (welche an ihme selbsten richtig, gut, leicht und bequemer ist,
nicht allein daraus zu schlagen, sondern auch daruff zu Componieren) sich gebrauchen . . ." See
the discussion by Johnson, *Vocal Compositions,* 123 – 125. Schonsleder, *Architectonice musices,* recommended tablature as one of the formats used by composers, along with the ten-line staff and score;
see chap. 3.

24. See Robert Hill, "Tablature versus Staff Notation: Or, Why Did the Young J. S. Bach
Compose in Tablature?," in *Church, Stage, and Studio: Music and Its Contexts in Seventeenth-Century
Germany,* ed. Paul Walker (Ann Arbor, 1990), 349 – 359. See also Marshall, *The Compositional
Process,* 1: 53.

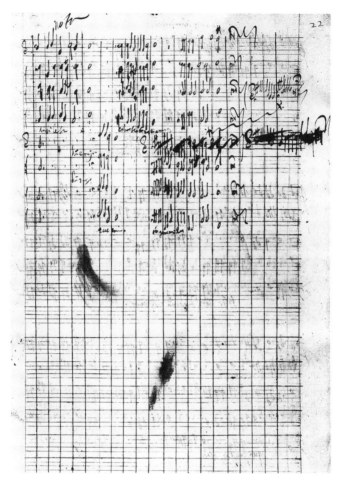

PLATE 7.9b   fol. 22ʳ

There are examples of composition in tablature, but from the realm of lute music.[25] The composer of the *Recercata a Joan Henrico Herwart* (Herwart himself?)

25. See, for example, Ness's identification of several different lutenist-composers among the lute manuscripts in Munich, including those of Melchior Newsidler (1541–after 1591): "A Letter from Melchior Newsidler," in *Music and Context: Essays for John M. Ward*, ed. Anne Dhu Shapiro (Harvard University, 1985), 352–369. Many of Newsidler's manuscripts preserve music subsequently published in a more highly ornamented form and thus constitute what Ness called "the bottom layers" of his output. Unfortunately, as far as I know, there has been no systematic examination of extant lute manuscripts from the sixteenth century to see what kinds of information they might contain concerning compositional process. Compositional process for the lute and other fretted stringed instruments has been approached primarily through a study of genre. See the work of John Griffiths, especially his edition of Esteban Daza, *The Fantasias for Vihuela*, Recent Researches in the Music of the Renaissance 54 (Madison, 1982); and the essays in *Une fantaisie de la Renaissance: Compositional Process in the Renaissance Fantasia. Essays for Howard Mayer Brown, in memoriam-Journal of the Lute Society of America* 23 (1990).

left evidence of his work on the ricercar scattered among the leaves of MunBS 267.[26] Göllner has offered the following characterization of the work:

> For this particular ricercar, composed rather typically on a series of different motives, there is considerable evidence in the sketches of instability in the choice of rhythmic unit. . . . Aside from this feature [differences in rhythmic units] the sketches for this independent instrumental work exhibit marked differences in character and function from those of the intabulations. Although some of the cadences are more elaborated in the final version, there is no clear distinction between a simple and an embellished version, and the main purpose of the sketches appears to have been the working out of the motives and the insertion of new sections into the piece. Their function, in other words, is directly related to the composition of the work in this case and not to its adaptation to the instrument.[27]

Although all the versions in MunBS 267 have not yet been published, it is clear from even the appearance of the music on the page that there are several different stages.[28] Despite the difference in notation, many of the characteristics found in mensural notation apply here as well. The sketches are fragmentary, often without indication of rhythmic notation or vertical lines (for example, fol. 45[r], staves 5–6). Drafts range from the very rough (for example, fol. 45[v], with many passages crossed out and replaced by others written in the margins) to the more polished (for example, fol. 48[v]; see plate 7.10). The fair copy of the ricercar (on fol. 32[r], olim fol. 40[r]) contains revisions as well (see plate 7.11). The composer inserted one phrase onto staff three (the added material is on the last staff) and another one at the end of staff 3 (the beginning of staff 4 is crossed out, and the added material is on hand-drawn staves in the right margin). What has apparently not been noticed before is that he sketched this added second phrase at the bottom of the next folio (fol. 33[r]), beneath the unfinished fair copy of another composition.

In only one instance (that I know of) is there a connection between the worlds of tablature and mensural notation. The portion of UppsU 76b that evidently served as Guillaume Morlaye's workbook preserves fragmentary sketches of an otherwise unknown six-voice chanson, *Nul n'est*, in both notations (see plate 7.12). In the version in mensural notation (fol. 146[r]), the superius is written out in full, with text, and the beginnings of the other voices are placed on the remaining staves in quasi-score (in the order altus 1, altus 2, taille 1, taille 2, bassus). On the facing page, the same composition exists in three different drafts, notated in French lute tablature.[29] The composer (Morlaye or someone else)

26. Ness, "The Herwart Lute Manuscripts," edition, no. 135, pp. 313–314; Marie Louise Göllner, "On the Process of Lute Intabulation," 93–94; and Taricani, "A Renaissance Bibliophile," 1370–1372. See also chap. 6.

27. Göllner, "On the Process," 94.

28. Professor Göllner has informed me by letter that she intends to publish the sketches at a future time.

29. The versions of *Nul n'est* were mentioned briefly by MacCracken, "The Manuscript Uppsala," 189; they were not included in Vaccaro's edition of Morlaye's music in the Uppsala manuscripts. For a transcription, see Hiroyuki Minamino, "Sixteenth-Century Lute Treatises with Emphasis on Process and Techniques of Intabulation," Ph.D. diss., University of Chicago, 1988, 82–88.

PLATE 7.10   MunBS 267, fol. 32ʳ: anonymous (Herwart?), ricercar, fair copy with revisions

PLATE 7.11   MunBS 267, fol. 48ᵛ: anonymous (Herwart?), ricercar, sketches

PLATE 7.12a   UppsU 76b, fol. 145ᵛ: Morlaye(?), *Nul n'est*, drafts in
tablature (fol. 145ᵛ), sketch in mensural notation (fol. 146ʳ)

focused on the melody, drafting it complete two times (once in tablature, once
in mensural notation), with revisions in the same places in both versions. The
second lute sketch, while incomplete, adds some of the harmonies. The ink
color suggests two different stages: light ink for the music of the superius and
most of the lute tablature, dark brown ink for the text of the superius, the
remaining vocal parts, and the revisions of the tablature.

Minamino, whose main topic was the process of intabulation, speculated (p. 84, n. 2): "Is it conceivable that the passage was composed by the intabulator, or the entire piece is a compositional
sketch?"

PLATE 7.12b   fol. 146ᵛ

FAIR COPIES

As in later periods, composers did not necessarily complete their work with
their sketches and drafts; they frequently continued composing and revising
during and after the preparation of the fair copy. Most fair copies were intended
for use in performance or transmission: they typically contained the full text (at
least for those genres that employed texts in all voices) and were written neatly
in the format associated with performance: separate parts (choirbook or partbooks) written in mensural notation for vocal music, tablature for instrumental
music.

While fair copies seem unlikely candidates for any contribution to an understanding of compositional methods, many of them contain significant revisions,
made either while the copy was being written down or afterwards as part of a
process of editing. Some of the changes in fair copies correct simple slips of the

pen. Others are "editorial": the new reading, which generally corrects grammatical errors or makes improvements in the counterpoint, replaces and is usually written over the earlier one. Determining precisely when the changes occurred is difficult; a sharp contrast in ink color can indicate that the changes were made at a time subsequent to the main copying.

While most of the changes in fair copies are probably later revisions, some were made as the copy was being prepared. An example is Giovanni Spataro's copy of his motet *Ave gratia plena*. He wrote each of the four voice parts on a separate half-sheet of paper and sent them in a letter to Pietro Aaron for comments; the motet has been preserved, glued to the end of the letter that accompanied it, in the collection of correspondence VatV 5318.[30]

The impetus for composing the motet came from a discussion of the genera that took place at the home of Monsignore Giambattista Casali. Casali, noting that ancient writers described the wonderful effects of using all the genera, wondered if it were possible to write in all three. The conclusion was that it was impossible not to, because the chromatic and enharmonic in effect aided the diatonic. By way of example Spataro mentioned the B–B octave, which, when divided into a fifth below and a fourth above, required a sharp before the F to create a perfect fifth. When one of the people present objected that he had never seen a composition that actually used that octave divided in that way, Spataro decided to write a piece to show that it was not only possible but reasonable to use the chromatic genus as well as the diatonic; the composition, in fact, even employs D♯ as the major third over B (m. 17). He wrote to Aaron that he had composed the motet (which he referred to throughout the letter as either "canto" or "concento") a few days ago ("a li giurni passati"); it had not yet been seen by anyone since the company had not reassembled since the initial discussion.

What nobody apparently realized before is that Spataro's autograph in VatV 5318 contains a number of revisions in voice-leading and text placement (see plate 7.13 and example 7.2). In passage no. 1 (mm. 5–9), Spataro changed from a rhythmically square imitation between altus and tenor (shown in the small staves) to a dotted figure beginning off the beat and including a passing tone. He also changed the voicing of the downbeat sonority in measure 8 by revising three voices (the original tenor is no longer legible). Another change involves the two inner voices. In passage no. 5 (m. 42), at the end of the text phrase "in tenebris," Spataro switched the two voices, giving the running passage that had been in the tenor to the altus, letting the tenor rest instead of the altus, and possibly improving the voice-leading.

Two of the revisions involve the text. In passage no. 2 (mm. 10–12) Spataro erased "gratia ple-" in the cantus (the text labeled "1") and replaced it with "Ave gratia plena," to bring it into line with the other two voices. In passage no. 4 (mm. 31–36) he erased "ex te enim ortus est" from altus and tenor and replaced it with "sol iustitie," thereby giving the inner voices the same text as the outer

---

30. Blackburn et al., *A Correspondence*, Letter 46, commentary, edition, and facsimile. The letter was written in autumn 1532.

PLATE 7.13   VatV
5318, fol. 245^r,
cantus and tenor:
Spataro, *Ave gratia
plena*, fair copy

two. The passage between measures 24 and 30 has a florid, quickly moving altus
and tenor over a slower bass. Spataro stretched the text very thin in the middle
voices, supplying "ex te enim ortus est" just once for eight measures (the editors
of the modern edition were able fit the text in twice); he added it a second time
in measures 31–36 but then replaced it. This change shows that he was not simply copying from a fully texted version, and furthermore it suggests he was not
seeing the music with its text in full score or he would presumably have noticed
the problem.

The versions of *Ave gratia plena* preserved in VatV 5318 are earliest extant versions of the piece. Spataro could very easily have been working from earlier
sketches or drafts that have not been preserved; we know from his correspondence that he used a *cartella* for composing and that he copied music from the
cartella onto paper to send to his correspondents.[31] It is difficult to be certain
when he made the changes; the fact that all the changes are in the same ink as

31. See chap. 5.

EXAMPLE 7.2   Spataro, *Ave gratia plena*

EXAMPLE 7.2   (*continued*)

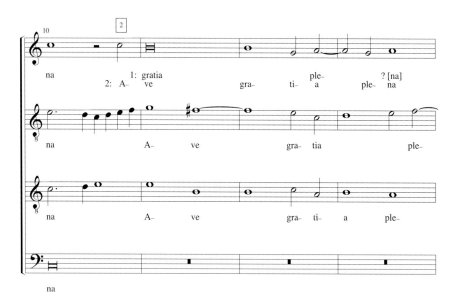

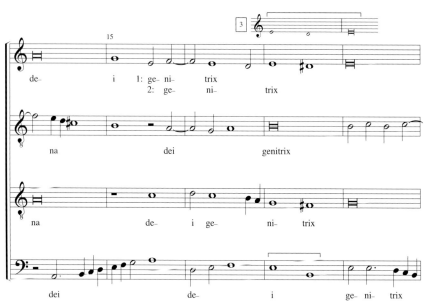

EXAMPLE 7.2   (*continued*)

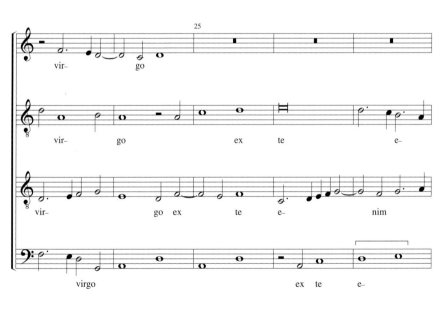

EXAMPLE 7.2   (*continued*)

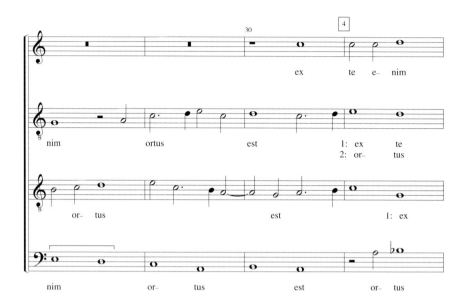

EXAMPLE 7.2 *(continued)*

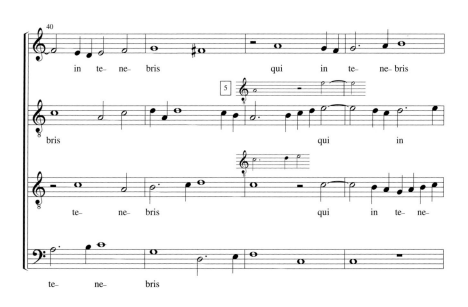

EXAMPLE 7.2   (*continued*)

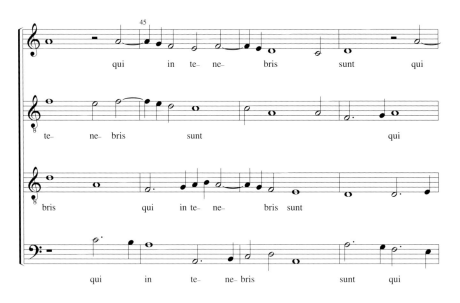

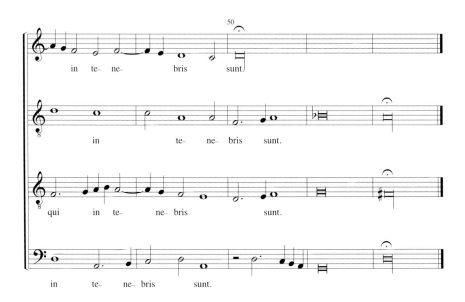

the surrounding notes suggests that he could have made them as he was writing these very pages to send to Aaron. One can only speculate what led him to make the changes: perhaps he noticed problems while studying the music himself, perhaps he detected them by hearing the piece performed.[32]

Spataro must have kept another written version of the piece—either on his *cartella* or on paper—because he subsequently reworked it, partly in response to Aaron's comments. Aaron's letter is lost, but its contents can be gleaned from Spataro's response of 2 January 1533. Aaron did not approve of the augmented octave in measure 14 or of the diminished fifth in measure 50. While defending himself in his answer, Spataro nonetheless accepted Aaron's criticisms and revised the piece before including it in one of the choirbooks he used at San Petronio.[33]

This example—and there are many others like it—show the kinds of polishing that could take place in the final stages of composition, even in the copies intended for performance or transmission.[34] Such corrections were not always easy to read, as a young cleric in Pontio's tutelage complained:

Io ne diro l'anno passato che lui compose una messa a otto et dove haveva lui falato l'haveva casso et fatte alcune notte molto mal de intenderle et si come dovea prima farmi cantar ciaschun di noi la parte nostra et poi unitamente come portava il dovere e insegnarme quelle cose falate e reconcie noi che non l'intendevemo me li faceva cantar come vi ho detto di compagnia et perche noi falavemo non conossendo ditte notte stegazate mi a datto di gran botte a Michel Angelo et a me dandome delle bochettate sopra la testa et molte fiate me la rotta . . .	I will tell you that last year he [Pontio] composed an eight-voice Mass and where he had made a mistake he crossed it out and added other notes that were very hard to understand; and since first he had me sing each one of us our part [alone] and then together as was proper and he taught me the wrong notes corrected in ways that we did not understand, he made me sing, as I said, with others on my part (*di compagnia*) and because we made mistakes, not understanding those crossed-out notes, he hit me and Michel Angelo many times on the head . . . [35]

We can only pity this poor singer trying to read Pontio's messy emendation.

---

32. As Blackburn has shown (*A Correspondence*, 123–124), Spataro also checked his work by adding an extra voice.

33. Frank Tirro ("Giovanni Spataro's Choirbooks in the Archive of San Petronio in Bologna," Ph.D. diss., University of Chicago, 1974) edited Spataro's later version of VatV 5318 and the revised version in BolSP 45 and discussed the changes. Spataro rewrote mm. 10–14, keeping the same melody but writing a new harmony, thus eliminating the offending dissonance in m. 14 and the B major sonority in m. 17. He also made other changes, substantially rewriting portions of the piece. Another change is in the text: only VatV 5318 has "virgo" ("Ave gratia plena dei genitrix virgo ex te enim ortus est sol iustitie illuminans qui in tenebris sunt").

34. For a discussion of Isaac's revisions for *Sanctissimae virginis votiva festa* and Rore's for *Sub tuum praesidium*, see chaps. 10 and 9.

35. BergBC 989, Pontio *processo*, testimony of Petrus de Medicis, clericus, fol. 12ᵛ. See Murray, "The Voice of the Composer," 2: 42; and Murray, "On the Teaching Duties."

This account of the various kinds of compositional documents illustrates the possibilities by means of a series of unrelated examples. Such a small fraction of composing manuscripts has been preserved that we rarely possess more than one or two documents for any composer, or indeed for any composition. In some instances we can watch a piece develop from one stage to the next, but most of the time we have only one snapshot of the work in progress and must try to imagine what came before or after. Some of the documents may be missing, or the composer may have been using an erasable tablet as well.

Despite the fragmentary nature of the evidence, I believe that each composer probably used several different formats, adjusting his methods to suit the composition, the paper available, and the stage of work. A vivid illustration of the variety can be found in the little-known but extremely interesting cache of compositional manuscripts written by a composer (possibly "J. R." or Jacomo Rosso) working at the collegiate church in Castell'Arquato during the second half of the sixteenth century.[36] He worked in many of the formats discussed here and composed both keyboard and vocal music. A brief survey of some of his procedures reveals the diversity of approach.

For example, he fit a series of sketches for the opening of a Magnificat into empty staves at the bottom of three of the fascicles of Veggio's vespers psalms (CastellC 47) (see plate 7.14). He had begun his sketching on the alto I part, with a pair of tenors and part of a bass. The next stage had all five voices; he achieved a nearly complete version, though one filled with parallel octaves and fifths. The third version, shown in plate 7.14 and example 7.3, demonstrates that he had rewritten two of the voices at the cadence. If he continued this piece elsewhere, it remains to be identified. One can imagine, however, from other examples of his work how he might have continued.

For a more extended draft he used quasi-score format. For example, he worked on two phrases on CastellC 32c, fol. [6^v]; the second one, like the first without text, consisted of twelve semibreves in the order c4c4c3c1F4 (see plate 7.15). He rewrote this phrase on CastellC 32b, fol. [6^v], this time with the text *Si ascendero in celum*, in slightly revised form, and continued it for another fourteen breves to the end of the section (cadence on A).

Longer passages were drafted one part to a page. One example is the draft of *De utero matris meae* (text reads: "matris meae de utero matris meae vocavit me dominus nomine meo"), found in CastellC 32a (bass), CastellC 32d (cantus), and CastellC 32e.[37] Vertical lines divide the music into several segments (see plate 7.16).

The same composer worked in instrumental as well as vocal idioms. Keyboard score (a five-line and an eight-line staff) was used for an unidentified

36. For a discussion of the manuscripts in the collection and the identity of this composer, see chap. 6. I visited Castell'Arquato during the final stages of work on this book, too late to pursue the material thoroughly; I had no idea that the collection contained such important material for compositional process.

37. The remaining part (or parts), as well as the final version, may very well be preserved in Castell'Arquato.

PLATE 7.14   CastellC 47.Tenore I, fol. 1ʳ: Rosso(?), Magnificat, sketch

EXAMPLE 7.3   Anonymous (Rosso?), Magnificat

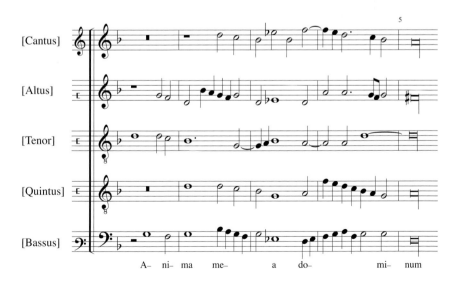

PLATE 7.15   CastellC 32c, fol. [6ᵛ]: Rosso(?), unidentified composition, sketch

PLATE 7.16   CastellC 32a, fol. [6ᵛ]: Rosso(?), *De utero matris meae*, draft

PLATE 7.17   CastellC 12a, fol. [6ᵛ]: Rosso(?), unidentified composition, keyboard score

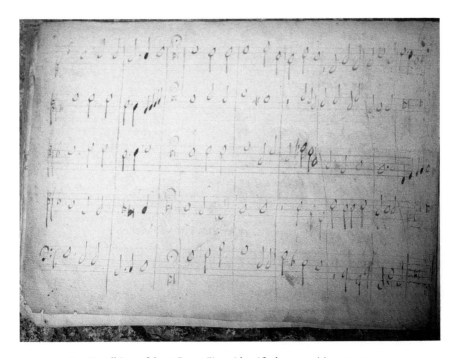

PLATE 7.18   CastellC 33, fol. 5ᵛ: Rosso(?), unidentified composition, open score

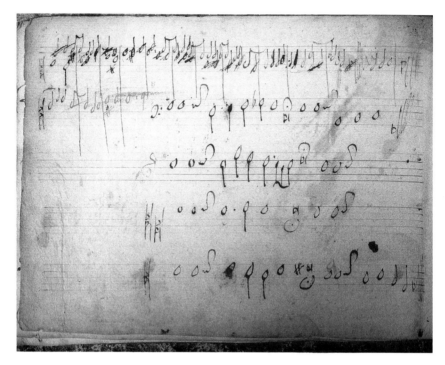

PLATE 7.19   CastellC 33, fol. 11ᵛ: Rosso(?), unidentified compositions

intabulation in CastellC 12a, fol. [6ᵛ] (see plate 7.17). He wrote out two phrases of a homophonic, five-voice composition in score (CastellC 33, fol. 5ᵛ), making a few revisions (see plate 7.18). And he sketched and heavily revised the cantus and the beginning of the altus of an unidentified composition, using open score format; he then abandoned the piece and used the rest of the page for a partial draft of a four-voice *falsobordone* in quasi-score (the voices are in the order bassus, cantus, altus, tenor) (see plate 7.19).

Although I have focused primarily on sketches and drafts that seemed at first glance both characteristic and representative, our nameless composer was also responsible for making fair copies of the music, presumably for use in performance. Many of them have revisions that suggest polishing or editing and can probably be seen as the final stage in an unusually well-documented process.

I hope that these preliminary observations serve to draw attention to this valuable collection of compositional documents. This composer—whoever he may be—left an unusually detailed picture of the variety of formats appropriate to the various stages of composition and to the available space.[38]

38. I hope that once the collection has been filmed and can become more accessible to scholars someone will undertake the task of identifying the composer, transcribing the music, and analyzing the sketches, drafts, and fair copies.

EVIDENCE FOR COMPOSITIONAL PROCESS

The most interesting information that can be gleaned from these composing manuscripts concerns how composers worked. There is no single process, but rather a variety of processes that reflect the structure of the music and the composer's priorities. Each of the examples I have selected tells its own story. Taken as a whole, these stories allow us to construct some general principles about compositional process in music from 1450 to 1600; taken individually, they reflect both changes in musical style over time and the variety of musical structures.

To put it simply, the main task in understanding how a composition from this period works is to identify the compositional points of departure. Was there pre-existent music—monophonic or polyphonic—that was reworked or adapted in some way? How were the voices related to one another: was one voice the most important or were the voices relatively equal in importance? Is the music based on a two-voice frame (typically, the superius and tenor)? Does the lowest sounding voice function as a bass? Is the structure imitative, with contrapuntal modules migrating among constantly varying pairs of voices? This list of questions, while hardly exhausting the possibilities, gives an idea of the variety of approach found over the course of the whole period. It is no surprise that the composer autographs not only reflect this variety but in many cases help to identify—by means other than music analysis—the compositional points of departure, the structure, the roles of the voices, and their relationships one to another.

By way of example, let us consider the three-voice chanson preserved among legal documents from the cathedral of Cambrai (LilleA 1081); it was probably written by Guillaume Bouchel, a notary and a friend of Dufay's, between 1440 and 1457 (see plate 7.20 and example 7.4).[39] The chanson, *A quoy passerai*, is written on a single blank page on four hand-drawn staves. The tenor—without text—is on the first staff. The superius—with text—is on the second and third staves. The contratenor—without text—immediately follows the superius on third staff, continuing to the fourth staff; it could not have been written (although of course it could have been composed) until the superius had been written out completely. Bonnie Blackburn, who discussed this piece in connection with fifteenth-century compositional process, saw this as an example of successive composition. The tenor was written out first, in a way that showed the phrase structure. Next the superius was added, and last the contratenor. Blackburn argued, "As long as composers wrote music successively, there was no need of a score; they could write 'upon the book,' that is, look at one line of music and write another, in the same way that they could 'sing upon the book.'"[40] Lending support to this view was Craig Wright's discovery that the pitches of the tenor derive from the inversion of the pitches of a tenor in a chanson in the Dijon chansonnier; in other words, Bouchel was working with a given line (to which he presumably had to give rhythm), not one newly com-

---

39. See chap. 6.
40. Blackburn, "On Compositional Process," 268, n. 116.

PLATE 7.20   LilleA 1081: Bouchel(?), *A quoy passerai*, draft

posed.[41] However, close examination of the manuscript suggests another possible scenario. Coincidence in ink color (light versus dark) suggests that Bouchel worked on—wrote down?—the tenor and superius together, phrase by phrase. For example, the final phrase in both voices is written in a noticeably lighter ink. Neither voice has any corrections (I am assuming that the two lines crossing out the stem of the A in measure 2 of the superius correct a slip of the pen). The two voices work well together and are harmonically self-sufficient. The contratenor is another story. Blackburn noted some of the problems: "A perusal of the transcription shows that this work was never verified aurally, either as a whole or in pairs of voices. A correction seems to have been made at measure 21 in the contratenor, with the result that the next five measures are displaced by a semibreve. Aside from these measures, the contratenor fits the tenor, but there are noticeable clashes with the superius."[42] In fact, I would describe the contratenor as a partially corrected draft; the several emendations (mm. 1, 15, 21) do not make it viable. (The earlier version is given on the small staff of example 7.4.) I think this is an example of a rather feeble attempt to add a contratenor to the superius–tenor frame.[43] The tenor, blocked out on the page in clear segments, is the foundation, designed with its superius as a pair.

41. Blackburn, "On Compositional Process," 268, n. 116.

42. Wright, "An Example of Musical Inversion," 145.

43. On another possible example (Sib HA3), see David Fallows, "English Song Repertories of the Mid-Fifteenth Century," *Proceedings of the Royal Musical Association* 103 (1976–1977): 74, to be discussed further in his forthcoming study of English song.

EXAMPLE 7.4   Anonymous (Bouchel?), *A quoy passerai*

PLATE 7.21　UppsU 76a, fol. 77ᵛ: Anonymous, *En contemplant*,
draft

Bouchel's autograph shows clearly, I think, that these two voices are the core of
the composition.

It is interesting to compare Bouchel's chanson with another three-voice
chanson composed perhaps half a century later. An anonymous composer, no
more skilled than Bouchel, added a draft of *En contemplant* to UppsU 76a (see
plate 7.21 and example 7.5). The chanson is brief, consisting of four sections (A
B C [A]), the last of which is identical with the first and not written out. Like
the Lille example, the three voices fit on one page, but in this case they are
arranged high to low: the superius (with the c1 clef) on staves 1–2, tenor (c3) on
3–4, and the contratenor (F3–F4) on staves 5–6.[44] The music looks like a rough
draft, with heavy revisions made both by writing over the first version and by

44. The voice names are taken from Brown, "Emulation, Competition, and Homage," 5.

EXAMPLE 7.5   Anonymous, *En contemplant*

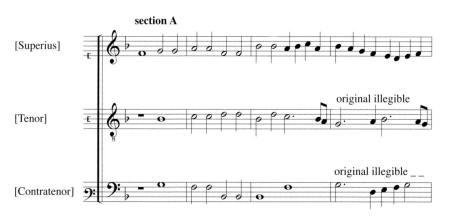

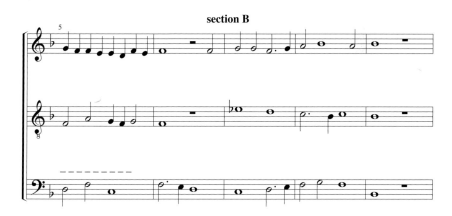

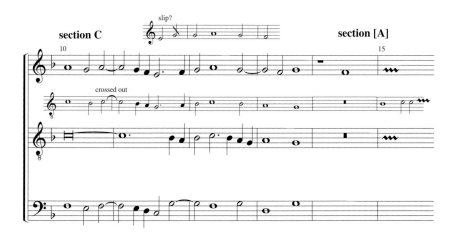

crossing it out and replacing it with another; there is no text, just an incipit that has been cancelled by a line drawn through it. Howard Mayer Brown described the draft as follows: "We seem . . . to be looking on at a composer's series of trials and errors, a fairly simple and unsophisticated composer, to be sure. The page can only be explained, it seems to me, as an early sixteenth-century compositional draft, written out from the very first as a set of parts."[45]

Brown noted that "the composer regarded the top line as the most important voice, and he probably wrote it first." He believed that the chanson was an example of emulation and imitation so frequently recommended to students and practiced by composers themselves, and he argued that the student-composer had worked from a polyphonic model, which he identified as the chanson *Vivent vivent en payx*, copied by the same composer/scribe on fol. 57ᵛ–58ʳ. Courtney Adams, however, challenged this view and suggested instead that the chanson was an early example of a *chanson rustique*, based on a monophonic tune. She found the same tune in the tenor voice of Gascogne's later three-voice setting.[46] As Adams noted, the discovery of a pre-existent melody did at least confirm Brown's hypothesis that the superius line was the first to be "composed," or in this case written down.

The discovery of a pre-existent melody helps to explain the differences among the voices in terms of the amount of revision. The superius has only a few changes, one a messy writing out of a flourish, another possibly just a slip of the pen, the third an emended passing-note figure. In contrast, both the tenor and contratenor have heavy changes made by writing the new version over the old at the end of Section A, and the tenor has an entirely new Section C (the original one was crossed out, the new one written next to it). (The original version is no longer legible in some places; where it is, it is given on small staves.) Brown used both the order of the voices on the page and Aaron's account of the order in which composers were to proceed (first a melody, then a tenor, then a contratenor) to argue that the composer "very likely did write out the Tenor after the Superius, and only later added the Contratenor." While this scenario may be correct, other possibilities seem more plausible to me. There is no way of knowing whether the composer wrote out the entire superius before working on the other voices, or whether he wrote it out phrase by phrase, as he worked on the other voices. The heavy overwriting at the end of section A occurred after section B had already been composed, so it tells us little. But it is interesting that there are two versions of the tenor, side by side, in section C. One of the emendations in the superius goes with the first version of the tenor, suggesting that the composer revised the superius as he worked on the tenor. But it is the absence of a second version of the contratenor that is most suggestive. The basic issue for the composer was, which voice would move in parallel motion with the superius: the tenor a sixth below (first version) or the contratenor a tenth below. The com-

---

45. "Emulation, Competition, and Homage," 5, the source for Brown's comments in the ensuing discussion.

46. "Communications," *JAMS* 36 (1983): 162–163; Professor Adams provided me with her unpublished transcription of Gascogne's setting.

poser tried the tenor first, rejected it, gave it to the contratenor, and then wrote a new tenor. Unfortunately, the fact that this was the final section of the piece (not counting the repeat of the first section) makes it impossible to be certain whether the composer was working one line at a time (as Brown suggested), phrase by phrase, or a combination of the two. In contrast to Bouchel's ungrammatical contratenor, this contratenor plays the role of a bass, integral to the essentially triadic harmonies. Though we will never know for sure, my guess is that this draft grew phrase by phrase. The very fact that the composer could be deliberating about which voice was to move in parallel motion with the superius bespeaks a different conception from Bouchel's: not a two-voice frame (even though superius and tenor always cadence together in the classic stepwise motion to the octave), but three integrated voices, each with its own function.

Adams drew attention to another version of *En contemplant*, found on a fragmentary folio at the end of the manuscript (fol. 78bis[v]; see plate 7.22). In fact, it appears to be a later version of the music on fol. 77[v]. The melisma at the end of the first phrase of the superius, messy on fol. 77[v], is written out cleanly on fol.

PLATE 7.22   UppsU 76a, fol. 78bis[v]: Anonymous, *En contemplant*, fair copy

PLATE 7.23 BerlS 40021, fol. 257aʳ: Anonymous, *In grandi cenaculo*, sketches and draft

78bisᵛ; furthermore, while the version on fol. 77ᵛ has no text, the version on fol. 78bisᵛ has enough words visible to show that the top line was fully texted. The draft on fol. 77ᵛ contains extensive revisions, while in the little that remains of fol. 78bisᵛ there are no changes at all. The first two staves on fol. 78bisᵛ contain fragments of a superius that is identical with the revised version on fol. 77ᵛ. The third staff, however, contains a brief fragment that is different from anything in the two lower voices on fol. 77ᵛ, suggesting that the composer either continued to revise or was composing another setting, with the same superius and different lower voices.

In some cases, sketches can help to identify the compositional point of departure. Consider, for example, the anonymous four-voice setting of an otherwise unknown Easter text, *In grandi cenaculo*. A page of a late fifteenth-century fascicle now bound into BerlS 40021, fol. 257a contains sketches and a draft (see plate 7.23). I describe the six distinct items on the page in some detail because the manuscript is hard to read. Staff 1 begins with [1] a sketch for the tenor, notated beginning on A (see example 7.6, mm. 1–6, Version 1). Immediately following on the same staff and continuing onto the next one is [2] a complete sketch of the tenor, this time up a step, beginning on B. The composer wrote one version of the final phrase at the beginning of staff 2 (example 7.6, mm. 15–18, Version 1), crossed it out and wrote a nearly final version (Version 2–3). The second half of the staff has [3] sketches for another melody, modified and worked out more completely [4] on staff 7.[47] Staves 3–6 contain a complete draft [5] of *In grandi cenaculo*, with the parts in the order [discantus], altus, tenor, bassus (the names are in the right-hand margin). The tenor is completely texted. Staves 8–11 contain an unidentified chant [6] written in *Hufnagel* notation.

The setting of *In grandi cenaculo* is homophonic in texture; there are four distinct phrases, corresponding to the four lines of the text:

Phrase/line	Text	Syllables
1	In grandi cenaculo	7
2	pascha manducatur	6
3	quo ritus legalium	7
4	rite terminatur.	6

The sketches reveal the composer's preoccupation with the tenor, something that would not necessarily be obvious just from examining the music.[48] The only clue from the music is that the tenor is the most interesting line, carefully balanced in range (for example, exploring first the fourth above B, then the fifth below). The composer started notating the tune, but quickly decided to change the pitch level (from A with a flat in the signature up a step to B in the *durus* system). He then wrote out the entire tenor, sketching a few notes of the top voice in phrase 3. He wrote the fourth and final phrase at the beginning of staff 2, then rejected it. He crossed it out and added another version right next to it. As is characteristic of sketches and drafts, this version has no text. Next the composer drafted the entire composition, writing the voices out on the page from high to low. Between the sketches and the draft he made two more changes in the tenor, modifying the cadences of phrases 2 and 4. He added a complete text to the tenor, and introduced a ligature not found in the earlier version, presumably to indicate text placement. After arriving at the final version of the tenor, he com-

47. Just, in *Der Kodex Berlin 40021*, 346, believed it to be another version of *In grandi cenaculo* and published a transcription underlaid with the text (not present in the source); differences in phrase structure and cadences suggest to me that the melody could be completely independent.

48. It is always possible, of course, that there were other sketches no longer extant that could challenge this interpretation.

EXAMPLE 7.6   Anonymous, *In grandi cenaculo*

EXAMPLE 7.6   *(continued)*

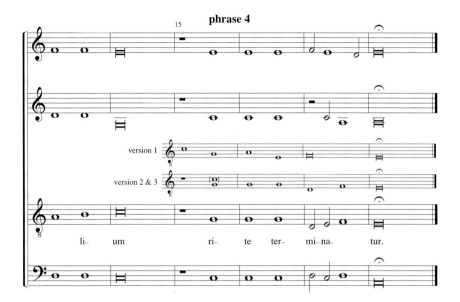

posed the other voices. The evidence for this order comes from measure 17; none of the other three voices works with earlier versions of the tenor.

There are a number of unanswered—and unanswerable—questions about this short composition. Was the composer sketching the other voices elsewhere, or does the music on this page constitute the entire (written) compositional history of this piece? Was it copied once again, perhaps in a format better suited to performance, or are we seeing a compositional effort so slight that the composer was happy to leave it written on a blank page of a fascicle that he then gave away?

In some cases, it is not sketches or drafts that yield information about compositional strategy, but rather a composition that was left unfinished. When composers broke off work part of the way through a composition, they sometimes revealed which voices they were working on first and which they were leaving to last. For example, the German sixteenth-century composer Caspar Othmayr wrote a portion of his four-voice setting of the Christmas hymn *Der Tag der ist so freudenreich* into a choirbook now preserved in Erlangen, but originally for use at Heilbronn (ErlU 473/4).[49] He wrote across the first opening "G. Othmayr calamo scripsit tumultuario a° 45" ("G. Othmayr wrote with a quill precipitously—or in a hurry—in the year [15]45") (see plate 7.24a–b). There is little reason to doubt either the statement or the authenticity of the music as an autograph.[50]

49. This setting is not known from other sources, but Othmayr did set the same tune as a *bicinium*; see Caspar Othmayr, *Ausgewählte Werke: Zweiter Teil*, ed. Hans Albrecht, Das Erbe deutscher Musik 26 (Frankfurt, 1956), no. 34.

50. Othmayr was in Heilbronn in 1545; see Hans Albrecht, *Caspar Othmayr: Leben und Werk* (Kassel, 1950), 12ff. "Othmayr" in the manuscript resembles the signature of an autograph letter

PLATE 7.24a ErlU
473/4, fol. 242^v:
Othmayr, *Der Tag
der ist so freudenreich,*
unfinished fair copy

Othmayr began to write out the piece at the end of the choirbook, but never finished it. The first opening (fols. 242^v–243^r) contains music for all four voices, but the altus is only partially texted and the bassus has no text at all. The second opening (see plate 7.24c–d) has no music for the altus, and no text for the other three parts. In the margin next to the tenor Othmayr wrote: "Restat tenoris apendix" ("The coda (?) of the tenor remains"); and next to the bassus: "Restat non nihil" ("Something remains"). While Othmayr could simply have been copying and not composing, the portions of the music that are written down suggest that he was actually composing even as he was writing it out as a fair copy suitable for performance.

(written in German script); see Carl Philipp Reinhardt, *Die Heidelberger Liedmeister des 16. Jahrhunderts,* Heidelberger Studien zur Musikwissenschaft 8 (Kassel, 1939), plate 8.

PLATE 7.24b   fol. 242ʳ

It is helpful to compare Othmayr's two settings—this unfinished four-voice setting from 1545 and the complete version for two voices that he published in 1547 (*Bicinia sacra. Schöne geistliche Lieder* [Nuremberg, 1547[18]])—from the point of view of both text and melody (see examples 7.7 and 7.8). The melody, as given in the 1547 version, consists of eight phrases, the poem of ten lines:

Section	Musical phrase	Text
A	1	Der Tag, der ist so freudenreich
	2	aller Kreature.
A [repeat]	1	Denn Gottes Sohn von Himmelreich
	2	über die Nature
B	3	von einer Jungfrau ist geborn.
	4	Maria, du bist auserkorn,
	5	daß du Mutter wärest.

PLATE 7.24c
fol. 243ᵛ

A'	6 [⁻1]	Was geschach so wunderlich?
	7	Gottes Suhn von Himmelreich,
	8	der ist Mensch geboren.

The melody in the bicinium is presented without elaboration in the upper voice ("vox vulgaris"). In the four-voice setting it occurs primarily in the tenor, with slight elaboration: brief phrases separated by rests (see example 7.8). In the four-voice version (see example 7.7) the bassus usually works closely with the tenor to form a series of two-voice modules. After the chordal texture of the opening measures, the cantus acts as the harbinger of the tenor, introducing the tune accompanied by the altus, and then serving as a countermelody to the tenor.

While it is hard to be certain of the order of events on these two openings, a few observations can be made and a few questions raised. Othmayr broke off

PLATE 7.24d
fol. 244ʳ

after the first few measures of the final section (A', phrase 6). It is suggestive that he wrote out the cantus—a voice that never rested—as well as the tenor (the main presenter of the melody) and the bassus (which functioned only to accompany the tenor), thus showing the bare bones of the piece, but left out the altus, a filler voice that could have been the last to be composed.

Why did he leave the piece unfinished? Two explanations seem plausible. He made a major mistake with the text on the first opening. The test, as found in the tenor, is:

Der tag der ist so freudenreich
aller creaturen
Gottes sun von himelreich
ist uber die nature.

EXAMPLE 7.7   Othmayr, *Der Tag der ist so freudenreich* (4 vv.)

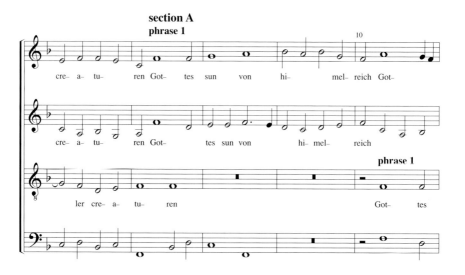

This agrees in all but minor details with the 1547 version. The problem lies with
the cantus.[51] In measure 13, instead of "ist uber die nature," the text reads "und
der ist mensch geboren der ist mensch ge: [boren] von einer Junckfrau ist." Perhaps Othmayr was thinking of the text for phrase 8 as found in his other setting

51. I have not seen this manuscript except on microfilm. The text of the altus appears to have
been emended but the earlier reading is not legible.

EXAMPLE 7.7   *continued*

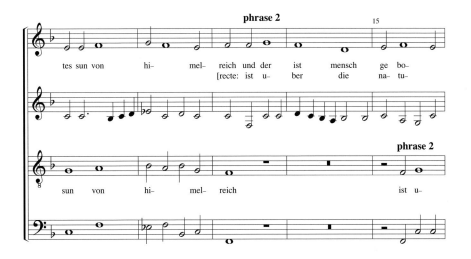

("der ist Mensch geboren"). The continuation, "von einer junckfrau ist," is correct. Presumably, it would not have been too hard to fix this mistake. A second,
potentially more serious, problem occurred on the second opening. The B section of the hymn has three phrases (nos. 3 – 5). In the published bicinium, Othmayr used each phrase once, but in this manuscript version he set phrase 4 twice.
The counterpoint is not exact, which means that it was not simply a copying
error. This seems to me to be a compositional error in handling the melody; it

EXAMPLE 7.7 *(continued)*

fols. 242ᵛ- 243ʳ altus missing on this folio

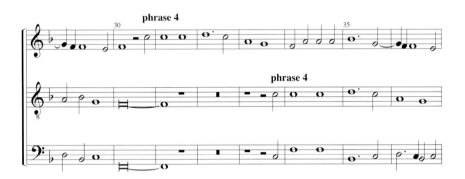

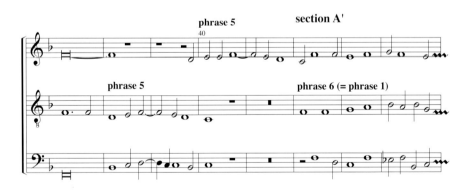

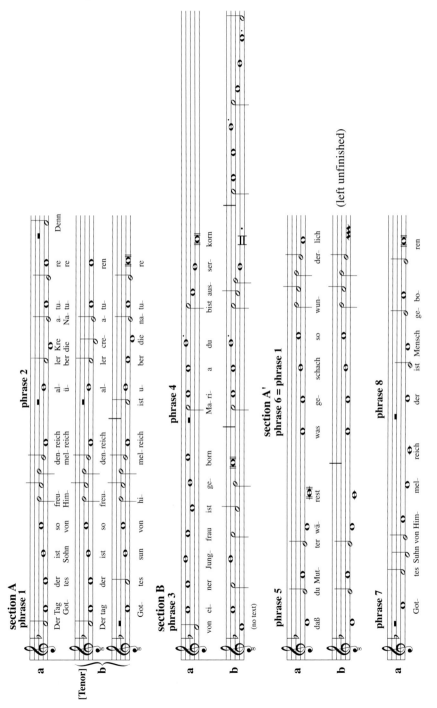

would be strange, given the style of this setting, for only this phrase to be repeated.

Were these mistakes the reason why he abandoned the piece? While the question must remain unanswered, this example does suggest that a careful study of pieces left incomplete even in formal manuscripts such as choirbooks may well yield clues about compositional process.

The examples presented thus far, spanning a period of nearly a century, show composers dealing in a variety of ways with a line serving as the point of departure, one of them newly composed (the tenor in the four-voice Easter song), three pre-existent to some extent (the tune in the superius of the Uppsala chanson, the chorale melody in the tenor of Othmayr's setting, the pitches of the tenor in Bouchel's chanson). The variety of approaches is striking, as is the diversity of musical structure and style.

The sketches also reveal some of the techniques that composers used to work, thus also conveying, though indirectly, important information about musical structure. There is considerable evidence that composers worked with individual segments—building blocks, as it were. The work of the Catalan composer Pujol is a good example. Pujol sketched a four-voice composition in quasi-score on fol. 57b of his commonplace book, BarcOC 28 (see plate 7.3, and example 7.9, Version A on page 189). He divided the music into seven segments, each identified by its own mark. Fortunately, the next stage—or at least a later stage—that this music passed through has been preserved elsewhere in the same manuscript. Folio 2 has Pujol's complete draft, dated "9 de iuy 1545," in choirbook format (see plate 7.4, and example 7.9, Version B on this page). The partial (or at least schematic) text identifies the piece as a Kyrie. This draft comes close to being a fair copy; it is virtually "clean," with only two minor changes.

EXAMPLE 7.9   Pujol, Kyrie

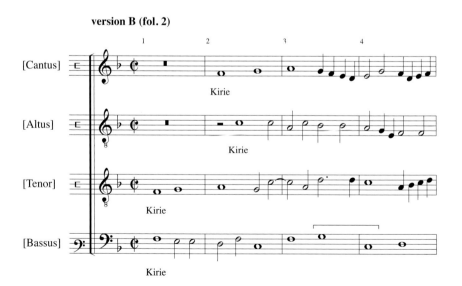

The changes suggest that Pujol was continuing to polish even as he prepared the draft in choirbook format.[52] The sketch on fol. 57b begins in the middle of measure 7; perhaps he sketched the beginning elsewhere. What is fascinating is that the segments of the sketch are not always contiguous. Did he leave the links between segments for the next stage of work?

This segmentation into minute particles—considerably smaller in some cases than phrases or musically meaningful units—is reminiscent of the recommen-

EXAMPLE 7.9   (*continued*)

version A (fol. 57)

52. My reason for calling it a draft comes from Pujol's work on the Agnus dei of the same Mass. Fol. 36 contains what is more readily identifiable as a draft, with erasures and cancellations, and with no text. The fair copy on fol. 33 is fully texted and written in a very clear hand.

EXAMPLE 7.9   *(continued)*

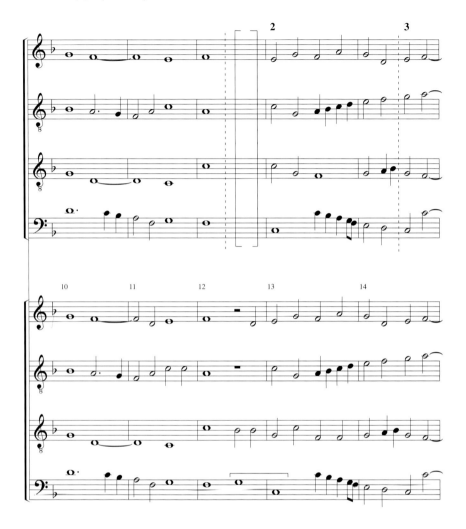

dations for beginning composers offered by the Lutheran theologian and music pedagogue Johannes Frosch.[53] The final chapter, "De ratione componendi, ut vocant, et condendis cantionibus," is a synopsis of a counterpoint treatise, addressing, for example, voice-leading, prohibition of the tritone, and the use of

53. *Rerum musicarum opusculum* (Strassburg, 1532; earliest extant edition, 1535). Frosch's treatise, a textbook intended for school use, is quite unusual in several respects. Instead of being a simple introduction to the rudiments of music (pitch and rhythm), it is a brief survey (only 39 fols.) of both *musica theorica* and *practica*; it is also written in an unusually abstruse and learned Latin. Hellmuth Christian Wolff, "Die ästhetische Auffassung der Parodiemesse des 16. Jahrhunderts," *Miscelánea en Homenaje a Monseñor Higinio Anglés*, 2 vols. (Barcelona, 1958–1961), 2: 1011–1019, first drew attention to the passages under consideration, which he cited as an example of parody. Lewis Lockwood,

EXAMPLE 7.9   *continued*

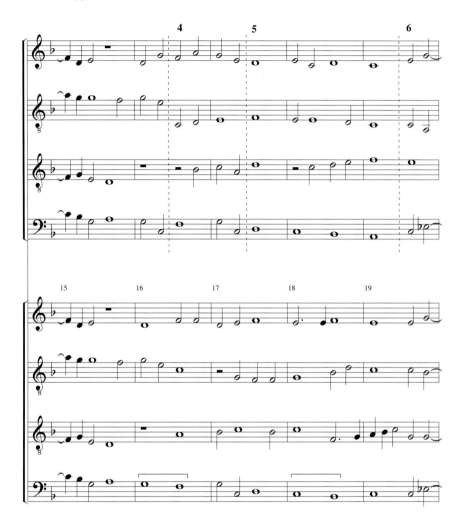

rests. Near the end of the chapter, Frosch recommended that the student study the compositions of good composers and select the best phrases to be assembled in a collection "so that when the need for them will come to you, you will have them ready, which you will adapt to your ways and in time insert into your own song."[54] He recognized that the benefits came from seeing how the phrases worked and from using them in compositions.

"On 'Parody' as Term and Concept in 16th-Century Music," in *Aspects of Medieval and Renaissance Music: A Birthday Offering to Gustave Reese*, ed. Jan LaRue (New York, 1966; repr. 1978), 569, quite rightly questioned that interpretation. On Frosch, see Clement A. Miller, "Frosch, Johannes," *NG*.

54. "Ut si quando tibi venerit illorum usus, tum in promptu habeas, quod similiter tuis modis adhibeas, & in tempore, tuo cantui inseras"; *Rerum musicarum*, sig. E.

EXAMPLE 7.9   *(continued)*

He illustrated his points with two motets, presumably his own compositions, the four-voice *Qui de terra est* and the six-voice *Nesciens mater*. For each
motet, Frosch first provided a series of examples, notated in choirbook format, consisting either of segments actually drawn from the two motets or passages that could be used in place of the ones in the motet. He labeled each
of these segments with a Roman numeral (the alternatives were identified as
"aliud"). Then he provided the music for the entire motet, also in choirbook
format, marked with lines and the same Roman numerals to show where the
segments occurred (see plates 7.25–26). On sig. F ii^r, at the end of the exam-

ples and before the six-voice motet, he added the note: "Here follows the application of examples of this kind in music (*in cantu*)." Most of the passages occur at the ends of phrases, in conjunction with cadences. For *Qui de terra* and its second part, *Et testimonium*, shown in example 7.10 (on pp. 197–202), there are ten segments, plus five alternatives (marked below in italics); curiously, one of the segments (VIII) does not occur in the motet:

First part:

I

Qui de terra est, de terra *loquitur,*

II, III

qui de celo venit, *super omnes est,*
et quod vidit et audivit, hoc testatur.

Second part:
Et testimonium eius nemo accipit,

         IIII, V   *VI, VII*

qui autem *acceperit eius* testimonium *signavit*

         IX, X

quia deus *verax est.*

For *Nesciens mater*, there are nine segments, and no alternatives. The segments for the four-voice piece are shorter, ranging from two to four measures, while those in the six-voice piece are as long as ten measures.

The choice of material is in some ways rather surprising. The segments do not coincide with musical phrases, nor do they present the material we would think of as characteristic or defining, such as the motivic opening of a point of imitation or a particular sequence of chords. Instead, it is the connective tissue, the measures leading up to cadences. The impression that these examples create—like Pujol's sketch in quasi-score—is of a piece constructed like a mosaic. In Frosch's case the stones are interchangeable. The segments are often contiguous, and as a result we see a passage divided up into tiny components, too small to make much sense musically, but evidently large enough to be thought of as building blocks.[55]

———

The examples show that there was no single "compositional process" for music of this period, any more than there can be for music of the nineteenth or twentieth century. Would we expect Copland, Stravinsky, and Bartók all to work the same way? How a composer worked depended on factors such as his skill level, the kind of space he had available for writing, the number of voices, the conventions of genre, and demands of style. The process is inextricably bound up with the musical ideas he is working out for each piece. Still, certain

<hr/>

55. The idea of composing by assembling stock phrases (like painting by the numbers) reflects the pedagogical approach used in organ fundamenta. Buchner, for example, provided examples of how to move from one sonority to another with schematic tables (if the tenor ascends by a second, if the tenor ascends by a third, etc.).

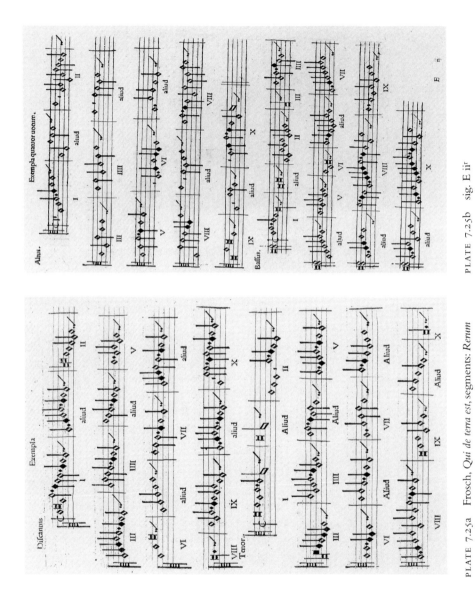

PLATE 7.25a   Frosch, *Qui de terra est*, segments: *Rerum musicarum*, sig. E i^v

PLATE 7.25b   sig. E ii^r

194

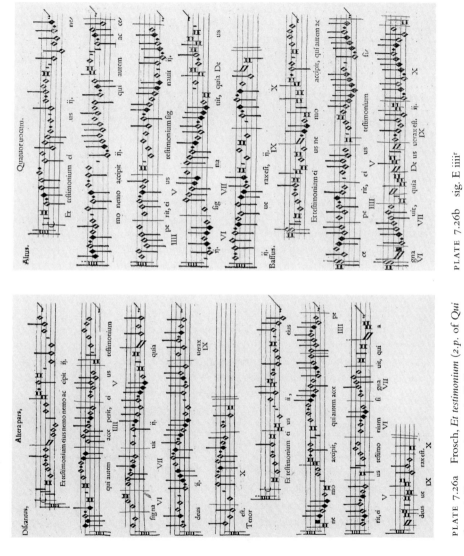

PLATE 7.26a   Frosch, *Et testimonium (2.p.* of *Qui de terra*): *Rerum musicarum,* sig. E iii^v

PLATE 7.26b   sig. E iiii^r

195

principles emerge that seem to cut across time, geography, genre, and even style.

Composers generally used the kind of notation characteristic of the type of music: mensural notation in separate parts for vocal music, one of the varieties of tablature (including open score) for instrumental music. Composers of instrumental music had the possibility of seeing the complete sonority at a glance, while composers of vocal music had to be able to read in separate parts. Because the notation of music for solo instruments had to convey the entire fabric of the composition (both the separate lines and the resulting harmonies), it would seem logical that these notations could have been useful for composers of vocal music as well as of instrumental music. While there is theoretical evidence linking tablature with composition, the manuscript evidence indicates that instrumental notations were used for composing *instrumental* music.

The nearly complete absence of scores used for composing vocal music is striking. The only example found to date—the eight-voice Magnificat from CoimU 48—was probably composed by an organist. We must conclude that composers could manage the complicated polyphony of the time without using the format that seems indispensable to us. Working on short segments using quasi-score format or on longer segments using separate parts, they were able to sketch and draft the early versions of their music. It is of course possible that scores used for composing vocal music will be discovered, but I suspect that at least for the period before the second half of the sixteenth century, newly discovered manuscripts will tell the same story as the sources already known to us.

The process was essentially additive. In many cases composers began at least the written phase of composition by sketching brief segments which they later combined in draft form. This way of working is readily comprehensible for compositions that consist of distinct phrases ("points of imitation"). In many cases it is clear that composers worked segment by segment even when they had a single line—either an existing tune or a newly composed tenor—as their point of departure. Sometimes they worked first with two "essential" voices and added a third, while at other times the grid of essential versus added shifted from phrase to phrase.

Composers of vocal music kept track by reading voices one against another, by adding vertical lines to demarcate segments, and by counting tactus. They also checked their work by performing it.

The process of composing could continue from the earliest sketches through the preparation of a fair copy and even beyond. It is also clear, however, that not every composition passed through every stage. Depending on the kind of music and the facility of the composer, it is conceivable that a composition could have been written out from the first as a draft or even as a fair copy.

These principles are only guidelines, a kind of paradigm. To test the paradigm and to see how the principles play out in the working methods of master composers, we turn now to a consideration of several test cases.

EXAMPLE 7.10   Anonymous (Frosch?), *Et testimonium* (*2.p.* of *Qui de terra*): motet and "aliud" segments

Altera pars

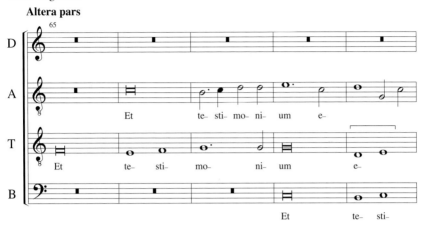

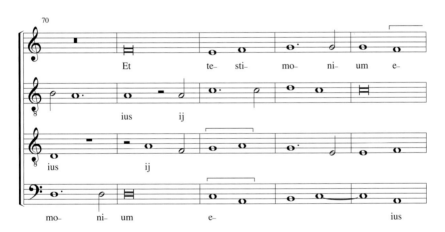

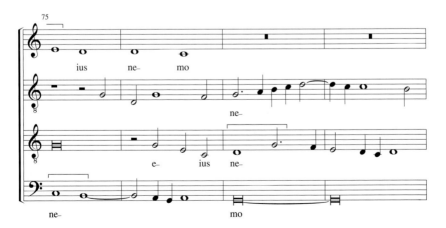

EXAMPLE 7.10   (*continued*)

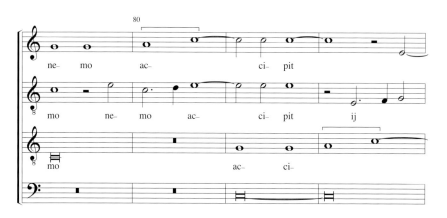

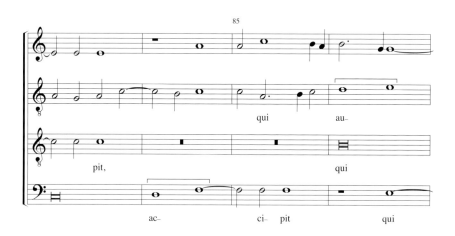

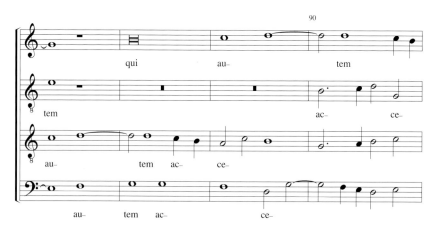

EXAMPLE 7.10   (*continued*)

EXAMPLE 7.10   (*continued*)

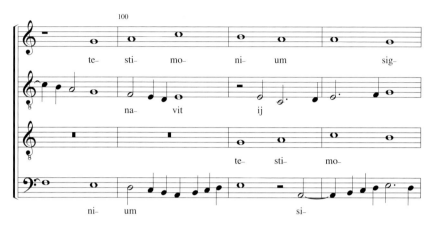

EXAMPLE 7.10   (*continued*)

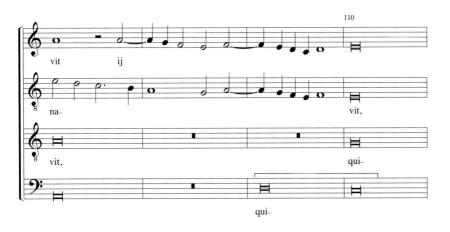

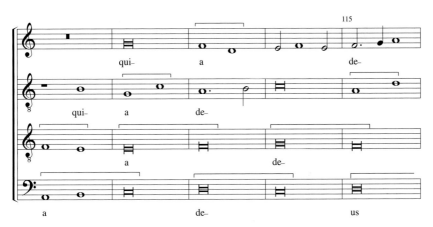

EXAMPLE 7.10 *(continued)*

PART II

FOUR CASE STUDIES

CHAPTER EIGHT

FRANCESCO CORTECCIA

In the previous chapters, I used manuscript, theoretical, documentary, and iconographic evidence to construct an abstract paradigm for how fifteenth- and sixteenth-century composers worked. The conclusions were inevitably— and intentionally—schematic. The goal of part II is to translate an abstract paradigm into concrete reality by examining the working methods of four major composers: Francesco Corteccia, Cipriano de Rore, Henricus Isaac, and Giovanni Pierluigi da Palestrina. The fortuitous preservation of autograph composing manuscripts by each one of them gives us a broad perspective on musical practices.

In considering their working methods, we will need to see what principles remain constant and what changes from composer to composer, style to style. We do not have the luxury afforded scholars working in later periods of seeing many pieces by a given composer pass through a number of different stages. The evidence we have concerns only a few pieces and then usually for only one or two stages in the entire process. But even so, it helps us to understand both the diversity of methods and the universality of some of the aspects of musical language.

––––––––

Francesco Corteccia was the leading Italian composer in Florence during the first half of the sixteenth century, one of the few Italians to achieve prominence in an era still dominated by composers from beyond the Alps.[1] Born in Florence in 1502, he spent his entire life in his native city, serving in the Medici-controlled institutions of the Cathedral and Baptistry, as well as San Lorenzo. In his capacity as canon of San Lorenzo, he kept records of financial agreements, providing examples of his handwriting from 1563 until 1570 (see plate 8.1).[2] In

---

1. Francesco Corteccia, *Collected Secular Works*, ed. Frank D'Accone, Music of the Florentine Renaissance, CMM 32, 8–10 (Rome, 1981); Mario Fabbri, "La vita e l'ignota opera-prima di Francesco Corteccia musicista italiano del Rinascimento (Firenze 1502–Firenze 1571)," *Chigiana* 22 (1965): 185–217; Andrew C. Minor, "Corteccia, (Pier) Francesco," *NG*; Alfred Einstein, *The Italian Madrigal* (Princeton, 1949; 1971).

2. FlorSL 2129 is entitled "Libro di ricordi" (1541–87). The document given in plate 8.1 dates from 18 May 1564; Corteccia attests that he wrote the document: "Io franc.⁰ Cortecci scrissi detto

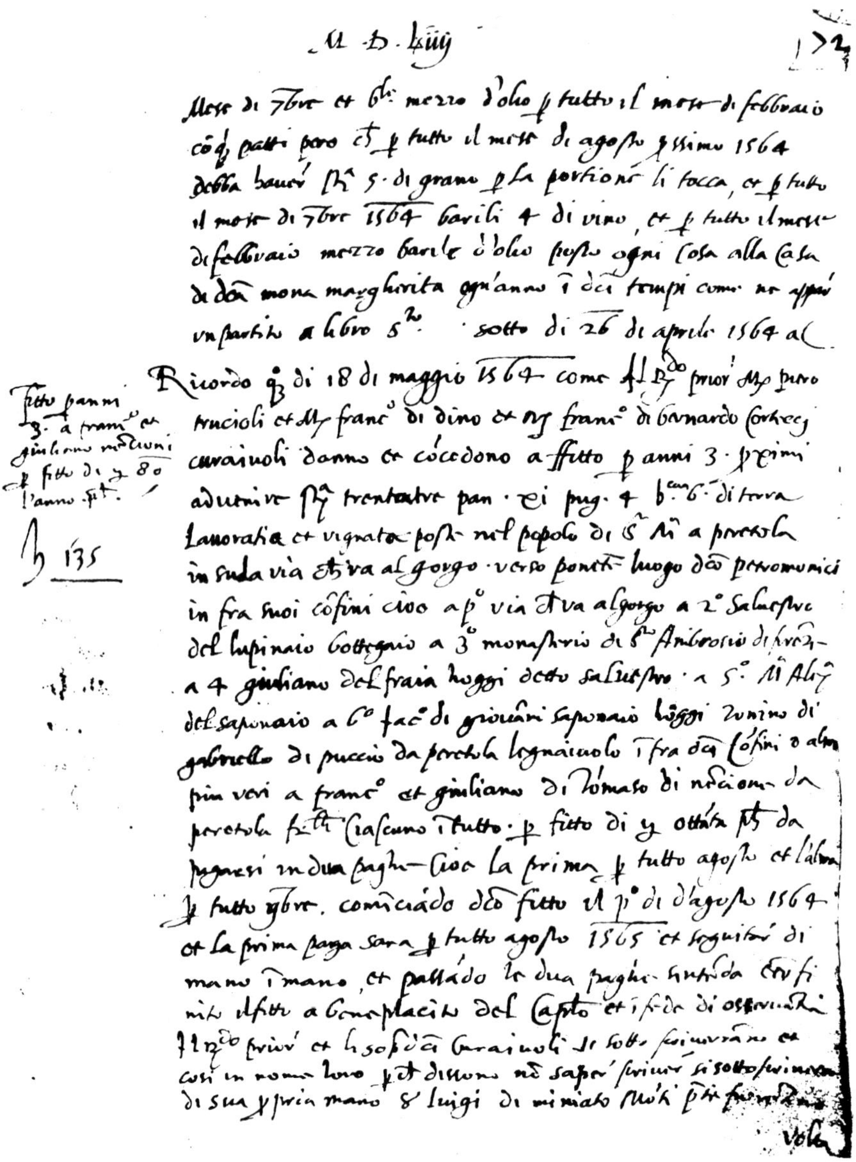

PLATE 8.1a   FlorSL 2129, fol. 72^r: Corteccia autograph

ricordo . . . et in fede mi sono sotto scritto di mia propria mano . . ." I found this rare example of Corteccia's hand while searching (in vain) for a "Libro di ricordi" from 1559 mentioned by Fabbri, "La vita," 208. Fabbri listed several other autographs, but the only one I was able to trace (courtesy of Enzo Settesoldi) was a 1559 *supplica* in Florence, Opera di S. Maria del Fiore, Suppliche, Rescritti e ordini del governo, fol. 399.

PLATE 8.1b   fol. 72ᵛ

his publications he called himself *maestro di cappella* to Duke Cosimo I, although the duke did not maintain a private chapel; Corteccia evidently functioned as the court composer, providing music for Medici festivities and theatrical events.[3] He composed over one hundred madrigals, for four, five and six

3. Kirkendale, *The Court Musicians*, 643–644 and passim; Anthony Cummings, *The Politicized Muse: Music for Medici Festivals, 1512–1537* (Princeton, 1992), 76–79.

voices.[4] A priest, he also composed a great deal of sacred music. He published two volumes of responsories in 1570, shortly before his death in 1571; two volumes of motets appeared posthumously. Other music (a cycle of hymns, a cycle of Mass propers, and two Passions) remained in manuscript; his vernacular setting of the Lamentations, which may have been published, is no longer extant.[5]

Most of Corteccia's activity as a madrigal composer probably dates from the 1530s and 1540s, and possibly as early as the 1520s. In the dedication to his *Primo libro de madriali a quattro voci* (1544), he referred to his madrigals as "these few blossoms of my youth" ("questi pochi fiori della mia giovenile età"). On the one hand, he seemed to distance himself from the music

> because madrigals are not only feeble and frivolous things for the most part, but also lascivious and unsuitable to a man of my years and of my calling, who, as a priest, should be occupied with the true praises of Most Holy God rather than with the incredible trifles of love, such as would be expected of a layman. . . .[6]

But on the other hand, he took the trouble to publish what was in effect a complete works edition of his madrigals. As the dedication makes clear, he was dismayed to find his name on music he had not composed, as well as the name of other composers on his own music; furthermore, the music was full of errors.[7]

> For the principal reason which moved me to do this is that some of these madrigals of mine had been printed by others (as anyone can verify) under the names of other authors, who in truth are more excellent and more famous than I. And it seemed wrong for me to permit my works to bring either injury or shame to

4. The madrigals have been edited by D'Accone in Corteccia, *Collected Secular Works*. On Corteccia's madrigals and their place in Italian theater, see Howard Mayer Brown, "A Typology of Francesco Corteccia's Madrigals: Notes towards a History of Theatrical Music in Sixteenth-Century Italy," in *The Well Enchanting Skill: Music, Poetry, and Drama in the Culture of the Renaissance. Essays in Honour of F. W. Sternfeld*, ed. John Caldwell, Edward Olleson, and Susan Wollenberg (Oxford, 1990), 3–28. See also Iain Fenlon and James Haar, *The Italian Madrigal in the Early Sixteenth Century: Sources and Interpretation* (Cambridge, 1988), esp. 264–273.

5. David A. Sutherland, "A Second Corteccia Manuscript in the Archives of Santa Maria del Fiore," *JAMS* 25 (1972): 79–85.

6. The translation is by D'Accone (Corteccia, *Collected Secular Works*, 8, p. xxvii). The original text of the letter of dedication is given in Fenlon and Haar, *The Italian Madrigal*, 265–266. Facsimiles of the title pages and letters of dedication are in Corteccia, *Collected Secular Works*. (Note that two of the plates were exchanged: the dedication identified as being in the 1547 edition of Corteccia's first book of madrigals is actually in the second book, while the lower of the two pages labeled as being in the second book actually belongs in the first book.) An early biographer, Michele Poccianti (*Catalogus Scriptorum Florentinorum* [Florence, 1589], 71), wrote, "While he was still a young man, he composed not a few madrigals, full of the greatest pleasantness" ("Elaboravit adhuc iuvenis madrigales non nullos, eximia iuncunditate refertos . . ."); translation and citation from Sutherland, "A Second Corteccia Manuscript," 85. None of the madrigals that Corteccia wrote after 1547 has survived.

7. Einstein, *The Italian Madrigal*, 276, first recognized Corteccia's volumes as an early example of a collected edition. Between 1539 and 1544, when his first book was published, fourteen madrigals that Corteccia would subsequently claim as his own and publish in one of his three books had appeared in print without his consent, some in Arcadelt's madrigal books, some in other anthologies. See Corteccia, *Collected Secular Works*, 8, p. xiii. For others that he never claimed, see Brown, "A Typology," 5.

someone else; also (to tell the truth) I questioned whether those composers, in attributing other people's errors to me, would themselves not judge me too vain and ambitious. On the other hand, printed under my name were some other [madrigals] which I freely confess to never having seen, let alone written, and thus I did not want anyone, being misled by such an ascription, to hold me in higher esteem than I actually merit . . . To these reasons one might add that my works, as well as the others, were full of the ugliest mistakes and of the gravest errors, both in words and music, which, as anyone who wishes will be able to see, has not occurred here, both because of our care and diligence and because of the good work and industry of the printer.[8]

Corteccia published his first book with the Venetian firm of Girolamo Scotto. Three years later, in 1547, during a hiatus in Scotto's activities as a music publisher, he reissued the volume in a second expanded and revised edition with the firm of Antonio Gardano. The same year he published two additional volumes: *Libro secondo de madriali a quatro voci* and *Libro primo de madriali a cinque & a sei voci*. These publications constitute Corteccia's canon, establishing not only the authentic works but also the readings most closely linked to the composer himself.[9]

Corteccia evidently took seriously the task of producing good editions. He wrote in the dedication to the second book of four-voice madrigals:

> I have sent the printer this second book of my Madrigals, having cleansed them first of the many errors of which they were full, either because of printing defects or because of whatever reason.[10]

He might have added that publishing these volumes afforded him the opportunity to make revisions in his music. In fact, he is one of the earliest composers for whom we have a significant number of compositions in several versions.[11] We know that much of Corteccia's music had a long period before reaching a final form. In 1544 he referred to his responsories for Holy Week as though they were complete. But Frank D'Accone has shown that he must have revised them a number of times before the final version was published in 1570.[12]

Until now, apart from this evidence of revision, the only other information we have had about Corteccia's practices as a composer came from his will. Like several other sixteenth-century composers, he used a stone tablet for composing,

8. Corteccia, *Collected Secular Works*, 8, p. xxvii.

9. The only piece whose authenticity might be questioned is *Quando prend'il camino*, included in the 1544 edition of the first book but not the second edition in 1547. This situation stands in stark contrast to the severe problems with authenticity that plague research on Verdelot's madrigals.

10. Corteccia, *Collected Secular Works*, 9, p. xxi. Fenlon and Haar, *The Italian Madrigal*, 269.

11. Einstein, *The Italian Madrigal*, 278, noted that Corteccia revised *Un dì lieto giamai*, eliminating the "Landini cadence-formula." For other examples of revisions, see Corteccia, *Collected Secular Works*, 8, p. xiii, and the critical notes; Frank D'Accone, "Updating the Style: Francesco Corteccia's Revisions in his Responsories for Holy Week," in *Music and Context: Essays for John M. Ward*, ed. Anne Dhu Shapiro (Harvard University, 1985), 32–53; Francesco Corteccia, *Collected Sacred Works*, ed. Frank D'Accone, Music of the Florentine Renaissance, CMM 32, 11: *Music for the Triduum Sacrum* (American Institute of Musicology, 1985).

12. D'Accone, "Updating the Style," 35–36.

which he bequeathed to his student, Michele Federighi.[13] He also left him his scores (*spartiti*), which are no longer extant; in the absence of any indication of their date or contents we should not assume that he used them for composing. They could easily be the sorts of manuscript anthologies recommended by Zacconi and Galilei, notebooks for copying and saving music.[14]

The discovery that Corteccia had used the blank staves of an old manuscript—FlorBN Magl. 117—for sketching and drafting his music gives us a rare view of the very earliest stages of composing and helps us understand more about Corteccia's compositional process.[15] Half of Corteccia's sketches in FlorBN Magl. 117 are for unknown compositions that may no longer be extant, if indeed they were ever finished; the absence of any text makes the search difficult (see table 8.2 at the end of this chapter for an inventory of the late additions to FlorBN Magl. 117). Five relate to *Domine non secundum*, a motet that has not survived elsewhere in a complete version.[16] Nine of the sketches are for three madrigals that he published in 1544 and 1547: *Fammi pur guerr'Amor, Con quel coltel,* and *Amanti i 'l vo pur dir*. The sketches in FlorBN Magl. 117 reveal in a general way how Corteccia worked, but they also let us watch several madrigals being transformed from sketches and drafts to completed compositions.

Corteccia used several different formats for sketching and drafting his music.[17] The choice depended partly on the space available to him—how many blank staves there were, and where they were located—and partly on the length of the music. For brief passages, ranging in length from as little as a few measures to as long as a phrase, he often employed a quasi-score format, in which the voices sometimes were sometimes placed in order from high to low, but often not (see plates 8.2 and 8.5). When the space did not even allow the four voices to be arranged in quasi-score, he simply fitted in the music as best he could (see plates 8.6 and 8.8). In one case, he used a kind of compact choirbook, cantus and bassus on the left, tenor and altus on the right (see plate 8.4). For extended passages, such as the draft of *Domine non secundum*, he usually wrote the voices as separate parts, deploying the space in the opening as if it were a choirbook, each voice in its own quadrant (see plate 8.3, half of an opening in choirbook format).

Corteccia employed different formats for different versions of the same piece. For example, he drafted the opening measures for all four voices of *Amanti i 'l vo pur dir* in quasi-score on the right-hand side of fol. 37ʳ (staves 2–5), in the order cantus, bassus, altus, tenor (see plate 8.2).[18] He made changes as he worked: there

13. See chap. 5. On Federighi, see D'Accone, "Updating the Style," 38.

14. Owens, "The Milan Partbooks," 294–295.

15. Jessie Ann Owens, "Francesco Corteccia's Sketchbook: New Evidence about Compositional Process," paper presented at the annual meeting of the American Musicological Society in November 1992. See chap. 6.

16. See Richard Sherr, "*Illibata dei virgo nutrix* and Josquin's Roman Style," *JAMS* 41 (1988): 434–464, which contains an appendix, "*Domine, non secundum peccata* and a Roman Motet Tradition," p. 455–464, listing eighteen settings.

17. See chap. 7.

18. The madrigal was first published under Corteccia's name in *Il primo libro de i madrigali di Maistre Ihan* (Venice, 1541), and later included in both editions of Corteccia's *Primo libro*. An error

are two versions of the tenor line and a minor emendation in the altus (slip of the pen E instead of F?) (see example 8.1, mm. 1–4, Version A). Then he shifted to choirbook format for drafting the cantus and tenor for the entire first part of the madrigal and the beginning of the second part (fol. 39ᵛ) (see plate 8.3 and example 8.1, mm. 1–20, Version B). It seems likely, given the nature of the music, that he was drafting all four voices at this point, and that only half of the draft has survived. He may have already filled fol. 40ʳ with sketches; perhaps he jotted down the altus and bassus on a loose scrap of paper or on an erasable tablet.

The sketches help to establish the chronology of work on the piece. Corteccia began with the four-voice opening, emending the tenor. Next he drafted at least two of the voices, and probably all four, using the emended tenor of measures 3–4; at this point he had arrived at virtually the final version of measures 1–8, although the tenor was still using the clef (c2) that would subsequently be assigned to the altus. The shift in clef may indicate that decisions about cleffing could have been made in response to the actual range of the parts rather than as a "precompositional" choice. Next he reworked the final measures of the first section (9–14), keeping the same cadence but altering the counterpoint. In drafting the beginning of the second section, he reached the final version of measures 15–19; he would subsequently change the continuation in the cantus. At some point during this process of drafting, he added a partial text in the tenor, indicating the beginning of each phrase with the first word or syllable.

The sketches show two different stages of work on this madrigal. In the first, Corteccia worked with a very short segment—just four measures—with the voices positioned close to one another, though not aligned or ordered high to low. In the second, he drafted an extended segment in separate parts. The sketches suggest that his choice of format was related not only to length but possibly also to the stage in the process. It would be interesting to know if he worked out every phrase of a composition in quasi-score, or just the hard parts, for example, the beginnings or the cadences.

It is striking that Corteccia did not use score format at all in his sketchbook. There is even evidence that he did not use score in the earlier versions that are no longer extant, for example, those possibly written on his slate. The music on fol. 20ʳ (see plate 8.4) is an eight-measure phrase from an unknown four-voice piece written in an imitative style (see example 8.2). The voices work in pairs, cantus and bassus presenting the motive on G an octave apart, and altus and tenor presenting the motive on D at the same pitch level. The placement on the page suggests that he worked out this phrase in terms of two-voice pairs, first the cantus–bassus frame on the left, then, on the right, the middle voices, which had to be accommodated by extending the staff with hand-drawn lines. Note that although cantus and bassus are first in terms of being written down, the tenor and altus come first in the actual music. That suggests that this passage is not the opening of a piece but rather fits in some way with a host composition whose identity is not now known. Significantly, Corteccia made a mistake in notating

in the bass of the 1541 print made the parts unsingable as printed. The text, a ballata-madrigal, is by Alfonso d'Avalos. See Corteccia, *Collected Secular Works*, 8: 80–82 and p. xxv.

PLATE 8.2   FlorBN Magl. 117, fol. 37ʳ: Corteccia, *Amanti i 'l vo pur dir*, sketches

PLATE 8.3   FlorBN Magl. 117, fol. 39ᵛ: Corteccia, *Amanti i 'l vo pur dir*, draft

EXAMPLE 8.I   Corteccia, *Amanti i 'l vo pur dir*, mm. I–20

EXAMPLE 8.1   *(continued)*

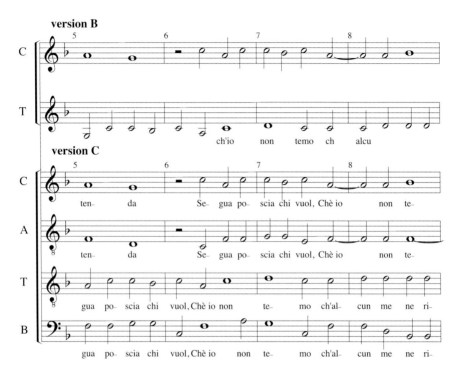

EXAMPLE 8.1   (*continued*)

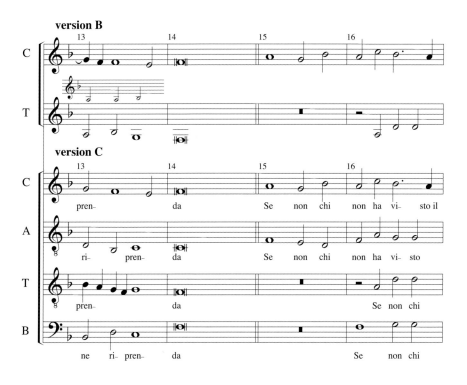

EXAMPLE 8.2   Corteccia, unidentified composition from FlorBN Magl. 117, fol. 20ʳ

PLATE 8.4   FlorBN Magl. 117, fol. 20ʳ: Corteccia, unidentified composition, sketch

the rhythm. In order for the four voices to work together to reach a cadence on G in measure 8, an extra semibreve rest at the beginning of cantus and bassus must be suppressed. If he had sketched out this passage on the slate in score, I do not believe that he would have made this particular mistake. In making a link between this passage and the host composition, he was evidently keeping track of the relative position of the outer voices and of the inner voices but not of all four together.

As interesting as it may be to watch how Corteccia actually set the music out on the page, it is even more interesting to consider the nature of the changes themselves. For two of the madrigals, the sketches and drafts permit us not only to trace the genesis of a composition, but also to learn something about his values as a composer.

Four of the sketches relate to *Fammi pur guerr'Amor*, a madrigal that Corteccia not only published but also continued to revise even after it appeared in print.[19] *Fammi pur guerr'Amor* appears anonymously in BrusC 27731, a manuscript that Haar and Fenlon date ca. 1535–40.[20] It also found its way (without reference to Corteccia's authorship) into Arcadelt's best-seller, the *Primo libro* of 1539 (or possibly 1538—both the first edition and the Milanese pirated edition are missing).[21] Corteccia included *Fammi pur guerr'Amor* in his *Primo libro* of 1544; three years later he included a slightly revised version in the second edition.

Fammi pur guerr'Amor (see example 8.3) is characteristic in many ways of the early madrigal as it developed in Florence and Rome.[22] The setting is syllabic, except for occasional flourishes at cadences. The texture is predominantly chordal, though there is also some imitation, for example, in the opening phrase. Corteccia chose a tonal type based on F, with a flat in the signature. Written in low clefs, the cantus and tenor occupy the plagal octave, an octave apart, while the altus and bassus occupy the authentic range, an octave apart.[23] The ambitus of the voices, while exceeding the usual range of an octave in both the tenor and bass, nonetheless is recognizable according to the patterns that were becoming standard just when this piece was published. A contemporary theorist or musician would likely have identified the piece as mode 6.

The text, by an unknown poet, consists of thirteen seven- or eleven-syllable lines; Frank D'Accone has classified it as a madrigal proper, the freest of the verse forms then in use.[24] The gist of the text is that Love, in the form of the arrow-

19. See the editions by D'Accone in Corteccia, *Collected Secular Works*, 8: 68–70 and by Albert Seay in Jacob Arcadelt, *Opera omnia*, CMM 31 (American Institute of Musicology, 1965-1970), 2: 29–31. Example 8.3 is based on D'Accone's edition, with the permission of American Institute of Musicology/Hänssler-Verlag.

20. *The Italian Madrigal*, 149. *Fammi pur guerr'Amor* appears on fols. 29ᵛ–30ʳ, followed by *Con quel coltel*, another Corteccia madrigal that we will be considering shortly.

21. See Thomas Bridges, "The Publishing of Arcadelt's First Book of Madrigals," Ph.D. diss., Harvard University, 1982; variants for *Fammi pur guerr'Amor* are listed on pp. 633–636. On the dating of the first edition, see p. 70.

22. For the early development of the madrigal, see Fenlon and Haar, *The Italian Madrigal*.

23. The ranges are: cantus c–cc; altus F–f; tenor C–c (plus extension to f); and bassus FF–F (plus extension to B♭).

24. Corteccia, *Collected Secular Works*, 8, p. xxiv. See Don Harrán, "Verse Types in the Early Madrigal," *JAMS* 22 (1969): 27–53. On Corteccia's musical response to verse types, see Brown, "A Typology," 14–19.

EXAMPLE 8.3   Corteccia, *Fammi pur guerr'Amor*

EXAMPLE 8.3   (*continued*)

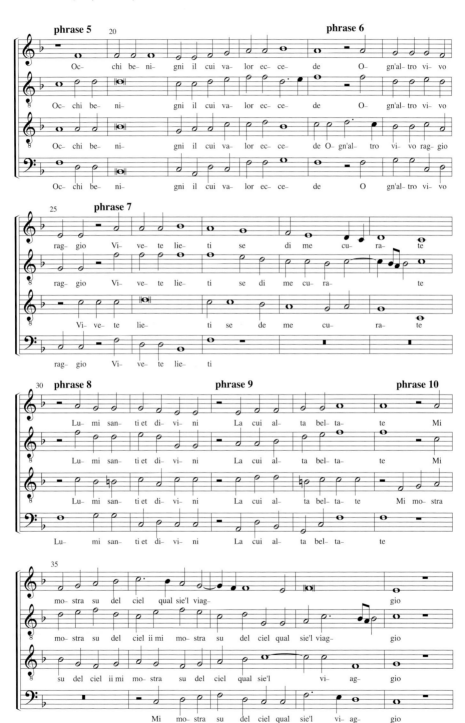

EXAMPLE 8.3   (*continued*)

wielding Cupid, can wage war all he wants because the lover is protected by the eyes of his beloved.

Fammi pur guerr'Amor	Rhyme
Fammi pur guerr'Amor quanto tu vuoi	A
Che gli occhi di costei pace mi danno,	B
Come veder tu puoi	a
Chè stimo poco de' tua lacci 'l danno.	B
Occhi benigni, il cui valor eccede	C
Ogn'altro vivo raggio,	d
Vivete lieti se di me curate;	E
Lumi santi et divini,	f
La cui alta beltate	e
Mi mostra su del ciel qual sie 'l viaggio,	D
Voi havete mercede	c
Così di me nel mio intens'ardore	G
Che poco curo le fiamme d'amore.	G

In terms of its rhyme scheme, the poem divides into three sections: ABaB CdEfeDc GG. But the syntax suggests a division into two parts. The first addresses Love: "[1] Make war against me, Cupid, as much as you want, since the eyes of her give me peace as you can see since I have little regard for the damage of your snares." The second addresses the eyes of the speaker's beloved, the source of his peace. It in turn consists of two parts of unequal length, each invoking the eyes with an imperative: "[2a] Kind *eyes*, whose worth exceeds that of any other living ray, *live happy* if you care for me; [2b] *lights* holy and divine, whose deep beauty shows me the path to heaven, *have pity* therefore on me in my intense ardor, since I care little for the flames of love." In terms of syntax, the structure is: [1] ABaB [2a] CdE [2b] feDcGG.

Corteccia let the verse structure determine the musical form, each line of poetry corresponding to a discrete musical phrase. But the larger-scale architecture of his setting, revealed by the cadences and structural points of division, shows the complexity of his reading of the text.[25] On one level, he seems to be dividing the text into four parts. The first corresponds to the opening quatrain (ABaB), the second to the first invocation of the eyes (CdE), the third to the first half of the second invocation (feD), and the fourth to the final demand, extended to a quatrain by repeating the final line (cGGG). Each part begins with a phrase starting on the downbeat (that is, at the beginning of the tactus), and continues with a series of phrases that all start off the beat. The contrast between phrases that have a clear sense of beginning and those that are continuations helps to articulate the piece as having four segments.

Cadences also help to define the large-scale structure see (table 8.1). Each part ends with a fully articulated cadence. The two strongest ones, in which the two primary voices, cantus and tenor, take on the main cadential functions (one voice

---

25. Brown, "A Typology," 9–12, independently reached much the same conclusion, working with a different madrigal.

TABLE 8.1   Corteccia, *Fammi pur guerr'Amor.* Cadence Scheme

Line/Phrase	Cantizans	Tenorizans	Pitch
1	—	—	[C]
2	T	B	C
3	T	A (to 3)	C
4	C	T	F
5	—	—	[F]
6	—	—	[C]
7	A	C	C
8	—	—	[C]
9	—	—	[F]
10	A	B	C
11	—	—	[C]
12	T	A (to 3)	C
13	—	—	[F]
14 = 13	C	T	F

Note: CATB in the second and third columns refer to the names of the parts; brackets in the fourth column mean a close rather than a formal cadence with the customary suspension and reso-lution. *Cantizans* means the voice taking the role of the cantus in a cadence, that is, stepwise motion upward to an octave or unison; *tenorizans* means the voice taking the role of the tenor, stepwise motion downward.

behaves like a cantus, the other like a tenor, in moving outward by step to the octave), close the first and last sections (although the last section does have a brief coda as well); both are on F, both reach the cadence pitch at the beginning of the tactus. In contrast, the other two, for the medial segments, use other voices to cadence on C; somewhat weaker than the first and last cadences, one occurs in the second half of a tactus, the other lasts only for a semibreve. In contrast to the strong cadences at the ends of segments, the rest of the phrases either end just with a chord but no formal cadence (indicated on the table with brackets), or with cadences that are weakened in some way (by brevity, for example, or by having one of the voices move to the upper third rather than to the unison or octave).

The large-scale structure built from these four sections can be interpreted in several different ways. Judging by length and cadence points, the four sections divide into two that mirror one another:

sections	1	2	/	3	4
cadences	F	C	/	C	F
measures	18	11	/	10	19+1
measures		29	/	29+1	

Of course, this could also be read as a large three-part structure:

sections	1	2		3
cadences	F	C	C	F
measures	18	11	10	19+1
measures	18	21		19+1
lines	4	3	3	4

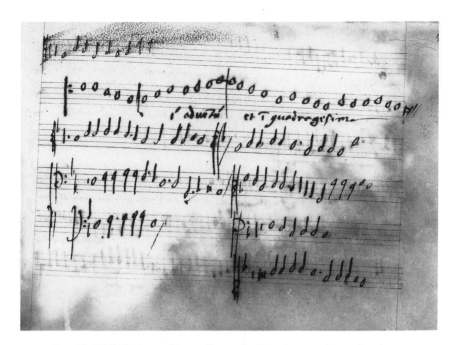

PLATE 8.5   FlorBN Magl. 117, fol. 44ʳ: Corteccia, *Fammi pur guerr'Amor*, sketch

But there is also another way to articulate the structure in two parts. Corteccia could have set up the first quatrain as the piece in microcosm: within the frame of F (at the beginning of the first phrase and at the major cadence at the double bar) are three contrasting cadences on C, at the ends of the first three lines of text. The double bar emphasizes this structure, setting the opening section apart from the rest of the piece. The second half of the piece mirrors, on a larger scale, the opening section. It starts and ends on F, and each of the sections cadences on C. The same music ends both sections ("Chè stimo poco de' tua lacci 'l danno" = "Che poco curo le fiamme d'amore"), bringing out the insouciance of the speaker toward both Cupid's snares and the flames of love.[26]

These sorts of questions about musical and textual structures are not only of interest to us today as we analyze this madrigal, but they concerned Corteccia as well. He worked out two separate sections of the madrigal in his sketchbook: the opening (mm. 1–14) and the beginning of the second section (mm. 19–29). In both he focused on the same issue: the placement of cadences to achieve structural clarity.

The drafts for the first section occur on two separate folios in different sections of the manuscript. Folio 44ʳ contains two brief sections in quasi-score format (see plate 8.5 and example 8.4). The opening of Version A (on the left-hand

26. Brown ("A Typology," 19) found that madrigals with this kind of musical repetition, which he called the *ballata* scheme, constituted the second largest group of Corteccia's madrigals.

EXAMPLE 8.4   Corteccia, *Fammi pur guerr'Amor*, mm. 1–7

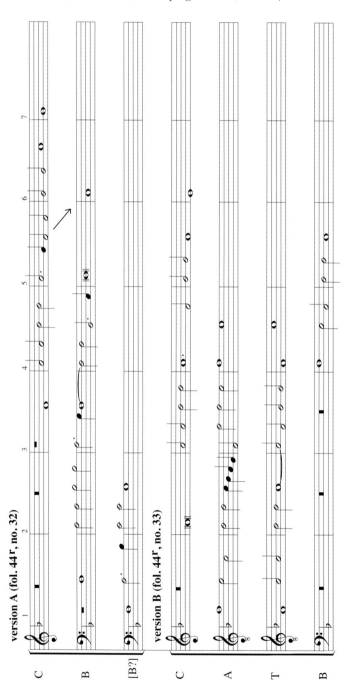

EXAMPLE 8.4 (*continued*)

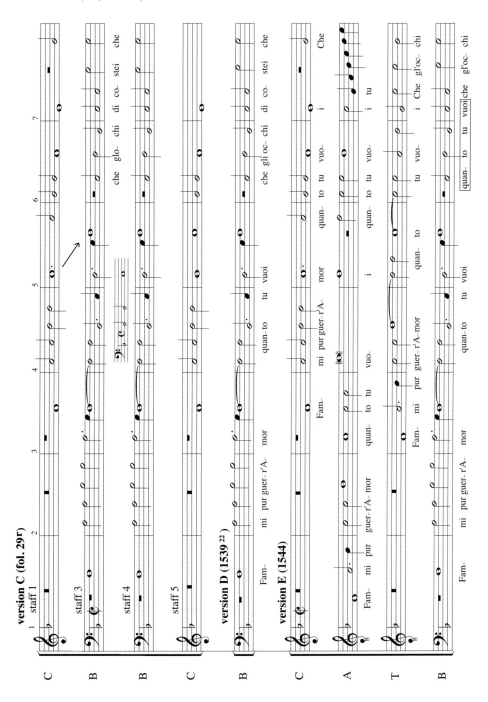

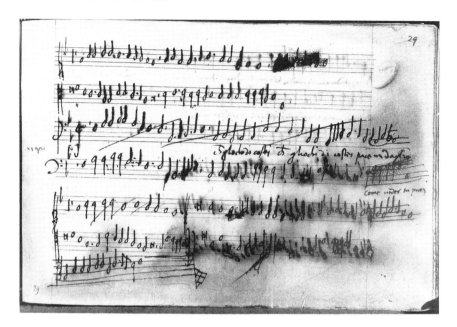

PLATE 8.6   FlorBN Magl. 117, fol. 29ʳ: Corteccia, *Fammi pur guerr'Amor* and *Con quel coltel*, sketches

side of fol. 44ʳ) presents the motives in the cantus and bassus in much the way they would appear in the final version. A third voice, notated as a bass part, might be an alternate version of the bass, but it seems more likely that it is presenting the first statement of the motive (against which the bassus and cantus must work), which in the final version was given to the altus. This sketch in effect presents the essential structure of the final version, though with a different conclusion. Version B, on the right-hand side of fol. 44ʳ, and most likely written after Version A, uses the same motive, but a different structure. Two of the voices present the motive, while the other two offer a countersubject. As we shall see, it is an alternative that he rejected.

Corteccia continued his work on the opening of the madrigal by flipping backward in the manuscript to fol. 29ʳ (see plate 8.6). This page is a striking example of his parsimonious use of space; it contains drafts of two madrigals, *Fammi pur guerr'Amor* and *Con quel coltel* (nos. 8 and 9, respectively, in figure 8.1). I would argue that he wrote *Fammi pur guerr'Amor* first and then squeezed the other madrigal, *Con quel coltel*, into the space that remained, adding a hand-drawn staff.

Example 8.4 contains a transcription of the sketches for *Fammi pur guerr'Amor* found on fol. 29ʳ, given in the order of their placement on the page: staff 1 cantus, staff 3 bassus (two versions), staff 4 bassus (two versions), and staff 5 cantus (beginning only). The work on this page is so complicated that assigning a letter to all of the stages is both confusing and perilous. For the sake of simplicity, I will refer to all the work on this folio as Version C.

cl	no. 8 [cantus]		
c3	no. 9 [altus]		
F4 ¢	no. 8 [bassus] [crossed out]		
F4	no. 8 [bassus]		
cl	no. 8 [cantus] [crossed out]	cl	no. 9 [cantus]
c4	no. 9 [tenor]	F4	no. 9 [bassus]
c4			

FIGURE 8.1   Diagram of FlorBN Magl. 117, fol. 29ʳ

There is good reason to think that Corteccia worked on this folio after work-ing on fol. 44ʳ: the several versions of the bassus all seem to be based on or derived from the bassus in Version A, but with several important changes: the cadence at the end of the first phrase is changed from C to F (marked with the arrows); the phrase continues to the end of the next line.

The work on fol. 29ʳ is very complicated and may never be sorted out com-pletely. An added difficulty is that the passage consists of three distinct segments, with different possible temporal combinations of voices within each segment. I was inclined initially to assume that Corteccia worked in order from top to bot-tom (that is, that versions closer to the top precede those closer to the bottom) and that the versions not crossed out come after those that are crossed out. I lean now toward a different interpretation: he began with a cantus–bassus frame con-sisting of bassus staff 4 (version 1) and cantus staff 5 (this is the only bass that works with this cantus); crossed out the cantus on staff 5 and abandoned it for good; wrote a new cantus on staff 1 and changed the bassus on staff 4 (version 2). At this point he had arrived at the final version of measures 1–7, at least as far as the notes for the outer voices were concerned. At some point—maybe now, maybe later—he copied out a neat version of this bass on staff 3 and added a time signature.

Figuring out a scenario for the rest of the passage is even more difficult because it requires sorting out three different bass lines, each of which cadences on a different beat (see example 8.5). Ironically, what I take to be the first of them, on staff 4, has the same music as the final version, arriving at C at the beginning of measure 11. Staff 3 has two versions, whose differences arise from the treatment of measure 9. If version 1 in fact continues to the end of the phrase, it cadences on the beginning of measure 12; version 2 is half a measure shorter. The version on staff 4 is even shorter, ending at the beginning of mea-sure 11. This first version, the bass on staff 4, works well with the first version of the cantus in staff 1 (with a G instead of an E in m. 10), as well as with the sec-ond version (the same as the final version). Neither version of staff 3 works with the cantus at this point. I suspect that the very end of staff 4—the part that is texted ("come veder tu poi")—is supposed to be read as contiguous with the

EXAMPLE 8.5   Corteccia, *Fammi pur guerr'Amor*, mm. 8–14

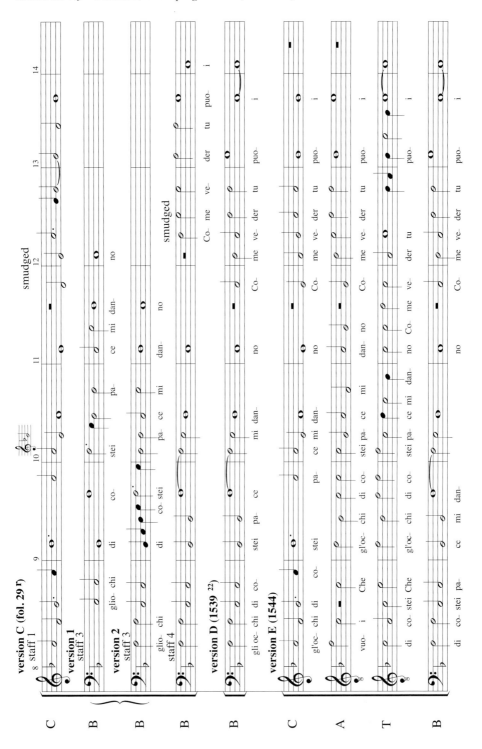

end of staff 3 (version 2), creating a viable cantus–bassus pair in measures 11–13, though one that would subsequently be altered. The curiosity is that staff 3 seems to have the final readings in legible form with text for all but two measures (mm. 10–11), yet it is crossed out. Could he have crossed it out after copying it on another page? This is a difficult and perhaps insoluble passage.

Though the details of the readings can be disputed, the overall position of fol. 29^r in the chronology of extant versions is clear. It is quite close to the earliest complete version that has survived, the Arcadelt *Primo Libro* (1539 or earlier), the bass of which is given as Version D. The final version, E, appeared in Corteccia's 1544 edition of his madrigals, published by Scotto.

During the course of work on the opening of this madrigal Corteccia altered the tonal architecture, perhaps to bring out features of the text. In the earliest draft, Version A, he arrived at a cadence on C at the end of line 1 (m. 5). The next draft, Version B, explored a different opening altogether, and plays no role in this evolutionary tale. In Version C, he changed the cadence to F in measure 5 and then continued directly with the words of the second line "che gl'occhi di costei." This is in fact the underlay found in the earliest printed version of the piece (see Version D). Version C has no text written out for the opening measures, but it is not unreasonable to infer from the text in measure 6 that the opening was the same as in the Arcadelt print. Sometime between 1539 and 1544, Corteccia changed his mind about the underlay from measure 6 on. In his own "authorized" edition (1544), he altered the text by repeating the final words of the phrase, "quanto tu vuoi" (shown in the box), thus treating measures 6–7 as an extension of line 1; by beginning the second line in measure 7, he established the cadence—in this case really only a brief resting place—for the first line as C. This change lets the cadence structure bring out the rhyme between lines 1 and 3: "vuoi" and "puoi." Version A has the idea of a cadence on C, but is not yet fully extended. Version C ends the phrase on F, reaching C only during the next phrase. Only in Version E, his final version, does the structure become clear.

Corteccia showed a similar concern with cadences in his drafts of the second portion of the madrigal (mm. 19–29). They occur near the end of the manuscript, on an opening that already had a chanson, fols. 58^v–59^r (see plate 8.7 and example 8.6). There are two versions. Version A is for two voices, cantus and bassus. Notice that the bassus continues for two measures beyond the cantus, as if Corteccia had tried out one possibility and rejected it before bothering to compose the cantus. Version B employs four voices. It takes the bass of Version A as its point of departure but soon arrives at quite a different solution to the temporal placement of the cadence. In Version B, he lengthened the B♭ sonority in measure 20, made the important F cadence fall on the beginning of the tactus in measure 23, and the subsequent C cadence at the beginning of measure 25. By eliminating the immediate return to F after the B♭ sonority in measure 20, he strengthened the subsequent arrival on F. Version C contains the final version as published in Corteccia's 1544 edition; it differs from Version B in only a few places, shown in brackets.

PLATE 8.7a   FlorBN Magl. 117, fol. 58ᵛ: Corteccia, *Fammi pur guerr'Amor*, sketches

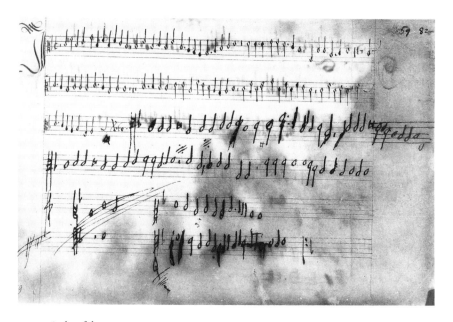

PLATE 8.7b   fol. 59ʳ

EXAMPLE 8.6   Corteccia, *Fammi pur guerr'Amor*, mm. 19–29

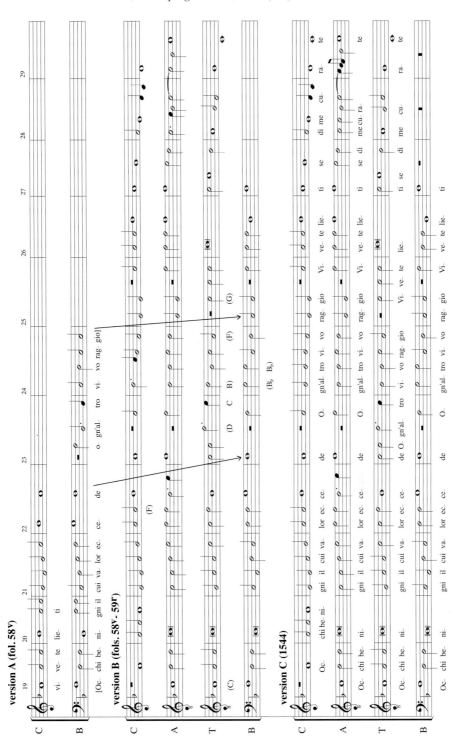

Corteccia's revisions for *Con quel coltel* reflect the same concerns we have seen in *Fammi pur guerr'Amor*: tonal coherence and temporal placement.[27] *Con quel coltel* is a canzone-madrigal, consisting of eleven lines:[28]

Line	Text	Rhyme
1	Con quel coltel col qual già t'uccidesti	A
2	Per crudeltà di core,	b
3	Uccidi un che si more	b
4	Della pietà qual in te nuov'havesti	A
5	Da te partendo, che se mai mi festi	A
6	Soffrir martir d'amore,	b
7	Adess'è il dolore	b
8	Qual tua pietà m'aggiunge, tal ch'io resti	A
9	Pei tuo' pietosi gesti,	a
10	Quasi senz'alma spirto et senza core	B
11	Quando partir da te mi forzan l'hore.[29]	B

Corteccia's setting is a very sophisticated response to both verse structure and syntax. He brought out the stanzaic structure of the poem by making the first two quatrains (AbbA AbbA) parallel (see figure 8.2).[30] Phrase 7 is an exact repeat of phrase 3, phrase 8 an altered version of 4. The harmonic differences at the beginning of the two strophes (cadences on G and C in the first, A and E in the second) are mediated by the repetitions at the end (cadences on C and G in both strophes). The closing tercet (treated as a quatrain by virtue of the repetition of line 11) takes elements from each of the two quatrains—a reworking of line 2 for line 10 to bring out the repetition of 'core' and a third use of the music of lines 3 and 7 in line 9—but ends with new material. Corteccia brought out the syntactic structure while still recognizing line endings by using different kinds of musical articulations. For example, in lines 3–5 he used simple closes (chords without the characteristic suspension formula typical of cadences) to mark line endings, while reserving formal cadences for syntactic divisions, the places where someone reading the poem aloud might pause ("Uccidi un che si more" [line ending, close] "Della pietà" [syntactic division, cadence] "qual in te nuov'havesti" [line ending, close] "Da te partendo," [syntactic division, cadence]).

27. The madrigal is found in BrusC 27731 (ca. 1535–1540) and in Corteccia's second book of four-voice madrigals (1547). FlorBN Magl. 117 shares with BrusC 27731 a version of the cantus, mm. 36–38, that Corteccia subsequently revised for publication.

28. I am indebted to Leofranc Holford-Strevens for the version of the text and for improving my translation; for a version that employs a different division into lines and a different punctuation, see Corteccia, *Collected Secular Works*, 9, p. xviii. The 1547 print has "tuo" in line 7; BrusC 27731 has "non havesti" in line 4.

29. "With that knife with which you have already killed yourself through cruelty of heart, you kill one who is dying from the new-found pity that you had in you as I part from you. So that if ever you made me suffer a torture of love, now it is the pain that your mercy inflicts on me, so that by your piteous conduct I am left all but a spirit without breath and heart when the hours make me depart from you."

30. Brown ("A Typology," 19) described this madrigal as having "unusually clear recognition of the stanzaic structure."

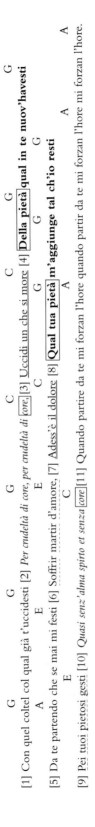

G   G   C   C   G

[1] Con quel coltel col qual già t'uccidesti [2] *Per crudeltà di core, per crudeltà di* core, [3] Uccidi un che si more [4] **Della pietà qual in te nuov'havesti**

A   E   C   G   G

[5] Da te partendo che se mai mi festi [6] Soffrir martir d'amore, [7] Adess'è il dolore [8] **Qual tua pietà m'aggiunge tal ch'io resti**

E   C   A   A   A

[9] Pei tuoi pietosi gesti [10] *Quasi senz'alma spirto et senza core* [11] Quando partire da te mi forzan l'hore quando partir da te mi forzan l'hore mi forzan l'hore.

FIGURE 8.2   Musical Phrases in *Con quel coltel*

EXAMPLE 8.7   Corteccia, *Con quel coltel*, mm. 1–12

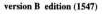

Corteccia worked on two sections of the madrigal in FlorBN Magl. 117: the first two and the last two lines. He squeezed a draft for the opening twelve measures onto fol. 29ʳ (see example 8.7 and plate 8.6). A comparison of this draft with the final version published in 1547 shows that he changed the opening segment (mm. 1–3) at some point after writing this passage into FlorBN Magl. 117. He altered the opening sonorities from a bass line of A D G C to one of E C A G, essentially a transposition downward by a fourth. He also partially rewrote the next segment (mm. 4–6). The cantus and bassus show extensive signs of revision in FlorBN Magl. 117; the revised version was close to the final version. He did not bother to revise the inner voices in FlorBN Magl. 117, perhaps intending to write them out from scratch in the next draft, unfortunately not preserved. The third segment (mm. 7–12) is virtually the same as the final version (there is a minor change in the altus).

The changes in sonorities in the opening may relate to Corteccia's vision of the overall structure of the madrigal. The first version of the bass created a line that spanned a ninth (from A down to G); the change created two phrases that both spanned just a sixth (from E down to G). This new point of arrival (G) also helped reveal the rhyme scheme (AbbA–GCCG).

While his main concerns at the opening appeared to be with the harmony, in his sketches for the conclusion Corteccia seemed to focus primarily on rhythm and placement within the tactus. There are five versions, counting the final printed version. He began on fols. 38ᵛ–39ʳ (see plate 8.8), working in choirbook format, and sketched two different endings (the first is only partly legible; see figure 8.3). He then turned back to fol. 34ᵛ (see plate 8.9) and sketched two more versions. Space was tight: there was almost room for conventional quasi-score format (tenor, cantus, and bassus on the bottom three staves, but the altus had to be squeezed onto the ends of staves 4 and 5 (see figure 8.4). Example 8.8 shows the gradual shift in placement of the final sonority from version to version (given the difficulties in reading these passages, the readings should be regarded as conjectural). The dotted barlines in Versions A–D show the original conception of the tactus; the solid barlines show the eventual solution as found in the final version (E). Even though a complete deciphering of this passage may not be possible, the main outlines of Corteccia's work are clear: he struggled with placement of the cadence within the tactus and with the overall duration of the cadence.

FlorBN Magl. 117 records only certain portions of Corteccia's process: sketches and very rough drafts. The music that has survived was too fragmentary and too messy to have been sung from or used to make copies. He must have written the music out in a fair copy, with text, neatly enough to serve as the model for subsequent copies—for the printer or for scribes making other manuscripts. In addition, while some of the early versions have survived, it is certainly possible that still earlier versions once existed, perhaps jotted on his slate.

Despite these evident lacunae, the sketchbook can offer valuable insight into Corteccia's methods. It is clear that he worked both with short segments and with longer drafts. He assembled the piece like a patchwork quilt, by fitting segments together. The sketches resemble the *giornate*—the areas painted in a single day—found in large frescoes.

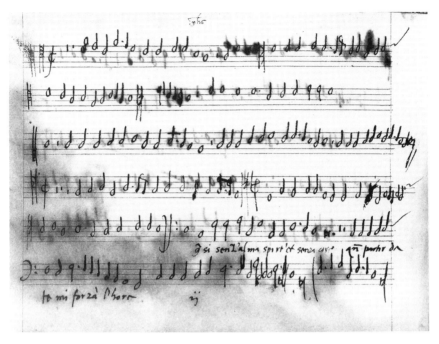

PLATE 8.8a   FlorBN Magl. 117, fol. 38ᵛ: Corteccia, *Con quel coltel*, sketches

PLATE 8.8b   fol. 39ʳ

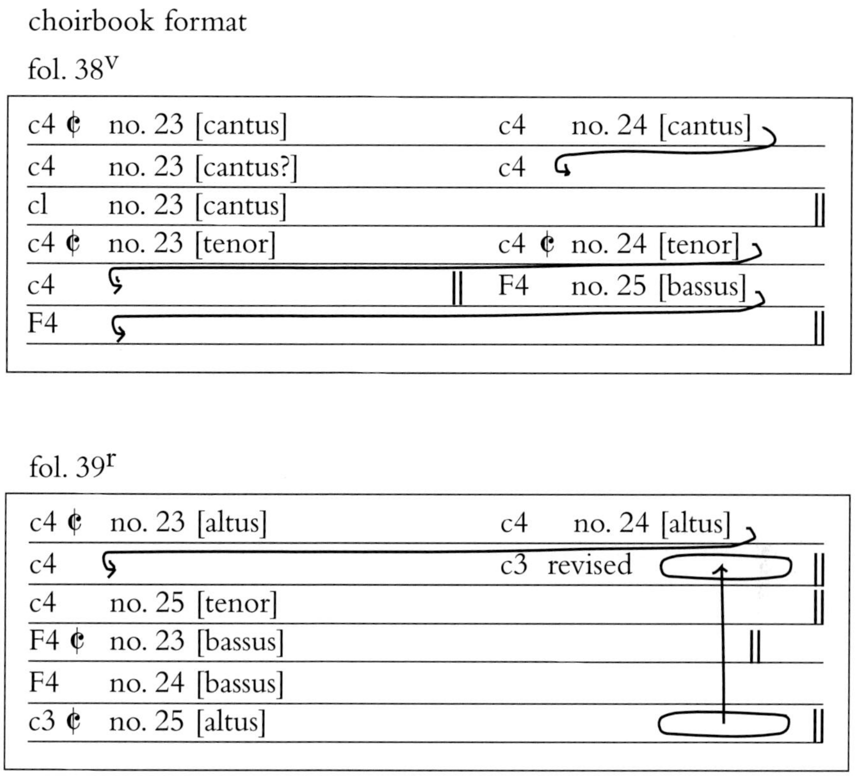

choirbook format

fol. 38^V

c4 ₵	no. 23 [cantus]		c4	no. 24 [cantus]
c4	no. 23 [cantus?]		c4	⌐
cl	no. 23 [cantus]			‖
c4 ₵	no. 23 [tenor]		c4 ₵	no. 24 [tenor]
c4	؟	‖	F4	no. 25 [bassus]
F4	؟			‖

fol. 39^r

c4 ₵	no. 23 [altus]		c4	no. 24 [altus]
c4	؟		c3	revised
c4	no. 25 [tenor]			‖
F4 ₵	no. 23 [bassus]			‖
F4	no. 24 [bassus]			
c3 ₵	no. 25 [altus]			‖

FIGURE 8.3   Diagram of FlorBN Magl. 117, fols. 38^v–39^r

Within each segment the process was additive, building from a line or pair of lines. Sometimes Corteccia worked with the entire sonority, but at other times he worked with a pair of voices. Perhaps it is not surprising, given the chordal texture of much of the music, that the cantus–bassus frame was in some cases the first to be composed.

In an essentially additive process like the one Corteccia used, the challenge was to get the temporal relationships right, both within and between segments. The sketches reveal that he had trouble with the placement of certain events, just the sort of problem it might be imagined a composer would have who is using an incremental process without benefit of a grid.

The changes show Corteccia to be profoundly interested in the text. Many of them make the musical representation of textual structure more evident. We know from his own words how important it was to him to express the meaning of the words. In the dedication that he wrote for the presentation copy of his hymn cycle, he explained some of the factors he had taken into consideration. He determined not to alter the chant, but at the same time, to avoid monotony, he treated it in various ways and placed it in various voices. He was concerned that the texts of the strophes that came after the first sometimes did not fit the melody, and so he took

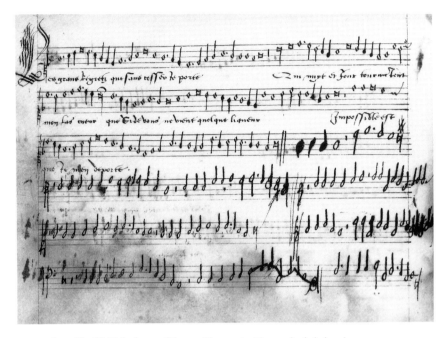

PLATE 8.9   FlorBN Magl. 117, fol. 34ᵛ: Corteccia, *Con quel coltel*, sketches

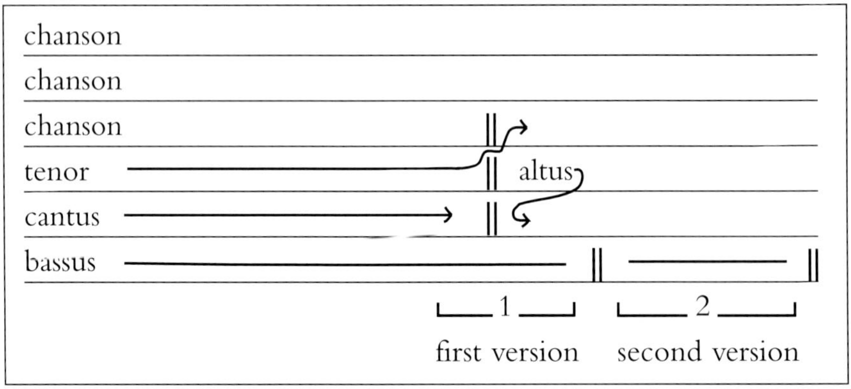

```
chanson  _____
chanson  _____
chanson  _____ ‖→_____
tenor    _____ ‖ altus _____
cantus   _____→   ‖ ↳_____
bassus   _____ ‖ _____ ‖
                            └─ 1 ─┘    └─ 2 ─┘
                         first version   second version
```

FIGURE 8.4   Diagram of FlorBN Magl. 117, fol. 34ᵛ

EXAMPLE 8.8   Corteccia, *Con quel coltel*, conclusion

care to hide the problem in his setting. His goal was to fit the notes ("note") and the melody ("aria") to the words, and to find ways to express their meaning:

> Which (as your excellency will see) we have freely varied in all verses not only to avoid the annoyance of similarity and to bring new pleasure to the ear of the worshiper with the variety as a whole, but also to keep the mind alert, attent, and steadfast in God by presenting to it always both the notes and the melody adapted to the words and in a certain manner expressive of the ideas, the highest goal of all our musical craftsmen in all their music.[31]

Though he was specifically writing about the hymns, the values he expressed applied to music in general: variety, careful accommodation of both melody and rhythm to the text, and expression of the meaning of the words. We know from his sketches that he "read" the text carefully, deciding how to express the structure of the text with the music, where to make the major points of articulation, what aspects to reflect in the music, what shape to give the whole. Thinking about the text must have been a constant part of his process, from the very beginning of sketching until he stopped revising.

Corteccia is the only composer, of the four whom we are considering, to have left sketches and drafts from such an early stage in the process. But as we turn to the drafts and fair copies made by the other three, we will see some of the same concerns, some of the same ways of working.

---

31. "Le quali (come vedra la ecc.tia v.a) habbiamo variate à tutti i versi non manco per fuggire il fastidio della similtudine con indulta, et con la novita insieme porger sempre nuovo piacere all'orecchi del contemplente, che per tener desto, attento et fermo in Dio lo intelletto col presentargli sempre et le note & l'aria accommodate alle parole, et in un certo modo espressive de lor concetti, fine principalissimo di tutti gli artefici nostri in tutte le musiche loro . . ." Text and translation from Glen Haydon, "The Dedication of Francesco Corteccia's Hinnario," *JAMS* 13 (1960): 115.

TABLE 8.2 Inventory of the Late Additions to Florence, Biblioteca Nazionale Centrale, Magl. XIX. 117

No.	Folio	Scribe	Voices	Mensuration	System and Cleffing	Format	Remarks
1	20ʳ	Corteccia	4	¢	♭c1c3c4F3	compact choirbook	imitation on D and G, cadence on G (8 mm.)
2	22ᵛ–23ʳ	Corteccia	3	¢	♭c1c3F3	choirbook	imitation on D and G, crossed out (11 mm.); related to (alternate beginning for?) *Domine non secundum*
3	22ᵛ–23ʳ	Corteccia	4		♭c1c3c4F4	choirbook	four brief phrases, cadence on G (13 mm.)
4	23ʳ	Scribe 2	2		♭c2c4	quasi-score	counterpoint exercise; canon, strict then free, cadence on E (16 1/2 mm.)
5	26ᵛ–27ʳ 27ᵛ–28ʳ	Corteccia	3	¢	♭c1c3F3	choirbook	*Domine non secundum peccata nostra* (draft of *prima pars*)
6	27ʳ	Corteccia	2		♭c4F4	quasi-score?	cadence on D (4 mm.) (two lines separated by a line from No. 5)
7	28ᵛ	Corteccia	3	¢	♭c1c3F3	parts	cantus of [*Domine ne memineris*], second part of *Domine non secundum*, followed by brief segments of tenor and bassus for cadence on G
8	29ʳ	Corteccia	2	¢	♭c1F4	quasi-score	[*Fammi pur guerr'Amor*] . . . che gl'occhi di costei, mm. 1–14 (Version C)
9	29ʳ	Corteccia	4		♭c1c3c4F4	parts	[*Con quel coltel*], mm. 1–12
10	29ᵛ	Scribe 3	2–3		♭F3F3c3	score	counterpoint exercise (8 mm.)

(continued)

TABLE 8.2 *(continued)*

No.	Folio	Scribe	Voices	Mensuration	System and Clefing	Format	Remarks
11	30ᵛ	Scribe 3	2		♮c1F4	score	counterpoint exercise (2 mm.)
12	31ᵛ	Scribe 3	2		♭c1F3	score	counterpoint exercise (6 mm.), long-note upper voice
13	32ʳ	Scribe 3	2		bc1F4	score	counterpoint exercise (three 1-m. beginnings)
14	33ʳ	Scribe 3	2		bc1F4	score	counterpoint exercise (7 mm.)
15	34ᵛ	Corteccia	4		♭c1c3c4F4	parts	[*Con quel coltel*], mm. 41–52
16	36ᵛ	Corteccia	1		♮F3	one line	margin: "1" (psalm tone?); cadence on A
17	36ᵛ–37ʳ	Corteccia	2	¢	♭c4F4	choirbook	margin: "2"; phrase, with cadence on G, two versions of c4 (11 mm.)
18	36ᵛ	Scribe 2	3	¢	♭c3c4F4	quasi-score	counterpoint exercise? three unrelated voices?
19	37ʳ	Corteccia	4		♭c1c3c4F4	quasi-score	cadence on C (5 mm.)
20	37ʳ	Corteccia	4		♭c1c2c3F3	quasi-score	[*Amanti i 'l vo pur dir*], mm. 1–4
21	37ᵛ–38ʳ	Corteccia	3		♭c1c3F3	choirbook	cadence on F, crossed out, possibly related to *Domine non secundum* (5 mm.) (cf. No. 5, mm. 25–29)
22	37ᵛ–38ʳ	Corteccia	3		♭c1c3F3	choirbook	contains at least two versions, possibly related to *Domine non secundum* (24 mm.)
23	38ᵛ–39ʳ	Corteccia	4		♮c4c4c4F4	choirbook	paired imitation (10 mm.)
24	38ᵛ–39ʳ	Corteccia	4		♮c4cc4c4F4	choirbook	paired imitation (12 mm.)

No.	Folio	Scribe	Voices		Clefs	Format	Description
25	38ᵛ–39ʳ	Corteccia	4		♭c1c3c4F4	choirbook	[*Con quel coltel*]. . . q[ua]si senz'alma spirt'et senza core q[ua]n[do] partir da te mi forza[n] l'hore, mm. 37–52
26	39ᵛ	Corteccia	2	¢	♭c1c2	choirbook (half)	[*Amanti i 'l vo pur dir*], mm. 1–20, cantus and tenor
27	40ʳ	Corteccia	4		♭c3c4c4F3	quasi-score	paired imitation (12 mm.); parts labeled cantus altus tenor bassus, barline in each voice after m. 10
28	40ʳ	Corteccia	3		♭c1c4F4	compact choirbook	cadence on D (4 mm.)
29	41ᵛ–42ʳ	Scribe 4?	2?		[♭c1?]♭c1	single lines	brief jottings; related?
30	44ʳ	Corteccia	1		♭c2	single line	smudged out
31	44ʳ	Corteccia	1		♮F4	single line	chant "in adventum et in quadragesima"
32	44ʳ	Corteccia	3		♭c1F3F3	quasi-score	[*Fammi pur guerr'Amor*], mm. 1–7, Version A
33	44ʳ	Corteccia	4		♭c1c3c4F4	quasi-score	[*Fammi pur guerr'Amor*]. mm. 1–6, Version B
34	58ᵛ–59ʳ	Corteccia	4		♭c1c3c4F4	parts	[*Fammi pur guerr'Amor*]. . . Vivete lieti, mm. 19–29, two versions (version A: 2v, ♭:c1F4; version B: 4v, ♭:c1c3c4F4)
35	59ʳ	Corteccia	2		♭c1c4	quasi-score	cadence, crossed out
36	59ʳ	Corteccia	2–3		♭c1c4 F4 [blank]	quasi-score [compact choirbook]	cadence on C; "Q"
37	59ᵛ	Scribe 2	3		♭c1c3c4	quasi-score	counterpoint
38	59ᵛ	Scribe 2	3		♭c1c2F4	quasi-score	counterpoint
39	60ᵛ	Scribe 2	2		♭c1c2	quasi-score	counterpoint

CHAPTER NINE

CIPRIANO DE RORE

Cipriano de Rore was one of the most important and celebrated composers of the sixteenth century, a pivotal figure whose innovations in musical style and technique would have ramifications for several decades after his death. No less a composer than Monteverdi would credit him with discovering a new relationship between music and text, the "seconda pratica."[1]

Rore was born in Ronse, a town in Flanders just west of Brussels.[2] He may have come to Italy as early as 1541, possibly to Brescia.[3] In 1542, the publication of his first book of madrigals established him as a major figure.[4] In 1546, he joined the Este court as *maestro di cappella*,[5] and stayed there until 1559, when he returned to Flanders to find his family ruined from the religious wars. Rore returned to Italy in 1561, serving at the Farnese court in Parma (1561–1563), then at San Marco in Venice (1563–1564), and then once again in Parma (1564–1565).[6] He died in Parma in 1565, only forty-nine years old.

1. Einstein, *The Italian Madrigal*, 384–423; Alvin Johnson, "Rore, Cipriano de," *NG*. I offered a preliminary interpretation of two later views of Rore—those of Monteverdi and Giovanni de' Bardi—in "Cipriano de Rore: Founder of the *Seconda Pratica*," a paper presented at the New England Chapter of the American Musicological Society, April 1985 and at Princeton University. For an extended examination of this topic, see Stefano La Via, "Cipriano de Rore as Reader and as Read: A Literary-Musical Study of Madrigals from Rore's Later Collections (1557–1566)," Ph.D. diss., Princeton University, 1991.

2. A. Cambier, "De grootste roome van de stad Ronse: De komponist Cypriaan De Ro[de]re, 'omnium musicorum princeps,'" *Annales Geschieden Oudheidkundige Kring van Ronse en het Tenement van Inde* 30 (1981): 5–56; idem, "Meer gegevens over de definitieve bevestiging van Cypriaan de Rore's Ronsische afkomst uit archiefstukken genealogie," ibid., 32 (1983): 221–249.

3. Richard Agee, "Ruberto Strozzi and the Early Madrigal," *JAMS* 36 (1983): 1–17, discovered two letters referring to Rore as being in Brescia. The date of the first is difficult to decipher (Agee lists it as 1541?), while the second one is clearly 1545.

4. See Martha Feldman, "Rore's 'Selva selvaggia': The *Primo Libro* of 1542," *JAMS* 42 (1989): 547–603, which contains references to the extensive earlier literature on this topic.

5. While the actual salary registers are missing for 1545–1546, I discovered among the original pay orders eventually used for compiling the registers the initial payment, dated 6 May 1546, to Rore as *maestro di cappella* (Modena, Archivio di Stato, Camera ducale, Mandati sciolti, Busta 13).

6. Jessie Ann Owens, "Cipriano de Rore a Parma (1560–1565): Nuovi Documenti," *Rivista italiana di musicologia* 11 (1976): 5–26.

Rore composed both sacred and secular music. His sacred music included motets, Masses, and a passion. His secular music included a number of dedicatory settings of Latin texts as well as settings of classical or neo-classical Latin poetry. He also composed several chansons. But his major contribution as a composer was through his madrigals. Five books of five-voice madrigals and two of four-voice were published, two of them posthumously.[7] While his early music was imitative and highly polyphonic in texture, his late music achieved a rhythmic transparency that enabled him to express the text in new ways.[8]

The evidence we have about Rore's working methods—apart from the music itself—comes from a set of five autograph partbooks now bound as a single volume, MilA 10, and from an affidavit written by Rore's pupil, the Ferrarese composer Luzzasco Luzzaschi.[9] We know from this affidavit that Rore worked first "in the mind" and that he used a *cartella* or erasable tablet.[10] The partbooks allow us to see Rore in the process of drafting three different compositions, each from a different stage in his process.

The three pieces are a five-voice setting in three parts of Ps. 50, *Miserere mei, Deus*; a four-voice setting of the Marian antiphon *Sub tuum praesidium*; and a five-voice fragment without text.[11] No other source is known for any of the pieces; so far as we know, they were never published.

Luzzaschi, in describing the partbooks, which he referred to by the name of the first piece, *Miserere mei, Deus*, explained that Rore had given him "the attached *Miserere*, composed by him in Flanders when he was young, and written in his hand. . . ." A comparison with extant autograph letters shows that Luzzaschi was correct about the manuscript being in Rore's hand, but he was wrong about its origins.[12] The paper is similar to that used in Brescia and Bergamo in the 1540s.[13] It seems more likely that Rore used the partbooks for composing after his arrival in Italy.

In contrast to the Corteccia sketchbook, the Milan partbooks do not record the earliest stages of composition, but instead the intermediate and near to final stages, the drafting and the copying out of a fair copy. It is possible that Rore, unlike Corteccia, never sketched on paper, but instead used the *cartella* or worked

---

7. In "Mode in the Madrigals of Cipriano de Rore," in *Altro Polo: Essays on Italian Music in the Cinquecento*, ed. Richard Charteris (Sydney, 1989) 1–15, I offer a list in chronological order of the madrigals by Rore that I consider to be authentic.

8. I discussed one such example (*Donec gratus eram tibi*) in "Music and Meaning" and others in "Cipriano de Rore: Founder."

9. Full text cited in chap. 4. The following discussion both draws on and develops the material presented in Owens, "The Milan Partbooks."

10. See chaps. 4 and 5.

11. Cipriano de Rore, *Opera Omnia*, ed. Bernhard Meier, CMM 14, 6 (American Institute of Musicology, 1975), 198–213, unfortunately lacking the critical apparatus.

12. The careful style of writing found in *Sub tuum praesidium* resembles the hand of the autograph letters, but there are clear points of congruence also with the faster and more informal style found in *Miserere mei* and the textless fragment.

13. The mark is a bull's head with a cross between the horns, similar to 14524–14525 in Charles Moïse Briquet, *Les Filigranes*, ed. A. Stevenson, 4 vols. (Amsterdam, 1968), 2: 734–735. The Bergamo organ book (BergBC 1143) also has a paper with a bull's head mark, though without a cross.

PLATE 9.1   MilA 10, fol. 17ᵛ: Rore, textless fragment (altus), draft

out many of the details in his mind before ever writing anything down. Such information as we can glean about Rore's methods, therefore, has to come from the drafts.

The textless composition seems to be the least advanced of the three pieces. It is written neatly, with relatively few corrections (see plate 9.1). There is no text, though the presence of ligatures probably indicates that the piece was conceived with a text in mind. The piece ends in mid-phrase, breaking off between measures 72 and 73 (see example 9.1). The ending suggests a point of imitation in the course of construction. A motive appears in the cantus (m. 66), then in the tenor (m. 68), beginning from B♭, and then in the altus (m. 69), on F. The bassus ends in measure 73, the tenor and quintus in measure 72, and the cantus and altus end in measure 71, while the altus is in the midst of presenting its motive. In both the quintus and altus, the piece stops at the end of a staff and the next note is indicated with a custos, as one would expect; the quintus indicates a C, which would clash with the other voices in measure 73. The other three voices stop mid-staff; only the tenor appears to have a custos, rather than a note, indicating a B♭ in measure 73. The way the voices end suggests that Rore was not copying from an earlier complete draft, but was instead composing as he wrote out this version.

A mistake at the beginning of the composition reinforces this impression (see example 9.2). The opening motive is an *inganno*: Rore is playing with three different articulations of the hexachord syllables *re fa mi fa sol la*. In the cantus and

EXAMPLE 9.1   Rore, textless composition, mm. 66–73

EXAMPLE 9.2   Rore, textless composition, mm. 1–13

tenor, they are D F E F G A, while in the altus the syllables become D B♭ A F G A, and in the bassus D E♭ D B♭ C D. Rore, perhaps thinking of the contour of the cantus and tenor, wrote a B♭ instead of the F in the altus in m. 5, and then over-wrote it immediately with the F. This mistake suggests that he was at the very least thinking through the music in his mind as he wrote, and not copying mind-lessly; it is possible that he was working out the altus as he wrote down the music.

However, there is also evidence that he may have been copying at least some of the music from an earlier written version, perhaps his *cartella*. In writing out the altus, he followed a pair of minim Ds with three wrong notes (m. 9), which he crossed out. This appears to be a typical copying error (*saut du même au même*), in which the eye jumps ahead to the next occurrence of an event (the minim Ds in m. 10).

We will probably never know precisely what earlier versions existed, if any. The draft, as it stands, is quite revealing, however. While Rore did make a few corrections, he left many other mistakes uncorrected.[14] A few of them have to do with pitch, causing momentary clashes, but most have to do with the nota-tion of rests, rendering the piece unplayable in its present form.[15] Some of the mistakes in the rests come between segments. For example, a semibreve rest is missing in both the altus and quintus in measure 14; as notated, the two voices would work well together but clash with the others. In another passage, the three of the five voices appear to be out of alignment. Both quintus and tenor as notated have an extra semibreve between measures 45 and 47, while the altus is a semibreve too short. The problems seem to occur at the end of a point of imitation. The next point, as notated, works well, assuming that the errors from the previous point are somehow corrected. These mistakes, which are similar to Corteccia's problems with the phrase notated as unaligned pairs on fol. 20ʳ, show that Rore was not working in score. The mistakes suggest that he had lost his place in the rhythmic scheme, encountering problems in joining individual segments correctly.

These problems in this abandoned draft suggest that the piece was growing as a series of units that made sense individually. Rore simply did not complete the work necessary to make the points fit together over the whole piece. The text-less fragment is essentially an uncorrected first draft.

In contrast to the draft of the textless fragment, Rore's draft of *Miserere mei* is considerably more advanced. It shows that his next step, after writing out an entire draft, was to correct errors, not only of pitch, but especially of rhythm. While the handwriting of *Miserere mei, Deus* is the same "quick" writing as that of the textless fragment, it is clear that he has taken the motet further in his com-

---

14. Rore used a "v" in a few places to indicate that a filled-in notehead was supposed to be empty. He crossed out a dot in the quintus, and changed one note in the tenor (m. 66₃ from G to E).

15. Only Meier's extensive editorial intervention makes the piece viable. He made the follow-ing changes: (1) pitch/rhythm: altus, m. 12₃ notated as C, changed to F; cantus, m. 64, G semibreve added; cantus, m. 53₂₋₃, A minim, F minim emended to A dotted minim, F semiminim; quintus, m. 45, rhythm minim, minim, semibreve, semibreve emended to semiminim, semiminim, minim, semi-breve); (2) rests: altus, m. 14, semibreve rest added; m. 46, semibreve rest changed to breve rest; quin-tus, mm. 1–10, longa rest added; m. 14, semibreve rest added; tenor, m. 28, semibreve rest added.

PLATE 9.2   MilA 10, fol. 10^v: Rore, *Miserere mei, Deus* (cantus), draft

positional process (see plate 9.2). For one thing, the piece is complete. It also has
at least a partial indication of text, similar to the technique Corteccia used. All of
the voices except the altus have the full text of the first part notated in a kind of
short-hand, mostly the first letter of a word.[16] The second part has no text,
except for the cantus, which has first letters for the first two staves (found on the
same folio as the first part, fol. 10^v). The third part is like the first, employing a
short-hand notation for the entire text in all parts.

Unlike the textless fragment, *Miserere mei, Deus* has many erasures and corrections. Some of them appear to be changes Rore made as he was composing,
in the sense of writing out the full draft, while others were revisions that he
made after completing the draft.

Unlike Corteccia, Rore did not leave any sketches of individual phrases. It is
nonetheless clear from the changes in the partbooks that, like Corteccia, he
worked segment by segment. *Miserere mei, Deus*, like Corteccia's madrigals, consists of a series of points of imitation, constructed around units of the text. The
music, however, is quite different from Corteccia's. Rather than the cantus–bassus
frame that Corteccia used for his predominately chordal settings, Rore worked
with a dense and highly imitative texture.

---

16. The altus has just "m"; the tenor has the full text written out on the first staff.

Typically, a point of imitation begins with a motive, or sometimes a pair of motives, treated in imitation in several or all of the voices. At any given time, one or two of the voices present motivic material while the others either rest or accompany the main voices with free contrapuntal material. Often, particularly when the segment is long, the opening words will have a clearly defined motive while the remainder will be set in free counterpoint. A point of imitation often ends with a cadence, here understood to be a two-voice contrapuntal structure, usually involving suspension and resolution (7–6 to 8 or 2–3 to 1). A point of imitation can often be further divided into smaller units of activity that could be called "contrapuntal events." Thus, for example, Rore could begin with a pair of voices that present the motive and form a "module," that is, a contrapuntal relationship that can be repeated. The next contrapuntal event within the same point of imitation could be the transposition of the module down an octave, with the addition of a third voice as a kind of decoration. Often, one voice will function as a link between points of imitation, presenting the new motive and text while the other voices are bringing the previous point to a close. The essence of this imitative style is the constantly changing combination of motivic and non-motivic material.

In some cases, the changes actually show how Rore built a particular point of imitation. For example, the point setting the text "Asperges me, Domine, hyssopo, et mundabor" ("You will wash me with hyssop, and I will be clean") has revisions in the quintus, showing two versions (see example 9.3). Rore could have begun with the quintus (mm. 113–117) in its role as a link between two points of imitation, then composed the altus and bassus (mm. 117–121), the central event of the point, and finally continued the quintus (mm. 118–120) as an accompaniment; or he could have begun with the altus and bassus, and then composed the quintus, first as a link and then as free counterpoint to the main pair. After writing this three-voice unit, Rore composed motive entries for the cantus and tenor to conclude the point of imitation. Unlike the first pair, these two voices were conceived not to be a self-sufficient pair but to fit with the other voices. Next Rore had to revise the quintus, originally conceived as part of the contrapuntal event that involved the altus and bassus, so that the next contrapuntal event—the motive entries in cantus and tenor—would work. The revisions, in fact, make sense only as a response to the cantus. Whatever he may have written on the *cartella*, he evidently wrote the first version of the quintus into the partbook before composing the motive entries in the cantus and tenor.

The work of crafting the composition focused in the first instance on the creation of a point of imitation, working outward from motive-bearing voices and from the combinations of motivic and non-motivic material. Even without any sketches, we can see in the many examples of this kind of change that Rore worked segment by segment.[17] He could have kept his place, while working with separate partbooks, because each part was growing at the same rate or by the same amount of music, one point at a time. As he worked on "Asperges me,"

---

17. Another example is discussed in Owens, "The Milan Partbooks," 287–292.

EXAMPLE 9.3   Rore, *Miserere mei, Deus*, mm. 113–122

he needed to know only where the voices began because the next point had not yet been written down.

While work on a single point of imitation sometimes required changes as voices or events were added, the real challenge was to keep track of the relationship between points of imitation, precisely the problems left uncorrected in the textless fragment. As he worked on the final thirty measures of the second part of *Miserere mei, Deus*, Rore made a mistake in temporal placement.[18] He wrote the music for the point of imitation "et omnes iniquitates" (mm. 149ff.), beginning with the motive in the cantus, thinking that the music began right after the beginning of the tactus. He wrote clear to the end of the section under this assumption. Before moving on to the third part, he realized his mistake as he was revising the final cadence. He corrected it by rewriting all the rests in all the voices so that they would show the tactus correctly; he fixed the mistake in the cantus by shortening the rests by a semibreve. This example shows how a segment could be viable musically as a discrete entity but not fit properly with the whole. It reveals that Rore—like Corteccia—was not seeing the whole piece in score.

The changes themselves, in this case, do not give us much insight into the piece itself. Many of them are corrections of small problems of voice-leading in a single part, or revisions of individual lines. Some are clustered in a way that suggests a whole-scale revision of a particular passage (for example, I, mm. 66–75, or II, mm. 166–177). But with only one exception, the changes have to do with counterpoint, not with the structure or placement of cadences. Their interest for us is in showing how the points of imitation came into being, and how they were eventually fit together to form a whole.

The third composition in the Milan partbooks, *Sub tuum praesidium*, represents the most advanced stage in Rore's compositional process. In contrast to the two drafts just discussed, it is a fair copy, with a full text, and the notes written out more carefully and neatly, in what looks like a "slower" hand. The text is a Marian antiphon, and the music is based on a familiar melody that Rore himself used again in a later setting.[19] Curiously, he altered the text, to make it appropriate to a particular patron or situation.

> Sub tuum praesidium confugimus, sancta Dei genitrix, nostras deprecationes ne despicias in necessitatibus, sed a periculis cunctis libera *me Franciscum* semper, virgo gloriosa et benedicta. Alleluia.

> Under your protection we flee, holy mother of God; do not despise our prayers in times of need, but ever free me, Franciscus, from all dangers, virgin glorious and blessed. Alleluia.

18. See Owens, "The Milan Partbooks," 271–276.

19. The other setting appears both in Munich, Bayerische Staatsbibliothek, Mus. Ms. B and in RISM 1563⁴. Also for four low voices (but with the cleffing c3c4c4F4), the setting is identical to the one in the Milan partbooks for the first five measures. Thereafter, the similarities derive from the use of the same melody. The specific source of the melody has not yet been identified; Willaert apparently used the same one.

EXAMPLE 9.4   Rore, *Sub tuum praesidium*, mm. 1–4

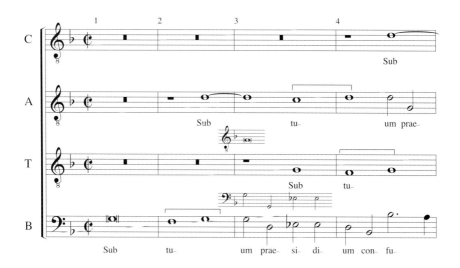

In the Milan partbooks Rore wrote the name variously as "francisce" (fol. 4), "francisse" (fol. 11ᵛ), "fra[n]cisse" (fol. 16ᵛ), and "fra[n]ciss[revised to c?]e" (fol. 20). Meier, in the edition, chose "Franciscum," the accusative singular of the male name, Franciscus.[20] The identity of this Francesco is unknown.

The changes all seem to be "editorial" revisions, that is, made afterwards as part of a process of polishing the composition. In one (fol. 20ʳ), Rore used the same ink as the surrounding notes (though the notes are heavier and thicker, suggesting the possibility that he may have been using a different quill) to rewrite a segment of the bass and change the text. While the original reading of the music is no longer legible, the text probably was "Libera me francisce semper francisce semper virgo gloriosa," amended to "Libera me francisce semper *virgo gloriosa* virgo gloriosa [new text in italics]."[21] Rore erased the original (actually digging a big hole in the paper) and put the new reading in its place; it fits awkwardly in the available space. For the other two revisions, he used a grey ink that is strikingly different from the prevailing brown. He made minor changes in two of the voices in the opening point of imitation (see example 9.4). And at the text "nostras deprecationes" (mm. 21–37), he changed the cantus, one of the voices bearing the main motive, to make it conform to other statements of the motive (see example 9.5). He also rewrote the tenor, which was functioning as a linking voice between two points of imitation; he delayed its entrance, eliminated a possibly awkward ornamental gesture, and created a clearer break with the previous point (see plate 9.3).

Rore's autograph partbooks preserve drafts for two compositions—one left unfinished and uncorrected, the other extensively revised—and a fair copy with revisions of a third. The partbooks evidently served two functions: first, to draft

20. Rore, *Opera omnia*, 6, p. xiv, n. 25.

21. Perhaps when the Biblioteca Ambrosiana reopens, an ultraviolet lamp may become available.

EXAMPLE 9.5   Rore, *Sub tuum praesidium*, mm. 21–37

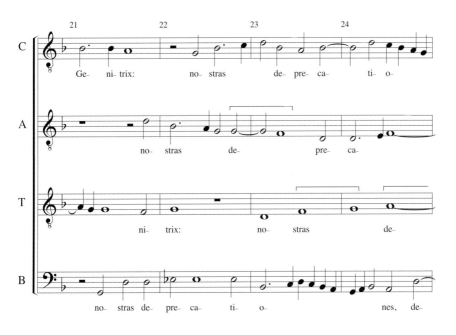

EXAMPLE 9.5   (*continued*)

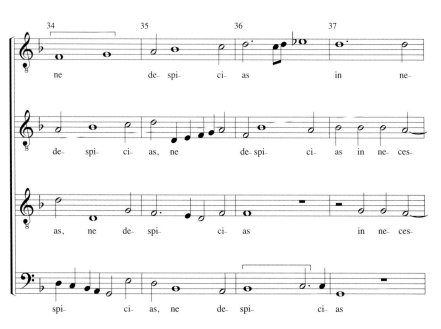

PLATE 9.3   MilA 10, fol. 4ʳ: Rore, *Sub tuum praesidium* (tenor), fair copy

compositions and second, to write out a fair copy that could then be recopied by a scribe or sent to a printer. While the Corteccia sketchbook revealed primarily the working out of brief segments, Rore's autograph gives us a view of work at a later stage. Despite the striking difference in style—Corteccia's chordal madrigals and Rore's highly contrapuntal motets—both composers were working at two levels: the individual phrases and the piece as a whole; and both were encountering similar difficulties as they worked.

CHAPTER TEN

HENRICUS ISAAC

Henricus Isaac was one of the most prominent and prolific composers of his time.[1] Born in Flanders probably in about 1450, he was called to Florence by Lorenzo de' Medici in 1485 to serve as composer and singer; he remained in Medici service until 1494. During these years, Florence must have become his real home; he married an Italian and purchased property there. After the expulsion of the Medici he left Florence and went to Pisa, probably in 1495. In 1496 he joined the chapel of the Emperor Maximilian I, and remained in imperial service until about 1512. During these years, Isaac traveled extensively, partly with Maximilian's court; there were frequent visits to Florence as well as sojourns in Torgau, Ferrara, and Constance. He retired to Florence in 1512 and died there in 1517.

Isaac was best known for his skill at transforming chant melodies into polyphonic compositions.[2] For example, the Swiss humanist and music theorist Heinrich Glarean wrote:

Sequitur haud imerito Symphonetas iam dictos et arte et ingenio Heinrichus Isaac Germanus. Qui et erudite et copiose innumera composuisse dicitur. Hic maxime Eccleasiasticum ornavit cantum videlicet in quo viderat maiestatem ac naturalem vim, non paulo superantem nostrae aetatis inventa themata. Phrasi aliquanto durior, nec tam sollicitus, ut consuetudini quid daret, quam ut elimata essent,

The Germanic Heinrich Isaac follows very justly the aforementioned composers [Josquin, Ockeghem, Obrecht and Brumel] both in art and talent. He also is said to have composed innumerable compositions, learnedly and prolifically. He embellished church song especially; namely, he had seen a majesty and natural strength in it which surpassed by far the themes invented in our time. Somewhat rough

1. The fundamental study on Isaac is Martin Staehelin's *Die Messen Heinrich Isaacs*. For a useful overview, with citation of the recent bibliography, see Martin Picker, *Henricus Isaac: A Guide to Research* (New York, 1991), 3–14.

2. Staehelin (*Die Messen*, 2) quotes all known references to Isaac by contemporary theorists and other writers; for a summary, see Picker, *Henricus Isaac*, 16–18.

quae ederet. Id etiam voluptati duxit copiam ostendere maxime Phthongis in una quapiam voce immobilibus, caeteris autem vocibus cursitantibus ac undique circumstrepentibus, velut undae vento agitatae in mari circa scopulum ludere solent. . . .

in *phrasis*, he was not so anxious to do something in the customary way as to bring forth the compositions which had been elaborated. It also gave him pleasure to show his versatility especially in tones remaining unchanged in any one voice, but with the other voices running about and clamoring around everywhere, just as waves moved by the wind are accustomed to play about a rock in the sea.[3]

In Glarean's view, Isaac used the chant to provide the motives or melodic ideas for the composition, rather than inventing them freely. He is portrayed as a fluent composer, a skilled melodist who excelled at handling the chant and understood its power.[4]

We can see some aspects of Isaac's craft at setting chant in the autograph manuscript of *Sanctissimae virginis votiva festa*, a sequence for St. Catherine. The autograph is a single bifolio, at one time a separate manuscript and now part of BerlS 40021, the choirbook that contains the sketches and draft of *In grandi cenaculo*.[5] Both *Sanctissimae virginis votiva festa* and *In grandi cenaculo* were part of a series of added fascicles sent to the anonymous compiler of the manuscript, identified by Martin Just as "Scribe Y"; Scribe Y came into the possession of the choirbook in about 1498 and added them soon thereafter as the final stage in its compilation.[6]

Three of the late additions to the choirbook contain music by Isaac. Even though each bears a heading identifying it as an Isaac autograph, Just showed that Isaac had in fact written only two of them.[7] One, the four-voice lied *In Gottes Namen fahren wir*, appears to be a fair copy, with no evidence of composing.[8] The other, Isaac's setting of *Sanctissimae virginis votiva festa*, is a manuscript used in

3. Glarean, *Dodecachordon* (Basel, 1547; repr. New York, 1967), 460; trans. Clement A. Miller, MSD 6 (American Intitute of Musicology, 1965). See Staehelin, *Die Messen*, 2: 114.

4. Isaac's pupil, Ludwig Senfl, in an autobiographical poem, praised his teacher: "Sein Melodey/was gstellt gar frey/darob man sich verwundern thett" (Staehelin, *Die Messen*, 2: 98–99).

5. See chapter 7. Martin Just, "Ysaac de manu sua," *Bericht über den internationalen Musikwissenschaftlichen Kongress Kassel 1962* (Kassel, 1963); Just, *Der Mensuralkodex Mus. ms. 40021*; *Der Kodex Berlin 40021*, ed. Just.

6. Just, introduction to *Der Kodex*, 76, pp. vii–xiii.

7. Pastedown to back cover: "h. Isaac de manu sua"; fol. 256ᵛ: "Ysaac de manu sua"; fol. 8ᵛ: "Ysacc de manu sua." Just ("Ysaac de manu sua") based his authentication of Isaac's hand on comparison with signed documents. He showed that *Missa Une mousse de Biscaye* (fols. 8ᵛ–10ᵛ) was not an autograph, but was instead copied by scribe P on northern Italian paper that dates from 1492 (watermark and information about the paper: *Der Kodex*, 78: 311). A facsimile of fol. 8ᵛ is in Johannes Wolf, *Musikalische Schrifttafeln* (Bückeburg and Leipzig, 1922), no. 49 and in *MGG* 6, cols. 1421–1422; and of fol. 9ᵛ in Just, *Der Mensuralkodex*, 2, pl. 18.

8. There are a few mistakes, but they appear to be of the kind that occurs during copying rather than during composition. For example, a phrase of the tenor was omitted; the missing notes were added at the end of the altus part, the next staff up, identified by an insertion mark. There is a fac-

composition. It is also a fair copy (in contrast to Corteccia and Rore, Isaac left neither sketches nor rough drafts), but it contains revisions and corrections that shed light on his methods.

To understand Isaac's work on this composition, we should try to imagine the stages he must have passed through. I think that at least three stages are discernible: first, a series of pre-compositional decisions; second, the writing out of a full draft in the Berlin bifolio; and third, the revision of this draft, also in the Berlin bifolio, to achieve a final version of the piece. Other stages may well have existed, about which we can only speculate.

Let us begin with the pre-compositional decisions. We know, because we have the music, that Isaac decided to compose a setting of the sequence *Sanctissimae virginis votiva festa*. We do not know precisely when or for what purpose. Just showed that the paper on which the piece was written came from Ravensburg, dated between 1498 and 1501, and was the same type that was used at the court of Emperor Maximilian.[9] It is hard to be certain of his whereabouts, and difficult, therefore, to fix the composition of the sequence. We know that he traveled with the court in 1500 and 1501, but he also visited Florence and stayed for a period at the Saxon court in Torgau.[10] Until better information emerges, Just's view—that Isaac composed the music ca. 1500 during his time at Maximilian's court, and sent it, together with the copy of *Missa Une mousse de Biscaye* and the song, to Scribe Y—remains the best available hypothesis.

Whatever the circumstances that led to the composition of the sequence, we can presume that Isaac's point of departure was the chant itself. The text, which dates from the end of the eleventh century, was probably German in origin, and it achieved widespread popularity in German-speaking realms.[11] It uses the melody known as *Laetabundus*, found with many other texts as well.[12] Characteristic of sequences of this period, it contains six sections of melody, each used

simile in Heinrich Isaac, *Weltliche Werke*, ed. Johannes Wolf, Denkmäler der Tonkunst in Österreich, Jg. 14/1 (Vienna, 1907).

9. Just, "Ysaac de manu sua," 114; Just, *Der Mensuralkodex*, 1: 39, 77–79; 2: 123–124, 190; *Der Kodex*, ed. Just, 78: 303.

10. For the most recent work on music at the electoral court of Frederick the Wise, see Kathryn Pohlmann Duffy, "The Jena Choirbooks: Music and Liturgy at the Castle Church in Wittenberg under Frederick the Wise, Elector of Saxony," Ph.D. diss., University of Chicago, 1995.

11. The full text is given in H. A. Daniels, ed., *Die Sequenzen des Thesaurus Hymnologicus*, Analecta Hymnica medii Aevi 55 (Leipzig, 1922; repr. 1961), 2/2: *Liturgische Prosen zweiter Epoche auf Feste der Heiligen*, no. 203, pp. 229–231. For an indication of its diffusion among Austrian Augustinians, see Franz Karl Prassl, *Psallat ecclesia mater: Studien zu Repertoire und Verwendung von Sequenzen in der Liturgie österreichischer Augustinerchorherren vom 12. bis zum 16. Jahrhundert* (Klagenfurt, 1987), 294 and 412.

12. For discussions and transcriptions of this melody, see Carl Allen Moberg, *Über die schwedischen Sequenzen* (Utrecht, 1927), 1: 183 and 247 ff.; 2, no. 4; and N. de Goede, *The Utrecht Prosarium*, Monumenta Musica Neerlandica 6 (Amsterdam, 1965), 17. See also Richard Crocker, "The Sequence," in *Gattungen der Musik in Einzeldarstellungen: Gedenkschrift Leo Schrade* (Berne, 1973), 1: 315–316; and John Stevens, *Words and Music in the Middle Ages: Song, Narrative, Dance and Drama, 1050-1350* (Cambridge, 1986), 91–100.

for two strophes.[13] The melody is built from recurring modules (here identified with capital letters) that follow the scheme:

Text	Melody: Phrases
strophes 1–2	section 1: ABA
strophes 3–4	section 2: CDA
strophes 5–6	section 3: ECA
strophes 7–8	section 4: FGH
strophes 9–10	section 5: IJGH
strophes 11–12	section 6: KKL

Example 10.1 shows the version of the sequence found in the nearly contemporary Passau Gradual and the chant-bearing voices in Isaac's polyphonic setting.[14] Isaac's text and the melody—to the extent that it can be deduced from its polyphonic reworking—differ in a few respects from the Passau version, but no better source has yet been found. Identifying the version of the melody that Isaac actually used may eventually help establish the context for which the music was composed.[15]

Almost as basic as the choice of the chant was a series of other decisions that presumably preceded any actual composition, that is, in the sense of actually writing down any music. Some were conventional, such as as his decision to set the even strophes of the sequence to polyphony, leaving the odd strophes (not written out in BerlS 40021) to be sung in plainsong.[16] Others were at the rather nebulous boundary where style, genre, convention, and performance practice

13. On sequence construction from this period, see Richard Crocker, "Medieval Monophony in Western Europe," in *The Early Middle Ages to 1300*, ed. Richard Crocker and David Hiley, *The New Oxford History of Music* 2 (2nd ed., Oxford, 1990), 288–293; Crocker, "The Sequence," 315–16; Richard Hoppin, "Exultantes collaudemus: A Sequence for Saint Hylarion," in *Aspects of Medieval and Renaissance Music: A Birthday Offering to Gustave Reese*, ed. Jan LaRue (New York, 1966; repr. Stuyvesant, N.Y., 1978); and Fassler, *Gothic Song*, 64–78.

14. *Graduale Pataviense (Wien 1511) Faksimile*, ed. Christian Väterlein, Das Erbe deutscher Musik, 87 (Kassel, 1982), fol. 267^r–v; pp. iv–v.

15. Väterlein pointed out that the *cantus firmi* in Isaac's settings, many of which were composed for use at Maximilian's court, differ somewhat from the usage of the Diocese of Passau, as exemplified by the *Graduale Pataviense*; he surmised that there may have been a chant book—now lost—used only at court. It is interesting to note that Isaac set the melody three other times, apparently following the same reading each time. The other settings are:

(1) [*Laetabundus . . .*] *Regem regum intactae*, in *Choralis Constantinus* II (1555), stanzas 2, 4, 6, 8, 10 and 12. The sequence is from the Mass for "Circumcisio Domini." For editions, sources, secondary literature, see Picker, *Henricus Isaac*, 57.

(2) [*Laetabundus . . .*] *Regem regum intactae*, in *Choralis Constantinus* III (1555), stanzas 2, 3, 5, 7, 8, and 11. The sequence is from the Mass "De beata virgine post festum nativitatis Christi." Picker, *Henricus Isaac*, 72–73.

(3) [*Laetabundus . . .*] *Sol occasum nesciens*, RISM 1541². This is a three-voice setting of verse 4 only. Picker, *Henricus Isaac*, 83.

16. Concerning the composition of Mass propers at this time, see Philip Stephen Cavanaugh, "A Liturgico-Musical Study of German Polyphonic Mass Propers, 1490–1520," Ph.D. diss., University of

EXAMPLE 10.1 *Sanctissimae virginis votiva festa*: (a) *Graduale Pataviense*, fol. 267ʳ and (b) Isaac, discantus (and tenor), BerlS 40021, fols. 255ᵛ–256ᵛ

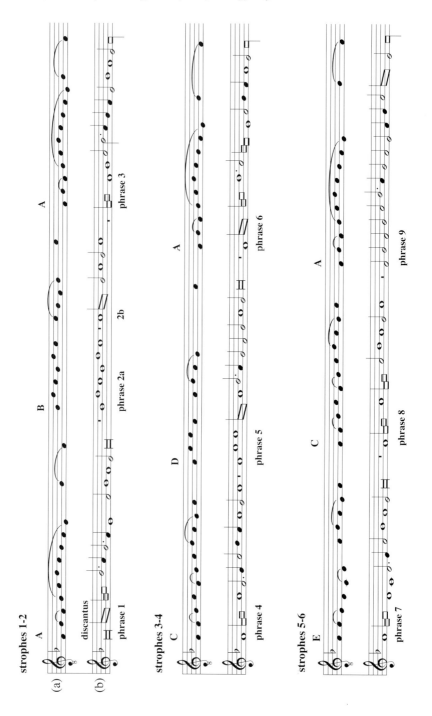

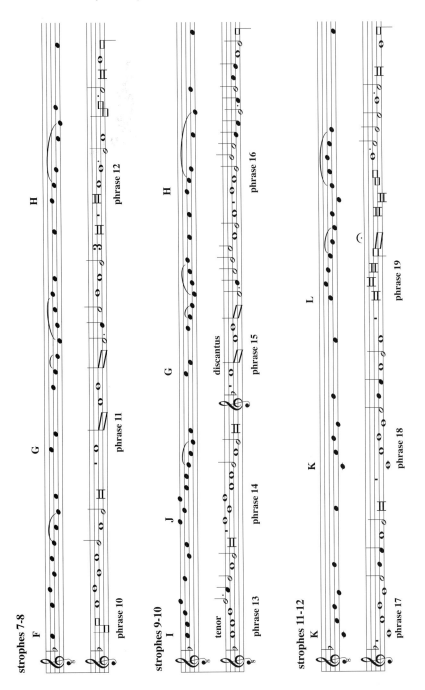

strophes 7-8

F

G

H

phrase 10

phrase 11

phrase 12

strophes 9-10

I

J

G

H

tenor

discantus

phrase 13

phrase 14

phrase 15

phrase 16

strophes 11-12

K

K

L

phrase 17

phrase 18

phrase 19

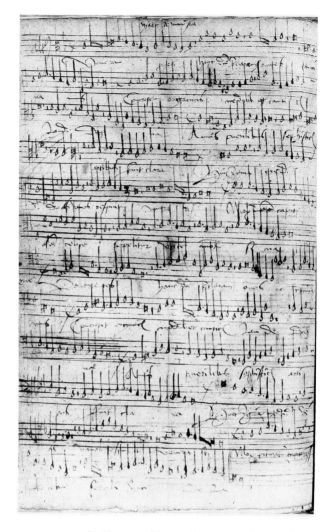

PLATE 10.1a   BerlS 40021, fol. 255ᵛ: Isaac, *Sanctissimae virginis,*
fair copy

intersect. Isaac chose to use a four-voice ensemble, with a relatively narrow
ambitus (see the transcription in the appendix to this chapter).[17] The discantus

Pittsburgh, 1972; and Gerhard-Rudolf Pätzig, "Liturgische Grundlagen und handschriftliche Überlieferung von Heinrich Isaacs 'Choralis Constantinus'," Diss., Eberhard-Karls-Universität zu Tübingen,
1956. See also Louise Cuyler, "The Sequences of Isaac's *Choralis Constantinus,*" *JAMS* 3 (1950): 3–16.

    17. In the transcription, (example 10.2), the numbers associated with each change correspond
to the list of changes and corrections given in table 10.1. I provide a partial underlay (of the cantus
firmus-bearing voices only) that attempts to reflect as closely as possible the placement of the text in
BerlS 40021. Just's excellent critical edition (fully texted, with reduced note values) presents only the
final version of the piece (*Der Kodex,* 78: 250–255).

PLATE 10.1b   fol. 256ʳ

and bassus, in the same range an octave apart, frame two inner voices occupying similar ranges midway between. Either at this point, or somewhat later when he actually began to notate the music, Isaac decided on the particular clefs to fix the ranges of the voices (c1c3c4F3).

A third and inevitably related decision concerned the treatment of the chant. Of the various options available to him for incorporating the melody in polyphony, Isaac chose the technique for which he was famous: an elaboration of the chant that would transform it into a rhythmicized, metrical line and make it into a strand in the polyphonic web that preserved the integrity of the melody while still functioning as an equal partner with the other voices.

These early stages are recorded only in the results of the deliberations and

PLATE 10.1C   fol. 256ᵛ

choices—the music itself. But some aspects of the actual crafting of the composition are revealed in Isaac's autograph.

The Berlin bifolio consists of two leaves (four pages), ruled in somewhat
irregular fashion with a rastrum (see plate 10.1). Three of the four leaves have
twelve staves drawn with the rastrum, while one (fol. 255ᵛ) has only eleven (the
twelfth staff was added crudely by hand at the bottom of the page). The uneven-
ness of the staves and of their spacing on the page, as well as the curious omis-
sion of a twelfth staff on one of the pages, hardly seems the work of a professional
scribe or the quality of paper that could be bought already lined. The irregularity suggests that Isaac himself may have ruled the paper.

The first page (fol. 255ʳ) is ruled, but has no other writing. Most of the

sequence (five of the six sections, settings of strophes 2, 4, 6, 8, and 10) is written in choirbook format on the central opening (plate 10.1a–b, fols. 255ᵛ–256ʳ).
For reasons that are unclear, Isaac used a rather unusual layout for the voices: altus
and tenor on the verso or left-hand side of the opening, discantus and bassus on
the recto. He wrote the final section (strophe 12) on the last page of the bifolio
(plate 10.1c, fol. 256ᵛ). Since he had only one page to work with, he had to use
a different format; rather than separating the voices into quadrants, he stacked
them in a quasi-score arrangement. He wrote two settings of the twelfth strophe,
both based on the same discantus.

Layout of BerlinS 40021, fol. 256ᵛ

staff 1: discantus for both settings (texted)
staff 2: bassus, first setting (texted)
staff 3: altus, first setting (texted)
staff 4: tenor, first setting (texted)
staff 5: residuum, bassus and altus, first setting
staff 6: tenor, second setting (incipit only)
staff 7: bassus, second setting (incipit only)
staff 8: altus, second setting (incipit only)
staves 9–12: blank

In composing the polyphonic setting of *Sanctissimae virginis votiva festa*, Isaac
took the chant as his point of departure. Transposing it up an octave and transforming it into a polyphonic line, he placed it in the discantus, the uppermost
line of the piece. It appears that he followed the chant closely—almost note for
note—at the beginning of each phrase, becoming freer at cadences to accommodate the conventions of polyphonic closure.[18] Isaac typically began the
phrases with relatively long note-values, then ended with quicker cadential ges-
tures. His procedure mirrors in its results (if not its methods) the recommendation that his pupil Hans Buchner made for beginning organists.[19]

Isaac let the melodic structure of the chant determine many of the structural
features of the polyphonic setting. The six large sections of the chant correspond
to the six sections of the polyphonic version. Within each section, the melody
divides into phrases corresponding to line divisions in the text. The polyphonic
version follows the same segmentation. Its phrases have an average length of
from five to seven breves (four phrases are longer or shorter than the average,
containing 4, 8, 9, or 11 breves).

The chant, employing the soft system with a flat in the signature, provides the
tonal orientation of the piece as well. A formal cadence, almost always involving
the discantus–tenor pair, concludes most of the phrases in the polyphonic setting.[20]
The cadence pitches correspond closely to those of the chant, emphasizing F (16),

18. Since we do not have the actual melody that Isaac worked with, we cannot be certain of
his exact procedure.
19. Buchner, *Sämtliche Orgelwerke*, 54: 22–24; see chap. 2.
20. Two phrases employ the tenor and bassus as the cadential voices; these occur in section
5/strophe 10 when the tenor bears the chant.

A (6), and C (2); in only one instance does the cadential pitch of the polyphony differ from that of the chant.[21]

Given the importance of the chant, it might seem reasonable to assume that Isaac began by composing the entire line that would bear the chant and then added the other voices. However, the physical evidence of the writing on the bifolio, as well as the music itself, suggests otherwise. It appears that he composed the piece one section at a time.

Part of the evidence comes from the layout of the music on the central opening. Isaac wrote the discantus for each section on a separate staff on fol. 256[r]. It is possible that he had originally intended to write all six sections on the central opening—he had left six staves for the discantus (as well as for the other voices). But the music for the other three voices was longer than a single staff per section. He wrote the music out continuously (that is, he began the new section right after the conclusion of the previous one, on the same staff), but he still could only fit the music for the first five sections on the opening. I suspect that if he had composed the entire cantus firmus-bearing voice first, he would likely have written it all down on the six staves of the central opening.

Another argument that he worked section by section comes from the music. Isaac could not set the entire chant using just the discantus because the fifth section went quite high, beyond the ambitus he had selected for the discantus. As a result, he placed the first two phrases of the fifth section down an octave in the tenor. While he could have written out the series of rests at the beginning of the discantus part without having first composed the tenor, he could not have written out these phrases in the tenor until he had composed everything leading up to them.

A third bit of evidence comes from ink color. Isaac wrote out the discantus for the twelfth strophe/sixth section on the top staff of the final page in an ink that is darker than the main ink used in the central opening and in the three lower voices in the two settings of the twelfth strophe. This suggests that he wrote down the discantus for the entire section as self-contained segment, and then came back to compose the other voices for both settings at another time. It is also possible that he used two pots of ink and possibly two quills for writing the music—a somewhat darker, denser brown for the solid note-heads and a more transparent brown for the open note-heads.[22]

Within each section, Isaac worked phrase by phrase, point by point. He had a number of different options for creating each point. One approach was to deploy the chant in two voices as a kind of frame. He did this in two ways. In one, either the discantus imitates the altus a fourth higher at the distance of a semibreve or a breve (phrases 1, 2, 3, 7, and 8), or the tenor imitates the discantus

---

21. In phrase 5 the altus and tenor cadence on F against the cantus firmus A in the discantus. Most of the A cadences have either an F or a D as the lowest sounding pitch, though not as part of the formal cadence.

22. See plates 6.1 and 6.2, showing a scribe with two pots of ink and two pens.

an octave lower at the distance of a breve (phrases 5 and 15). In the other, he placed the chant in one voice only and then used a variety of different textures in the accompanying voices. The texture can be essentially chordal, either strict (phrases 9, 12, 19, 22) or free (phrases 4, 10, 17, 18, 20, 21), or the other voices can have a free polyphonic texture, occasionally using specific motives (phrases 6, 11, 13, 14, 16).

As Isaac worked on the Berlin bifolio, he occasionally made mistakes that he corrected before going on (see table 10.1 at the end of this chapter). Sometimes he simply crossed out notes and added the correct ones directly to the right; other times he erased (i.e., scraped the ink from the paper) and wrote a new version on top of the old.

One of these corrections (no. 11) suggests that Isaac was actually composing as he wrote the music down on the bifolio, and not simply copying. He had initially decided to write a three-voice cadence in measure 51 (discantus, tenor, and bassus) and to use the altus as a link between phrases 8 and 9. He then decided to change to a four-voice cadence with a complete break in all voices and to begin the next phrase with a strict chordal texture in fauxbourdon style. He crossed out the first version of the altus and wrote the second version next to it (the ink is the same for both versions). When he wrote the first version of the altus, he evidently had not yet decided on the approach he would use in phrase 9. The changes in the altus seem to show him in the midst of composing phrase 9.

Other corrections reinforce this impression. Isaac wrote the wrong clef in the tenor (c3 instead of c4) three times and each time caught the error almost immediately (nos. 10, 15, 21). These mistakes show that he did not write out all the clefs before writing the music, nor did he simply copy the music from a source using the same layout. Is it possible that he was working from a format like the ten-line staff, which could not easily distinguish the staves of the individual voices, or like German organ tablature, which indicated pitches for the lower voices with letter notation? Or was he simply confused, going back and forth between two inner voices that were similar in range?

Isaac added the text soon after the music, probably before beginning the next section. In one instance (no. 8), adding the text may have helped him see the need for a revision. The change involves an accompanying voice that together with the tenor presents a repeated four-note motive as a kind of counterpoint to the long-note cantus firmus presented in imitation in altus and cantus. Isaac may have written the entire bass line from measure 45 through to the end of the phrase. Then when he went back to add the text and started to write "so-" under the motive in measure 45, he realized that he had three consecutive statements beginning F D F. He made the change in the pitches, erased the syllable "so-," and then placed the text under the second statement of the motive. This scenario and the fact that the ink color was the same suggest a correction during the initial phase of work on the piece.

After Isaac had drafted the entire piece, he revised it. These revisions, unlike the corrections and changes discussed above, were always done by erasing or overwriting, never by crossing out, and always in a different, darker ink. I suspect that, as in other instances we have encountered, Isaac either checked the voices one against the other or had the piece performed.[23]

The changes in the first phrase illustrate the character of the revisions as well as the difficulties in interpreting them. The chant appears in both the discantus and altus (the altus is down a fourth and precedes the discantus by a semibreve). The bass appears to function at least for the first five measures as the foundation of the sonority, working as a unit with the two upper voices. The tenor seems to be fit in in a way that does no damage to the counterpoint, but that also seems rather shapeless. At the end of the phrase, however, it assumes a major structural role, working with the discantus to arrive at a cadence on F. The bass continues its supporting role, and the altus, no longer presenting the chant, now has the appearance of contrapuntal filler. There are two changes in this first phrase, both in the tenor. The first one, in measure 2, is no longer legible. The second, in measure 5, may indicate that the tenor had already been written and needed to be changed once the altus was added.

The changes or corrections in *Sanctissimae virginis votiva festa* occur at some twenty-six different places. For a good number of them, it is possible to speculate, on the basis of factors such as ink color and the way the correction is made, about when they may have taken place: during the first phase of writing or during the process of revision. In some instances it is possible to decipher the original reading, but in others the erasure was too thorough.

The location of the changes may reflect Isaac's order of work. It is surely significant that there are only two instances of a change or correction in one of the voices bearing the chant. In no. 19, he changed the final breve of the phrase to a semibreve followed by a rest in order to show the phrase division, thus following his usual practice of using a rest to divide the discantus into phrases. In no. 13, he rewrote three of the voices, including the discantus, altering the opening sonorities of strophe 8. Unfortunately, the original version is not visible. It is noteworthy that this is one of very few places where the polyphonic version apparently differs from the chant (at least the version found in the *Graduale Pataviense*) at the beginning of a phrase. The chant begins C C D B♭, while the discantus, in the revised version, begins F C C D B♭.[24]

All the rest of the changes involve either the accompanying voices or the voices that function as links between phrases. The location of the changes suggests that Isaac wrote the individual points working first from the chant-bearing voices, then adding the accompanying voices, and finally making links between points of imitation.

For this piece, it is not possible to posit a single order of composition, for example, discantus, tenor, bassus, altus. Even the suggestive placement of the three lower voices on the final page (bassus, altus, tenor in the first setting; tenor, bassus, and altus in the second) does not help determine the order of work

---

23. The singers at the Cathedral in Constance checked Isaac's music by singing it to be sure that it was complete and correct before he was paid. See Staehelin, *Die Messen*, 2: 69.

24. The scribe in Jena, Universitätsbibliothek 33, one of the two other extant sources of this composition, replaced the offending F with a semibreve rest.

within the individual point. Instead, it is necessary to see how each voice functions in each point: chant-bearing, accompanying, linking. For example, in
phrase 5, discantus and tenor bear the chant. The altus is an added voice; Isaac
changed the rhythm in measure 28 (no. 6) to maintain some rhythmic interest in
a passage where the outer voices were moving stolidly in semibreves. In phrases
2 and 3, however, the altus functions with the discantus to present the chant in
imitation. The changes occur in the bass (no. 3, mm. 13–14) and then in the
tenor (no. 4, mm. 14–17), functioning as accompanying or linking voices. This
evidence suggests that the typical advice about the order for composing given by
theorists or music teachers is too simplistic.[25]

The distribution of changes phrase by phrase reveals that most phrases have
either no changes or at most one change. Only six phrases have two or more:
phrases 1, 3, 8, 10, 11, and 17. They represent three of the four types of texture:
only the strict chordal texture is free of multiple changes. That means that it is
impossible to point to a particular technique as presenting greater difficulties for
Isaac. Two phrases—8 and 11—each contain four changes, but neither the character of the changes nor the nature of the music itself suggests any special explanation for the higher number.

A few of the changes are at the beginning or middle of phrases, but most
come at the end. They often involve either the cadence or the link between two
phrases. For example, in no. 5, Isaac rewrote the altus, which is functioning as the
link between phrase 4 and 5; the original reading is no longer legible. The location of the changes suggests that the many of the problems came at the seams
between phrases.

In a few instances it is tempting to speculate that the change involved the second or third voice to be composed and that it was necessitated by a kind of chain
reaction. The first version worked fine until new material was added. The striking
number of changes found in the tenor voice (more than twice as many as all the
other voices combined) may suggest that the tenor was often the second voice to
be composed and therefore often the voice that needed to be changed once the
rest of the music was written.[26] However, the variety of texture and procedure
from phrase to phrase means that the voices assumed different roles in each phrase.

Where does the Berlin bifolio fit in Isaac's process? Just described it as a copy
("Abschrift") and provided a stemma that posits a lost exemplar (a) from which
the Berlin bifolio descended.[27] But as we have seen, it is not a simple fair copy
made after the composition was complete: there are too many erasures, overwritten notes, and crossed-out notes.

Does the bifolio represent Isaac's only complete draft, containing changes
made both while he was composing and afterward while he was revising? Was he

---

25. See, for example, the advice given by Pietro Aaron, in Blackburn, "On Compositional
Process," 210–219.

26. The changes do not occur equally in all voices. The tenor is changed most frequently (13
instances as the only voice, as well as 3 instances as one of two or more voices), followed by altus
(4+1) and bassus (4+3).

27. Just, in *Der Kodex*, 78: 345.

composing directly onto this bifolio in a fashion neat enough for it to be sent to the compiler of BerlS 40021, or was there an earlier written version? Did Isaac sketch the music elsewhere, or did he write in the first instance directly on the Berlin bifolio?

If we can believe the testimony of Lampadius, writing some twenty years after Isaac's death, Isaac and Josquin used some sort of tablet for composing.[28] It is certainly possible that Isaac could have used a tablet; many other composers did. But the character of the changes on the Berlin bifolio suggests that at the very most the sketches would have been partial or fragmentary. Why else would he have needed to make so many corrections?

To try to answer the question about the existence of earlier written versions, we can invoke what we know about Isaac's reputation as a composer. Some composers were known to be slow and to revise their music over a long period of time. Glarean described Josquin as a composer who kept his music for years, making many corrections, before letting go of it.[29] Zarlino made similar comments about Willaert.[30] Others, like Obrecht, had a reputation for speed.[31] Several different bits of evidence portray Isaac as a quick writer. In an often-cited letter of 2 September 1502 to Duke Ercole I d'Este, the Ferrarese secretary Gian de Artiganova compared Josquin and Isaac as candidates for the position of *maestro di cappella*:

> I must notify your Lordship that Isaac the singer has been in Ferrara, and he has written a motet on a fantasy entitled 'La mi la so la so la mi' which is very good, and he wrote it in two days. From this one can only judge that he is very rapid in the art of composition; besides, he is good-natured and easy to get along with, and it seems to me that is the right man for Your Lordship. . . . To me he seems well suited to serve Your Lordship, more so than Josquin, because he is of a better disposition among his companions and will compose new works more often. It is true that Josquin composes better, but he composes when he wants to, and not when one wants him to.[32]

28. See chap. 5.

29. *Dodecachordon*, 363.

30. Zarlino, in *Sopplimenti musicali* (Venice, 1588; repr. New York, 1979), 326, translated by Einstein, *The Italian Madrigal*, 445, reported an exchange between a certain *maestro* Alberto, who bragged that he had composed a Mass in one night, and Parabosco, who claimed that Willaert would have spent two months: "He studies and ponders very carefully what must be done before he considers a piece finished and presents it to the world." Giulio Ongaro ("The Chapel of St. Mark's at the Time of Adrian Willaert (1527-1562): A Documentary Study," Ph.D. diss., University of North Carolina at Chapel Hill, 1986, 89–90) found a document that supports this view. Baldassare Donato, a singer and scribe for the chapel, had the following task: "And since the said *maestro* Adriano is busy, Baldissera shall have the duty to keep *maestro* Adriano occupied in composing . . . and as soon as *maestro* Adriano will hand him some new compositions, he must write them down . . . and notify the Most Illustrious *Procuratori*, so that they might see what the said *maestro* Adriano has done."

31. According to Glarean (*Dodecachordon*, 456), Obrecht composed a Mass in one night: "Hunc praeterea fama est, tanta ingenii celeritate ac inventionis copia viguisse, ut per unam noctem, egregiam, & quae doctis admirationi esset, Missam componeret."

32. Lewis Lockwood, "Josquin at Ferrara: New Documents and Letters," in *Josquin des Prez: Proceedings of the International Josquin Festival-Conference*, ed. Edward E. Lowinsky (London, 1976), 132–133.

There have been several different interpretations of the letter, trying to make it fit surviving music. There is a four-voice composition that uses the solmization 'La mi la sol la sol la mi' as an ostinato; it exists in two versions, one without text, and one with the Marian text *Rogamus te*, published by Petrucci in 1504.[33] In one interpretation, Isaac brought the textless piece with him and spent the time in Ferrara turning it into the motet *Rogamus te* by adding text. In another, he was actually composing the textless piece (in which case Gian's use of the term "motet" is simply an anomaly).[34] The latest theory, proposed by Willem Elders, is that while he was in Ferrara Isaac composed a motet that has not survived but that may have used the text *O praeclara*; the textless, instrumental version existed by about 1500, and Petrucci, not Isaac, was responsible for adding the text *Rogamus te* to it for the 1504 publication. Whatever the eventual outcome of this debate, the thrust of Gian's letter is clear: since Isaac was able to write a motet in just two days, he was a rapid composer.

A second reference to Isaac's speed comes from Paolo Cortese's *De cardinalatu*:

Ex eodemque studio Herricus Isachius Gallus maxime est appositus ad eiusmodi praecentoria construenda iudicatus: nam praeterquam, quod multo est caeteris in hoc genere fundendo celerior, tum valde eius illuminat cantum florentior in struendo modus, qui maxime satus communi aurium naturae sit: sed quamquam hic unus excellat e multis, vitio tamen ei dari solere scimus, quod in hoc genere licentius catachresi modorumque iteratione utatur, quam maxime aures fastidii similitudine in audiendo notent.

For a similar inclination Herricus Isachius Gallus [Heinrich Isaac of France] is judged to be most apt to compose such precentorial songs; for, in addition to being much quicker than all the others in pouring forth this genre, his style of composition brightens the singing so floridly that it more than satiates the ordinary capacity of the ear. But, although he is the one who excels among many, nevertheless we know that it happens to be blamed on him that he uses in this genre *catachresis* [literally, improper use of words] and repetition of modes more liberally than the most the ear can take without sense of annoyance because of uniformity in what it listens to (*similitudo in audiendo*).[35]

33. The textless version was edited by Johannes Wolf in Isaac, *Weltliche Werke* I, 87–89, and the texted version by Richard Sherr in *Selections from Motetti C (Venice, 1504)*, Sixteenth-Century Motet 2 (New York, 1991), 199–206.

34. For surveys of the arguments, see Picker, *Henricus Isaac*, 9–10 and 122, and Willem Elders, "Zur Frage der Vorlage von Isaacs Messe *La mi la sol* oder *O praeclara*," in *Von Isaac bis Bach: Studien zur älteren deutschen Musikgeschichte. Festschrift Martin Just zum 60. Geburtstag* (Kassel, 1991), 9–13.

35. *De cardinalatu libri tres* (Castel Cortesiano, 1510), bk. 2, fols. 73ᵛ–74ᵛ. "Precentorial songs" refers to motets. Text taken from Staehelin, *Die Messen*, 2: 93. The translation is by Nino Pirrotta, "Music and Cultural Tendencies in Fifteenth-Century Italy," in Pirrotta, *Music and Culture in Italy from the Middle Ages to the Baroque* (Cambridge, Mass., 1984), 104–105; a facsimile of the portions of the treatise concerning music is found on pp. 97–101. Staehelin correctly takes issue with Pirrotta's translation of *florentior* as floridly, suggesting instead flourishing (*blühend*) or splendid (*prächtig*).

The third piece of evidence regarding Isaac's speed concerns the composition of Mass propers that would eventually be published, long after his death, as Book II of the *Choralis Constantinus*. Pay documents show that the church officials commissioned the composition on 14 April 1508.[36] On 18 May 1509 they engaged a scribe to copy the music, and on 29 November 1509 Isaac was paid for the completed work, which the singers tried out and found "gantz und gerecht." Book II contains propers for twenty-five Masses, each consisting typically of four compositions (drawn from among the chants approprate to the feast: introit, alleluia, gradual, tract, sequence or prosa, and communion).[37] If he had completed the entire commission by May 1509, he was working at the rate of approximately two Masses per month.

What are the implications for his working process that Isaac could compose quickly? Perhaps we could conclude that he was able to work without needing many written stages. While he could have sketched some of the music first, perhaps using the same format that he used for writing the music on the final page of the bifolio, it seems at least possible that he worked directly on the Berlin bifolio, without sketching first. The notation of the music in choirbook format on the central opening, despite being neat enough to send in a letter, has some of the characteristics of a composer's draft. The presence of the various kinds of changes shows that Isaac could compose as well as revise while working with the music notated in separate parts.

Once Isaac had finished composing and revising his setting of the sequence, he presumably sent the bifolio to Scribe Y, who added it to BerlS 40021.[38] He may have made another copy for himself, for the piece exists in two other manuscripts that Just suggests may be independent of BerlS 40021.[39] Only the Berlin bifolio contains two settings of the final section; the other manuscripts have just the first one.

The Berlin bifolio offers a valuable glimpse of several stages of Isaac's work. The compositional method, reflecting a master composer working quickly and confidently at his craft, seems well suited to the demands of convention.

36. Staehelin, *Die Messen*, 2: 67.

37. See Picker, *Henricus Isaac*, 56–67.

38. Y added the heading "Ysaac de manu sua" on fol. 255ᵛ, "Sequent.a" on fol. 256ʳ, the foliation, the two entries in the index, and the six part names written in the margin of fol. 256ᵛ. Isaac wrote the part names on staff 5 of fol. 256ᵛ and those on fol. 255ᵛ; he may have written "de santa katerina" at the top of fol. 256ʳ.

39. One is the choirbook Jena, Universitätsbibliothek 33, copied for All Saints Church in Wittenberg; the other is Dresden, Sächsische Landesbibliothek, 1/D/506, copied for the St. Annenkirche in Annaberg in 1510-1530. Just, in *Der Kodex*, 78: 345; *CC*, 1: 297 and 175.

TABLE 10.1 Provisional List of Changes and Corrections in Isaac, *Sanctissimae virginis votiva festa*

No.	Measure	Voice	Change	Ink	Stage	Explanation
1.	2	T	erased, overwritten	dark	2	ligature erased?
2.	5	T	erased, overwritten	dark	2	tenor changed after altus added?
3.	13	B	crossed out, overwritten	?	?	bassus worked with discantus, changed after tenor added?
4.	14–16	T, B	erased, overwritten	dark	2	revision in linking voice; new version added after text
5.	25–26	A	erased, overwritten	dark	2	new linking voice
6.	28	A	stem, rest added	dark	2	adds rhythmic variety
7.	33–34	T	notes erased, rests added	dark	2	thins texture
8.	45	B	erased, overwritten	same	1	text may have prompted change, to avoid repetition
9.	48	T	erased, overwritten	dark?	2?	improves voice–leading
10.	50	T	crossed out	same	1	incorrect clef
11.	49–51	A	crossed out	same	1	revision in linking voice
12.	54–57	T, B	erased, notes added	dark	2	problem with counterpoint at cadence?
13.	57–58	D, A, T	erased, overwritten	dark	2	revision of opening sonorities
14.	58–59	T	overwritten	dark?	2?	change in rhythm, alters sounding of sonority
15.	62	T	crossed out	same	1	incorrect clef; pitches in correct position
16.	63	T	overwritten	dark?	2?	two corrections: (1) to shorten tenor, prevent clash with discantus; (2) to avoid going to same pitch as altus (changed after altus added?)
17.	65–66	B	crossed out	same	1	original reading makes little sense; text "respuit" added in dark ink (?) after the correction

(continued)

TABLE 10.1 (continued)

No.	Measure	Voice	Change	Ink	Stage	Explanation
18.	68	A	overwritten	same	1	slip of pen (semibreve C overwritten as 3)
19.	88	D	overwritten	dark?	2?	note shortened, rest added to articulate phrase
20.	90	T	overwritten	same?	1?	slip of pen? (rest written on the right line for the corrected pitch)
21.	94	T	crossed out	same	1	incorrect clef
22.	94	T	overwritten	dark	2?	opening sonority altered. Version beginning with C not transmitted in other sources, suggesting that Isaac could have changed his mind after maining the Berlin bifolio and switched to an opening on G (as in the repeat). Just (*Der Kodex*, 78: 345) speculated that the second reading (with C) could be either Isaac's final version or a change made by Scribe Y.
23.	95	T	overwritten	same	1	improves voice-leading
24.	123	B	erased, overwritten	same	1	bassus changed after altus added to avoid parallel fifths?
25.	128	B	overwritten	?	1?	slip of pen? original reading makes no sense
26.	142	T	overwritten	dark	2	change in rhythm to minimize dissonance

APPENDIX

EXAMPLE 10.2   Isaac, *Sanctissimae virginis votiva festa* (BerlS 40021, fols. 255ᵛ–256ᵛ)

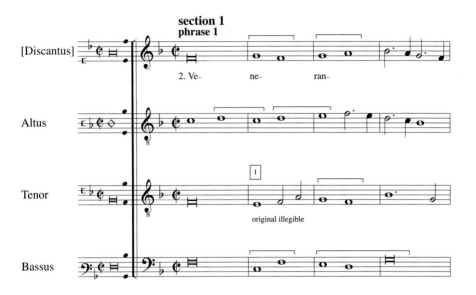

EXAMPLE 10.2   (*continued*)

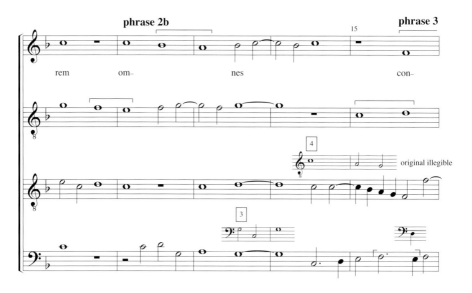

EXAMPLE 10.2   (*continued*)

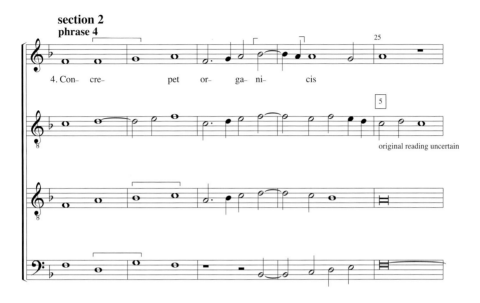

section 2
phrase 4

4. Con– cre– pet or– ga– ni– cis

original reading uncertain

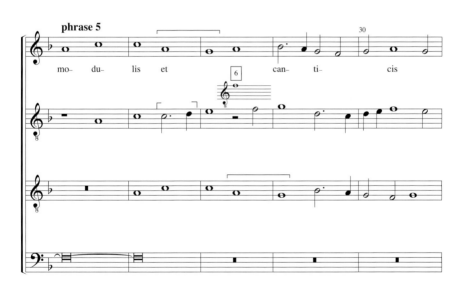

phrase 5

mo– du– lis et can– ti– cis

EXAMPLE 10.2   (*continued*)

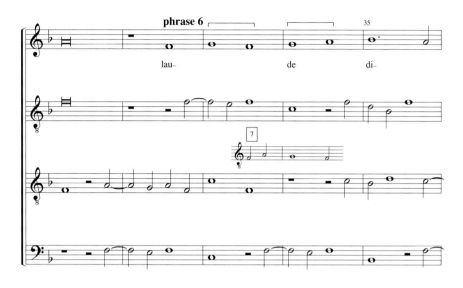

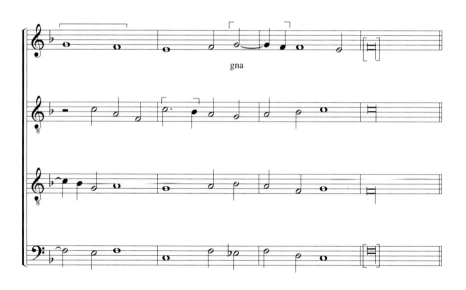

EXAMPLE 10.2   (*continued*)

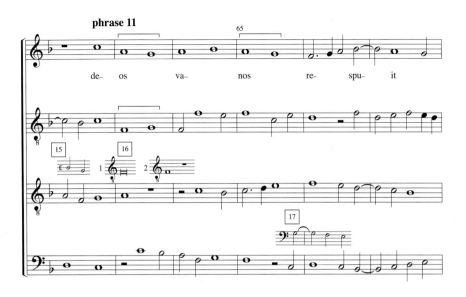

phrase 11

de- os   va- nos   re- spu- it

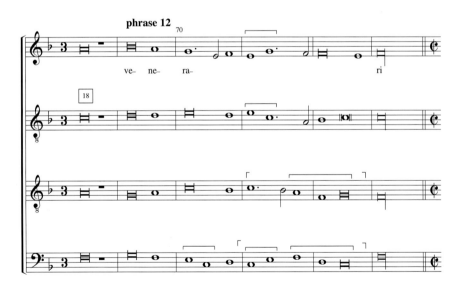

phrase 12

ve- ne- ra-   ri

EXAMPLE 10.2   *(continued)*

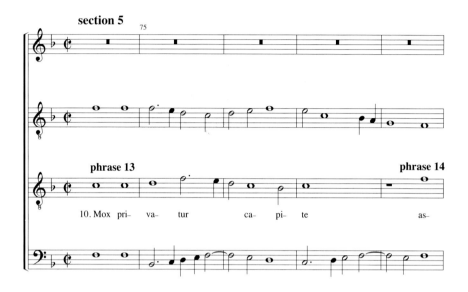

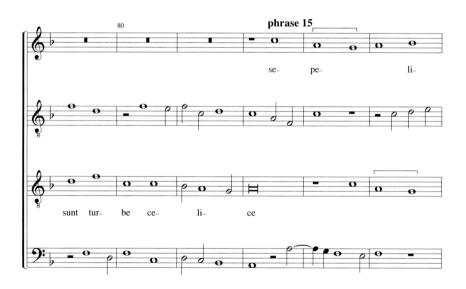

EXAMPLE 10.2   *(continued)*

EXAMPLE 10.2   (*continued*)

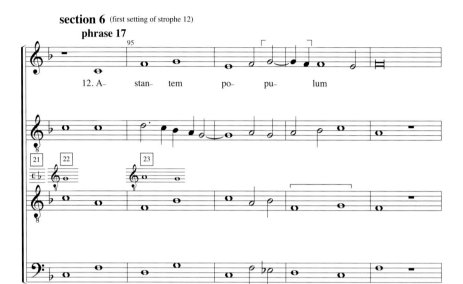

section 6 (first setting of strophe 12)

phrase 17

12. A- stan- tem po- pu- lum

phrase 18

Lau- dan- tem te cle- rum

EXAMPLE 10.2   (*continued*)

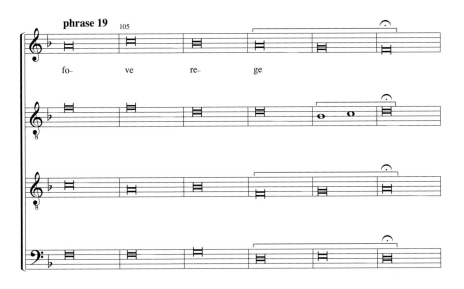

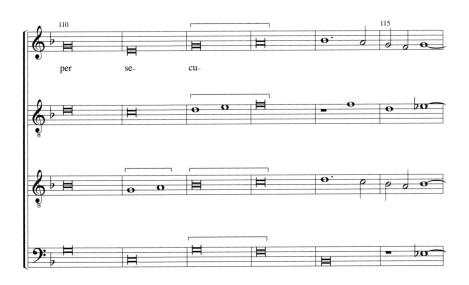

EXAMPLE 10.2   (*continued*)

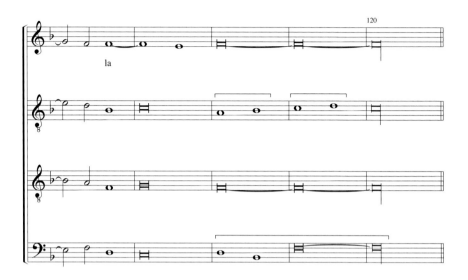

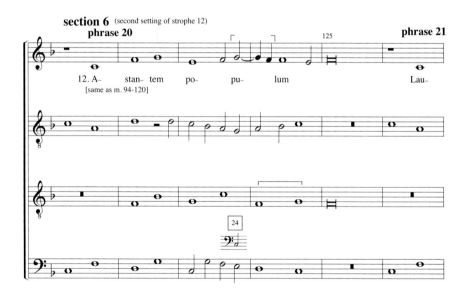

EXAMPLE 10.2   (*continued*)

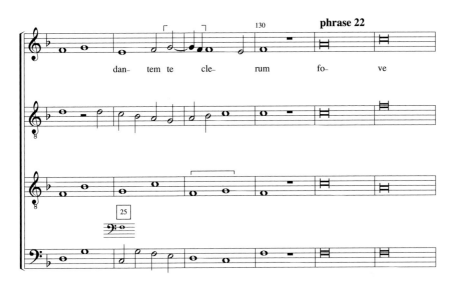

dan- tem te   cle-   rum   fo-   ve

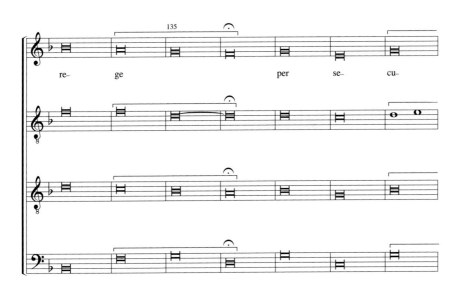

re-   ge   per   se-   cu-

EXAMPLE 10.2   *(continued)*

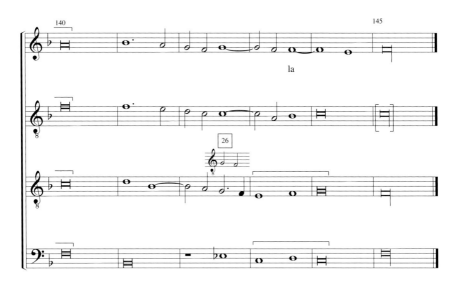

CHAPTER ELEVEN

GIOVANNI PIERLUIGI
DA PALESTRINA

Giovanni Pierluigi da Palestrina was the most important composer of sacred music in Italy during the final quarter of the sixteenth century. He composed 104 Masses and several hundred motets, as well as liturgical music: litanies, Magnificats, hymns, and Lamentations.[1] He stood apart from most of his contemporaries not only in the sheer volume of music that he composed but also in its unusually wide dissemination both in print and manuscript: he published twenty-one volumes of sacred music during his lifetime, and most enjoyed many subsequent editions.

It is surprising, given Palestrina's prominence in his own time and his place in history, that there has never been a comprehensive examination of the evidence concerning his working methods. The only scholar to have considered this topic at any length was Raffaele Casimiri, who discussed some of the revisions in RomSG 59, a manuscript largely in Palestrina's hand.[2] But there is other evidence not considered by Casimiri, much of which was first uncovered by Knud Jeppesen, that can help clarify aspects of Palestrina's working methods. The following discussion, rather than presenting new discoveries, offers a new interpretation of existing evidence from the broader perspective outlined in this book. As in the other three case studies, we see but part of the picture.

THE MANTUAN COMMISSION

The only source of information about the early stages of Palestrina's process comes from a series of letters preserved in the Mantuan archives.[3] Palestrina enjoyed a long-standing connection with Guglielmo Gonzaga, Duke of Mantua, an avid patron of music and amateur composer. In 1568 he composed a Mass for

1. Lewis Lockwood, "Giovanni Pierluigi da Palestrina," *The New Grove High Renaissance Masters* (New York, 1984).
2. Casimiri, *Il "Codice 59"*.
3. The letters were first published by Bertolotti, *Musici alla corte*, 47–55. See the appendix to this chapter for the relevant extracts.

the duke. The terms of the commission must not have been clear, for Palestrina's letter accompanying the Mass reveals his concern that it might not be what the duke wanted:

> Since I have been ordered by so excellent a lord as yourself and by the hand of so exceptional a virtuoso as master Giaches [Wert] to compose the Mass that is enclosed here, I have fashioned it as I have been instructed by master Annibale Capello. If in this first attempt I shall not have fulfilled the wishes of your Excellency, I beg you to inform me how you prefer it—whether short, or long, or written so that the words can be understood.[4]

Over the years, Palestrina continued to send music, including motets and *falsibordoni*, various *canti* and *canzoni*. In 1572 he dedicated his second book of motets for five, six, and eight voices to Guglielmo, and received 25 ducats. In the letter of dedication, Palestrina thanked him for his generosity toward his family; the collection includes music by his brother and two of his sons, one of whom was set to enter Gonzaga service but then died unexpectedly.[5]

Palestrina also commented on the duke's own musical compositions.[6] In a letter of 3 March 1570, he gave his reactions to a motet:

> In order to study it more satisfactorily I have set the motet into score, and have observed its beautiful workmanship, far removed from the common run, and the vital impulse given to its words, according to their meaning. I have indicated certain passages in which it seems to me that if one can do with less, the harmony will sound better—such as the sixth and unison, when both parts are moving with sixth and fifth ascending and at the same time certain unisons are descending; since the imitations cause the parts to move in this way, it seems to me that because of the dense interweaving of the imitations, the words are somewhat obscured to the listeners, who do not enjoy them as in ordinary music.[7]

4. Mantua, Archivio di Stato, letter from Palestrina to the duke, 2 February 1568, facsimile: Giovanni Pierluigi da Palestrina, *Le messe di Mantova, inedite dai manoscritti di S. Barbara*, ed. Knud Jeppesen, *Le opere complete di Giovanni Pierluigi da Palestrina*, 18–19 (Rome, 1954), 18, p. xiii; see also the appendix to this chapter, no. 1. The translation is by Lewis Lockwood, in his edition of Palestrina, *Pope Marcellus Mass*, Norton Critical Scores (New York, 1975), 24. Knud Jeppesen, "Pierluigi da Palestrina, Herzog Guglielmo Gonzaga und die neugefundenen Mantovaner-Messen Palestrina's," *Acta musicologica* 25 (1953): 149–152, identifies the Mass as the untitled four-voice Mass (usually referred to as "Sine nomine") preserved in MilC 109. Palestrina received the handsome sum of 50 ducats for composing it.

5. The collection contains two motets that Palestrina presumably composed for Santa Barbara, *Gaude Barbara beata* and *Beata Barbara*. Another collaborative effort, in addition to this motet collection, may have been a *Missa domenicalis* with movements composed by Palestrina and the three other members of his family who were composers, preserved in MilC 55, and available in a modern edition: *Sei missae dominicales*, ed. Siro Cisilino (Padua, 1981).

6. On Gonzaga as a composer, see Richard Sherr, "The Publications of Guglielmo Gonzaga," *JAMS* 31 (1978): 118–125. See also Guglielmo Gonzaga, *Sacrae cantiones quinque vocum* (Venice, 1583), ed. Richard Sherr (New York, 1990) and Guglielmo Gonzaga, *Madrigali a cinque voci* (Venice, 1583), ed. Jessie Ann Owens and Megumi Nagaoka (New York, 1995).

7. Letter from Palestrina to the duke, 3 March 1570, text in Jeppesen, "Pierluigi da Palestrina," 156–157, and below, appendix, no. 2. The translation is by Lockwood, *Pope Marcellus Mass*, 25. For a translation into period English, see Piero Weiss, *Letters of Composers through Six Centuries* (Philadelphia, 1967), 16-17.

The letter reveals what Palestrina thought was important: a close relationship between text and music, and a texture that is thin enough for the words to be heard.[8] It also shows how he functioned as teacher: writing out the music he wanted to evaluate in score, marking problematic passages.[9] In 1583 there were discussions about Palestrina becoming *maestro di cappella* in Mantua, but in the end nothing came of it. The death of Duke Guglielmo in 1587 ended his association with Mantua.

For our purposes, the most important evidence is the correspondence surrounding Palestrina's commission to compose Masses for the palatine basilica, Santa Barbara.[10] Duke Guglielmo commissioned a series of Masses that were to be: (1) *alternatim* (that is, divided between chant and polyphony), (2) based on the newly revised chants of the Santa Barbara liturgy, and (3) imitative throughout. Palestrina thought that he could compose one Mass every ten days. In fact, the chronology drawn from the correspondence shows that he was working at the rate of approximately one Mass every three weeks between October 1578 and April 1579.[11]

The evidence about Palestrina's working methods comes from the beginning of the series of letters from 1578–1579. The duke's agent in Rome, Don Annibale Capello, reported on 18 October 1578:

> Having passed recently through a serious illness and being thus unable to command either his wits or his eyesight in the furtherance of his great desire to serve Your Highness in whatever way he can, M. Giovanni da Palestrina has begun to set the Kyrie and Gloria of the first mass on the lute, and when he let me hear them,

---

8. For a discussion of the letter, see Knud Jeppesen, "Über einen Brief Palestrinas," in *Festschrift Peter Wagner zum 60. Geburtstag*, ed. K. Weinman (Leipzig, 1926), 100–106. In a second letter, from 1574, Palestrina sent the duke a score of his Mass, marked with crosses and his comments. The *Pleni* was evidently beyond help; Palestrina hoped that the duke would be able to find the time to do it over. Letter from Palestrina to the duke, 17 April 1574; see Jeppesen, "Pierluigi da Palestrina," 158, and below, appendix, no. 3.

9. See chap. 2.

10. Oliver Strunk, "Guglielmo Gonzaga and Palestrina's *Missa Dominicalis*," *MQ* 33 (1947), reprinted in Strunk, *Essays on Music in the Western World* (New York, 1974), 94–107, the version cited here, offered a convincing interpretation of the letters and of the nature of Palestrina's commission from Guglielmo that enabled Jeppesen to identify the Masses among the music of the Fondo Santa Barbara, now in Milan, Biblioteca del Conservatorio. See Knud Jeppesen, "The Recently Discovered Mantova Masses of Palestrina," *Acta musicologica* 22 (1950): 36–37; Jeppesen, "Pierluigi da Palestrina," 132–179; and Palestrina, *Le messe di Mantova*. See also Fenlon, *Music and Patronage*, ch. 3.

11. An outline of the main events can be derived from the extant letters: (1) 18 October 1578: Palestrina has set the Kyrie and Gloria to the lute. (2) 1 November 1578: Palestrina is sending the first Mass; he will send one every ten days. (3) 5 November 1578: Palestrina has sent the first Mass (fourth mode, cantus firmus transposed up a fifth or an octave, *Missa In duplicibus minoribus* I or II). (4) 15 November 1578: Capello has sent the second Mass. (5) 10 December 1578: Capello has sent the fourth Mass (one which Palestrina particularly liked). (6) 17 March 1579: payment (by Strozzi on behalf of the duke) of 100 scudi to Palestrina. (7) 18 March 1579: Strozzi has sent a Mass. (8) 21 March 1579: Palestrina has sent three *ultime* [last? or most recent? or latest?] Masses, composed according to Capello's most recent instructions ("ultimo avertimento"), i.e., with a different disposition of chant in the Sanctus. (9) 1 April 1579: Strozzi has sent a Mass.

I found them in truth full of great sweetness and elegance. And now that His Holiness has commanded that there are to be two choirs at St. Peter's, each choir of twelve singers (for he has discovered that Julius II so ordered when he provided the chapter with revenues sufficient for this purpose), and has for this reason also caused the dismissal of all the married singers save only Palestrina by special privilege, if with the gracious permission of Your Highness it may be so, Palestrina wishes also to have the second parts and to use them in the church in question instead of the organ on occasions of high solemnity, for he affirms that Your Highness has in truth purged these plainsongs of all the barbarisms and imperfections that they contained. I trust that he will not do this without your permission. And as soon as his infirmity permits he will work out what he has done on the lute with all possible care.[12]

Jeppesen discovered the reply to this letter among chancellery documents; written by an unknown court official, it is preserved in draft form, in two slightly different versions. The first version reads:

His Highness commands that Your Lordship tell Messer Giovanni di Palestina that he should take care to get well and not hurry to set to the lute the Kyrie and the Gloria with other compositions, because having at hand many other talented men there is no need for compositions for lute, but instead for compositions made with great care. His Highness thinks that the music composed for Santa Barbara would not succeed there (i.e., in Rome) because of the amount of imitation that it contains, since they use simple (plain) music; however, if it is pleasing to Messer Giovanni and if he wants to use it, His Highness will order that just as he has already been sent half of the chants, he can have sent to him the whole chant.[13]

The second draft of the duke's letter adds several important details:

His Highness orders that you tell Messer Giovanni di Palestina that he take care to get well and not hurry to set the Masses to the lute, since he desires that they employ imitation throughout and be written on the chant as the other composers have done and as he himself did in the Mass for Major Double feasts.

This response suggests that the duke thought that Palestrina was composing music for the lute, and it is clear that he had a rather low opinion of it. He valued music "fatto con molto studio," by which he implied that lute music was not so carefully crafted. The idea that Palestrina might have been using the lute for composing vocal music seems not to have occurred to him, perhaps an indication that neither he nor other composers whom he knew used the lute.

Ten "Santa Barbara" Masses by Palestrina have survived.[14] A document recently discovered by Paola Besutti records the copying of a lost "Missa in duplicibus

---

12. The translation is by Strunk, "Guglielmo Gonzaga," 99–100. For the original text, see below, appendix, no. 4.

13. Jeppesen, "Pierluigi da Palestrina," 161–162, including a facsimile of the *recto*. Mantova, AS, Archivio Gonzaga, Serie F.II.7, Busta 2207, Minuta di lettere del Duca Guglielmo Gonzaga al Capello, Pietole, 23 ottobre 1578. See appendix, no. 5.

14. MilC 164 and 166, 1592¹: two settings of Masses "in duplicibus minoribus," three "in festis beatae Mariae virginis," two "in festis apostolorum," two "in semiduplicibus maioribus," and one "in dominicis diebus."

majoribus" by Palestrina in 1574, an indication that the commission had already begun as much as four years earlier.[15] It now appears that he provided settings for the first six of the ten Masses in the "Kyriale ad usum ecclesie Sancte Barbare."[16]

Capello's letter is difficult to interpret. Does "porre sul leuto" mean that Palestrina was using the lute as a tool in composing, or was it merely a convenient way to perform the music for Capello in the absence of a choir?[17] Was Palestrina playing the Mass as it would have sounded as a choral composition, or was he simply giving Capello a taste, perhaps playing the essential sonorities, the main motives, playing a kind of reduction for lute?

Capello's remarks about Palestrina's "indispositione grave havuta la testa ne la vista" ("the serious illness that the head had in the vision or sight," to translate literally) raise other questions. Did the illness interrupt Palestrina's activities altogether, or did it simply prevent him from writing anything down? And what exactly does "spiegarà cio ch' ha fatto col leuto" mean? *Spiegare* can have the sense of making something clear or accessible, extending something, unfolding a map.[18] Florio defines it as "to displaie, to explaine, to expound, to unfold, to spred abroad."[19] Was Capello describing Palestrina's normal procedure, or did his illness cause Palestrina to alter his practices in some way? We have seen that some composers—Monteverdi, for instance, and Rore—worked first "in the mind."[20] Was Palestrina composing in the mind, and simply playing the music on the lute, waiting until he was well to write it down? Is it possible that Palestrina was jotting down his ideas in lute tablature?[21]

While I doubt that we can arrive at a definitive interpretation of Capello's letter, it is possible to suggest a hypothesis. Given the problem with Palestrina's health, particularly his eyesight, it seems unlikely that he notated the music at all—in tablature or mensural notation—while he was sick. Nor was Palestrina one of the beginners whom Finck ridicules who needed to sound out conso-

15. Paola Besutti, "Giovanni Pierluigi da Palestrina e la liturgia mantovana (II)," read at the III Convegno Internazionale di Studi Palestrina e l'Europa, October 1994. Besutti also found a payment for a *Missa Dominicalis*, which probably refers to the Mass published in 1592.

16. Namely, in duplicibus maioribus, in duplicibus minoribus, in festis beatae Mariae viriginis, in festis apostolorum, in Dominicis diebus, and in semiduplicibus maioribus. On the Santa Barbara liturgy see Jeppesen, "Pierluigi da Palestrina," 138–142. See also Iain Fenlon, "Patronage, Music and Liturgy in Renaissance Mantua," in *Plainsong in the Age of Polyphony*, ed. Thomas F. Kelly (Cambridge, 1992), 220–224. On the Kyriale and chant at Santa Barbara, see Paola Besutti, "Catalogo tematico delle monodie liturgiche della Basilica Palatina di S. Barbara in Mantova," *Le fonti musicali in Italia, studi e ricerche* 2 (1988): 53–66 and Besutti, "Giovanni Pierluigi da Palestrina e la liturgia Mantovana," in *Atti del II Convegno Internazionale di Studi Palestriniani*, ed. Lino Bianchi and Giancarlo Rostirolla (Palestrina, 1991), 157–164.

17. See chap. 4.

18. The *Vocabolario degli Accademici della Crusca*, 834, defines it as "allargare, e aprir le cose ristrette, in pieghe, contrario di ripiegare."

19. *A Worlde of Wordes*, 389.

20. See chap. 4.

21. Casimiri, *Il "Codice 59,"* 10 and 27, assumed that Palestrina worked first in *tabulatura*, which I take to mean score.

nances on an instrument before writing them down.[22] If Palestrina used the lute for composing, I suspect that it was to hear his ideas; he could also have been using it to show the duke's agent that he had been working on the commission. The description suggests the same two-step process to which Monteverdi alluded when he claimed that a piece was composed already in his mind, implying that all that remained was to write it down.

The Mantuan correspondence offers tantalizing hints about Palestrina's methods, but little concrete information. For a better understanding, we need to consider the documents in light of his extant autograph manuscripts.

PALESTRINA AUTOGRAPHS

Palestrina left a large number of compositions in manuscript when he died in 1594. For example, only forty-three of his Masses were published during his lifetime, while thirty-eight appeared in print after his death, presumably taken from autograph manuscripts or from manuscripts copied from his autographs.[23] Of this legacy only four autographs have survived, all of them written in mensural notation.[24]

Knud Jeppesen identified Palestrina's hand in the choirbook VatV 10766.[25] Palestrina added his (otherwise unknown) *falsobordone* setting of Psalm 109, *Dixit Dominus*, on a blank opening at the end of the choirbook, and corrected a mistake in the text of one of the hymns (see plate 11.1). The opening, while not containing any significant revisions, does perhaps reflect Palestrina's writing out or writing down of the piece rather than a simple copying from another source. He initially identified the four quadrants—cantus, altus, tenor, bassus—with the part names in the middle of the staff, but when space ran short, he crossed out "Tenor" and "Bassus" because he needed the staff. A rather sharp change in ink color for the last two verses may indicate that he worked on the piece at two different times.

The other three manuscripts, in contrast, all contain revisions of one sort or another, to which I return later. Two sets of parts are now found in the library at the Conservatorio di Musica Santa Cecilia; each contains the music for an eight-voice motet, copied on eight sheets of paper, front and back. *Omnis pulchritudo* (RomeSC O.232) is in upright format, with nine staves per side (see plate 11.2).[26]

22. See chap. 4

23. Palestrina's son and heir, Iginio, supervised the printing of the Masses. He tried to sell a portion of the gradual that he claimed his father had revised, but the manuscript was determined to be a fake. See Robert F. Hayburn, *Papal Legislation on Sacred Music 95 A.D. to 1977 A.D.* (Collegeville, Minn., 1979), 44–57. The case eventually went to trial and the son lost; he is said to have given the manuscript away.

24. Jeppesen, "Palestrina," *MGG*.

25. Knud Jeppesen, "Palestriniana: Ein unbekanntes Autogramm und einige unveröffentlichte Falsibordoni des Giovanni Pierluigi da Palestrina," in *Miscelánea en Homenaje a Monseñor Higinio Anglés* (Barcelona, 1958–1961), 417–430; color reproductions in *Rome Reborn: The Vatican Library and Renaissance Culture*, ed. Anthony Grafton (Washington, 1993), plate 162.

26. Giovanni Pierluigi da Palestrina, *Omnis pulchritudo domini*, ed. V. Mortari (Rome, [1950]); facsimile of fol. 1.

Beata es Virgo Maria (*2.p. Ave Maria*) (RomeSC O.231) is in oblong format, six staves per page (see plate 11.3).[27] The motets are both responsories, set as polychoral pieces for two four-voice choirs.

We do not know the context for the composition of these two motets. There are a number of possibilities.[28] One is the Chiesa Nuova, the center of Filippo Neri's activities. According to Noel O'Regan, eight-voice music by Lasso, Palestrina, Giovanni Animuccia, and Marenzio—published using a full eight-voice texture—was revised in manuscript to create true *cori spezzati* (that is, with harmonically self-sufficient choirs) for use in the Chiesa Nuova. While the two Santa Cecilia motets have not been specifically linked to the Chiesa Nuova, they conform in style to music that can be. Other possibilities, also suggested by O'Regan, are the Oratory of Santissima Trinità dei Pellegrini, where Palestrina led the music for Holy Week in 1576 and 1578, and Santo Spirito in Sassia. He could also have written the music for St. Peter's. Capello's letter of 18 October 1578 transmits Palestrina's request for the complete chant for the Mass (not just the portions he was to set polyphonically) and mentions Gregory XIV's interest in music for two choirs. *Beata es* also occurs in a source associated with the Cappella Giulia, VatG XIII.24, a set of partbooks containing polychoral music.[29]

The fourth and most substantial of the manuscripts is the Lateran choirbook studied by Casimiri, RomeSG 59.[30] Quite small in size (ca. 15.5 by 11 in.), at least in comparison with many of the choirbooks of the time, the manuscript contains sixty-four compositions, written on ninety-four folios: office hymns, Lamentations, a few canticles, the responsory for the Dead, the Improperia, and a motet.[31] While the other three autographs might be considered fair copies suitable for performance or, in the case of the two motets, for transmission as well as for performance, RomeSG 59, in contrast, seems to be Palestrina's personal copy of some of his music.

We know that that composers kept personal copies of their music.[32] The title

27. Facsimile (complete): *Atti del II Convegno Internazionale di Studi Palestriniani* (Palestrina, 1991). Palestrina, *Le opere complete*, 34: 41.

28. On Roman polychoral music, see Noel O'Regan, "The Early Polychoral Music of Orlando di Lasso: New Light from Roman Sources," *Acta musicologica* 56 (1985), 234–251; O'Regan, "Palestrina and the Oratory of Santissima Trinità dei Pellegrini," in *Atti del II Convegno Internazionale di Studi Palestriniani* (Palestrina, 1991), 95–121; and O'Regan, "'Blessed with the Holy Father's Entertainment': Roman Ceremonial Music as Experienced by the Irish Earls in Rome, 1608," *Irish Musical Studies*, 2: *Music and the Church* (1991): 41–61.

29. O'Regan, "The Early Polychoral Music," 238–239. José M. Llorens, *Le opere musicali della Cappella Giulia*, 1: *Manoscritti e edizioni fino al '700*, Studi e Testi 265 (Vatican City, 1971), no. 34 (with a list of contents).

30. Casimiri, *Il "Codice 59"*. For the past decade at least, this manuscript was not accessible. I am grateful to Dott. Giancarlo Rostirolla for helping me gain access; I was able to spend four hours with it in October 1990. He is preparing a facsimile edition of the manuscript, which I hope will provide information about physical aspects such as watermarks, gathering structure, and ink color that I was unable to consider.

31. Casimiri, *Il "Codice 59"*, gives a list of contents. There are facsimiles in Casimiri, *Il "Codice 59"*; Giovanni Pierluigi da Palestrina, *Werke*, ed. F. X. Haberl (Leipzig, 1862–1907), vol. 31; and Jeppesen, "Palestriniana: Ein unbekanntes Autogramm."

32. BarcOC 28 is an example of a composer's personal notebook; see chap. 7.

PLATE 11.1a   VatV 10776, fol. 55ᵛ: Palestrina, *Dixit Dominus*, fair copy

298

PLATE 11.1b   fol. 56ʳ

299

page of the 1555 print of Ruffo's motets, for example, boasts that the music was corrected from his "proprii originali," his own "original" manuscript: *Cantus Motetti, a sei voci composti da Vincentio Ruffo, maestro della capella, del domo, di Verona, dedicati, al signor Luca Grimaldi, novamente posti in luce da li suoi proprii originali, corretti, & stampati* (Venice: Girolamo Scotto, 1555). "Proprii originali" is synonymous with the more common designation "proprii essemplari," found fre-

PLATE 11.2   RomeSC O.232, tenor (chorus secundus): Palestrina, *Omnis pulchritudo*, fair copy

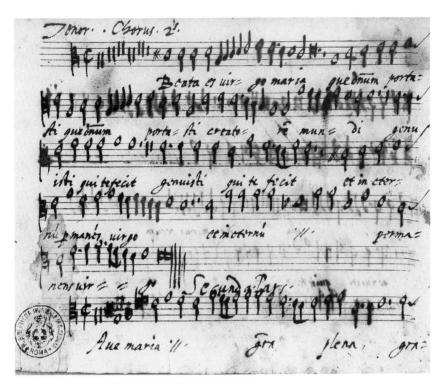

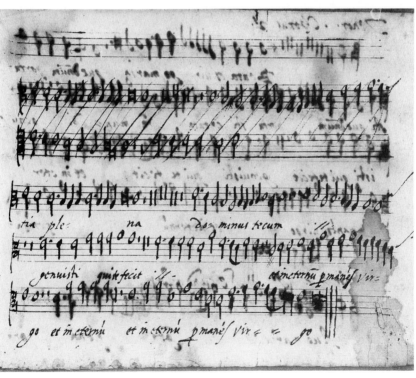

PLATE 11.3   RomeSC O.231, tenor (chorus secundus): Palestrina, *Beata es* (*2.p. Ave Maria*), fair copy

quently in Scotto prints.[33] The scribe of MunBS 239 used the same word in noting (on fol. 7ᵛ) that he copied Obrecht's *Missa Fors seulement* from Obrecht's own copy, presumably an autograph: "ab exemplari eiusdem descripta."[34] One of Pietro Pontio's pupils kept his *originale* of a Magnificat on a *cartella*.[35] *Originale* seems to imply a final version, a fair copy with revisions. Other terms may also have been used. The Ferrarese copyist Jean Michel lent his "registre" to another copyist; "registre" could be either a book or a list of pieces.[36]

I consider RomeSG 59 to be Palestrina's *originale* in part because of the revisions he made in the music and in part because of the ordering of the music in the manuscript. The order suggests that it was a working manuscript, not a polished or final copy. The manuscript falls into four main sections. The Lamentations for Holy Week are divided between the first and third sections. The hymns are in the second and fourth sections. The rest of the pieces in the manuscript seem to have been fit in wherever space would permit.

Casimiri recognized that the manuscript had not been written at one time. He used the appearance of the writing to posit three main stages in the manuscript's genesis.[37] Until there is a systematic study of the paper, gathering structure, and other physical evidence that could help determine the chronology of its compilation, this issue will have to remain open.

Dating the manuscript has also proven difficult. The presence of the year "1560" on the first page led some scholars (for example, Baini and Haberl) to assign it to Palestrina's time at San Giovanni in Laterano, from October 1555 until July 1560. Casimiri, however, realized that "1560" was a later addition to the

---

33. For example, Ruffo's 1554 *Madrigali a sei a sette et a otto voce . . . novamente da li suoi proprii essemplarii corretti & post'In Luce*. Facsimile of the title page in *Die Musik des 15. und 16. Jahrhunderts*, 78.

34. Barton Hudson, "On the Texting of Obrecht's Masses," *MD* 42 (1988): 102–103.

35. See chap. 5. Another witness, Petrus di Solzia, referred to a book he kept containing his music. He said that he had shown Pontio one of the *canti* he had composed and that he realized that Pontio was not conscientious as a teacher because he put a cross by a good passage ("qualche bel ponto") and left two parallel fifths or sixths stand unremarked; Solzia testified that he still had the book (*libro*) marked by Pontio. See Murray, "The Voice of the Composer," and Murray, "On the Teaching Duties."

36. Lewis Lockwood, "Jean Mouton and Jean Michel: French Music and Musicians in Italy, 1505–1520," *JAMS* 32 (1979): 224–229. In 1494 Compère explained that he was unable to provide music for Ferrante d'Este because he had left his music books with his new compositions in France; Lockwood, "Music at Ferrara in the Period of Ercole I d'Este," *Studi musicali* 1 (1972): 115–116, 129–130.

37. Casimiri, *Il "Codice 59,"* 11–21. The first stage was for the rather neat, small hand that entered the Lamentations on fols. 2ᵛ–6 and 23ᵛ–26. The second stage represents the bulk of the manuscript, including almost all of the hymns. The third stage, characterized by a larger, bolder script and a different kind of text repetition mark, included the Magnificat on fols. 77ᵛ–80 and *Hodie Christus natus est* on fols. 90ᵛ–91. He noted two other scribal appearances, a slightly later "calligraphic" hand for fols. 39ᵛ–42 and 45ᵛ–46, and a hand that he thought was not necessarily Palestrina's, on fols. 33ᵛ–34 and 42ᵛ–45. I suspect that a careful check of Roman manuscripts will turn up scribal concordances for Casimiri's "calligraphic" hand, his "altra mano," his "third" stage, and possibly even the "first" stage, leaving as Palestrina's work the hymns and some of the miscellaneous liturgical pieces of his "second" stage.

manuscript, and that the presence of the manuscript in the Archivio musicale of San Giovanni in Laterano was unrelated to Palestrina's service as *maestro di cappella*—simply an accident of history.[38] His suggestion that the manuscript belonged to Palestrina himself, and was among the manuscripts left to his son after his death, seems quite plausible.

Casimiri was intent on establishing as broad a range of dates for the creation of the manuscript as possible, between 1555, when Palestrina began to work at San Giovanni in Laterano, and 1588 or 1589, the date of publication of one of the Lamentations (1588) and most of the hymns (1589). I think it far more likely that the manuscript dates from Palestrina's second period as *maestro di cappella* in the Cappella Giulia from 1571 until his death in 1594. The evidence actually suggests an even narrower time frame, from about the mid-1570s until the mid-1580s.

Palestrina may have stopped using the manuscript by 1587. The final piece is a draft of a *falsobordone* setting of *Benedictus Dominus* (fol. 94^v) that was published in Giovanni Guidetti's *Cantus ecclesiasticus* of 1587.[39] At the early end of the temporal spectrum, two of the pieces bear the names of singers from the Cappella Giulia.[40] Matching the names against archival evidence shows that the Improperia on fols. 89^v–90 were sung in 1573. The Lamentation on fol. 1, however, could have been sung anywhere between 1573 and 1578. We know, however, from the Mantuan correspondence that Palestrina was busy composing Lamentations in 1574.[41] Documents preserved in Rome indicate that the scribe Johannes Parvus copied a set of Lamentations in 1575 (the manuscript has unfortunately not survived).[42] Jeppesen assumed, quite reasonably, that the Lamentations Palestrina was working on in 1574 were the same as this set from the Lateran choirbook; the presence of the names of the singers on fol. 1 seems like convincing evidence (see plate 11.4).

The hymns probably date from somewhat later. Casimiri noticed that many of them had barlines dividing the music and speculated that RomeSG 59 had

38. Casimiri (*Il "Codice 59"*, 1, 23–26) recognized that the portion of the title bearing the date "1560" was an eighteenth-century addition by Girolamo Chiti. He noted that the manuscript was not included in an inventory of the Lateran collection made in 1620–1622; it first appeared in an inventory of 1748, under its present collocation.

39. Jeppesen, "Palestriniana: Ein unbekanntes Autogramm," 429–430, 432, with a facsimile of fol. 94^v.

40. Casimiri, *Il "Codice 59"*, 17–18. The most recent archival work (Giancarlo Rostirolla, "La Cappella Giulia in San Pietro negli anni del magistero di Giovanni Pierluigi da Palestrina," *Atti del Convegno di Studi Palestriniani*, ed. F. Luisi [Palestrina, 1977], 117; 174–181) confirms Casimiri's dates for the Improperia, but suggests a wider span for the Lamentation. Rostirolla (p. 17) made the interesting suggestion that the presence of individual singers' names indicated performance by soloists (one on a part). I think it could also indicate rehearsal.

41. Jeppesen, "Pierluigi da Palestrina," 157; letter of Annibale Capello of 17 April 1574, cited by Bertolotti, *Musici alla corte*, 50; see below, appendix, no. 6. Casimiri, *Il "Codice 59"*, 19, proposed a date of 1574 for the Lamentation.

42. Jeppesen, "Palestrina," *MGG*, col. 699. On Parvus, see Mitchell Brauner, "The Parvus Manuscripts: A Study of Vatican Polyphony, ca. 1535 to 1580," Ph.D. diss., Brandeis University, 1982. Rostirolla, "La Cappella Giulia," 252–253.

PLATE 11.4   RomeSG 59, fol. 1ʳ (after Casimiri): Palestrina, Lamentation, *Miserere mei*

been used as the source for the 1589 print; the barlines sometimes coincided with page turns. In fact, RomeSG 59 served as the source for the Cappella Giulia manuscript XV.19 (VatG XV.19), which Alessandro Pettorini copied in 1581–1582 (he was paid in February 1582).[43] By a wonderful coincidence, Pet-

43. Jeppesen, "Palestrina," col. 699. Llorens, *Le opere musicali della Cappella Giulia*, no. 31 (with a list of contents). It contains all of the hymns from RomeSG 59 except for a rejected version of *Tibi Christe splendor patris*, an incomplete setting of *Conditor alme siderum*, and the (extra) even strophes

torini was the tenor from the Cappella Giulia whose name Palestrina had written in the margin of fol. 90 in 1573. VatG XV.19 is in a very poor state of preservation and has apparently never been filmed. A comparison of several openings
in good enough condition to be examined shows exact correspondence
between the barlines in RomeSG 59 and page turns in VatG XV.19 as well as in
the rubrics (for example, the names of feasts) on both manuscripts.[44]

It seems likely that Palestrina used RomeSG 59 for gathering the earliest
known version of his hymns. It is not a neat copy, with the hymns written out
in the characteristic liturgical order, but instead a rather rough working manuscript. For reasons that are not clear, the hymns for the first part of the liturgical
year (*temporale*) occur in the middle of the manuscript (hymns that appear in
VatG XV.19 as nos. 1–23 are written out on fol. 46^v–92), while those from the
middle of the *sanctorale* are at the beginning (hymns that appear in VatG XV.19 as
nos. 24–41 are on fols. 6^v–23).

The physical placement of the hymns in RomeSG 59 may help determine the
chronology of Palestrina's work on the cycle. It is curious, for example, that he fit
two hymns, *Tristes erant apostoli* and *Deus tuorum militum*, onto blank staves on pages
already occupied by other hymns. Was he just being parsimonious, or should we
conclude that this was the last available space and he needed to fit the whole cycle
into this manuscript? He rejected the version of *Tibi Christe splendor patris* that he
had written on fols. 9^v–10 (no. 10), and added the final version on fols. 22^v–23 at
the end of a group of sixteen hymns, presumably in the next available space.

Perhaps as an aid to the scribe using the disordered contents of RomeSG 59
for preparing a formal choirbook, Palestrina put in a series of cross-references.
For example, he wrote on the rejected version of *Tibi Christe splendor patris* a reference to the location of the final version: "For [the hymn for the feast of] St.
Michael Archangel, turn thirteen folios" ("In S.ti Michaelis Archangeli voltate
tredici carte"). Another is the reference on fol. 39^v to the first Lamentation for
Holy Saturday at the beginning of the book. The presence of such references
among both the hymns and the Lamentations suggests that the manuscript could
have served as the source not only for the hymns but also for the Lamentations.

The choirbook, in short, seems to have functioned like a notebook for pre-
serving compositions, for writing them out so that they could be performed and
then revised if necessary, and also for providing scribes or typesetters with an
authoritative source from which to make copies for public transmission.

While the autographs—particularly RomeSG 59—need more thorough
study, it is possible to offer some preliminary conclusions about Palestrina's com-

---

of several hymns. On Pettorini, see Rostirolla, "La Cappella Giulia," 140–142, 256. On Palestrina's
hymns, see Daniel Zager, "The Polyphonic Latin Hymns of Orlando di Lasso: A Liturgical and
Repertorial Study," Ph.D. diss., University of Minnesota, 1985, 167–178. Zager (p. 173) speculated
that RomeSG 59 "may well be the earliest complete source of Palestrina's hymns and the exemplar
from which Cappella Giulia XV 19 was copied in 1582. Certainly the identical content of these two
manuscript sources strongly suggests that the one is linked to the other very closely, with both pre-
dating the 1589 print."

44. A careful study of the sources of Palestrina's hymns that takes into consideration both contemporary settings and changes in the liturgy is badly needed.

positional procedures, particularly by considering the sources in light of other autograph manuscripts of the period.

Palestrina, unlike Corteccia or Rore, left no sketches or rough drafts. The only possible examples of drafts are the two *falsobordone* settings in RomeSG 59, both in quasi-score. Their placement on the first and last page of the manuscript suggests that they were casual additions to staves that happened to be available. The one on fol. 1, *Miserere mei*, has no text (see plate 11.4); the one on fol. 94ᵛ, *Benedictus Dominus*, is texted and has a slight revision (see plate 11.5). These two examples may indicate that Palestrina, like many of his contemporaries, used quasi-score for sketching or drafting. We cannot be certain, however, since both the chordal style of the settings and the fact that he was working in both cases with just a single page rather than a full opening make quasi-score the logical choice of format (like Isaac's use of quasi-score for the final strophe of *Sanctissimae virginis votiva festa*). It is certainly possible that these pages do reflect his first written version of the material.

The rest of Palestrina's surviving autographs are fair copies. Three of the four sources contain revisions that reflect either the correction of copying mistakes or substantive musical changes, the kind of polishing that took place at the final stage of composition, perhaps following a performance.

Casimiri listed many of the revisions he found in RomeSG 59, some among the hymns, but many in the two Lamentations he thought belonged to the earliest period of work on the manuscript.[45] Some of them were subtle changes in voice-leading or text placement, just a note or two, perhaps a rest.[46] But there were also more extensive revisions.[47] In one place Palestrina thought a canon would work, but when it did not he crossed out the rubric indicating canon and added the fifth voice on a hand-drawn staff at the bottom of the page. In another instance mentioned above, he crossed out an entire setting of *Tibi Christe splendor patris*, and added another one.

The evidence culled from changes in all three autographs suggests that Palestrina was not working from score. That may be a surprising conclusion given the fact that he scored Duke Guglielmo's music so that he could study it ("per meglio contemplarlo"), but it fits the evidence of all other known manuscripts of vocal music. With but a single exception, examples of composition in score come not from vocal but from keyboard music.[48]

For example, in the hymn *Christe redemptor* (see example 11.1), he rewrote altus and bassus, eliminating the more pungent passing sixth chord on the last beat of measure 29 as well as the D in the bassus and the F in the altus that worked against the cadence on A in measure 30 between the cantus and tenor. These

45. Casimiri, chap. 4: "*Il Codice—autografo*, documento d'autocritica del Palestrina," 27–45.
46. Fols. 6; 34; 51ᵛ; 54; 61; 62v; 63.
47. The revisions included: fols. 5ᵛ–6, Lamentation, rewriting cantus at "novi diluculo" and rewriting two voices at "convertere"; fol. 23ᵛ, rewriting "et respice," condensing three measures into two and eliminating a repeat at "lassis"; fols. 26ᵛ–27, changing the harmonies in "Ecce nunc"; fols. 57ᵛ–58 shortening a phrase at "sustulit"; and fol. 15ᵛ, changing a canon into a notated fifth voice.
48. See chap. 7.

PLATE 11.5
RomeSG 59, fol.
94ᵛ: Palestrina,
Benedictus Dominus,
draft

changes—improvements or corrections of errors—are precisely the kinds of problems that would have been quite obvious in score but harder to detect in parts.

It is hard to say what format he was using for any possible earlier drafts. The only evidence is circumstantial and derives from the corrections and revisions to the fair copies. When he copied *Ave Maria*, the second part of the eight-voice motet *Beata es*, he wrote portions of the music into the wrong part three times (see plate 11.3). For example, he began the second part of the tenor of Choir II on the last staff, turned the page over and continued for a while with the correct music, but after the rests in the middle of the line he mistakenly began to copy music from the bass. He wrote the music first, without the text, and copied quite a bit before realizing that there was a mistake. Then he crossed out the wrong notes and added the correct ones directly after the ones he had crossed out, a clear indication that these corrections took place during the actual copying rather than afterwards, as was usually the case with the revisions. It seems

EXAMPLE 11.1   Palestrina, *Christe redemptor . . . conserva*, str. 5, mm. 29–30

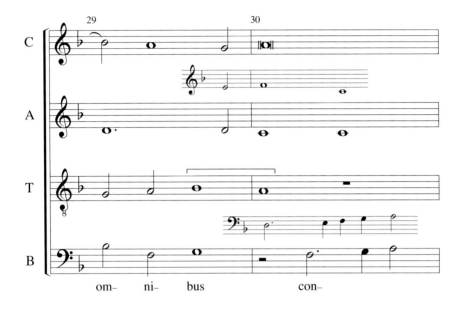

unlikely that his eye skipped from one staff to another since in each case the passages were a number of measures apart.

Another copying error, this time in RomeSG 59, may indicate indirectly the format he was using. Palestrina wrote out the first verse of the four-voice hymn, *Plasmator*, in the usual choirbook format: Cantus/Tenor facing Altus/Bassus. The first strophe calls for CATB, while the third (the next one to be set polyphonically) calls for ATTB. He made a mistake at the beginning of the third strophe, beginning to write music for the top voice, in this instance the altus, in the customary place for the cantus and with the cantus clef. Realizing his mistake, he crossed out the music and added the rubrics: "cantus tacet" and "tenor 2.s." It seems that he instinctively tried to write the top line where it is usually found. Thus he was probably working either from a version notated in quasi-score like the *falsobordone* examples, with the top line at the top of a page, or from one in choirbook format with the altus as the top voice in the upper left-hand corner.

The changes in *Omnis pulchritudo domini* are particularly suggestive, given Capello's remarks about Palestrina's use of the lute. *Omnis pulchritudo* is a responsory, with the overall form ABCB. All the corrections are in the two B sections, the *repetenda*. Some of the mistakes in the first do not recur the second time, suggesting that once he had fixed something he would not make the same mistake twice. Some he had to fix in both B sections, suggesting that the changes came after the entire piece was written out. But the second B does have one error not found in the first. Furthermore, the second B is not an exact repeat: he switched voices within the choirs (lines 2 and 3 are exchanged in the lower choir, lines 1 and 2 in the upper choir), and also altered some of the details of ornamentation. Was he working from the first B and deliberately making slight changes, or can we just possibly imagine him working from a kind of chordal grid—whether written or "in the mind"—that he realized twice, in slightly different ways?[49]

The evidence is fragmentary but we can make a few observations. First, Palestrina may have used the lute in composing, either as a way of sounding out the music or as a way of notating it. Second, he probably did not compose in score, but instead may have used the quasi-score format or choirbook format, or even some kind of chordal grid for the early stages of work. Third, he continued to revise and polish his music both while he prepared fair copies and afterward.

———————

It is clear that Corteccia, Rore, Isaac, and Palestrina—all of whom are usually referred to as "Renaissance" composers—wrote very different kinds of music. Isaac's polyphonic elaboration of a monophonic sequence stands in sharp contrast to Corteccia's soprano–bass framework for his madrigals; and both contrast with the imitative style used by Rore in the Milan partbooks and by Palestrina. The surviving manuscripts let us see their work at different stages in the process—from very early sketches to the final polishing of a fair copy. Clearly, each composer had his own habits or methods of working, appropriate to the music and to his own psyche.

49. For a more extended discussion of the changes in *Omnis pulchritudo* and *Beata es* (*2.p. Ave Maria*) see Jessie Ann Owens, "Palestrina at Work," forthcoming in *Papal Music and Papal Musicians in Late Medieval and Renaissance Rome*, ed. Richard Sherr (Oxford, in press).

APPENDIX. EXCERPTS FROM THE CORRESPONDENCE BETWEEN PALESTRINA, THE DUKE OF MANTUA, AND ANNIBALE CAPELLO

1. Letter from Palestrina to the duke, 2 February 1568

   . . . essendomi comandato da si Eccellente signore, et per mano di virtuoso cosi raro, come m. Giacches di far questa Messa, qui inclusa, la quale ho fatta cosi come m'ha instrutto m. Aniballe Cappello, se in questa prima volta non havrò sodisfatta la mente di V.ra Eccel.za se li piacera comandarmi, come la voglia, o, breve, o, longa, o che si sentan le parole, io mi provarò servirla secondo il mio potere . . .

2. Letter from Palestrina to the duke, 3 March 1570

   Havendomi fatto favore di farmi udir il Motetto ed il Madrigale di V. Excel.za il suo virtuoso, mi comandò da sua parte che dicessi liberamente il mio parere, io dico che così come l'E. V.ra avanza in ogni sua opera la natura, così nella musica eccede quelli che ne fanno degnamente professione, et per meglio contemplarlo, ho partito il Motetto, et visto il bello artifitio lontano dal commune, et il dare spirito vivo alle parole, secondo il significato, ho segnati alcuni luoghi, che mi par che quando si può far di meno soni meglio l'harmonia, com'è sesta e unisono, movendosi ambe le parti et sesta et quinta ascendendo et discendendo similmente alcuni unisoni, che le fughe à forza ci conducono le parti, mi pare ancora che per la stretta tessitura delle fughe, si occupino le parole alli ascoltanti, che non le godono come nella musica commune, ben si vede che l'Ecc.za V.ra sa meglio di me tutte queste minuzzole, ma per obedirla ho ditto questo e così l'obedirò sempre quando mi farra favore di comandarmi come servitore affettionato et obbligatissimo . . .

3. Letter from Palestrina to the duke, 17 April 1574

   Io credo che m. Don Aniballe scriva a V. Ecc.za perche la messa è stata tarda al ritornare, la quale è stata revista da me, più tosto per ubedire, che per bisogno che havesse di avertimento alcuno, cosi la mando ripartita e dove dico il parer mio vi sono alcune crocette, il pleni non lho tocco perche spero un giorno V. Ecc.za havendo un poco d'otio si pigliara piacere di rinovare quel terzetto . . .

4. Letter from Don Annibale Capello to the duke, 18 October 1578

   . . . M. Gio. da Palestina non servendogli per l'indispositione grave havuta di fresco la testa, ne la vista, per essercitar La gran voluntà di servir in quel modo che puo ha cominciato a porre sul Leuto le chirie et la Gloria della prima messa, et me le ha fatti sentire pieni veramente di gran suavita et leggiadrie.

Et quando con buona gratia di lei potesse farlo hora che N. S. in San Pietro ha comandato che si canti con due chori di xii per choro come ha trovato che ordinò Giulio ii quando lascio per tal effetto intrade bastanti a quel capitolo et ha per questo ancho fatto mandar via tutti i cantori coniugati salvo lui per privilegio spetiale. Vorebbe anche le seconde parti et servirsene nella detta chiesa in molte sollenita in luogo dell'organo poichè afferma che nel vero V. A. ha purgati quei canti fermi di tutti i barberismi e di tutte l'imperfettioni che vi erano. Il che pero non farà senza sua licenza, ma quando prima dalla debolezza gli sara permesso, spiegarà ciò ch'ha fatto col liuto con tutto il suo studio . . .

5. Draft of a letter from an unidentified court official to Capello, 23 October 1578

first version

Al capello

. . . S. Alt.a ordina che V.S. dica à M. Giovanni di Palestina che attenda à risanarsi, ne si affretti di porre sul leuto li chirie et la gloria con l'altre compositioni, perche havendovi posto mano tant'altri valent'huomini non bisogna compositione di leuto, ma si bene compositione fatta con molto studio. Reputa S. Altezza che la musica fatta per S.ta Barbara non riuscirebbe forse costi, per le molte fughe quali vi sono dentro, usandosi costi musica piana, tuttavia s'ella piace al detto m. Giovanni et se ne vole servire, S. Altezza darà ordine che si come ella gli è stata mandata sin hora spezzata gli sia mandata intiera.

second version

Al capello

. . . S. Alt.a ordina che V.S. dica à M. Giovanni di Palestina che attenda à risanarsi, ne si affretti di porre sul leuto le messe disid[erando] ella ch'esse siano fugate continovamente et sopra'l soggetto come hanno fatto gl'altri, et esso istesso nel Doppio maggiore, et perche questo stile che si usa in S.ta Barbara è differente da quello che V.S. scrive usarsi costi, non mi ha l'Altezza Sua ordinato che [word crossed out] nel capo del servirsene costi in S. Pietro in luogo del organo io le dica altro, se non se quei canti fermi cosi acconci piacino a esso m. Gio la glieli mandera intieri da servirsene come li verra commodo. Di Pietolo a 23 d'ottobre 1578.

6. Letter from Capello to the duke, 17 April 1574

Non sopportando il mio grandissimo desiderio d'honorarmi con servire a V. E. che la scusa della tardanza fatta in rimandarle la messa da lei giudiosissimamamente composta sia portata da altri che da me stesso, sara cagione, che questa volta usi soverchio ardire con lo scrivere imediatamente a V Ecc. La qual supplico ad attribuire a questo sol rispetto tanta licenza che mi ho preso. Et a credere insieme che l'occupationi di M. Gio. da Palestina in comporre alcune lamentationi per ordine del Papa et nelle cappelle di questi giorni santi hanno fatto tardare esso M. Gio. a fare alcune poche consideration et avertimenti sopra la detta compositione.

POSTSCRIPT

I end with a "postscript" rather than a "conclusion" because the topic I consider here is so new and so large that it is premature to claim any conclusions. While I have tried to be as broad as possible in the kinds of evidence I consider, I know full well that I have not been able to be comprehensive in any area. That said, I would like to state briefly what I take to be the main results of this investigation.

First, there are far more manuscripts used in composition than anyone ever suspected, and more are certain to be discovered. These manuscripts need to be the basis for future work on compositional process and on the genesis of musical compositions. Understanding the kinds of manuscripts that preserve composer autographs should help identify additional sources.

Second, the surviving autograph manuscripts contain documents from the very earliest stages of composition until the final revisions. The sketches, drafts, and fair copies have certain characteristic features, though with important variations from composer to composer and genre to genre.

Third, composers of complex vocal polyphony during the period from roughly 1450 to 1600 neither needed nor used scores for composing. Scores were used for studying music, particularly after the middle of the sixteenth century, and they were used in composition by composers of keyboard music accustomed to using them in performance. Instead of scores, composers worked on short segments in quasi-score format and on longer segments in separate parts (for example, choirbook format).

Fourth, we need to invoke a different kind of memory to explain how composers could read and compose in separate parts. We need to free ourselves from the habit of score-based thinking and try to enter a very different conceptual world.

Fifth, the process of composition was essentially additive, lines added to lines, segments to segments. The hypothesis of a dichotomy between successive and simultaneous composition as an explanation for the shift from cantus-firmus or line-based music to imitative music does not fit the evidence of the autograph manuscripts. Even when there is a pre-existent line, there is an implied harmony; even when lines share equally in the presentation of a motive in imitation, there is a process of addition.

I am conscious of many areas of great importance for our understanding of compositional process that I have not addressed. Because I was concentrating on manuscript evidence, I chose not to consider the vast and rich domain of musical analysis as a technique for accounting for the compositional history of a piece. Many pieces will yield the secret of how they came into existence. Another promising area involves borrowing of all sorts; an important subtopic is the transformation of music from one realm to another, usually vocal to instrumental. A third is what John Milsom calls "recomposition," when composers leave us two or more complete and viable versions of their music.[1] It is my hope that the techniques and insights we gain from working with the music for which we have direct manuscript evidence will help our investigations in these other crucial areas.

1. John Milsom, "Tallis's First and Second Thoughts," *Journal of the Royal Musical Association* 113 (1988): 203–222.

BIBLIOGRAPHY

Primary Sources (before 1800)

Aaron, Pietro. *Thoscanello de la musica.* Venice, 1523. Reprint, New York, 1969.

Agricola, Martin. *Musica instrumentalis deudsch.* Wittenberg, 1529; 2d. ed., 1545. Reprint of the 1529 edition, Hildesheim, 1969. Translated by William E. Hettrick under the title *The 'Musica instrumentalis deudsch' of Martin Agricola.* Cambridge, 1994.

Anonymous. "Ars discantus secundum Johannem de Muris." Edition in CS 3: 68 – 113.

Anonymous. Cambridge, Corpus Christi College, MS 410. Edition in CS 1: 182 – 250.

Anonymous. *Curial e Güelfa.* Edited by A. Rubio y Lluch. Barcelona, 1901. Translated by P. Waley under the title *Curial and Guelfa.* London, 1982.

Anonymous. "Juxta artem conficiendi." Göttingen, Niedersächsische Staats- und Universitätsbibliothek, Mus. IV 3000 Rara. Edited by Carl Dahlhaus, "Eine deutsche Kompositionslehre des frühen 16. Jahrhunderts," *Kirchenmusikalisches Jahrbuch* 40 (1956): 33 – 43.

Arcadelt, Jacob. *Opera omnia.* Edited by Albert Seay. CMM 31. American Institute of Musicology, 1965 – 1970.

Avianius, Johannes. *Isagoge in libros musicae poeticae.* Erfurt, 1581.

Bakfark, Valentinus. *Opera Omnia.* Edited by István Homolya and Dániel Benkő. 3 vols. Budapest, 1981.

Banchieri, Adriano. *Cartella musicale nel canto figurato fermo, & contrapunto.* Venice, 1614. Reprint, Bologna, 1968.

―――. *Contraponto bestiale alla mente.* In *Festino nella sera del giovedi grasso.* Venice, 1608.

Bermudo, Juan. *El arte tripharia.* Osuna, 1550. Reprint, n.p., n.d.

―――. *Declaración de instrumentos musicales.* Osuna, 1549; 2d ed., 1555. Reprint of 1555 edition, Kassel, 1957.

Beurhaus, Friedrich. *Erotematum musicae libri duo.* Dortmund, 1573; 2d ed., 1580. Reprint of 1580 edition, Cologne, 1961.

The Board Lute Book. Introduction by Robert Spencer. Leeds, 1976.

Bontempi, Giovanni Andrea Angelini. *Historia musica.* Perugia, 1695. Reprint, Bologna, [1971].

―――. *Nova quatuor vocibus componendi methodus.* Dresden, 1660. Reprint, Lucca, 1993.

Borsieri, Girolamo. *Il supplimento della nobiltà di Milano.* Milan, 1619.

The Bottegari Lutebook. Edited by Carol MacClintock. The Wellesley Edition 8. Wellesley, Mass., 1965.

Buchner, Hans. "Fundamentum." *Sämtliche Orgelwerk.* Edited by Jost Harro Schmidt. Das Erbe deutscher Musik, 54–55. Frankfurt, 1974.

Burmeister, Joachim. *Musica poetica.* Rostock, 1606. Reprint, Kassel, 1955. Translated by Benito Rivera under the title *Musical Poetics.* New Haven, 1993.

Burtius, Nicolaus. *Musices opusculum.* Bologna, 1487. Reprint, Bologna, 1969. Edited by G. Massera, *Nicolai Burtii Parmensis Florum libellus* (Florence, 1975). Translated by Clement A. Miller. MSD 37. Neuhausen-Stuttgart, 1983.

Calvisius, Seth. *Exercitationes musicae duae.* Leipzig, 1600. Reprint, Hildesheim, 1973.

———. Draft (ca. 1589) for *Melopoiia sive melodiae condendae ratio* (Erfurt, 1592), Göttingen, Niedersächsiche Staats- und Universitätsbibliothek, Ms. Philos. 103. Edited by Carl Dahlhaus, "Musiktheoretisches aus dem Nachlaß des Sethus Calvisius," *Musikforschung* 9 (1956): 129-139.

Carrara, Michele. [*Intavolatura di liuto.*] Rome, 1585. Edited by B. Disertori. Florence, n.d.

[Cimello, Tomaso.] Bologna, Civico Museo Bibliografico Musicale, B 57. "Discorso sulle prolazioni e sui tempi dagli antichi di Tomaso Cimello."

Cleriadus et Meliadice. Roman en prose du XVe siècle. Edited by Gaston Zink. Geneva, 1984.

Cochlaeus, Johannes. *Musica activa.* N.p., [ca. 1504]; 2d ed., [ca. 1505]; 3d ed., Cologne, 1507. Second edition edited by Hugo Riemann, "Anonymi Introductorium Musicae (c. 1500)," *Monatshefte für Musikgeschichte* 29 (1897): 147–154 and 157–164, and 30 (1898): 1–8 and 11–19.

———. *Tetrachordum musices.* Nuremberg, 1511. Reprint, 1512 edition, Hildesheim, 1971. Translated and edited by Clement A. Miller. MSD 23. American Institute of Musicology, 1970.

Cocker, Edward. *England's Pen-man; or Cocker's New Copy-book.* London, 1703.

Coclico, Adrianus Petit. *Compendium musices descriptum ab Adriano Petit Coclico discipulo Iosquini de Pres in quo praeter caetera tractantur haec: De modo ornate canendi, De regula contrapuncti, De compositione.* Nuremberg, 1552. Reprint, Kassel, 1954. Translated by Albert Seay under the title *Musical Compendium.* Colorado Springs, 1973.

Contino, Giovanni. *Cinque Messe Mantovane.* Edited by Ottavio Beretta. Monumenti musicali italiani 14. Milan, 1988.

Coprario, John. *Rules How To Compose: a facsimile edition of a manuscript from the library of the Earl of Bridgewater (circa 1610) now in the Huntington Library, San Marino, California.* Introduction by Manfred F. Bukofzer. Los Angeles, 1952.

Corteccia, Francesco. *Collected Sacred Works.* Edited by Frank D'Accone. Music of the Florentine Renaissance. CMM 32, 11. *Music for the Triduum Sacrum.* American Institute of Musicology, 1985.

———. *Collected Secular Works.* Edited by Frank D'Accone. Music of the Florentine Renaissance. CMM 32, 8–10. Rome, 1981.

Cortese, Paolo. *De cardinalatu libri tres.* Castel Cortesiano, 1510.

Cretin, Guillaume. "Plainte sur le trepas de feu maistre Jehan Braconnier, dit Lourdault, chantre." In *Oeuvres poétiques de Guillaume Crétin.* Edited by Kathleen Chesney. Paris, 1932.

Daza, Esteban. *The Fantasias for Vihuela.* Edited by John Griffiths. Recent Researches in the Music of the Renaissance 54. Madison, 1982.

Diruta, Girolamo. *Seconda parte del Transilvano.* Venice, 1609. Reprint, Buren, Netherlands, 1983. Translated by Murray C. Bradshaw and Edward J. Soehnlen under the title *The Transylvanian.* Henryville, 1984.

Doni, Giovanni Battista. *Lyra barberina.* Edited by A. F. Gori. Florence, 1763. Reprint, Bologna, 1974.

Dressler, Gallus. "Praecepta musicae poeticae" (1564). Berlin, Staatsbibliothek zu Berlin,

Mus. ms. autogr. theor. Edited by Bernhard Engelke, *Geschichtsblätter für Stadt und Land Magdeburg* 49/50 (1914–1915): 214–250.

Elizabethan Consort Music I. Edited by Paul Doe. Musica Britannica, 44. London, 1979.

Ensemble Ricercars. Cristofano Malvezzi, Annibale Padovano. Edited by Milton A. Swenson. Recent Researches in Music of the Renaissance 27. Madison, 1978.

Faber, Heinrich. "Musica poetica." Berlin, Staatsbibliothek zu Berlin, Mus. ms. theor. 1175; Zwickau, Ratsschulbibliothek, Mus. 13,3; Hof, Gymnasium, Paed. 3713.

Fernandes, Gaspar. *Obras sacras.* Edited by Robert Snow. Portugaliae Musica 49. Lisbon, 1990.

Finck, Hermann. *Practica/musica Hermanii Finckii.* Wittenberg, 1556. Reprint, Bologna, 1969. Shorter edition (ends with f. [Ttiiii]): *Practica/Musica Her=/manni Finckii.* Wittenberg, 1556. Reprint, Hildesheim, 1971.

Florio, John. *Queen Anna's New World of Words.* London, 1611. Reprint, Menston, 1968.

———. *A Worlde of Wordes.* London, 1598. Reprint, New York, 1972.

Freig, Johannes Thomas. *Paedagogus.* Basel, 1582. Translated and edited by Jeremy Yudkin under the title *Paedagogus. The Chapter on Music.* MSD 38. Neuhausen-Stuttgart, 1983.

Frosch, Johann. *Rerum musicarum opusculum rarum ac insigne, totius eius negotii rationem mira industria & brevitate complectens.* Strassburg, 1535. Reprint, New York, 1967.

Gaffurius, Franchinus. *Practica musice.* Milan, 1496. Reprint, New York, 1979. Translated by Irwin Young under the title *The* Practica musicae *of Franchinus Gafurius.* Madison, 1969.

Galilei, Vincenzo. *Dialogo della musica antica et della moderna.* Florence, 1581. Reprint, New York, 1967.

———. *Fronimo dialogo . . . nel quale si contengono le vere et necessarie regole del intavolare la musica nel liuto.* Venice, 1568; 2d ed., 1584. 1584 edition translated by Carol MacClintock under the title *Fronimo, 1584.* MSD 39. American Institute of Musicology, 1985.

———. "Il primo libro della prattica de contrapunto . . . intorno all'uso delle consonanze." *Die Kontrapunkttraktate Vincenzo Galileis.* Edited by Frieder Rempp. Cologne, 1980.

Galliculus, Johannes. *Isagoge de composicione cantus.* Leipzig, 1520. Translated by Arthur A. Moorefield under the title *The Introduction to Song Composition.* Ottawa, 1992.

Glarean, Heinrich. *Dodecachordon.* Basel, 1547. Reprint, New York, 1967. Translated by Clement A. Miller. MSD 6. American Institute of Musicology, 1965.

Gonzaga, Guglielmo. *Madrigali a cinque voci.* Venice, 1583. Edited by Jessie Ann Owens and Megumi Nagaoka. New York, 1995.

———. *Sacrae cantiones quinque vocum.* Venice, 1583. Edited by Richard Sherr. New York, 1990.

Graduale Pataviense. Vienna, 1511. Reprint, with an introduction by Christian Väterlein. Das Erbe deutscher Musik 87. Kassel, 1982.

Gumpelzhaimer, Adam. *Compendium musicae.* Augsburg, 1591; 1625.

Herbst, Johann Andreas. *Musica poetica sive compendium melopoeticum.* Nuremberg, 1643.

Heyden, Sebald. *De arte canendi.* Nuremberg, 1540.

Holtzmüller, Heinrich. *Liber perutilis.* Basel, 1553.

Isaac, Heinrich. *Weltliche Werke I.* Edited by Johannes Wolf. Denkmäler der Tonkunst in Österreich, Jg. 14/1. Vienna, 1907.

Johannes of Lublin. *Tablature of Keyboard Music.* Edited by John R. White. CEKM, 6. American Institute of Musicology, 1967. Facsimile: *Tablatura organowa Jana z Lublina.*

Monumenta musicae in Polonia. Seria B., vol. 1. Edited by Krystyna Wiłkowska-Chomińska. Warsaw, 1964.

Keyboard Music at Castell'Arquato. Edited by H. Colin Slim. CEKM 37. American Institute of Musicology, 1975 – .

Der Kodex Berlin 40021. Edited by Martin Just. Das Erbe deutscher Musik 76 – 78. Kassel, 1990 – 1991.

Lampadius, Auctor. *Compendium musices, tam figurati quam plani cantus ad formam dialogi, in usum ingenuae pubis ex eruditis musicorum scriptis accurate congestum*. Berne, 1537; edition consulted for this study: Berne, 1554.

LeRoy, Adrian. *A Briefe and easye instruction to learne the tableture*. London, 1568.

———. *Oeuvres. Les instructions pour le luth (1574)*. Edited by J. Jacquot, P.-Y. Sordes, and J.-M. Vaccaro. 2 vols. Paris, 1977.

Lippius, Johannes. *Synopsis musicae novae*. Strassburg, 1612.

Luscinius, Othmar. *Musurgia seu praxis musicae*. Strassburg, 1536.

Machaut, Guillaume de. *Le livre du Voir-Dit*. Edited by Paulin Paris. Paris, 1875. Reprint, Geneva, 1969.

Monteverdi, Claudio. *Lettere*. Edited by Éva Lax. Florence, 1994.

The Letters of Claudio Monteverdi. Translated and introduced by Denis Stevens. Oxford, 1995.

Morlaye, Guillaume. *Oeuvres pour le luth, 2: Manuscrits d'Uppsala*. Edited by Jean-Michel and Nathalie Vaccaro. Paris, 1989.

Morley, Thomas. *A Plaine and Easie Introduction to Practicall Musicke*. London, 1597. Reprint, Amsterdam, 1969. Edited by Alec Harman under the title *A Plain and Easy Introduction to Practical Music*. New York, 1952; 2d ed., 1963.

Munich, Bayerische Staatsbibliothek. Mus. Ms. 9437. *Eine neue Quelle zur italienischen Orgelmusik des Cinquecento*. Edited by Marie-Louise Göllner. Münchner Editionen zur Musikgeschichte 3. Tutzing, 1982.

Nucius, Johannes. *Musices poeticae sive de compositione cantus praeceptiones*. Neisse, 1613. Reprint, Leipzig, 1976.

Ornithoparcus, Andreas. *Musice active micrologus*. Leipzig, 1517. Translated by John Dowland under the title *Andreas Ornithoparcus His Micrologus* (London, 1609). Reprint of the 1517 and 1609 editions, with an introduction by Gustave Reese and Steven Ledbetter, as Ornithoparcus/Dowland, *A Compendium of Musical Practice*. New York, 1973.

Othmayr, Caspar. *Ausgewählte Werke: Zweiter Teil*. Edited by Hans Albrecht. Das Erbe deutscher Musik 26. Frankfurt, 1956.

Palestrina, Giovanni Pierluigi da. *Le messe di Mantova, inedite dai manoscritti di S. Barbara*. Edited by Knud Jeppesen. *Le opere complete di Giovanni Pierluigi da Palestrina*, 18 – 19. Rome, 1954.

———. *Omnis pulchritudo domini*. Edited by V. Mortari. Rome, [1950].

———. *Pope Marcellus Mass*. Norton Critical Scores. Edited by Lewis Lockwood. New York, 1975.

Philomathes, Venceslaus. *De nova domo musicorum libri quattuor compendioso carmine elucubrati*. Vienna, 1512.

Playford, John. *An Introduction to the Skill of Musick*. London, 1655. 12th ed., 1694. Reprint, New York, 1972.

Poccianti, Michele. *Catalogus Scriptorum Florentinorum*. Florence 1589.

Pontio, Pietro. *Ragionamento di musica*. Parma, 1588. Reprint, Kassel, 1959.

Praetorius, Michael. *Syntagma musicum*. Wolfenbüttel, 1619. Reprint, 1958.

Puteanus, Erycius. *Modulata Pallas, sive septem discrimina vocum*. Milan, 1599.

Quercu, Simon de. *Opusculum musices.*Vienna, 1509; edition cited, Landshut, 1516.

Reisch, Gregor. *Margarita philosophica.* Strassburg, 1503.

Rore, Cipriano de. *Opera Omnia.* Edited by Bernhard Meier. CMM 14. American Institute of Musicology, 1959 - .

Rossetti, Biagio. *Libellus de rudimentis musices.*Verona, 1529. Reprint, New York, 1968.

Rossi, Giovanni Battista. *Organo de cantori per intendere da se stesso ogni passo difficile che si trova nella musica.*Venice, 1618. Reprint, Bologna, 1984.

Sancta Maria, Thomas de. *Libro llamado Arte de tañer Fantasia.*Valladolid, 1565. Reprint, Geneva, 1973. Translated by Almonte C. Howell, Jr. and Warren E. Hultberg under the title *The Art of Playing the Fantasia.* Pittsburgh, 1991.

Scaletta, Horatio. *Primo scalino della scala di contrapunto.* Milan, 1622.

Schanppecher, Melchior. *Musica figurativa.* In *Opus aureum*, pars III/IV. Cologne, 1501. Edited by K.W. Niemöller as *Die Musica figurativa des Melchior Schanppecher.* Beiträge zur rheinischen Musikgeschichte 50 (Cologne, 1961).

Schonsleder, Wolfgang. *Architectonice musices universalis ex qua melopoeam per universa et solida fundamenta musicorum, proprio marte condiscere possis.* Ingolstadt, 1631.

Sebastiani, Claudius. *Bellum musicale.* Strassburg, 1563.

Sei missae dominicales. Edited by Siro Cisilino. Padua, 1981.

Selections from Motetti C (Venice, 1504). Edited by Richard Sherr. Sixteenth-Century Motet 2. New York, 1991.

Tabulaturen des XVI. Jahrhunderts. Edited by H. J. Marx. Schweizerische Musikdenkmäler 6 - 7. Basel, 1967.

Tigrini, Orazio. *Il compendio della musica nel quale brevemente si tratta dell'arte del contrapunto.* Venice, 1588. Reprint, New York, 1966.

Tinctoris, Johannes. *Liber de arte contrapuncti. Opera theoretica.* Edited by Albert Seay. CSM 22. American Institute of Musicology, 1975. Translated by Albert Seay under the title *The Art of Counterpoint.* MSD 5. American Institute of Musicology, 1961.

The Tudor Church Music of the Lumley Books. Edited by Judith Blezzard. Recent Researches in the Music of the Renaissance 65. Madison, 1985.

Uppsala, Universitetsbiblioteket, Vokalmusik i handskrift 76a. Edited by Howard Mayer Brown. Renaissance Music in Facsimile 19. New York, 1987.

Uppsala, Universitetsbiblioteket, Vokalmusik i handskrift 76b. Edited by Thomas MacCracken. Renaissance Music in Facsimile 20. New York, 1986.

Valderrábano, Enríquez de. *Libro de musica de vihuela, intitulado silva de sirenas.* Valladolid, 1547. Edited by E. Pujol. Monumentos de la Música Española 22 - 23. Barcelona, 1965.

Vanneo, Stephano. *Recanetum de musica aurea.* Rome, 1533. Reprint, Kassel, 1969.

Venegas de Henestrosa, Luis. *Libro de cifra nueva para tecla, harpa, y vihuela, en el qual se enseña brevemente cantar canto llano, y canto de organo, y algunos avisos para contrapunto.* Alcalá de Henares, 1557. Edited by Higinio Anglés. *La música en la Corte de Carlos V.* Monumentos de la Música Española 1/2. Barcelona, 1944.

Vicentino, Nicola. *L'antica musica ridotta alla moderna prattica.* Rome, 1555. Reprint, Kassel, 1959.

Vienna, Österreichische Nationalbibliothek, Musiksammlung, Mus. Hs. 18.744. Edited by Jessie Ann Owens. Renaissance Music in Facsimile 25. New York, 1986.

Virdung, Sebastian. *Musica getutscht.* Basel, 1511. Translated and edited by Beth Bullard as *Musica getutscht: A Treatise on Musical Instruments (1511) by Sebastian Virdung.* Cambridge, 1993.

*Vocabolario degli Accademici della Crusca.*Venice, 1612. Reprint, Florence, 1987.

Walther, Johann Gottfried. *Musicalisches Lexikon oder Musicalische Bibliothec.* Leipzig, 1732.

Wollick, N. *Opus aureum*. Cologne, 1501.

Zacconi, Lodovico. *Prattica di musica*. Venice, 1596. Reprint, Bologna, 1983.

———. *Prattica di musica seconda parte*. Venice, 1622. Reprint, Bologna, 1983.

Zarlino, Gioseffo. *Le istitutioni harmoniche*. Venice, 1558. Reprint, New York, 1965. Translated by Guy A. Marco and Claude V. Palisca under the title *The Art of Counterpoint. Part Three of* Le Istitutioni harmoniche, *1558*. New York, 1968.

———. *Sopplimenti musicali*. Venice, 1588. Reprint, New York, 1979.

Secondary Sources

Abert, Adolf. "Das musikalische Studienheft des Wittenberger Studenten Georg Donat (um 1543)." *Sammelbände der Internationalen Musikgesellschaft* 15 (1913–14): 68–98.

Adams, Courtney. "Communications." *JAMS* 36 (1983): 162–163.

Agee, Richard. "Ruberto Strozzi and the Early Madrigal." *JAMS* 36 (1983): 1–17.

Albrecht, Hans. *Caspar Othmayr: Leben und Werk*. Kassel, 1950.

Apfel, Ernst. *Geschichte der Kompositionslehre von Anfängen bis gegen 1700*. Wilhelmshaven, 1981.

Armstrong, James. "How to Compose a Psalm: Ponzio and Cerone Compared." *Studi musicali* 7 (1978): 103-139.

Arlt, Wulf. "Vom Überlieferungsbefund zum Kompositionsprozeß: Beobachtungen an den zwei Fassungen von Busnois' *Je ne puis vivre ainsy*." In *Festschrift Arno Forchert zum 60. Geburtstag am 29. Dezember 1985*, edited by G. Allroggen and D. Altenburg. Kassel, 1986.

Baltzer, Rebecca. "The Thirteenth-Century Motet and the Role of Manuscript Makers in Defining a Genre." Paper read at the annual meeting of the American Musicological Society, Chicago 1991.

Bate, R. S. "Musical slates." *Notes and Queries from Somerset and Dorset* 31, n. 49 (1936): 50–51.

Becherini, Bianca. *Catalogo dei manoscritti musicali della Biblioteca nazionale di Firenze*. Kassel, 1959.

Beebe, Ellen. "Text and Mode as Generators of Musical Structure in Clemens non Papa's *Accesserunt ad Jesum*." In *Music and Language*. Studies in the History of Music 1. New York, 1983.

Bent, Margaret. "A Contemporary Perception of Early Fifteenth-Century Style: Bologna Q15 as a Document of Scribal Editorial Initiative." *MD* 41 (1987): 183–201.

———. "Pycard's Double Canon: Evidence of Revision?" In *Sundry Sorts of Music Books: Essays on the British Library Collections. Presented to O. W. Neighbour on his 70th Birthday*, edited by Chris Banks, Arthur Searle, and Malcolm Turner, 10–25. The British Library, 1993.

———. "*Resfacta* and *Cantare Super Librum*." *JAMS* 36 (1983): 371–391.

———. "Some Factors in the Control of Consonance and Sonority: Successive Composition and the *Solus tenor*." In *International Musicological Society: Report of the Twelfth Congress, Berkeley 1977*. Kassel, 1981.

Bernstein, Lawrence. "A Florentine Chansonnier of the Early Sixteenth Century: Florence, Biblioteca Nazionale Centrale, Ms. Magliabechi XIX 117." *Early Music History* 6 (1986): 1–107.

Bertolotti, Antonino. *Musici alla corte dei Gonzaga in Mantova dal secolo XV al XVIII*. Milan, 1890. Reprint, Bologna, 1969.

Besseler, Heinrich, and Peter Gülke. *Schriftbild der mehrstimmigen Musik*. Musikgeschichte in Bildern 3/5. Leipzig, 1973.

Besutti, Paola. "Catalogo tematico delle monodie liturgiche della Basilica Palatina di S. Barbara in Mantova." *Le fonti musicali in Italia, studi e ricerche* 2 (1988): 53–66.

—. "Giovanni Pierluigi da Palestrina e la liturgia Mantovana." In *Atti del II Convegno Internazionale di Studi Palestriniani*, edited by Lino Bianchi and Giancarlo Rostirolla, 157–164. Palestrina, 1991. The second part was read at the III. Convegno Internazionale di Studi "Palestrina e l'Europa," October 1994.

Blackburn, Bonnie J., "On Compositional Process in the Fifteenth Century." *JAMS* 40 (1987): 210–284.

—. "The Printing Contract for the *Libro primo de musica de la Salamandra* (Rome, 1526)." *Journal of Musicology* 12 (1994): 345–356.

—, Edward E. Lowinsky, and Clement Miller, eds. *A Correspondence of Renaissance Musicians*. Oxford, 1991.

Blezzard, Judith. "The Wells Musical Slates." *Musical Times* 120 (1979): 26–30.

Bliss, A. J. "The Inscribed Slates at Smarmore." *Proceedings of the Royal Irish Academy* 64 (1965–1966), Section C, 33–60.

Bloxam, M. Jennifer. "Newly-discovered Fragments of Renaissance Polyphony in Bruges: A Glimpse of Sixteenth-Century Composers at Work." Paper read at the annual meeting of the American Musicological Society, Pittsburgh, 1992.

Brauner, Mitchell. "The Parvus Manuscripts: A Study of Vatican Polyphony, ca. 1535 to 1580." Ph.D. diss., Brandeis University, 1982.

Brennecke, W. "S. Hemmel." *MGG* and *NG*.

Bridges, Thomas. "The Publishing of Arcadelt's First Book of Madrigals." Ph.D. diss., Harvard University, 1982.

Briquet, Charles Moïse. *Les Filigranes*. Edited by Allan Stevenson. Amsterdam, 1968.

Britton, Derek, and Alan J. Fletcher. "Medieval Hiberno-English Inscriptions on the Inscribed Slates of Smarmore: Some Reconsiderations and Additions." *Irish University Record* 20 (1990): 71–72.

Brown, Howard Mayer. "Carpentras." *NG*.

—. "Cleriadus et Meliadice: A Fifteenth-Century Manual for Courtly Behavior." In *Iconography at the Crossroads*, ed. Brendan Cassidy, 215–225. Princeton, 1993.

—. "Emulation, Competition, and Homage: Imitation and Theories of Imitation in the Renaissance." *JAMS* 35 (1982): 1–48.

—. "Songs After Supper: How the Aristocracy Entertained Themselves in the Fifteenth Century." In *Musica Privata: Die Rolle der Musik im privaten Leben. Festschrift zum 65. Geburtstag von Walter Salmen*, edited by Monika Fink, Rainer Gstrein, and Günter Mössmer, 37–52. Innsbruck, 1991.

—. "A Typology of Francesco Corteccia's Madrigals: Notes towards a History of Theatrical Music in Sixteenth-Century Italy." In *The Well Enchanting Skill: Music, Poetry, and Drama in the Culture of the Renaissance. Essays in Honour of F. W. Sternfeld*, edited by John Caldwell, Edward Olleson, and Susan Wollenberg. Oxford, 1990.

Bush, Helen. "The Recognition of Chordal Formation by Early Music Theorists." *MQ* 32 (1946): 227–243.

Cahn, Peter. "Zur Vorgeschichte des 'opus perfectum et absolutum' in der Musikauffassung um 1500." In *Zeichen und Struktur in der Musik der Renaissance*, ed. Klaus Hortschansky, 11–26. Kassel, 1989.

Cambier, A. "De grootste roome van de stad Ronse: De komponist Cypriaan De Ro[de]re, 'omnium musicorum princeps'." *Annales Geschieden Oudheidkundige Kring van Ronse en het Tenement van Inde* 30 (1981): 5–56.

—. "Meer gegevens over de definitieve bevestiging van Cypriaan de Rore's Ronsische afkomst uit archiefstukken genealogie." *Annales Geschieden Oudheidkundige Kring van Ronse en het Tenement van Inde* 32 (1983): 221-49.

Cametti, Alberto. "L'insegnamento privato della musica alla fine del Cinquecento." *Rivista musicale italiana* 37 (1930): 74-77.

———. "La scuola dei pueri cantus di S. Luigi dei francesi in Roma e i suoi principali allievi (1591-1623)." *Rivista musicale italiana* 22 (1915): 593-641.

Carey, Frank. "Composition for Equal Voices in the Sixteenth Century." *Journal of Musicology* 9 (1991): 300-342.

Carpenter, Hoyle. "Microtones in a Sixteenth Century Portuguese Manuscript." *Acta musicologica* 32 (1960): 23-28.

Carruthers, Mary. *The Book of Memory: A Study of Memory in Medieval Culture.* Cambridge, 1990.

Carter, Tim. "Music-Selling in Late Sixteenth-Century Florence: The Bookshop of Piero di Giuliano Morosi." *Music & Letters* 70 (1989): 483-504.

Casademunt i Fiol, Sergi. "Un manuscript català inèdit del segle XV [*sic, recte:* XVI]." *Recerca musicologica* 3 (1983): 39-58.

———. *Il "Codice 59" dell'Archivio Musicale Lateranense, autografo di Giov. Pierluigi da Palestrina.* Rome, 1919.

Casimiri, Raffaele. "Lettere di musicisti (1579-1585) al Cardinal Sirleto." *Note d'archivio* 9 (1932): 102-105.

Cattin, Giulio. "Un processionale fiorentino per la settimana santa: studio liturgico-musicale sul ms. 21 del'Opera di S. Maria del Fiore." *Quadrivium* 15/2 (1974): 53-204.

Cavanaugh, Philip Stephen. "A Liturgico-Musical Study of German Polyphonic Mass Propers, 1490-1520." Ph.D. diss., University of Pittsburgh, 1972.

Census-Catalogue of Manuscript Sources of Polyphonic Music 1400-1550. Renaissance Manuscript Studies 1. 5 vols. American Institute of Musicology, 1979-1988.

Chailley, Jacques. "Tabulae Compositoriae." *Acta musicologica* 51 (1979): 51-54.

Charteris, Richard, and Gertraut Haberkamp. "Regensburg, Bischöfliche Zentralbibliothek, Butsch 205-210: A Little-known Source of the Music of Giovanni Gabrieli and his Contemporaries." *MD* 43 (1989): 195-249.

Chew, Geoffrey. "Notation, III.5." *NG.*

Chybinski, Adolf. "Polnische Musik und Musikkultur des 16. Jahrhunderts in ihren Beziehungen zu Deutschland." *Sammelbände der Internationalen Musikgesellschaft* 13 (1911-1912): 463-505.

Clercx, Suzanne. "D'une ardoise aux partitions du XVIe siècle . . ." In *Mélanges d'histoire et d'esthétique musicales offerts à Paul Marie Masson.* Paris, 1955.

Cohen, David E. "Contrapunctus, Improvisation, and *Res Facta.*" Paper read at the annual meeting of the American Musicological Society, Austin, 1989.

Coussemaker, Charles Edmond Henri de. *Scriptorum de musica medii aevi.* 3 vols. Paris, 1864-1876. Reprint, Hildesheim, 1963.

Crawford, David, and Scott Messing. *Gaspar de Albertis' Sixteenth-Century Choirbooks at Bergamo.* Renaissance Manuscript Studies 6. American Institute of Musicology. Stuttgart, 1994.

Crocker, Richard. "Medieval Monophony in Western Europe." In *The Early Middle Ages to 1300,* edited by Richard Crocker and David Hiley. *The New Oxford History of Music,* 2. 2d ed., Oxford, 1990.

———. "The Sequence." In *Gattungen der Musik in Einzeldarstellungen: Gedenkschrift Leo Schrade.* Berne, 1973.

Culley, Thomas D., S.J. *Jesuits and Music I: A Study of the Musicians connected with the Ger-*

man College in Rome during the 17th Century and of their Activities in Northern Europe. Rome, 1970.

Cummings, Anthony. *The Politicized Muse: Music for Medici Festivals, 1512–1537.* Princeton, 1992.

Cuyler, Louise. "The Sequences of Isaac's *Choralis Constantinus.*" *JAMS* 3 (1950): 3 – 16.

D'Accone, Frank A. "Repertory and Performance Practice at Santa Maria Novella at the Turn of the 17th Century." In *A Festschrift for Albert Seay: Essays by his Friends and Colleagues,* edited by Michael D. Grace, 71 – 136. Colorado Springs, 1982.

———. "Updating the Style: Francesco Corteccia's Revisions in his Responsories for Holy Week." In *Music and Context: Essays for John M. Ward,* edited by Anne Dhu Shapiro, 32 – 53. Harvard University, 1985.

Dahlhaus, Carl. "Musiktheoretisches aus dem Nachlaß des Sethus Calvisius." *Musik-forschung* 9 (1956): 129 – 139.

Daniels, H. A., ed. *Die Sequenzen des Thesaurus Hymnologicus.* Analecta Hymnica Medii Aevi 55. Leipzig, 1922. Reprint, New York, 1961.

Dart, Thurston. "Tablature." *NG.*

David, Hans T., and Arthur Mendel, eds. *The Bach Reader.* New York, 1945; rev. ed. 1966.

de Goede, N. *The Utrecht Prosarium.* Monumenta Musica Neerlandica 6. Amsterdam, 1965.

Denk, Rudolf. *"Musica Getutscht": Deutsche Fachprosa des Spätmittelalters im Bereich der Musik.* Munich, 1981.

DeVoto, G., and G. C. Oli. *Dizionario della lingua italiana.* Florence, 1971.

Disertori, B. *La musica nei quadri antichi.* Calliano, 1978.

Dobbins, Frank. "Morlaye, Guillaume." *NG.*

Duffy, Kathryn Pohlmann. "The Jena Choirbooks: Music and Liturgy at the Castle Church in Wittenberg under Frederick the Wise, Elector of Saxony." Ph.D. diss., University of Chicago, 1995.

Durante, Elio, and Anna Martellotti. "Terminorum musicae diffinitiones overo puntual-izzazioni sul lessico musicale del tardo rinascimento e del barocco." *Annali della facoltà di lingue e letterature straniere,* 3d ser., 6/1 (1985): 147 – 170; 7/1 – 2 (1986): 49 – 90.

Eberlein, Roland. "The Faenza Codex: Music for Organ or for Lute Duet?" *EM* 20 (1992): 461-466.

Edwards, Rebecca A. "Claudio Merulo: Servant of the State and Musical Entrepreneur in Later Sixteenth Century Venice." Ph.D. diss., Princeton University, 1990.

Einstein, Alfred. *The Italian Madrigal.* Princeton, 1949; 2d ed., 1971.

Eitner, Robert. "Mittheilungen." *Monatshefte für Musikgeschichte* 5 (1873): 29 – 31.

Elders, Willem. "Zur Frage der Vorlage von Isaacs Messe *La mi la sol* oder *O praeclara.*" In *Von Isaac bis Bach: Studien zur älteren deutschen Musikgeschichte. Festschrift Martin Just zum 60. Geburtstag.* Kassel, 1991.

Fabbri, Mario. "La vita e l'ignota opera-prima di Francesco Corteccia musicista italiano del Rinascimento (Firenze 1502 –Firenze 1571)." *Chigiana* 22 (= II n.s.) (1965): 185 – 217.

Fabbri, Paolo. *Tre secoli di musica a Ravenna dalla controriforma alla caduta dell'Antico Regime.* Ravenna, 1983.

———. "Vita musicale nel Cinquecento ravennate: Qualche integrazione." *Rivista italiana di musicologia* 13 (1978): 30 – 59.

Fallows, David. "English Song Repertories of the Mid-Fifteenth Century." *Proceedings of the Royal Musical Association* 103 (1976 – 1977): 61 – 79.

Une fantaisie de la Renaissance: Compositional Process in the Renaissance Fantasia. Essays for Howard Mayer Brown, in memoriam-Journal of the Lute Society of America 23 (1990).

Fassler, Margot. *Gothic Song: Victorine Sequences and Augustinian Reform in Twelfth-Century Paris.* Cambridge, 1993.

Febvre, Lucien, and Henri-Jean Martin. *L'Apparition du livre.* Paris, 1958. Translated by David Gerard under the title *The Coming of the Book: The Impact of Printing 1450–1800* (1976; London, 1990).

Feldman, Martha. "Rore's 'Selva selvaggia': The *Primo Libro* of 1542." *JAMS* 42 (1989): 547–603.

Fenlon, Iain. *Music and Patronage in Sixteenth-Century Mantua.* Cambridge, 1980.

———. "Patronage, Music and Liturgy in Renaissance Mantua." In *Plainsong in the Age of Polyphony,* edited by Thomas F. Kelly, 209–235. Cambridge, 1992.

———, ed. *Cambridge Music Manuscripts, 900–1700.* Cambridge, 1982.

———, and James Haar. *The Italian Madrigal in the Early Sixteenth Century: Sources and Interpretation.* Cambridge, 1988.

———, and John Milsom. "'Ruled Paper Imprinted': Music Paper and Patents in Sixteenth-Century England." *JAMS* 37 (1984): 139–163.

———, Nan C. Carpenter, and Richard Rastall. "Education in Music. II and III." *NG.*

Ferand, Ernest T. "Bemerkungen zu der neuen Quelle von Heinrich Fabers 'Musica poetica'." *Musikforschung* 11 (1958): 340–341.

———. "Improvised Vocal Counterpoint in the Late Renaissance and Early Baroque." *Annales musicologiques* 4 (1956): 129–174.

———. *Die Improvisation in der Musik.* Zürich, 1939.

Flynn, Jane. "A Reconsideration of the Mulliner Book (British Library Add. MS 30513): Music Education in Sixteenth-Century England." Ph.D. diss., Duke University, 1993.

———. "The Education of Choristers in England during the Sixteenth Century." In *English Choral Practice, 1400–1650,* edited by John Morehen. Cambridge, 1996.

Forney, Kristine. "'Nymphes gayes en abry du Laurier': Music Instruction for Women in Renaissance Antwerp." Paper read at the annual meeting of the American Musicological Society, Pittsburgh, 1992.

Frati, L. "Memorie per la storia della musica in Bologna dal secolo xv al xvi." *Rivista musicale italiana* 24 (1917): 449–478.

Frey, Herman-Walther. "Die Kapellmeister an der französischen Nationalkirche San Luigi dei Francesi in Rom im 16. Jahrhundert." *AfMw* 22 (1965): 32–60 and 23 (1966): 272–293.

Genesi, Mario. *Castell'Arquato, Archivio della Chiesa Collegiata, Catalogo dei manoscritti musicali.* I Quaderni musicali di Castell'Arquato, 1. Piacenza, [1987].

Georgiades, Thrasybulos. "Zur Lasso-Gesamtausgabe." In *Bericht über den Internationalen Musikwissenschaftlichen Kongress Wien 1956,* 216–219. Graz, 1958.

Gibbons, Felton. *Dosso and Battista Dossi: Court Painters at Ferrara.* Princeton, 1968.

Göllner, Marie Louise. [Martinez-Göllner]. "Die Augsburger Bibliothek Herwart und ihre Lautentabulaturen: Eine Musikbestand der Bayerischen Staatsbibliothek aus dem 16. Jahrhundert." *Fontes Artis Musicae* 16 (1969): 29–48.

———. "On the Process of Lute Intabulation in the Sixteenth Century." In *Ars Iocundissima: Festschrift für Kurt Dorfmüller zum 60. Geburtstag,* edited by Horst Leuchtmann and Robert Münster, 83–96. Tutzing, 1984.

———, ed. *Tabulaturen und Stimmbücher bis zur Mitte des 17. Jahrhunderts.* Bayerische Staatsbibliothek. Katalog der Musikhandschriften 2. Munich, 1979.

Grendler, Paul. *Schooling in Renaissance Italy: Literacy and Learning, 1300–1600.* Baltimore, 1989.

Grier, James. "*Ecce sanctum quem deus elegit Marcialem apostolum*: Adémar de Chabannes and the Tropes for the Feast of Saint Martial." In *Beyond the Moon: Festschrift Luther Dittmer*, edited by Bryan Gillingham and Paul Merkley, 28 – 74. Wissenschaftliche Abhandlungen 53. Ottawa, 1990.

Gurlitt, Willibald. "Die Kompositionslehre des deutschen 16. und 17. Jahrhunderts." In *Bericht über den Internationalen Musikwissenschaftlichen Kongress Bamberg 1953*, 103 – 113. Kassel, 1954.

Gushee, Lawrence. "Analytical Method and Compositional Process in Some Thirteenth- and Fourteenth-Century Music." *Forum musicologicum*. Basler Beiträge für Musikgeschichte 3. Basel, 1982.

———. "New Sources for the Biography of Johannes de Muris." *JAMS* 22 (1969): 3 – 26.

Haack, H. "Partitur." *Riemann Musik Lexikon: Sachteil*. 12th ed. Mainz, 1967.

Haar, James. "Lessons in Theory from a Sixteenth-Century Composer." In *Altro Polo: Essays on Italian Music in the Cinquecento*, edited by Richard Charteris, 51 – 81. Sydney, 1990.

Haas, Robert. *Aufführungspraxis der Musik*. Potsdam. 1931.

Haase, Hans. "Komposition." *MGG*.

Haller, Klaus. "Partitur." *Handwörterbuch der musikalischen Terminologie*. Wiesbaden, 1976.

———. *Partituranordnung und musikalischer Satz*. Tutzing, 1972.

Hammond, Frederick. *Girolamo Frescobaldi: A Guide to Research*. New York, 1988.

Hannas, Ruth. "Communication on the 'tabula compositoria' of Lampadius." *JAMS* 2 (1949): 130 – 132.

———. "Reply to Lowinsky." *JAMS* 3 (1950): 63 – 64.

———. "Reply to Lowinsky." *JAMS* 9 (1956): 70.

Harrán, Don. "Verse Types in the Early Madrigal." *JAMS* 22 (1969): 27 – 53.

———. *Word-Tone Relations in Musical Thought from Antiquity to the Seventeenth Century*. MSD 40. American Institute of Musicology, 1986.

Hayburn, Robert F. *Papal Legislation on Sacred Music 95 A.D. to 1977 A.D.* Collegeville, Minn., 1979.

Haydon, Glen. "The Dedication of Francesco Corteccia's Hinnario." *JAMS* 13 (1960): 114 – 116.

Hell, Helmut. "Ist der Wiener Sibyllen-Codex wirklich ein Lasso-Autograph?" *Musik in Bayern* 28 (1984).

———. "Senfls Hand in den Chorbüchern der Bayerischen Staatsbibliothek." *Augsburger Jahrbuch für Musikwissenschaft* (1987): 65-137.

Hermelink, Siegfried. "Chiavette." *NG*.

———. *Dispositiones Modorum: Die Tonarten in der Musik Palestrinas und seiner Zeitgenossen*. Münchner Veröffentlichungen zur Musikgeschichte 4. Tutzing, 1960.

———. "Die Tabula compositoria. Beiträge zu einer Begriffstimmung." In *Festschrift Heinrich Besseler zum sechzigsten Geburtstag*, 221 – 230. Leipzig, 1961.

Higgins, Paula. "Music and Musicians at the Sainte-Chapelle of the Bourges Palace, 1405 – 1515." In *Atti del XIV Congresso della Società Internazionale di Musicologia*, 3, 689 – 701. Turin, 1990.

Hill, Robert. "Tablature versus Staff Notation: Or, Why Did the Young J. S. Bach Compose in Tablature?" In *Church, Stage, and Studio: Music and Its Contexts in Seventeenth-Century Germany*, edited by Paul Walker. Ann Arbor, 1990.

Hoke, Hans Gunter. "Partitur." *MGG*.

Hollstein's Dutch and Flemish Etchings, Engravings, and Woodcuts ca. 1450–1700, 21. Amsterdam, 1980.

Holman, Peter. *Four and Twenty Fiddlers: The Violin at the English Court 1540–1690*. Oxford, 1993.

Hoppin, Richard. "Exultantes collaudemus: A Sequence for Saint Hylarion." In *Aspects of Medieval and Renaissance Music: A Birthday Offering to Gustave Reese*, edited by Jan LaRue. New York, 1966. Reprint, Stuyvesant, N.Y., 1978.

Hudson, Barton. "On the Texting of Obrecht's Masses." *MD* 42 (1988): 101–127.

Hughes, Anselm. "Sixteenth-Century Service Music: The Tudor Church Music Series." *Music and Letters* 5 (1924): 145–154, 335–346.

Jeffery, Peter. "The Autograph Manuscripts of Francesco Cavalli." Ph.D. diss., Princeton University, 1980.

———. "Music Manuscripts on Microfilm in the Hill Monastic Library at St. John's Abbey and University." *MLA Notes* 35 (1978-1979): 7–30.

Jeppesen, Knud. "Palestrina." *MGG*.

———. "Palestriniana: Ein unbekanntes Autogramm und einige unveröffentlichte Falsibordoni des Giovanni Pierluigi da Palestrina." In *Miscelánea en Homenaje a Monseñor Higinio Anglés*, 417–432. Barcelona, 1958–1961.

———. "Pierluigi da Palestrina, Herzog Guglielmo Gonzaga und die neugefundenen Mantovaner-Messen Palestrina's." *Acta musicologica* 25 (1953): 132–179.

———. "The Recently Discovered Mantova Masses of Palestrina." *Acta musicologica* 22 (1950): 36–37.

———. "Über einen Brief Palestrinas." In *Festschrift Peter Wagner zum 60. Geburtstag*, edited by K. Weinmann, 100–107. Leipzig, 1926.

Johnson, Alvin. "Rore, Cipriano de." *NG*.

Johnson, Cleveland. *Vocal Compositions in German Organ Tablatures 1550–1650: A Catalogue and Commentary*. New York, 1989.

Jones, Pamela M. *Federico Borromeo and the Ambrosiana: Art Patronage and Reform in Seventeenth-Century Milan*. Cambridge, 1993.

Judd, Robert F. "The Use of Notational Formats at the Keyboard. A Study of Printed Sources of Keyboard Music in Spain and Italy c. 1500–1700, Selected Manuscript Sources Including Music by Claudio Merulo, and Contemporary Writings Concerning Notations." D.Phil. thesis, Oxford University, 1988.

Just, Martin. *Der Mensuralkodex Mus. ms. 40021 der Staatsbibliothek Preußischer Kulturbesitz Berlin*. Tutzing, 1975.

———. "Heinrich Isaacs Motetten in italienischen Quellen." *Analecta musicologica* 1 (1963): 1–19.

———. "Ysaac de manu sua." In *Bericht über den Internationalen Musikwissenschaftlichen Kongress Kassel 1962*, 112–114. Kassel, 1963.

Kämper, Dietrich. *Studien zur instrumentalen Ensemblemusik des 16. Jahrhunderts in Italien*. Analecta musicologica 10. Cologne, 1970.

Kanazawa, Masakata. "Antonius Janue and Revisions of his Music." In *Memorie e contributi alla musica dal medioevo all'età moderna offerti a F. Ghisi nel settantesimo compleanno (1901–1971)*, 1: 177–194. Bologna, 1971.

Kastner, Macario Santiago. "Los manuscritos musicales n.s 48 y 242 de la Biblioteca General de la Universidad de Coimbra." *Anuario musical* 5 (1950): 78–96.

Kendrick, Robert L. "Musical Self-Expression in Federico Borromeo's Milan." Paper read at the annual meeting of the Renaissance Society of America, New York 1995.

Kerman, Joseph. "Sketch Studies." In *Musicology in the 1980s: Methods, Goals, Opportunities*, ed. D. Kern Holoman and Claude V. Palisca, 53–65. New York, 1982.

Kinkeldey, Otto. *Orgel und Klavier in der Musik des 16. Jahrhunderts*. Leipzig, 1910.

Kirby, Frank E. "Hermann Finck's *Practica musica*: A Comparative Study in 16th Century German Musical Theory." Ph.D. diss., Yale University, 1957.

Kirkendale, Warren. *The Court Musicians in Florence during the Principate of the Medici*. Florence, 1993.

Kmetz, John. "The Drafts of Jodocus Fabri and Company: New Evidence of Compositional Process from Renaissance Basel." Paper read at the annual meeting of the American Musicological Society, Minneapolis, 1994.

————. *Die Handschriften der Universitätsbibliothek Basel. Katalog der Musikhandschriften des 16. Jahrhunderts*. Basel, 1988.

————. "The Piperinus-Amerbach Partbooks: Six Months of Music Lessons in Renaissance Basle." In *Music in the German Renaissance*, edited by John Kmetz, 215–234. Cambridge, 1994.

Knighton, Tess. "The *a cappella* Heresy in Spain: An Inquisition into the Performance of the *Cancionero* Repertory." *Early Music* 20 (1992): 561–581.

Konrad, Ulrich. *Mozarts Schaffensweise: Studien zu den Werkautographen, Skizzen und Entwürfen*. Göttingen, 1992.

Ladewig, James. "Frescobaldi's "Recercari, et canzoni franzese" (1615): A Study of the Contrapuntal Keyboard Idiom in Ferrara, Naples, and Rome, 1580–1620." Ph.D. diss., University of California at Berkeley, 1978.

————. "Luzzaschi as Frescobaldi's Teacher: A Little-Known Ricercare." *Studi musicali* 10 (1981): 241–264.

La Via, Stefano. "Cipriano de Rore as Reader and as Read: A Literary-Musical Study of Madrigals from Rore's Later Collections (1557–1566)." Ph.D. diss., Princeton University, 1991.

Leech-Wilkinson, Daniel. *Compositional Techniques in the Four-Part Isorhythmic Motets of Philippe de Vitry and his Contemporaries*. New York, 1989.

————. "Machaut's *Rose, Lis* and the Problem of Early Music Analysis." *Music Analysis* 3 (1984): 9–28.

————. "*Le Voir Dit* and *La Messe de Nostre Dame*: Aspects of Genre and Style in Late Works of Machaut." *Plainsong and Medieval Music* 2 (1993): 43–73.

————. "*Le Voir Dit*: A Reconstruction and a Guide for Musicians." *Plainsong and Medieval Music* 2 (1993): 103–140.

Lester, Joel. *Compositional Theory in the Eighteenth Century*. Cambridge, 1992.

Lichtenthal, Pietro. *Dizionario e bibliografia della musica*. Milan, 1826.

Limentani Virdis, Caterina, Franca Pellegrini, and Gemme Piccin, eds. *Una dinastia di incisori, i Sadeler*. Padua, 1992.

Litterick, Louise. "The Revision of Ockeghem's 'Je n'ay dueil.'" In *Musique naturelle et musique artificielle: In memoriam Gustav Reese-Le Moyen français* 5 (1980): 29–48.

Llorens, José M. *Le opere musicali della Cappella Giulia, I: Manoscritti e edizioni fino al '700*. Studi e Testi 265. Vatican City, 1971.

Lockwood, Lewis. "Jean Mouton and Jean Michel: French Music and Musicians in Italy, 1505–1520." *JAMS* 32 (1979): 191–246.

————. "Josquin at Ferrara: New Documents and Letters." In *Josquin des Prez: Proceedings of the International Josquin Festival-Conference*, edited by Edward E. Lowinsky, 103–137. London, 1976.

————. "Music at Ferrara in the Period of Ercole I d'Este." *Studi Musicali* 1 (1972): 101–131.

————. "Palestrina, Giovanni Pierluigi da." *The New Grove High Renaissance Masters*. New York, 1984.

————. "'Parody' as Term and Concept in 16th-Century Music." In *Aspects of Medieval and Renaissance Music: A Birthday Offering to Gustave Reese*, edited by Jan LaRue, 560–575. New York, 1966. Reprint, New York, 1978.

Lowinsky, Edward E. "Early Scores in Manuscript." *JAMS* 13 (1960): 126–173; reprinted in *Music in the Culture*, 803–840.

———. *Music in the Culture of the Renaissance and Other Essays*, edited by Bonnie J. Blackburn. 2 vols. Chicago, 1989.

———. "Musical Genius—Evolution and Origins of a Concept." *MQ* 50 (1964): 321–340; 476–95; reprinted in *Music in the Culture*, 40–66.

———. "On the Use of Scores by 16th-Century Musicians." *JAMS* 1 (1948): 17–23; reprinted in *Music in the Culture*, 797–800.

———. "Reply to Ruth Hannas." *JAMS* 2 (1949): 132–134; reprinted in *Music in the Culture*, 800–802.

Luther, W. M. "Autograph." *MGG*.

———. *Gallus Dressler. Ein Beitrag zur Geschichte des protestantischen Schulkantorats im 16. Jahrhunderts*. Kassel, [1945].

MacClintock, Carol. "A Court Musician's Songbook: Modena MS C311." *JAMS* 9 (1956): 177–192.

———. *Giaches de Wert (1535–1596): Life and Works*. MSD 17. American Institute of Musicology, 1966.

MacCracken, Thomas. "The Manuscript Uppsala, Universitetsbiblioteket, Vokalmusik i Handskrift 76b." Ph.D. diss., University of Chicago, 1985.

Mandel, George Thomas. "Paper—Growth without Profit." *IPH Yearbook* 1 (1980): 77–88.

Marshall, Robert L. *The Compositional Process of J. S. Bach: A Study of the Autograph Scores of the Vocal Works*. Princeton, 1972.

Martin, Henri-Jean. *L'Histoire et pouvoirs de l'écrit* (1988). Translated by Lydia G. Cochrane under the title *The History and Power of Writing* (Chicago, 1994).

McGee, Timothy. "Instruments and the Faenza Codex," *EM* 14 (1986): 480–490.

———. "Once again, the Faenza Codex, a Reply to Roland Eberlein." *EM* 20 (1992): 466–468.

Meier, Bernhard. "Die Harmonik im Cantus firmus-haltigen Satz des 15. Jahrhunderts." *AfMw* 9 (1952): 27–44.

———. *Die Tonarten der klassischen Vokalpolyphonie*. Utrecht, 1974. Translated by Ellen Beebe under the title *The Modes of Classical Vocal Polyphony* (New York, 1988).

———. "Eine weitere Quelle der 'Musica poetica' von H. Faber." *Musikforschung* 11 (1958): 76.

Mertens, J. "Recherches archéologiques dans la collégiale Saint-Feuillen." *Bulletin de la Commission Royale des Monuments et des Sites* 4 (1953): 135–181.

Miller, Clement A. "Frosch, Johannes." *NG*.

Milsom, John. "Tallis's First and Second Thoughts." *Journal of the Royal Musical Association* 113 (1988): 203–222.

Minamino, Hiroyuki. "Sixteenth-Century Lute Treatises with Emphasis on Process and Techniques of Intabulation." Ph.D. diss., University of Chicago, 1988.

Minor, Andrew C. "Corteccia, (Pier) Francesco." *NG*.

Mischiati, Oscar. "Un'antologia manoscritta in partitura del secolo XVI. Il ms. Bourdeney della Bibliothèque Nationale di Parigi." *Rivista italiana di musicologia* 10 (1975): 265–328.

———. *La prassi musicale presso i canonici regolari del Ss. Salvatore nei secoli XVI e XVII e i manoscritti polifonici della Biblioteca Musicale 'G. B. Martini' di Bologna*. Rome, 1985.

Moberg, Carl Allen. *Über die schwedischen Sequenzen*. Utrecht, 1927.

Moyer, Ann. *Musica scientia: Musical Scholarship in the Italian Renaissance*. Ithaca, 1992.

"La musica nella storia delle università." In *Atti del XIV Congresso della Società Internazionale di Musicologia*, I: 27–89. Turin, 1990.

Murray, Russell E. "On the Teaching Duties of the Maestro di Cappella in Sixteenth-Century Italy: The Processo against Pietro Pontio." *Explorations in Renaissance Culture* 14 (1988): 115–128.

———. "The Voice of the Composer: Theory and Practice in the Works of Pietro Pontio." Ph.D. diss., University of North Texas, 1989.

Musikalische Edition im Wandel des historischen Bewußtseins, edited by Thrasybulos Georgiades. Kassel, 1971.

Die Musik des 15. und 16. Jahrhunderts, edited by Ludwig Finscher. Neues Handbuch der Musikwissenschaft 3. Laaber, 1990.

Musik in Bayern. II. Ausstellungskatalog. Tutzing, 1972.

Ness, Arthur J. "The Herwarth Lute Manuscripts at the Bavarian State Library, Munich: A Bibliographical Study with Emphasis on the Works of Marco dall'Aquila and Melchior Newsidler." Ph.D. diss., New York University, 1984.

———. "A Letter from Melchior Newsidler." In *Music and Context: Essays for John M. Ward*, edited by Anne Dhu Shapiro, 352–369. Harvard University, 1985.

New Grove Dictionary of Music and Musicians. Edited by Stanley Sadie. London, 1980.

Newes, Virginia. "Writing, Reading and Memorizing: The Transmission and Resolution of Retrograde Canons from the 14th and Early 15th Centuries." *EM* 18 (1990): 218–234.

Nickell, Joe. *Pen, Ink, & Evidence: A Study of Writing Materials for the Penman, Collector, and Document Detective.* Lexington, Ky., 1990.

Niemöller, Klaus Wolfgang. "Nicolaus Wollick und sein Musiktraktat." *Beiträge zur rheinische Musikgeschichte* 13 (1956).

———. *Untersuchungen zu Musikpflege und Musikunterricht an den deutschen Lateinschulen vom ausgehenden Mittelalter bis um 1600.* Regensburg, 1969.

———. "Zum Einfluss des Humanismus auf Position und Konzeption von Musik im deutschen Bildungssystem der ersten Hälfte des 16. Jahrhunderts." In *Musik in Humanismus und Renaissance*, edited by Walter Rüegg and Annegrit Schmidt, 77–97. Weinheim, 1983.

Ongaro, Giulio. "The Chapel of St. Mark's at the Time of Adrian Willaert (1527–1562): A Documentary Study." Ph.D. diss., University of North Carolina at Chapel Hill, 1986.

O'Regan, Noel. "'Blessed with the Holy Father's Entertainment': Roman Ceremonial Music as Experienced by the Irish Earls in Rome, 1608." *Irish Musical Studies* 2: *Music and the Church* (1991): 41–61.

———. "The Early Polychoral Music of Orlando di Lasso: New Light from Roman Sources." *Acta musicologica* 56 (1984): 234–251.

———. "Palestrina and the Oratory of Santissima Trinità dei Pellegrini." In *Atti del II Convegno Internazionale di Studi Palestriniani*, 95–121. Palestrina, 1991.

Osley, A. S. *Scribes and Sources: Handbook of the Chancery Hand in the Sixteenth Century.* Boston, 1980.

Owens, Jessie Ann. "Cipriano de Rore a Parma (1560–1565): Nuovi Documenti." *Rivista italiana di musicologia* 11 (1976): 5–26.

———. "Cipriano de Rore: Founder of the *Seconda Pratica*." Paper read at the New England Chapter of the American Musicological Society, April 1985.

———. "Francesco Corteccia's Sketchbook: New Evidence about Compositional Process." Paper read at the annual meeting of the American Musicological Society, Pittsburgh, 1992.

———. "An Illuminated Manuscript of Motets by Cipriano de Rore (München, Bayerische Staatsbibliothek, Mus. Ms. B)." Ph.D. diss., Princeton University, 1978.

————. "An Isaac Autograph." In *Music in the German Renaissance: Sources, Styles, and Context*, edited by John Kmetz, 27–53. Cambridge, 1994.

————. "The Milan Partbooks: Evidence of Cipriano de Rore's Compositional Process." *JAMS* 37 (1984): 270–298.

————. "Mode in the Madrigals of Cipriano de Rore." In *Altro Polo: Essays on Italian Music in the Cinquecento*, edited by Richard Charteris, 1–15. Sydney, 1989.

————. "Music and Meaning in Cipriano de Rore's Setting of 'Donec gratus eram tibi.' " In *Music and Language*. Studies in the History of Music 1, 95–117. New York, 1983.

————. "Music Historiography and the Definition of 'Renaissance'." *MLA Notes* 47 (1990): 305-330.

————. Review of Bonnie J. Blackburn et al., *A Correspondence. JAMS* 46 (1993): 313–318.

Pätzig, Gerhard-Rudolf. "Liturgische Grundlagen und handschriftliche Überlieferung von Heinrich Isaacs 'Choralis Constantinus'." Diss., Eberhard-Karls-Universität zu Tübingen, 1956.

Page, Christopher. "The Performance of Songs in Late Medieval France, A New Source." *EM* 19 (1982): 441–450.

Page, Daniel B. "Composition at Nonesuch: The Consort Dances of British Library, MSS Royal Appendix 74–76." Paper read at the symposium "Creative Process in Renaissance Music," Brandeis University, 1992.

————. *G. B. Doni's Lyra Barberina. Commentary and Iconographical Study; Facsimile Edition with Critical Notes*. Bologna, 1981.

Palisca, Claude. *Humanism in Italian Renaissance Thought*. New Haven, 1985.

Petroski, Henry. *The Pencil: A History of Design and Circumstance*. New York, 1990.

Piattoli, Renato. "Un documento fiorentino di apprendistato musicale dell'anno 1504." In *Collectanea Historiae Musicae* 2, 351–353. Florence, 1957.

Picker, Martin. *Henricus Isaac: A Guide to Research*. New York, 1991.

Pirrotta, Nino. "Music and Cultural Tendencies in Fifteenth-Century Italy." *JAMS* 19 (1966); reprinted in *Music and Culture*, 80–112.

————. *Music and Culture in Italy from the Middle Ages to the Baroque: A Collection of Essays*. Cambridge, Mass., 1984.

Polk, Keith. *German Instrumental Music of the Late Middle Ages*. Cambridge, 1992.

Prassl, Franz Karl. *Psallat ecclesia mater: Studien zu Repertoire und Verwendung von Sequenzen in der Liturgie österreichischer Augustinerchorherren vom 12. bis zum 16. Jahrhundert*. Klagenfurt, 1987.

Preece, Isobel Woods. " 'Cant Organe': A Lost Technique?" Paper read at the Annual Conference on Medieval and Renaissance Music, Edinburgh, 1988.

————. "W$_3$—Some Fragments of Scottish Fourteenth-Century Polyphony." Paper read at the Annual Conference on Medieval and Renaissance Music, Glasgow, 1994.

Pritchard, V. *English Medieval Graffiti*. Cambridge, 1967.

Quoika, Rudolf. *Das Positif in Geschichte und Gegenwart*. Kassel, 1957.

Rainbow, Bernarr. *Music in Educational Thought and Practice: A Survey from 800 BC*. Aberystwyth, 1989.

Randel, Don Michael. "Dufay the Reader." In *Music and Language*, 38–78. Studies in the History of Music 1. New York, 1983.

Rees, Owen. "Newly-identified Holograph Manuscripts from Late-Renaissance Portugal." *EM* 22 (1994): 261–277.

————. "Sixteenth- and Early Seventeenth-century Polyphony from the Monastery of Santa Cruz, Coimbra, Portugal." Ph.D. diss., Cambridge University, 1991.

Reese, Gustave, and Jeremy Noble. "Josquin Desprez." *The New Grove High Renaissance Masters*. New York, 1984.

Reinhardt, Carl Philipp. *Die Heidelberger Liedmeister des 16. Jahrhunderts*. Heidelberger Studien zur Musikwissenschaft 8. Kassel, 1939.

Rempp, Frieder. "Elementar- und Satzlehre von Tinctoris bis Zarlino." In *Italienische Musiktheorie im 16. und 17. Jahrhundert*. Geschichte der Musiktheorie 7. Darmstadt, 1989.

Reynolds, Christopher. "Musical Evidence of Compositional Planning in the Renaissance: Josquin's *Plus nulz regretz*." *JAMS* 40 (1987): 53–81.

Riemann, Hugo. *Geschichte der Musiktheorie*. Leipzig, 1898; 2d ed., Berlin, [1920]. Translated by Raymond H. Haggh under the title *History of Music Theory Books I and II by Hugo Riemann* (Lincoln, 1966). Translated by William C. Mickelsen under the title *Hugo Riemann's Theory of Harmony: A Study and History of Music Theory, Book III* (Lincoln, 1977).

Ristory, Heinz. "Notationstechnische Modifikationen von Vokalvorlagen im Codex Vind. 5094 der österreichischen Nationalbibliothek (Wien)." *MD* 39 (1986): 53–86.

Rivera, Benito. *German Music Theory in the Early 17th Century: The Treatises of Johannes Lippius*. Madison, 1980.

———. "Harmonic Theory in Musical Treatises of the Late Fifteenth and Early Sixteenth Centuries." *Music Theory Spectrum* 1 (1979): 80–95.

———. "The *Isagoge* (1581) of Johannes Avianius: An Early Formulation of Triadic Theory." *Journal of Music Theory* 22 (1978): 43–64.

Rome Reborn: The Vatican Library and Renaissance Culture. Edited by Anthony Grafton. Washington, 1993.

Rostirolla, Giancarlo. "La Cappella Giulia in San Pietro negli anni del magistero di Giovanni Pierluigi da Palestrina." In *Atti del Convegno di Studi Palestriniani*, edited by F. Luisi. Palestrina, 1977.

Rowan, Ruth Halle. *Music Through Sources and Documents*. New York, 1979.

Ruhnke, Marin. *Joachim Burmeister. Ein Beitrag zur Musiklehre um 1600*. Kassel, 1955.

Sachs, Klaus-Jürgen. "Arten improvisierter Mehrstimmigkeit nach Lehrtexten des 14. bis 16. Jahrhunderts." *Basler Jahrbuch für historische Musikpraxis* 7 (1983): 166–183.

———. "Die Contrapunctus-Lehre im 14. und 15. Jahrhundert." *Die mittelalterliche Lehre von der Mehrstimmigkeit*. Geschichte der Musiktheorie 5. Darmstadt, 1984.

———. "Contrapunctus/Kontrapunkt." *Handwörterbuch der musikalischen Terminologie*. Edited by H. H. Eggebrecht. Wiesbaden, 1982.

Salmen, Walter. *Musiker im Porträt*, 1: *Von der Spätantike bis 1600*. Munich, 1982.

———. *Musikleben im 16. Jahrhundert*. Musikgeschichte in Bildern 3/9. Leipzig, 1976.

Sartori, Antonio. *Documenti per la storia della musica al Santo e nel Veneto*. Edited by E. Grossato. Vicenza, 1977.

Scherliess, Volker. *Musikalische Noten auf Kunstwerken der italienischen Renaissance bis zum Anfang des 17. Jahrhunderts*. Hamburg, 1972.

Schreurs, Eugeen. *Anthologie van muziekfragmenten uit de Lage Landen*. Leuven, 1995.

———, and Bruno Bouckaert, eds. *Bedreigde klanken? Muziekfragmenten uit de Lage Landen*. Leuven, 1995.

Schwartz, Rudolf. "Zur Partitur im 16. Jahrhundert." *AfMw* 2 (1919–1920): 73–78.

Sherr, Richard. "*Illibata dei virgo nutrix* and Josquin's Roman Style." *JAMS* 41 (1988): 434–464.

———. "Notes on Two Roman Manuscripts of the Early Sixteenth Century." *MQ* 63 (1977): 66–73.

———. "The Publications of Guglielmo Gonzaga." *JAMS* 31 (1978): 118–125.

Silbiger, Alexander. "Is the Italian Keyboard *Intavolatura* a Tablature?" *Recercare* 3 (1990): 81–103.

———. *Italian Manuscript Sources of 17th Century Keyboard Music*. Ann Arbor, 1980.

Die Singenden in der graphischen Kunst 1500–1900. Kunstsammlung der Veste Coburg. Essen, 1962.

Slim, H. Colin. "Dosso Dossi's Allegory at Florence about Music." *JAMS* 43 (1990): 43–98.

———. "Images of Music in Three Prints after Maarten van Heemskerck." In *Iconography at the Crossroads*, ed. Brendan Cassidy, 229–240. Princeton, 1993.

———. "Keyboard Music at Castell'Arquato by an Early Madrigalist." *JAMS* 15 (1962): 35–47.

———. "The Keyboard Ricercar and Fantasia in Italy c. 1500–1550 with Reference to Parallel Forms in European Lute Music of the Same Period." Ph.D. diss., Harvard University, 1960.

———. "The Music Library of the Augsburg Patrician, Hans Heinrich Herwart (1520–1583)." *Annales musicologiques* 7 (1964–1977): 67–109.

———. "Some Puzzling Intabulations of Vocal Music for Keyboard, C. 1600, at Castell'Arquato." In *Five Centuries of Choral Music: Essays in Honor of Howard Swan*, edited by Gordon Paine. Stuyvesant, N.Y., 1989.

———. "Veggio." *NG*.

Smits van Waesberghe, Jos. *Musikerziehung: Lehre und Theorie der Musik im Mittelalter*. Musikgeschichte in Bildern 3/3. Leipzig, 1969.

Staehelin, Martin. *Die Messen Heinrich Isaacs*. Bern and Stuttgart, 1977.

———. "Obrechtiana." *Tijdschrift van de Vereniging voor Nederlandse Muziekgeschiedenis* 25 (1975): 1–37.

Stevens, John. *Words and Music in the Middle Ages: Song, Narrative, Dance and Drama, 1050–1350*. Cambridge, 1986.

Stevens, Kevin M., and Paul F. Gehl. "Giovanni Battista Bosso and the Paper Trade in Late Sixteenth-Century Milan." *La Bibliofilia* 91 (1994): 43–62.

Stevenson, Robert M. *Juan Bermudo*. The Hague, 1960.

———. *Spanish Cathedral Music in the Golden Age*. Berkeley, 1961.

Strohm, Reinhard. *The Rise of European Music, 1380–1500*. Cambridge, 1993.

Stroux, Christoph. *Die Musica Poetica des Magisters Heinrich Faber*. Inaugural-Diss., Albert-Ludwigs-Universität zu Freiburg im Breisgau, 1967. Port Elizabeth, 1976.

———. *Essays on Music in the Western World*. New York, 1974.

Strunk, Oliver. "Guglielmo Gonzaga and Palestrina's *Missa Dominicalis*." *MQ* 33 (1947); reprinted in *Essays on Music in the Western World*, 94–107.

Summers, William J. "English 14th-Century Polyphonic Music: An Inventory of the Extant Manuscript Sources." *Journal of Musicology* 8 (1990): 173–226.

———. "Fourteenth-Century English Music: A Review of Three Recent Publications." *Journal of Musicology* 8 (1990): 118–139.

Sutherland, David A. "A Second Corteccia Manuscript in the Archives of Santa Maria del Fiore." *JAMS* 25 (1972): 79–85.

Tancke, Gunnar. *Die italienischen Wörterbücher von den Anfängen bis zum Erscheinen des Vocabolario degli Accademici della Crusca (1612)*. Tübingen, 1984.

Taricani, JoAnn. "A Renaissance Bibliophile as Musical Patron: The Evidence of the Herwart Sketchbooks." *MLA Notes* 49 (1993): 1357–1389.

Tarrini, Maurizio. "Una gara musicale a Genova nel 1555." *Note d'archivio per la storia musicale*, nuova serie, 3 (1985): 159–170.

Taruskin, Richard. "Settling an Old Score: A Note on Contrafactum in Isaac's Lorenzo Lament." *Current Musicology* 21 (1976): 83–92.

Thoene, Walter. *Friedrich Beurhusius und seine Musiktraktate*. Beiträge zur rheinischen Musikgeschichte 31. Cologne, 1959.

Tirro, Frank. "Giovanni Spataro's Choirbooks in the Archive of San Petronio in Bologna." Ph.D. diss., University of Chicago, 1974.

————. *Renaissance Musical Sources in the Archive of San Petronio in Bologna*. Renaissance Manuscript Studies 4, I: *Giovanni Spataro's Choirbooks*. American Institute of Musicology, 1986.

Towne, Gary. "Music and Liturgy in Sixteenth-Century Italy: The Bergamo Organ Book and its Liturgical Implications." *Journal of Musicology* 6 (1988): 471–509.

Turrini, Giuseppe. *L'Accademia filarmonica di Verona*. Verona, 1941.

Van, Guillaume de. "La Pédagogie musicale à la fin du moyen âge." *MD* 2 (1948): 75–97.

Vanhulst, Henri. "Le Manuscrit 41 des Archives Communales de Bruges." In *Le Concert des voix et des instruments à la Renaissance*, ed. Jean-Michel Vaccaro, 231–42. Paris, 1995.

Veldman, Ilja M. *Maarten van Heemskerck and Dutch Humanism in the Sixteenth Century*. Translated by Michael Hoyle. Maarssen, 1977.

Ward, John M. "The So-called 'Dowland Lute-Book'." *Journal of the Lute Society of America* 9 (1976): 5–29.

Warren, Charles. "The Music of Derick Gerarde." Ph.D. diss., Ohio State University, 1966.

————. "Gerarde, Derick." *NG*.

Wéber, Édith. "L'Enseignement de la musique dans les écoles humanistes et protestantes en Allemagne: Théorie, pratique, pluridisciplinarité." In *L'Enseignement de la musique au Moyen Age et à la Renaissance*, 108–129. Fondation Royaumont, [1987].

————. *Musique et théâtre dans les pays rhénans*, I: *La Musique mesurée à l'antique en Allemagne*. Paris, 1974.

Weiss, Piero. *Letters of Composers through Six Centuries*. Philadelphia, 1967.

Whalley, Joyce Irene. *Writing Implements and Accessories*. Detroit, 1975.

Wolf, Jean K., and Eugene Wolf. "Rastrology and its Use in Eighteenth-Century Manuscript Studies." In *Studies in Musical Sources and Style: Essays in Honor of Jan LaRue*, edited by Eugene K. Wolf and Edward H. Roesner. Madison, 1990.

Wolf, Johannes. *Musikalische Schrifttafeln*. Bückeburg and Leipzig, 1922.

Wolff, Hellmuth Christian. "Die ästhetische Auffassung der Parodiemesse des 16. Jahrhunderts." In *Miscelánea en Homenaje a Monseñor Higinio Anglés*, 2: 1011–1019. Barcelona, 1958–1961.

Wright, Craig. "An Example of Musical Inversion from the Circle of Dufay." In *Dufay Quincentenary Conference*, edited by Allan Atlas, 144–148, 182. Brooklyn, 1976.

————. *Music and Ceremony at Notre Dame of Paris 500-1550*. Cambridge, 1989.

Zager, Daniel. "The Polyphonic Latin Hymns of Orlando di Lasso: A Liturgical and Repertorial Study." Ph.D. diss., University of Minnesota, 1985.

INDEX

Aaron, Pietro, 15, 22, 163, 174, 271n
    letters from Spataro, 80–81, 98–99, 100, 124,
        155, 163
    Thoscanello de la musica, 23–25, 25 pl, 36, 97
Achatius zu Dolma, 131
Adams, Courtney, 174, 175
Agricola, Martin: *Musica instrumentalis
    deudsch*, 40, 42, 43 pl
Albertis, Gaspar de, 111, 122, 131
Alberto, 272n
Alleluia post pascha, 122
Altus, 18–19, 24–25, 26, 27, 32, 33, 250
Amerbach, Bonifacius, 14
Animuccia, Giovanni, 297
Annaberg, St. Annenkirche, 274n
anonymous compositions
    Agnus Dei, 145n
    Al carmoneso, 145n
    Benedictus, 14
    Bon temps vient, 130
    Deprecor te, 80
    Domine adiuvandum me à8, 145n
    En contemplant à3, 130, 172–176, 173 ex, 172
        pl, 175 pl, 188
    Gloria à2, 130
    In grandi cenaculo, 117, 126, 177–179, 176 pl,
        178–179 ex, 259
    Jamais de ma femme à6, 119, 127
    Je ne complains amour, 127
    L'amy complais, 119
    Lord, now let thy servant, 128
    Lord now let us, 127
    Magnificat à8, 123, 127, 147, 196
    Matris meae, 123n
    Mère de Dieu, 119
    Miserere, 14
    Missa Alles soubdain mon desir, 111, 129

    Missa Christus resurgens, 127
    Pavana, 145n
    Pavana dela bataglia, 145n
    Salve Regina, 117
    To iours, 129
    Todeschina, 145n
    Vivent vivent en payx à3, 130, 174
    See also Bouchel; Del Rio; Frosch; Morlaye;
        Rosso
Antonio di Frari, dit il Campanaro, 129
Antwerp, educational institutions, 12n
Arcadelt, Jacques, 208n, 217, 229
    Occhi miei, 144n
Ars discantus secundum Johannem de Muris, 25n,
    28–29
Augsburg, 82, 120
autograph manuscripts
    attribution of, 3, 109–110
    extant examples of, 126–134
    typology of, 110–125, 135
Avalos, Alfonso d', 211n
Avianus, Johannes: *Isagoge in libros musicae
    poeticae*, 67

Baccusi, Hippolito, 93
Bach, Johann Sebastian, 48n, 149
Bakfark, Bálint, 131
    Intabulatura, 72, 72 pl
Banchieri, Adriano
    Cartella musicale, 76, 89, 97
    Contraponto bestiale alla mente, 68
barlines
    on the compositional sheet, 17–18, 60, 62,
        94, 99, 148, 153
    at the distance of a breve/tempus, 18, 41, 57,
        60, 62–63, 122
    at the distance of 1 or 2 tactus, 59, 94–95

in keyboard scores, 50, 94, 122
not used in composition, 5, 98–99
in scores, 42, 61, 94
in tablature, 43, *43 pl*, 45
on the tablet, 99
used to divide examples in treatises, *26 pl*, 27, 36–37, 38, 92, 192, *194 pl*
used to divide sections, not measures, 30, 53, 139, 164, 196, 298–299, *298–299 pl*, 303–305
Bartók, Béla, 193
bassus, 18–19, 22–25, 27–30
first part composed, 29, 32
Beauvais, St-Pierre, 79, 90
Bergamo, 245
Santa Maria Maggiore, 13, 76, 111, 122
Bermudo, Juan
Declaración de instrumentos musicales, 36, 49–52, 62–63, *63 pl*
El arte tripharia, 42n, 45n
Besutti, Paola, 294
Beurhaus, Friedrich: *Erotematum musicae*, 58n
Blackburn, Bonnie J., 83, 98–99, 100, 169–170
Bloxam, M. Jennifer, 119
Bologna, 88
San Petronio, 100, 111, 134, 163
Bolzano, 89n
Bontempi, Giovanni Andrea Angelini: *Historia musica*, 76
Bordogna, Francesco: *Magnificat*, 101
Borromeo, Federico, *Cardinal*, 64–65, 87
Borsieri, Girolamo, 96–97
Bosso, Giovanni Battista, 112
Bottegari, Cosimo, 111, 131
Bouchel, Guillaume, 117, 128, 131, 169–172, 175
A quoi passerai, 117, 128, 169–172, *170 pl*, 171 *ex*, 188
Bourges, 14, 76, 89
Bracconier, Jehan (Lourdault), 76, 95, 102
Brescia, 244n, 245
Breu, Jörg, the Elder, 823
Brown, Howard Mayer, 15, 72, 174–175
Bruges, 118
Brumel, Antoine, 258
Buchner, Hans: *Fundamentum*, 30–32, *31 ex*, 193n, 267
Burmeister, Joachim: *Musica poetica*, 48, *49 pl*, 76, 101
Burtius, Nicolaus: *Musices opusculum*, 20, 21, 39
Buus, Jacques, 121n
Byrd, William, 44, 73

cadences
in composing, 164, 229, 251, 267–268, 269
in compositional planning, 221–222, 232

discussed in treatises, 15, 16, 17, *18 pl*, 22, 40, 43, 54, 56, 92
examples of, 14, 241–243
Caimo, Gioseffo, 97
Calvisius, Seth, 60
Exercitationes musicae duae, 59n
Melopiia sive melodiae condendae ratio, 38n, 41n, 58–59
Cambio, Perissone, 91
Cambrai, Cathedral, 117, 169
cantus. *See* soprano
cantus firmus or pre-existent melody
as used in compositions, 19, 21, 30, 242, 258–268, 293–294
in counterpoint exercises, 14, 67–68, 90–91
in keyboard music, 30, 122, 147
taken from another composition, 19, 169, 174, 181
canzona, 121
Capello, Annibale, 73, 292, 293, 295, 297, 303n, 308, 311–312
Carpentras (Elzéar Genet): *Salve Regina*, 124, 131
Carrara, Michele: *Intavolatura di liuto*, 42n
cartella, 75, 78, 80–81, 89, *90–91 pl*, 91, 302
not to be interpreted as "score," 98n
See also tablets, erasable
Carver, Robert: *O bone Jesu*, 131
Casali, Giambattista, 155
Casati, Girolamo, 97
casella, 91–92
Casimiri, Raffaele, 3n, 302–303, 306
Castell'Arquato, Chiesa Collegiata, 111, 116, 133, 164
Cavalli, Francesco, 3, 109
Césaris, Johannes, 89n
Chailley, Jacques, 90
chanson rustique, 174
chant, used as the basis for compositions, 30, 67, 122, 145–147, 258–267, 293
Chiti, Girolamo, 303n
choirbook format
in extant autographs, 126–134
playing a composition from, 49–50
used when composing, 57, 308–309
used when drafting, 144, 189, 210–211, 241–243, 267, 274, 309
used in fair copies, 111, 124, 144, 288, 297
used in finished manuscripts, 116, 296, 305
used in sketching, 119, 137, 210, 235, 241–243
used in treatises, 36–37, 192
chords, 43
and acceptable intervals, 15, 16, 24–26, 28–29, 32

chords (*continued*)
  manner of constructing, 16–17, 21, 23,
    27–28, 29
Cimello, Giovan Tomaso, 15, 55, 92n
clavichord, used in composition, 70
Clavijo del Castillo, Bernardo, 48
clef
  combinations, 39, 42, 63, 217, 241–243, 265
  and range, 57, 211, 217, 265, 268
Clercx, Suzanne, 4, 74
Cleriadus et Meliadice, 72
Cochlaeus, Johannes, 38, 56–57
  Musica activa, 38n, 40, 41, 56
Cocker, Edward: *England's Pen-man*, 76,
    135–136
Coclico, Adrianus Petit, 15
  Compendium musices, 11, 67, 77, 81, 90–92,
    92 pl, 93 ex
  on Josquin, 11–12
Coimbra, Santa Cruz monastery, 14, 111, 123,
    131, 147
color, in organ intabulations, 30–32
commonplace book, 111, 116, 123, 130, 132,
    133. *See also originale*; sketchbook or
    workbook
Compère, Loyset, 302n
composer, as scribe, 111
composition
  with the aid of instruments, 70–73,
    293–294, 309
  over a cantus firmus, 14, 67–68, 170 (*see also*
    cantus firmus)
  of imitative writing, 32, 241, 249, 250–253,
    294
  in the mind, 64–70, 245, 309
  order of composing voices, 17–19, 21–24,
    169–172, 180–183, 211, 235–236,
    270–271 (*see also* bassus; soprano;
    tenor)
  rules for, 15–16
  in score, 60–63
  in segments, 139, 169–170, 175, 188–190,
    192–193, 196, 211, 221–223, 227,
    249–253, 268, 312
  in separate voice parts, 5, 7
  speed of, 272–274, 293
  on the tablet, 65
  and text, 69, 97, 229, 232–233, 235, 269,
    292–293
  See also revisions; sketches and drafts; staff of
    ten lines
compositional planning, 69–70, 221–223, 229,
    232, 235, 260–267
concento, 155
consonance and dissonance, 15, 16, 39, 92

Constance, 258, 270n, 274
Contino, Giovanni, 131
contrabasso, 21, 24
contrapponto alla mente, 68, 93
contratenor, 169–170
Coornhert, Dirck Volkertszoon, 85, *85 pl*
Copland, Aaron, 193
Coprario, John: *Rules how to compose*, 14–15
cori spezzati, 297
corrections
  made to completed compositions, 99–100,
    124, 131, 163, 296
  made to drafts, 151, 246, 249, 250, 253, 269,
    271
  made during sketching, 136, 139, 174
  made to fair copies, 81, 155, 259n, 260,
    306–309
  made on the tablet, 95
  See also revisions
Corteccia, Francesco, 205–243, *206–207 pl*,
    245, 249, 253, 306, 309
  Amanti i'l vo pur dir, 210–211, 213–216, *212
    pl, 213–215 ex*, 243
  Con quel coltel, 137, 210, 226, 232–239, *234
    ex, 236 pl, 238 pl, 239 ex*, 241–243
  Domine ne memineris, 241
  Domine non secundum à3, 143, 210, 241–242
  Fammi pur guerr'Amor, 144, 210, 217–229,
    *218–220 ex, 223 pl, 224–225 ex, 226 pl, 228
    ex, 230 pl, 231 ex*, 241, 243
  madrigal editions, 208, 209, 210n, 217
  Quando prend'il camino, 209n
  Responsories, 209
  sketching and drafting, 114–115, 128, 131,
    136–137, 139, 143–144, 205–243, *216 pl*,
    257
  Un dì lieto giamai, 209n
  and his will, 77, 87n, 95, 105
Cortese, Paolo: *De Cardinalatu*, 273
counterpoint
  described, 20
  exercises in, 14, 67, 94, 123, 241–243
  improvised, 67–68, 92–93
  rules for, 13–14, 24, 33
Crecquillon, Thomas: *Alles soubdain mon desir*,
    111
Cretin, Guillaume: *Plainte sur le trepas
    de . . . Bracconier*, 76, 95, 102
Cristo, Pedro de, 109n, 111, 131
Curial e Güelfa, 76, 95, 101–102

D'Accone, Frank, 95, 209, 217
Dahlhaus, Carl, 57
Daza, Esteban, 150n
Del Lago, Giovanni, 78, 80–81, 82

Del Rio, Carlo, 121, 128, 133, 147, *148 pl*

Diruta, Girolamo: *Il Transilvano*, 76, 92n, 94–95, *94 pl*, 106

discantus. *See* soprano

Doni, Giovanni Battista: *La Lyra barberina*, 76, 97n, 107

Donat, Georg, 14

Donato, Baldassare, 91, 272n
   Fiamma amorosa, 133

Dossi, Dosso: *Allegory of Music*, 86

Dowland, John, 131
   Andrea Ornithoparcus His Micrologus, 29n, 57n
   What if a day, 131

drafts
   by Corteccia, 210–211, 223, 226, 229, 235, 241–243
   defined, 110, 141–142
   by Gerarde, 115
   for keyboard, 145–148
   for lute, 120, 151
   by Palestrina, 303, 305, 306
   in parts, 210–211, 245–253
   by Rore, 245, 249–253, 254
   on the tablet, 100–101
   various examples of, 117–120, 123, 164, 170, 172–174, 177–179, 188
   See also sketches

Dressler, Gallus: *Praecepta musicae poeticae*, 15–16, 21–22, 38n, 41n, 57–58

Dublin, National Museum, 79

Du Bois, Jean, 14n

Dufay, Guillaume, 117, 169

Elders, Willem, 273

Erasmus, 78n

Este, d'
   Ercole I, Duke of Ferrara, 272
   Ercole II, Duke of Ferrara, 65, 82
   Ferrante, 302n

Fabbri, Paolo, 13

Faber, Heinrich: *Musica poetica*, 38n, 40, 41

Fabri, Jodocus, 54n, *119 pl*, 123, 126, 131
   Magnificat, 126, *143 pl*, 144

fair copies
   defined, 110–111, 154
   by Isaac, 259–260, 267, 269–271
   for keyboard, 121
   for lute, 120, 151
   by Palestrina, 296, 297, 306
   for performance, 124–125
   by Rore, 245, 253–257
   on the tablet, 101
   various examples of, 116, 118–129, 123

falsobordone, 168, 292, 296, 303, 308

fascicles
   collected into manuscripts, 111, 126–128, 133, 177
   used for composition, 112, 116–117, 120–121, 266

Federighi, Michele, 95, 105, 210

Fenlon, Iain, 217

Fernandes, Gaspar, 109n, 131

Ferrara, 244, 258, 272–273

Festa, Andrea, 55

Festa, Costanzo, 14

Finck, Hermann: *Practica musica*, 69–70, 295

Florence, 89, 205, 258, 260
   Baptistery, 205
   San Lorenzo, 205
   Santa Maria del Fiore, 205, 206n
   Santa Maria Novella, 76, 105

Florio, John: *A Worlde of Wordes*, 75, 76, 78, 295

Fogliaris, Johannes de, 122, 126, 132, 145–147, *146 pl*
   Misit Dominus, 147
   O quam suavis, 147
   Sicut novelle, 147

foglio rigato, 78, 80, 81

Forkel, J.N., 48n

form, of compositions. *See* compositional planning

format, or layout of parts, in treatises, 34–48.
   See also choirbook format; parts and part-books; quasi-score; score

Fosse (Belgium), St-Feuillien, 79, 83

Freig, Johannes Thomas: *Paedagogus*, 12n

Frescobaldi, Girolamo, 121

Frosch, Johann
   Nesciens mater à6, 192–193
   Qui de terra est à4, 192–193, *194–195 pl*, *197–202 ex*
   Rerum musicarum opusculum, 53, 190–191, *194–195 pl*

fuga (and imitation), 15, 16, 20, 22, 54, 67, 69

Gaffurius, Franchinus: *Practica musice*, 25n, 34n, *35 pl*, 36,

Galilei, Vincenzo, 15, 45, 70–72, 111, 132, 210
   as composer, 4n
   Dialogo della musica antica et della moderna, 71
   Fronimo dialogo, 42n

Galliculus, Johannes, 25
   Isagoge de compositione cantus, 25, 38n, 39n, 58n

Gardano, Antonio, 209

Gascogne, Matthieu: *En contemplant*, 174

Gerarde, Derick, 115, 124, 128, 132, 137–141, *137–138 pl*

German theoretical tradition, 56, 62–63
Gesner, Konrad, 136n
Ghent (Belgium), 79
Gian de Artiganova, 272–273
Giovannelli, Ruggiero, 78
Girona (Spain), 122
Glarean, Heinrich, 258–259
  Dodecachordon, 36, 272
Göllner, Marie Louise, 151
Gonzaga, Duke Guglielmo
  buys cartelle, 88, 95–96
  and Palestrina, 13n, 55n, 291–295, 306,
    310–311
  as patron, 73
Gonzaga, Duke Vincenzo, 65
Graduale Pataviense (1511), 261–263, 270
Graziani, Tommaso, 13, 133
Gregory XIV, Pope, 297
Guami, Giuseppe, 70
Guidetti, Giovanni, 303
Guido: Micrologus, 39n, 48
Gumpelzhaimer, Adam
  autographs, 111, 132
  Compendium musicae, 87
  as composer, 13n, 96, 96 pl

Haar, James, 217
harp, 49, 52, 72
Heilbronn, 179
Hemmel, Sigmund, 76, 95, 105
Herbst, Johann Andreas: Musica poetica, 41n,
    62n, 75, 76, 99–100
Hermelink, Siegfried, 4–5, 74
Herwart, Johann Heinrich, 120, 129, 150, 152 pl
hexachord syllables, 82, 246
Hofhaimer, Paul, 110, 132
Holman, Peter, 115
Höltzel, Hieronymus, 82, 83 pl
Holtzmüller, Heinrich: Liber perutilis, 113n
Hufnagel notation, 86, 177

Iberti, Annibale, 66n
Ijsselstein (Netherlands), 79
imitation. See composition; fuga
improvised counterpoint, 67–68
inganno, 246
Innocenzo da Ravenna, 13, 133
instruction in music, 82
  in composition, 11–33, 67, 122
  in counterpoint, 11, 24, 89, 122, 133
  including checking exercises, 11, 91,
    292–293
  including copying manuscripts, 111
  including singing, 11–12, 13
  on the organ, 12n

as organized in institutions, 12
using tablets, 68, 88, 89–94
instruments of music. See clavichord; harp; key-
    board; lute; organ; spinet; vihuela; viola;
    violin
intabulation
  for keyboard from vocal models, 117, 121,
    122, 144
  for lute from vocal models, 120, 151–154
  techniques for, 30–31, 40, 94–95
intonations for Psalms, 14
Isaac, Henricus, 30, 82n, 97, 111, 205, 258,
    272–273, 309
  Choralis Constantinus, II, 274
  In gottes namen fahren wir, 132, 259
  La mi la sol la sol la mi, 272–273
  Missa Une mousse de Biscaye, 259n
  O praeclara, 273
  Regem regum intactae, 261n
  Rogamus te, 273
  Sanctissimae virginis vitova festa, 125, 126, 132,
    259–272, 262–263 ex, 275–290, 277–290
    ex, 306
  Sol occasum nesciens, 261n
  Ite cunctipotens missa est, 90n

Jambes (Belgium), 79
Jan of Lublin, 47, 148
Janequin, Clément: La guerre, 120
Jeffery, Peter, 3, 109
Jeppesen, Knud, 296, 303
Josquin des Prez, 4, 11–12, 60n, 97, 117, 258, 272
Judd, Robert, 51
Julius II, Pope, 294
Just, Martin, 117, 259, 260
Juxta artem conficiendi, 38n, 57

Kerman, Joseph, 3
keyboard
  playing from choirbook, 49–50
  playing from parts, 48–49
  sketches and drafts, 117, 123, 144–150
  See also clavichord; organ; spinet
keyboard score (partitura), 37, 46, 94, 94 pl, 113,
    126, 144–147, 164–168
Kilian, Lucas, 96, 96 pl
Kinkeldey, Otto, 4
Kmetz, John, 119
Konrad, Ulrich, 98
Kyrie Pater cuncta, 90n

Laetabundus, 260, 261n
Lampadius, Auctor
  Compendium musices, 4, 26–29, 26 pl, 29 pl,
    38n, 39–40, 40–41 pl, 41–43, 57n, 58n, 97

on composing in the mind, 66–67
composing with a tablet, 272
on tablets, 76, 78, 103–104
Lasso, Orlando di, 89n, 110, 132, 297
   Ce faux amours, 132
Leech-Wilkinson, Daniel, 19n, 21n, 33n, 54n
Leonardus de Brixia, 91, 101
Le Roy, Adrian: *A Briefe and easye instruction*,
   42n
Liechtenthal, Pietro, 89n
ligatures, 246
Lippius, Johannes
   order of composing parts, 32–33
   Synopsis musicae novae, 32–33, 58n, 60, 75, 76,
   99
Lowinsky, Edward, 4, 23, 33, 45, 51
Luscinius, Othmar: *Musurgia seu praxis musicae*,
   47–48, 76
lute
   used when composing, 72, 73, 293–294,
   308–309
   sketches and drafts for, 116, 120, 150–153
   songs with, 131
   tablature for, 45–47, 116, 120, 129–132,
   150–153
Luzzaschi, Luzzasco, 70
   refers to Rore, 64–65, 76, 81, 87, 95, 101,
   245

Machaut, Guillaume de: *Le Voir Dit*, 21n, 56
Macque, Giovanni de, 121
madrigals, 5, 121, 207–208, 217
Málaga, Cathedral, 48
Malvezzi, Cristofano, 121n
Mantua, 93
   Santa Barbara, 131, 292n, 293, 294
Marenzio, Luca, 297
Massera, Giuseppe, 21n
Master AE, 82n
Maximilian I, Emperor, 258
   court of, 260, 261n
Medici
   Cosimo I, Duke, 207
   Lorenzo de', 258
Meier, Bernhard, 254
memory, 54–55
Merulo, Claudio, 70, 76, 88, 104
Michel, Jean, 302
Milan, Biblioteca Ambrosiana, 64,
   254n
Miller, Clement A., 21n
Milsom, John, 314
Minerbetti, Tommaso, 78, 83, 95, 105
Mischiati, Oscar, 13
modes, in composition, 22, 70, 217

Monteverdi, Claudio, 110, 244, 295
   on composing, 65–66
   Ohimè il bel viso, 66n
   Zefiro torna, 66n
Moorefield, Arthur A., 25n
Morlaye, Guillaume, 116, 130, 132, 151
   Nul n'est, 116, *153–154 pl*
Morley, Thomas: *A Plaine and easie introduction*,
   37, 44, 69n
Morosi, Piero di Giuliano, 78n
Mozart, Wolfgang Amadeus, 98
Mudgley (England), 79
Munich, Hofkapelle, 133

Nanino, Giovanni Maria, 12n
Nenna, Pomponio, 121
Neri, Saint Filippo, 297
Newsidler, Melchior, 132, 150n
Niccolò il Giolfino: *La Musa Tersicore*, 87n
notation
   Hufnagel, 86, 177
   stroke, 79
Nucius, Johannes: *Musices poeticae*, 58n

Obrecht, Jacob, 110, 133, 258, 272, 302
Occagna, Gottardo, 55
Ockeghem, Jean, 258
O'Regan, Noel, 297
organ, 73
   instruction for, 12n
   intabulation technique, 30–31, 40
   See also keyboard
originale (composer's file manuscript), 111,
   123–124, 129, 133, 300–302. *See also*
   commonplace book
Ornithoparcus, Andreas, 38, 40–41
   Musice active micrologus, 29n, 36, 38n, 39n, 40n,
   57, 86, *88 pl*
   rules for chord structure, 29
Othmayr, Caspar, 179
   Der Tag, der ist so freudenreich à2, 181, *187 ex*
   Der Tag, der ist so freudenreich à4, 12, 133,
   179–188, *180–183 pl*, *184–187 ex*

Padovano, Annibale, 70, 121n
Padua, Sant'Antonio, 76
Paindavoine, Robinet, 14n
Palatino, Giovanni Battista: *Libro nuovo d'im-*
   parare a scrivere, 136n
Palestrina family, 292n, 296n
Palestrina, Giovanni Pierluigi da, 55n, 129, 133,
   205, 291–295, 297, 309
   autographs, 129, 133, 296, *298–301 pl*, *304 pl*,
   307 pl
   Beata Barbara, 292n

Palestrina, Giovanni Pierluigi da, (*continued*)
  Beata es virgo Maria à8, 129, 297, *301 pl*, 307
  Benedictus Dominus (*falsobordone*), 303, 306,
    307 pl
  Christe redemptor, 306–308, *308 ex*
  Conditor alme siderum, 304n
  Deus tuorum militum, 305
  Dixit Dominus (*falsobordone*), 296, *298–299 pl*
  fair copies, 306
  Gaude Barbara beata, 292n
  and Guglielmo Gonzaga, 13n, 55n, 291–295,
    306, 311–312
  Hodie Christus natus est, 302n
  Hymns, 303–305
  Lamentations, 303, 305
  Masses for Santa Barbara, Mantua, 73, 292–295
  Miserere mei (*falsobordone*), *304 pl*, 306
  Missa Domenicalis, 292n
  Missa Ecce sacerdos magnus, 44
  Missa in duplicibus majoribus (lost), 294–295
  Missa sine nomine à4, 292n
  Omnis pulchritudo domini à8, 129, 296, *300 pl*,
    308–309
  Plasmator, 308
  revisions, 306–307
  and RomeSG 59, 124, 133, 297–306
  Tibi Christe splendor patris, 304n, 305, 306
  Tristes erant apostoli, 305
  used the lute when composing, 73, 293–294,
    308–309
paper
  cost of, 112, 114
  ruled for lute tablature, 112
  ruled for music, 62, 112–113
  specified for composition, 62, 65, 67, 70–72,
    74, 92
  used for fair copies, 156
Parabosco, Girolamo, 272n
Parma, Farnese court, 244
Parsley, Osbert: *Salvator mundi*, 44
parts and partbooks, 111, 132
  used for composing, 116, 121, 142, 164, 210,
    245, 251
  used for fair copies, 155, 296–297
  used for keyboard realisations, 48–54
  used as an *originale*, 124
  used in treatises, 34–35
Parvus, Johannes, 303
Passau, diocese of, 261n
Paumann, Conrad, 68n
performance
  of intabulations, 50, 54
  as a means of testing compositions, 55–56,
    65–66, 81, 99–100, 270
  from parts at the keyboard, 48–54

Petrucci, Ottaviano de, 273
Petrus de Medicis, 163n
Pettorini, Alessandro, 304–305
Pevernage, Andreas: *Gloria in excelsis Deo*, 85,
    86 pl
Philomathes, Venceslaus, 38, 40
  De nova domo musicorum, 17–19, *18 pl*, 38n, 78
Piperinus, Christoph, 14, 30n
Pisa, 258
Plantin, Christopher, 77n
Playford, John: *An Introduction to the Skill of
    Musick*, 39n
Poccianti, Michele, 208n
Pollet, Johannes, 132
Pontio, Pietro, 15, 302
  processo against, 13, 76, 91, 101, 104, 163, 302n
  Ragionamento di musica, 37, 69n
  teaching responsibilities, 13, 91
Porta, Costanzo, 13, 110,   133
Praetorius, Michael, 148
  Syntagma musicum, 62n, 76, 149n
Prioris, Johannes: *Ne recorderis*, 95
pseudo-score. *See* quasi-score
Pujol, ?Juan, 122, 126, 133, 139, 193
  Agnus, 189n
  Kyrie, 139, *142 pl*, 188–189, *188–192 ex*
Puteanus, Erycius: *Modulata Pallas*, 76, 93n

Quantz, Johann Joachim, 98
quasi-score
  on a tablet, 9–91, 96, *96 pl*
  in treatises, 35–38, 43, 57, 87
  used in composing, 4, 7, 96–97, 309
  used in counterpoint exercises, 14,
    241–242
  used for drafts, 126–130, 164, 168, 223,
    241–243, 267, 306, 309
  used for sketches, 119, 126–130, 137–139,
    151, 188, 196, 210, 235, 241–243
Quercu, Simon de: *Opusculum musices*, 25

Radous, Matous, *114–115 pl*
Raphael: *A School of Athens*, 77n
rastrum, 112–113, *114–115 pl*, 144, 266
Ravenna, 13n
Ravensburg, 260
Rees, Owen, 147
rehearsal, 53, 54
Reisch, Gregor: *Margarita philosophica*, 86, *87 pl*
Renaldi, Giulio, 44
revisions
  after circulation of the composition, 124,
    163, 209, 217
  in drafts, 154, 172–175, 176, 211, 235,
    250–251, 253, 269–271, 274–276, 306

as evidence of the act of composition, 174, 270
in fair copies, 110, 124–125, 151, 154–156, 168, 254, 260, 302, 306–307, 308–309
reflecting concern with the text, 155–156, 237, 269
in sketches, 137, 227–229
See also corrections
Reynolds, Christopher, 69
ricercar, 120, 121, 151–152
Rivera, Benito, 58n
Rodio, Rocco, 44
Rome
    Chiesa Nuova, 297
    Collegio Germanico, 76, 89n, 105
    San Giovanni in Laterano, 302–303
    San Luigi dei Francesi, 76, 89n, 105–106
    Santissima Trinità dei Pellegrini, 297
    Santo Spirito in Sassia, 297
Ronse (Flanders), 244
Rore, Cipriano de, 205, 244, 306, 309
    his *cartella*, 65, 75, 87
    composing on a *cartella*, 65, 75, 81–82, 95, 101
    composing in the mind, 65, 295
    composing in parts, 5
    drafts and fair copies, 121, 133, 143n, 244–257
    Mass, 65, 82
    Miserere mei, Deus à5, 65, 128, 245, 249–253, 250 pl, 252 ex
    Per mezzo i boschi, 55
    published books of madrigals, 244, 245, 253n
    Sub tuum presidium à4, 128, 245, 250 pl, 253–257, 254–256 ex
    Untexted fragmentary composition, 245–249, 246 pl, 247–248 ex
Rossi, Giovanni Battista: *Organo de cantori*, 44
Rosso, Jacomo, 116, 127, 133, 164, 165–168 pl
    De utero matris meae, 164, 166 pl
    Magnificat, 164, 165 pl, 165 ex
    Si ascendero in celum, 164
Ruffo, Vincenzo, 300

Sadeler, Johannes
    Annunciation to the Shepherds, 85, 86 pl
    Arithmetica, 77
    St. Cecilia at prayer, 48
Salamanca, University, 48
Sancta María, Thomas de: *Arte de tañer fantasia*, 37, 54
scala decemlinealis. See staff of ten lines
Scaletta, Horatio: *Primo scalino*, 76
Schanppecher, Melchior: *Musica figurativa*, 28–29, 39

Schonsleder, Wolfgang: *Architectonice musices universalis*, 41n, 61–62, 75, 76, 99–100, 149n
Schwartz, Rudolf, 4
score
    in a composer's file, 132, 210
    for making intabulations, 94–95
    as the medium for composition, 23, 45, 57, 58n, 60, 62, 97, 99–101, 168
    as not the medium for composition, 5, 7, 98–99, 196, 211, 217, 249, 253, 306, 309, 312
    open, for keyboard, 42–43, 46–47, 51, 113, 121, 196, 306, 312
    prepared from parts, 50, 52
    for sketching and drafting, 147–149
    for study, 55, 94, 292
    in treatises, 36–37, 42–45, 59–61, 92
    in written-out examples of counterpoint, 14, 36–37, 44, 92–94, 241–243
    See also keyboard score
Scotto, Girolamo, 209, 229, 302
Sebastiani, Claudius: *Bellum musicale*, 39n, 45–46, 47 pl
Senfl, Ludwig, 111, 133, 259n
Sherr, Richard, 124
Sirleto, Cardinal, 55
sketchbook or workbook, 121–123, 131, 132, 235. *See also* commonplace book
sketches
    by Corteccia, 114–115, 137, 210–211, 217, 223, 226–229, 235, 241–243
    defined, 110, 136
    by Gerarde, 115, 137–141
    for keyboard, 117, 121, 123, 144–148, 168
    for lute, 116, 120, 151
    on the tablet, 100–101
    various examples, 117–120, 123, 139, 164, 177
slate tablets. *See* tablets, erasable
Slim, H. Colin, 3n, 117
Smarmore (Eire), 79, 90n
Solzia, Petrus di, 302n
soprano (*see also* cantus, discantus), 19, 26, 29, 32
    composed after the tenor, 17–18, 28, 169
    the first voice composed, 21, 23, 30, 33, 174
    the last voice composed, 33
Spataro, Giovanni, 33, 95, 98–99, 100, 102, 134
    Ave gratia plena, 81, 100, 124, 130, 134, 155–163, 156 pl, 157–162 ex
    and correspondence with Del Lago, 75, 76–77, 78, 80–81, 82, 88, 103
    and letters to Aaron, 80–81, 98–99, 100, 124, 155, 163
    Virgo prudentissima, 81, 100

spinet, 48
Spinone, Benedetto, 55
staff
    of eleven lines, 36, 59–60
    of fourteen lines, 25
    of nine lines, 36
staff of ten lines, 26–27, 74, 97
    discussed in treatises, 38–39, 56–61, 97
    examples in treatises, 17, 18 pl, 26, 26 pl, 36,
        38–41, 43
    on tablets, 5, 74
    useful for beginners, 56–58, 60, 63
    used for composing, 5, 17, 26, 36, 57, 59, 61,
        100
Steen, Jan: Der Streit beim Spie, 77n
Stevenson, Robert, 48, 51n
Stravinsky, Igor, 193
Strozzi, Pompeo, 293n
subject for a composition, 19–21

tablature, 113
    for composition, 62, 100, 144, 148–150, 196,
        269
    for keyboard, 40, 42, 43 pl, 46–48, 50–51,
        144–145, 149
    for lute, 45–47, 120, 129–132, 150–153
    See also intabulation
tablets, erasable, 60, 61, 74–107
    containing counterpoint exercises, 89–91,
        90–92 pl
    containing a hexachord, 82, 86, 87 pl
    containing polyphony, 85, 86, 88 pl
    made of slate, 4, 74, 77, 95
    not used for scores, 98
    size and shape of, 81, 82–87, 100
    used in composition, 4–5, 64–65, 80–81,
        87n, 92, 95–101, 156, 209, 211–212, 245,
        249, 251, 272
    used in instruction, 68, 89–94
    used in intabulating for keyboard, 94–95
    used for scores, 99–100
    used for tablature, 100
    See also slate tablets
tabulae compositoriae, 4, 60, 74. See also tablets,
    erasable
Taverner, John, 134
tenor, the first voice composed, 17–19, 21, 22,
    28, 33, 169–170, 177
Tigrini, Orazio: Il compendio della musica, 43
Tinctoris, Johannes, 15, 68n
    Liber de arte contrapuncti, 69n
Torgau, court, 258, 260
Towne, Gary, 122

Tubal, 82n
tuning, for string instruments, 14

Vaccaro, Jean-Michel, 116
Vaccaro, Nathalie, 116
Valderrábano, Enríquez de: Libro de musica de
    vihuela, 53, 53 pl
Van Heemskerck, Maarten, 85, 85 pl
Vanneo, Stefano, 24
    Recanetum de musica aurea, 36
Vatican, choral institutions, 294, 297, 303
Vecchi, Orfeo, 96
Veggio, Claudio, 117, 134, 164
Venegas de Henestrosa, Luis: Libro de cifra nueva,
    42n
Venice, 80, 88–89
    San Marco, 48n, 55, 244
Verdelot, Philippe, 209n
    Sancta Maria succurre miseris, 42
Verona, Accademia Filarmonica, 76
Vicentino, Nicola, 15
    L'antica musica, 36, 69n
vihuela, used for playing a score from parts, 49,
    52
viola, tuning instructions, 14
violin, tuning instructions, 14
Virdung, Sebastian: Musica getuscht, 48n
Vos, Martin de, 85

Walther, Johann Gottfried: Musicalisches Lexicon,
    75, 76, 78
Wells (England), Wells Museum, 79, 90n
Wert, Giaches, 292
    Jesu redemptor omnium, 129, 134
    Missa in festis B. M. virginis, 124, 134
    Missa in festis duplicibus maioribus, 124, 129,
        134
    Subite proni ianuas, 134
Wieck, Clara, 98
Willaert, Adrian, 55, 73, 91, 272
    Qual anima ignorante, 55
Wittenberg, All Saints Church, 274n
Wright, Craig, 117, 169
Wyss, Urban: Libellus valde doctus, 136n

Young, Irwin, 25n

Zacconi, Lodovico, 93, 210
    Prattica di musica, 37, 44, 67–68, 76, 82,
        92–93, 94, 106–107
Zarlino, Gioseffo, 15, 19–20, 272
    Le istitutioni harmoniche, 19–20, 24n, 32, 37, 43
    Sopplimenti musicali, 272n

INDEX OF MANUSCRIPTS

Barcelona, Biblioteca de l'Orfeó Català
  Music, Item 12–VII-28: 122–123, 126, 133, 139, *142 pl*, 188, 297n
Basel, Öffentliche Bibliothek der Universität
  F.I.8a: 30n
  F.VI.26: 119–120, *119 pl*, 123, 131–132, 144, *145 pl*
Bergamo, Biblioteca Civica
  Misericordia Maggiore 989: 91n, 101n
  Misericordia Maggiore 1143: 122, 126, 132, *143 pl*, 145–147, 245n
  Misericordia Maggiore 1207: 131
  Misericordia Maggiore 1208: 131
  Misericordia Maggiore 1209: 131
Berlin, Staatsbibliothek zu Berlin
  Mus.ms.theor.1175: 38n, 41
Berlin, Preussischer Kulturbesitz
  Mus.ms.40021: 117, 125, 126, 132, *176 pl*, 177, 259–260, 264–267, *264–266 pl*, 269, 271–272, 274–277
  Mus.ms.40027: 4n, 111n, 132
  Mus.ms.40028: 4n, 111n, 132
Bologna, Civico Museo Bibliografico Musicale
  B.140: 4n, 13–14, 133
  Q.25: 111n, 127
  Q.116: 13
Bologna, Archivio Musicale della Fabbriceria di San Petronio
  A.29: 134
  A.31: 134
  A.38: 124, 134
  A.40: 134
  A.45: 100, 134, 163n
  A.46: 124, 134
Bourges, Archives Départmentales du Cher
  fragments: 14
  8 G 1634: 89n

Bruges, Stadarchief
  41: 127
  538: 54n, 118–119, *118 pl*, 127
Brussels, Bibliothèque du Conservatoire royale de musique
  27731: 217
Cambridge, Corpus Christi College Library
  410: 21n
Cambridge, University Library
  Bux.96: 127
Castell'Arquato, Archivio Communale
  MS s.s.: 116n
Castell'Arquato, Chiesa Collegiata, Archivio, 47, 123, 127, 133
  Exactiones et expensae 2: 116n
  2: 144–145, *146 pl*
  3: 145n
  5: 134
  6: 145n
  12a: *167 pl*, 168
  32: 164, *166 pl*
  33: 168, *167–168 pl*
  47: 117, 164, *165 pl*
Coimbra, Biblioteca Geral da Universidade
  8: 131
  18: 131
  33: 131
  36: 131
  48: 14, 123, 127, 147–148, *149–150 pl*, 196, 203
  242: 123
Dijon, Bibliothèque Municipale
  517: 169
Dresden, Sächsische Landesbibliothek
  1/D/506: 274n
Edinburgh, National Library of Scotland
  5.1.15: 131

Erlangen, Universitätsbibliothek
   473/4: 127, 133, 179, *180–183 pl*
Faenza, Biblioteca comunale
   117: 46
Florence, Archivio di Stato
   Corp.Rel.Sop.N.o 102: 78n
   Libri di Commercio 553: 78n
Florence, Archivio Musicale dell' Opera di
   Santa Maria del Fiore
   21: 128
Florence, Archivio San Lorenzo
   2129: 205n, 206, *206–207 pl*
   2344: 95n
   N: 131
Florence, Biblioteca Nazionale Centrale
   Ant. di Galileo 1: 132
   Ant. di Galileo 6: 132
   Ant. di Galileo 9: 4n, 111, 132
   Magliabechi XIX.106bis: 4n, 121, 128, 133
   Magliabechi XIX.117: 5, 14, 114–115, 128,
      131, 137, 143n, 210–211, *212 pl, 216 pl, 223
      pl, 226 pl*, 223–227, *230 pl*, 235–238, *236 pl,
      238 pl*, 241–243
   II.I.295 (=Magliabechi XIX.107): 121, 128,
      133, 147, *148 pl*
Gdańsk, Biblioteki Polskiej Akademii Nauk
   E.2165:   132
Göttingen, Niedersächsische Staats- und Uni-
      versitätsbibliothek
   Mus.IV 3000 Rara: 38n
   Philos.103: 38n
Guatemala City, Catedral, Archivio Capitular
   1: 131
Hradec Králové, Muzeum východních Čech
   II A 13: 113, *114–115 pl*
Jena, Universitätsbibliothek
   33: 270n, 274n
Königsberg, Stadtbibliothek
   Gen 2.150: 131
Kraków, Biblioteka Polskiej Akademii Nauk
   1716: 47, 148–149, *149–150 pl*
Lille, Archives départementales du Nord
   4 G 1081: 117, 128, 131, 169, *170 pl*
London, British Library
   Add. 30513: 12n
   Royal Appendix 17–22: 132
   Royal Appendix 23–25: 128, 132, 137–139,
      137–138 pl
   Royal Appendix 26–30: 132
   Royal Appendix 31–35: 132
   Royal Appendix 49–54: 132
   Royal Appendix 74–76: 115, 128
Mantua, Archivio di Stato, Archivio Gonzaga:
   292n
   Carteggio Diversi (di Venezia), B.1498: 88n

Milan, Biblioteca Ambrosiana
   A.10.Sup.: 64, 76, 121, 128, 133, 245–246,
      246 pl, 250 pl, 253–257, *257 pl*
Milan, Biblioteca del Conservatorio di Musica
      "Giuseppe Verdi"
   Santa Barbara 42: 131
   Santa Barbara 109: 292n
   Santa Barbara 142: 124, 129, 134
   Santa Barbara 143: 124, 129, 134
   Santa Barbara 164: 294n
   Santa Barbara 166: 294n
   Santa Barbara 195/17: 129, 134
   Santa Barbara 195/18: 134
Modena, Archivio di Stato
   Camera ducale, Mandati sciolti, Busta 13:
      244n
Modena, Biblioteca Estense e Universitaria
   C.311: 111n, 131
Munich, Bayerische Staatsbibliothek
   Mus.Ms.B: 253n
   Mus.Ms.239: 302
   Mus.Ms.266: 132
   Mus.Ms.267: 120–121, 129, 151, *152 pl*
   Mus.Ms.1503f: 133
   Mus.Ms.1627: 132
   Mus.Ms.2987: 132
   Mus.Ms.3155: 111, 133
   Mus.Ms.9437: 129
Oaxaca, Catedral
   MS s.s.: 131
Oxford, Bodleian Library
   Music School e.420–2: 134
Padua, Archivio di S. Antonio Confessore
   b.70: 87n
Paris, Bibliothèque nationale
   Fonds du Conservatoire, Rés. 429: 132
Parma, Archivio di Stato
   Rac. ms., busta 75, no.2: 111, 129
Regensburg, Bischöfliche Zentralbibliothek
   Butsch 205–210: 132
Rome, Biblioteca Musicale Governativa del
      Conservatorio di Musica "Santa Cecilia"
   G.384: 14, 92n
   0.231: 129, 133, 297, *301 pl*
   0.232: 129, 133, 296, *300 pl*
Rome, San Giovanni in Laterano, Archivio
      Musicale
   59: 124, 129, 133, 291, 297–306, *304 pl, 307
      pl*, 309
Rome, San Luigi dei Francesi, Archivio
   Mandati, filza 41: 89n
Schlägl, Prämonstratenser-Stift, Stiftsbibliothek
   10: 197n
Segovia, Archivo Capitular de la Catedral
   MS s.s.: 133

Sibton Abbey, private possession
    H.A.3:50/9/15.7(1): 129, 170n
Uppsala, Universitetsbiblioteket
    Vok.i Hdskr.76a: 5, 130, 172, *172 pl*, *173 ex*,
        175 pl
    Vok.i Hdskr.76b: 116, 130, 132, 151–154,
        153–154 pl
    Vok.i Hdskr.76c: 130, 132
    Vok.i Hdskr.87: 132
    Vok.i Hdskr.412: 132
Vatican City, Biblioteca Apostolica Vaticana
    Cappella Giulia XIII.24: 297
    Cappella Giulia XV.19: 304–305
    Cappella Sistina 42: 124, 131
    Vaticani Latini 5318: 54, 74, 124, 130,

155–156, *156 pl*, 163n (*see also* the
    references to Del Lago and Spataro
    correspondence)
Vaticani Latini 10776: 133, 296–299,
    298–299 pl
Vienna, Österreichische Nationalbibliothek,
    Handschriften- und Inkunabelsammlung
    11883: 111n
    18744: 132
Washington, Folger Shakespeare Libraries
    V.b.280: 131
Wolfenbüttel, Herzog August Bibliothek
    499 (W$_3$): 130
Woodford Green, private collection
    MS s.s. (Board Lute Book): 131